CHRONICLE OF YOUTH

Great War Diary

1913–1917

Vera Brittain

Edited by Alan Bishop

PHOENIX
PRESS

5 UPPER SAINT MARTIN'S LANE
LONDON
WC2H 9EA

A PHOENIX PRESS PAPERBACK

First published in Great Britain in 1981
by Victor Gollancz
This paperback edition published in 2000
by Phoenix Press,
an imprint of Orion Books Ltd,
Orion House, 5 Upper St Martin's Lane,
London WC2H 9EA

Phoenix Press
Sterling Publishing Co. Inc.
387 Park Avenue South
New York
NY 10016–8810
USA

Second impression
Reissued 2002

A CIP catalogue record for this book
is available from the British Library.

ISBN 1 84212 542 7

Typeset at The Spartan Press Ltd,
Lymington, Hants

Printed and bound in Great Britain by
Clays Ltd, St Ives plc

CONTENTS

CHRONICLE OF YOUTH

ILLUSTRATIONS

Vera Brittain at the front window of Melrose, Buxton, about 1913

Mr and Mrs Brittain outside Melrose, Buxton, about 1913

Vera Brittain in Buxton

Vera Brittain as a V.A.D nurse

Roland Leighton: the portrait he sent to Vera Brittain in December 1914

Ploegsteert Wood: a photograph taken by Roland Leighton

Vera Brittain: the portrait she sent to Roland Leighton in December 1914

The Three Musketeers – Edward Brittain, Roland Leighton and Victor Richardson: the enlargement from a photograph taken at Uppingham School O.T.C. Camp in July 1914

Geoffrey Thurlow

Edward Brittain

Vera Brittain with fellow nurses below St George's Hospital, Malta, about 1917

Vera Brittain outside Nurses' Quarters, St George's Hospital, Malta, about 1916

Vera Brittain with some of her patients at St George's Hospital, Malta, in 1916

A page from Vera Brittain's diary

ACKNOWLEDGEMENTS

I am very grateful to Miss Terry Smart for her excellent collaboration on this edition. Over the past few years she has been responsible for cataloguing the Vera Brittain Archive in McMaster University Library, Hamilton, Ontario, Canada. To this Archive belong the photographs reproduced in this book, the prefatory pieces by Vera Brittain quoted in the Introduction, and the diary itself.

Mr Graham Hill, the University Librarian, gave me invaluable help and advice; and from Dr William Ready, Librarian Emeritus, I received early encouragement. I am greatly indebted to them both, as well as to Mrs Charlotte Stewart, Mrs Kate Donkin, Mr Laszlo Jambor, Miss Carol Mazur, and other members of the Library Staff.

Mrs Margaret Chan drew the map of the Western Front; Mrs Ora Orbach typed the final manuscript; and the English Department and the Faculty of Humanities, McMaster University, provided some timely financial aid.

Friends and colleagues were generous with their help and encouragement. I wish particularly to thank Mrs Audrey Alexander, Miss Yvonne Bennett, Prof. Andrew Brink, Prof. John Ferns, Prof. James King, Mr Arthur McCalla, Prof. Richard Morton, Mrs Sandra O'Grady, Prof. Richard Rempel, Miss Cornelia Starks and Mrs Sheila Turcon.

Very useful information was kindly provided by Lady Anne de Villiers, Fellow of Somerville College, Oxford, who is currently at work on a history of the College; by Mr C. Macdonald, Headmaster of Uppingham School; and by Mrs Norma Barclay, Editor of the *Buxton Advertiser*, and the Buxtonians who responded to the appeal she made on my behalf.

To Clare Leighton I owe a great debt: for her moving Preface to this book, as well as for permission to print poetry by her brother Roland, and excerpts from his letters, as quoted in the diary. I wish also to acknowledge the kindness of David Leighton, Alastair Gornall, and other members of the family.

I am very grateful indeed to Mrs Shirley Williams, Vera Brittain's daughter, for her generous and helpful consideration of the book's text, in spite of the many demands on her time. And the encouragement, advice, efficiency and utterly good heart of Paul Berry, Vera Brittain's literary executor, have meant more than I can say.

Finally: this book has gained greatly from the guidance of Miss Livia Gollancz.

No one mentioned above is in any way responsible for deficiencies in this edition. Nor is my wife Judith, who has sustained me from day to day with her enthusiasm and good sense.

Alan Bishop
1981

PREFACE

It is over half a century since Roland was killed. Time is supposed to hold the power of softening the effect of grief, but as I read this diary of Vera Brittain's with its vivid account of life in the First World War, I found myself as emotionally destroyed as though my brother's death had happened but a short while before.

When Dr Alan Bishop asked me to write this Preface I hesitated before saying I would do so. Why, I felt, must I relive that terrible time of wholesale destruction? But, as I wavered, my decision was forced upon me. A friend reproached me. 'It is your duty to write this and it is also your contribution to history,' she insisted. 'Don't forget that you are, today, the sole living person who closely experienced the tragedy of your brother's death. You would never forgive yourself if you were a coward and shrank from this. The world needs to be reminded of the wanton horror of that war, with its destruction of the flower of a generation of young men.'

Perhaps, too, it is of importance to chronicle a war as seen and experienced through the eyes and emotions of the young. It is strange how vividly a visual memory can be stamped into the soft wax of the very young. The impression is deep and hardens over the years, never to be softened and erased by time. So it is that to this day the sound of a bugle or even the sight of a soldier in uniform can frighten me.

As I write this I find myself back in childhood. It is a cold morning in January and I am in the garden of our cottage in Sussex. My father is with me. I carry two heavy kettles. They are filled with boiling water, for we are about to bury the tunic – blood-stained and bullet-riddled – in which Roland has been killed . . . Father watches the windows of the house, for my mother must not see this tunic that Father has hidden from the packages of Roland's effects returned from France. I am to thaw the frozen earth so that it may be buried out of sight.

Over here, in America, where I am now living, children have not been so directly exposed to the fears and horrors of war. War is something you see on television or read about in history books. It does not impinge upon one's daily life. But my generation in England chanced to grow up with the repeated associations of war. Behind the brave, happy trivia of daily life loomed this hideous spectre.

I think my first encounter with it was in 1914. Our nannie had taken me and my little brother to the fish-market at Lowestoft so that we might watch the arrival of the Belgian refugees fleeing from the Germans. They were huddled together on the decks of tiny little boats. I remember that I started to cry, out of concern and pity, and begged the old nannie to let us take them home with us. When, naturally, she refused, I was inconsolable.

But this was just a beginning. The full moon brought fears of Zeppelin raids, with nights spent in the cellar of our house, and, as the fury of the war increased, fears of an actual German invasion. On these nights we two children were provided with food, a little money and extra clothes, so that we could flee. None of these disasters happened to us, but the fears were spawned in our sensitive little minds.

Roland, by now, was in the army in France. But I was not afraid, for I knew he could never be killed. It was as though my adoration of him must act as a charm. Besides, I also knew that he was destined to do wonderful things in life. He *could* not be killed. This certainty persisted with me, as an amulet against fear, over the time he was fighting in France. When the telegram came, on the morning after Christmas Day, something of faith in life snapped inside me.

All that was so long ago. But it has left me with a deep terror of war and a pleading with the world to see that we are not beguiled into it. The wages of war continue long after the young men are forgotten, and we who lived through it have a deep responsibility.

Thus it is that I feel the importance of this book. Vera Brittain knew and suffered, and we are fortunate to be able to read and learn the lesson of the waste and horror of war.

Clare Leighton
August 1980

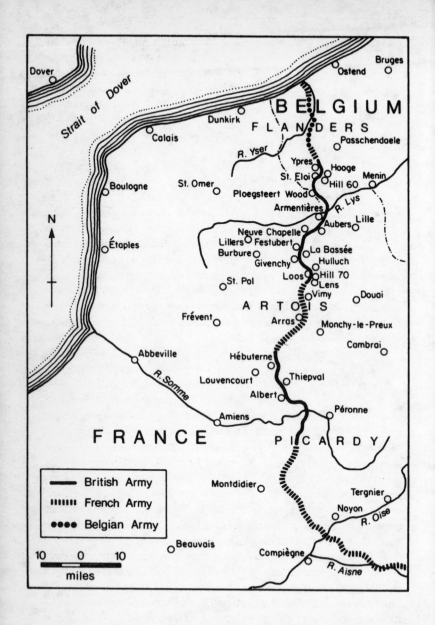

The Western Front in December 1915

INTRODUCTION

Chronicle of Youth was first published nearly twenty years ago, in 1981. Its close connection with *Testament of Youth*, Vera Brittain's famous 'autobiographical study of the years 1900–1925', was signalled not only by title and author but by its appearance in the wake of the popular, award-winning BBC television adaptation by Elaine Morgan. *Testament of Youth*, the book – a bestseller on publication in 1933, never out of print, and firmly established as a classic in the literature of war and peace – gained from the television series a new prominence, a new readership, and increased reputation and critical attention; *Chronicle of Youth* also profited.

However, the relationship between *Chronicle of Youth* and the television series was largely fortuitous. When, during the early 1970s, I first read Vera Brittain's 1913–17 diary – in McMaster University Library, among the Vera Brittain Papers (then newly acquired, after her death in 1970, and in process of being sorted and catalogued) – I knew nothing about a proposed television adaptation. Several years earlier, I had been impressed and moved by *Testament of Youth* on reading it as background to the poetry of the Great War. Then, soon after joining the McMaster English Department as an assistant professor, I recognised my good fortune in having ready access to significant documents relating to the War, among them the diary and correspondence represented by quotations in *Testament of Youth*.

It was quickly obvious to me that the diary was, as Vera Brittain had herself believed, worthy of publication in its own right – and not only because it contained much that she could not find room for in *Testament of Youth*. Immediacy, unsparing honesty, intimacy, emotional force, fluent vivid writing, sharp expression of a complex individuality, and of course a detailed almost-daily recording of personal experience and of the international catastrophe that would destroy all four of the young men she loved (and then dominate the rest of her life): these are qualities of a superb diary – of a superb war diary. When I first read it, I wept over several passages, all the more poignant in her clear assertive handwriting; and there are some passages – above all, those expressing, nakedly, the depth of her grief after her fiancé Roland Leighton's death – that I recoil still from re-reading.

In 1975, I was fortunate to meet Paul Berry, senior Literary Executor to the Vera Brittain Estate, who was visiting McMaster University Library to do research among the Papers for his biography. I too was writing a biography at the time – of Joyce Cary, the novelist. Paul and I became friends; and when, in 1977, I asked for permission to edit the diary for publication, he gave me immediate approval and warm encouragement. He had known Vera Brittain well in her later years, and was a fount of generous information about her personality, her life and her work. He also told me, while I was working on the edition, that the television adaptation of *Testament of Youth* was in process. *Chronicle of Youth* would connect well with it, and with a sharply increasing interest (partly achieved by his assiduous work as literary executor) in Vera Brittain's pacifist and feminist thought, activities and writing.

We both also knew that Vera Brittain had wished the diary to be published, and had twice set out to publish it herself. In 1922 she had submitted it for a literary prize that included publication of the winning autobiographical entry: 'I selected and typed sections of the diary . . . and sent it in. I called it "Chronicle of Youth". It was not chosen . . .' A few years later, inspired by Robert Graves' *Goodbye to All That* (1929) and other just-published Great War memoirs, she began to use the diary as 'raw material for Testament of Youth'. Yet, even after the great international success of her masterpiece, she again set out, in the months before the outbreak of the Second World War, to publish the diary itself (presumably in the edition she had prepared earlier); arguing, in notes she wrote then for an Introduction, that it was significantly different in nature and effect. *Testament of Youth* was a broad, retrospective account of her early life and of the War – 'the forest, not the trees themselves'; and she conceded that, in the diary, 'because one sees the trees one by one, the forest never becomes quite clear'. Yet, as she went on to insist, the diary's close focus, detailed personal record of daily experience, and ignorance of the future, convey

> one effect which *Testament of Youth*, because of its very perspective and the long period it covered, could only partially convey – the cumulative effect of day-by-day suspense & anguish, the unillumined length of the night which had done so much permanent quenching of youthful hope & energy before it was finished.

Several reviewers of *Chronicle of Youth* echoed that opinion. One wrote that, 'Whereas in a novel the love story is designed by the omnipotent writer, in the diary it is spontaneous and immediate, recorded moment by moment as it happens. The result is a story so absorbing it is difficult to stop reading.'

And *Chronicle of Youth* is, in large part, a love story – a movingly tragic love story, as Vera Brittain's editing stressed. In the dark, tense days of 1938–39, she hoped that it would be 'a warning & challenge to both modern youth & its elders'; that it might help avert the lowering international disaster. But her intention was overtaken by the events of September 1939, and she turned her energies to the hard, brave work of pacifist activism throughout the new World War. She did not again seek to publish the diary; but hoped and expected that it would be published after her death.

The relationship between the diary and *Testament of Youth* is more complex than Vera Brittain indicated in her Introductory notes. Inevitably, there are significant differences, in content and emphasis, resulting from such obvious facts as dissimilar scope and genre, lapse of time and the changed point of view of the writer. The memoir – written more than a decade after the diary, when its author had become prominent, through her writing and lecturing, as a feminist and anti-war activist – represents the young Vera as more consistent and peace-loving, in her response to militarism, than the diary reveals her to have

been. As noted by one reviewer, in *Testament of Youth* Vera
Brittain did not include facts starkly revealed in the diary: that,
for instance, in the general jingoistic euphoria after the declaration of war, she had strongly supported, indeed encouraged, her
younger brother Edward's desire to volunteer for military
service (even though he was under age) and had ridiculed her
father's reservations; while only intermittently expressing com-
passionate concern about the war's toll of death and destruction. As Vera Brittain seems to have realised, the diary in some
respects corrects or qualifies *Testament of Youth*; and the confused
and conventional young Vera of the diary enforces, much more
than the tidied-up, morally-correct Vera of the memoir, the
mature Vera Brittain's memorable statement in *Testament of
Youth* that 'the pacifist's real problem' is the powerful effect of
'this glamour, this magic, this incomparable keying up of the
spirit in a time of mortal conflict';

> the challenge to spiritual endurance, the intense sharpening of
> all the senses, the vitalizing consciousness of common peril for
> a common end [that] allure those boys and girls who have just
> reached the age when love and friendship and adventure call
> more persistently than at any later time.

Is the diary itself entirely trustworthy, then? Many readers,
encouraged by critical theorists and by writers who have
deliberately mixed generic qualities (one recent biography
incorporated its author, in a fictional relationship with his
subject!), have become radically sceptical of claims that literature can represent reality, express 'the truth'; and now explicitly
or implicitly define truth-claiming genres like autobiography
and biography as essentially fiction. Rejecting such simplistic
analysis, one must still recognise that – especially in the diary of
a young woman who aspired, as Vera Brittain did, to be a
novelist – some imaginative infusion into experience is inevitable. One notes this in, for instance, the references by both
Vera and Roland, as their relationship develops, to Lyndall and
Waldo, the central characters of a novel they both admired
extravagantly, Olive Schreiner's *Story of an African Farm*. But this
does not invalidate the diary's recording of events, and in fact

serves to strengthen the diary's realism, since it springs from and very effectively renders their complex, highly-literate personalities, and the nature of the love that flowered between them. More damaging to the diary's credibility, perhaps, is the fact that some entries seem to have been composed several days after the events recorded (the poignant account of Vera's receiving news of Roland's death at the end of 1915 is one instance). Yet this, too, is not incompatible with the conventions of a diary – whose value, after all, is necessarily located in the individual writer's expression of experience and observation, often in unpropitious circumstances or after interruption by complex events that both repel and demand expression, analysis. The question of integrity must always be under some scrutiny by the reader of a diary, and cannot be disentangled from the trust a reader gives to – or withholds from – its writer, on the basis of evidence in the text. Indeed, the tense, ever-unfolding relationship between writer and reader imposed by a diary is one of the genre's sharpest delights. And, paradoxically (or as a healthy antidote to critical pessimism about literary truth-telling), we thirst above all for trustworthy personal accounts of lives and events in crisis – demonstrated, as I write these words, by reviews of a war diary that parallels Vera Brittain's, *The Klemperer Diaries, 1933–1945: I Shall Bear Witness to the Bitter End*. Just as those reviews reflect utter confidence in Klemperer's account, so, in my observation, do readers of Vera Brittain's diary ultimately give its writer their full trust.

In her own edition of it, Vera Brittain abridged the 1913–17 diary, reducing its length by almost a half (from over 250,000 words to about 155,000 words, at her own estimate); and made many substantial changes whose cumulative effect was to weaken the text's authenticity. For instance, she replaced all names with pseudonyms, and decided to end the edited text at April 1916, soon after the death of Roland, so shaping it emphatically as a tragic love-story: for, without the events and developed relationships of 1917 – including her Malta V.A.D service, and the deaths of her close friends Victor Richardson and Geoffrey Thurlow – the diary ends climactically with the death of 'Vincent Farringdon' (Roland Leighton) and her own grief. She even created, some five years after its date, a long entry for Easter Sunday, April 23rd 1917, as a peroration (there is no entry for that date in the diary itself):

> Perhaps one can never rise to the heights until one has gone down into the depths – such depths as I have known of late. Perhaps I shall one day rise, and be worthier of him who in his life both in peace and war, and in his death on the fields of France, has shown me 'the way more plain'. At any rate, if ever I do face danger and suffering with some measure of heroism, it will be because I have learnt through him that love is supreme, that love is stronger than death and the fear of death.

Of course the diary was her own, and intimately known to her in all that it recorded; so Vera Brittain surely felt no qualms in making changes in its edited text, for literary or other reasons. A general justification was always present, too, in the need to reduce its length by about half if it were to be published in one volume for the general reader. When I began the task of editing the diary, more than fifty years later, that same requirement was fundamental. After reading Vera Brittain's edition carefully, and knowing that time had eroded some constraints but also imposed the need to take account of *Testament of Youth*, I decided to edit the diary quite independently, while respecting her principles and implied wishes as far as I could. (For that reason, omissions are not indicated, so presenting the diary text to readers without complication or impediment.) However, I found myself subject to some constraints similar to those Vera Brittain had experienced. In approving my edited text, her family requested several omissions, some of which, after discussion, I accepted. Similarly, to avoid hurting the widow and family of a man ridiculed in the diary, I omitted passages that were not needed to reveal the young Vera's state of mind at the beginning of the War. Throughout my editing, I received and considered valuable advice – notably from Paul Berry, and Clare Leighton, Roland's sister, who also became a friend, and whose generosity and courage in writing a fine Preface for the book increased my debt to her immeasurably.

Twenty years later – and possibly more mature in judgement

– I would like to have had the time to reconsider and even re-edit the diary; but that has not been possible. One reviewer predicted in 1981 that *Chronicle of Youth* would become 'a classic in its own right'; I must take comfort in that judgement, hoping again that my editing has done no harm to Vera Brittain's incomparably moving and valuable testimony. It was a privilege to have edited her diary so as to make it available to readers around the world; so I am delighted that Phoenix Press are republishing the edition now, for a new generation of readers. I hope that one day the diary will be published in full: its historical and literary importance – as indicated by substantial quotation and reference – has been firmly established by *Chronicle of Youth* in the period since its publication.

Complementing its original close relationship with *Testament of Youth* (and, later, with Vera Brittain's second major diary, of 1932–1945, edited and published as *Chronicle of Friendship* and *Wartime Chronicle*), *Chronicle of Youth* now also connects closely with two publications of the past few years: the authorised biography of Vera Brittain (1995), and *Letters of a Lost Generation* (1998). The latter, an edition of the extensive surviving corres-pondence of Vera Brittain and the four young men she lost in the Great War – Roland Leighton in 1915, Victor Richardson and Geoffrey Thurlow in 1917, and her brother Edward in 1918 – has very close links to the diary, in which passages from many of the letters are quoted. But the letters continue beyond the point when, after she returned to England from Malta in May 1917, Vera Brittain's diary lapsed; and in many other ways, they extend and complement both *Testament of Youth* and *Chronicle of Youth* – not least in giving a full, defining, public voice to each of the four young men. I first read those letters in the early 1970s, immediately after reading the diary, and was so deeply moved and impressed that, in 1977, I requested permission to edit them for publication. Over the years, I renewed that request at intervals, and transcribed the letters in readiness; but it was only a few years ago that the opportunity came (with, as so often, all too close a deadline!) for the publication of a selective edition, in collaboration with Mark Bostridge and in connection with the 80th anniversary of the end of the First World War. Published a few years earlier, the biography – *Vera Brittain: A*

Life, by Paul Berry and Mark Bostridge – drew on the correspondence, as well as on *Chronicle of Youth* and *Testament of Youth*; so bringing together all four books – diary, letters, memoir, biography – in a profoundly moving and informative record of the Great War, as experienced by Vera Brittain, Roland Leighton, Victor Richardson, Geoffrey Thurlow, Edward Brittain, representatives of a lost generation whose testimony lives on in truths we inherit through their words.

Alan Bishop
May 2000

A NOTE ON THE TEXT

Vera Brittain's diary of 1913 to 1917 was written in seven octavo notebooks, each of about 200 pages. These are now in the Vera Brittain Archive in McMaster University Library.

Apart from an early gap mentioned in the entry of October 18th 1913 and a second one from October 18th to November 24th 1915, the diary was kept with great regularity and fullness until the death of Roland Leighton at the end of 1915. Thereafter entries are variable. Gaps of several weeks occur in January and February 1916, and again from April 20th to June 3rd and from July 6th to September 14th (except for the brief 'End of August' entry). A very large gap occurs near the diary's conclusion, from December 24th 1916 to April 15th 1917. Entries on several loose sheets found at the back of the 1916–17 volume have been interpolated in the text; and the concluding list which commemorates the dead has been taken from a separate notebook containing memorabilia.

The diary's length of more than 250,000 words has been reduced by about half for this book. The selection of passages is not Vera Brittain's, although it seemed appropriate to use her title since this book is generally similar to the one she intended to publish. Because her selection was compiled shortly after the First World War, she clearly felt obliged to omit many passages for fear of hurting relatives or friends; among other textual changes, she also replaced all names with pseudonyms and omitted the 1917 entries. The present selection was made independently, after a close study of the diary, and then reconsidered in relation to Vera Brittain's selections. It attempts to represent the nature and concerns of the diary as closely as possible. Excisions from the original text were made to avoid insignificant repetition and unimportant detail, to reduce the overall length, and in a few instances to avoid causing offence unnecessarily. In addition, since *Testament of Youth* is so widely known and readily available, some passages were omitted largely because they appear at length there. In accordance with Vera Brittain's practice in editing her selection, and in order to avoid textual complication, the excisions are not indicated.

To retain as far as possible the informal nature of a diary, inconsistencies in abbreviation (such as '&/and'), in capitalisation ('the Front/the front') and in representation of numbers ('3/three'), have not generally been altered; and errors in quotation have not been corrected. But, to help the reader, some abbreviations have been expanded, at a few points the punctuation and paragraphing have been adjusted, some minor shifts in typographical convention have been imposed, and entry-headings have been generally regularised. All these changes – as with the corrections of obvious slips of the pen – have been made silently, but any uncertain or altered readings have been placed within square brackets.

The Notes have been grouped after the text and keyed to page numbers. They aim to identify Vera Brittain's quotations, to give essential or useful information, and to explain any obscurities in the text. Where possible and appropriate, the Index includes reference to the Notes. And a brief Chronology, placed between the Notes and Index, lists important events of the diary against page-references to the text.

Alan Bishop

1913

Wednesday January 1st Melrose, Buxton

We danced the New Year in at the Garnetts' yesterday evening; I don't know why I enjoyed it so much, except that I suppose it is gratifying, when there are too many girls at a dance, never to have to dance with girls or sit out. Oh! I was so relieved to hear those twelve strokes which announced the departure of 1912 for good & all. I don't know why it was such a miserable year, but I am glad to get rid of it & forget it. It was my year of being eighteen too, which is supposed to be a girl's traditional age for happiness – but it is like me to go contrary to this tradition as to so many others! *I* have been far from blameless; I shudder to think how I have thrown a year away – save in experience, which one cannot throw away! – how little I have read, & written practically nothing, how unenergetic, unenterprising I have been, after so many good resolutions, too, last New Year! Well, this is a chronicle of 1913, not a complaint of 1912! At any rate I have made no special resolutions this time, so let us hope my year of being nineteen will be kinder to me, & I to it, than the last one.

Friday January 3rd

Nothing of any interest happened all day until the Cottage Hospital Ball at the Peak Hydro – 9 till 2 – but it was till 3.0 for me! I am really beginning to love dancing for dancing's sake. I danced every one, including three extras & could have gone on for hours. The only thing that spoilt my enjoyment was the supper business, which was all my own fault & made me feel mean. We went with Maurice & Dorothy & Mr James Ellinger, & at golf in the morning I promised Maurice to have supper with him, & according to himself and Dorothy he went only to have supper with me. At the dance Dr Shipton asked me for supper & I refused him on Maurice's account, but when Mr Duncan asked me I began to think I would like an older person instead of quite a boy for my partner, & Mr D. was urgent. I know it was just to gratify my vanity that I wanted an older man as really I think far away more of Maurice than of that brainless Duncan youth, but I asked or rather urged Maurice to cancel the supper engagement. Of course he had no choice but he was terribly hurt & I knew it; I regretted it as soon as I had done it & should, apart from the feeling of meanness, have liked supper ever so much better with him. It was not worthy of me to break my promise – I feel so insincere & unkind, & I know he won't forgive me for ages.

Saturday January 4th

I have by no means heard the last of Maurice's cancelled supper dance! Mrs Ellinger telephoned this morning to thank Mother for chaperoning Dorothy, also to inform her that they were all hurt & offended with me for my treatment of Maurice. Daddy was inclined to scold & be agitated; of course I would take none of it, though also of course it was quite right & proper as I know I was in the wrong though I wouldn't admit it anywhere but in here.

Sunday January 5th

Maurice & Dorothy came to tea. Maurice hardly spoke a word to me the whole time. After tea Edward & I played the violin & piano and Dorothy sang. Oh! how I envy such a glorious voice – it is like one's dreams of Heaven. There is no gift that I would possess in preference to this one, – this voice that can not only win fame but move hearts as well.

Monday January 6th

In the afternoon Mother, Edward & I went to a musical party at the Harleys'. Bertram Spafford sang quite well; his voice is sympathetic & he has much improved. Miss Harley also attempted to sing & the pianist to recite to the piano – a rather weak performance as she accompanied herself, so couldn't do any actions. Edward was quite the redeeming feature; Mrs

Ellinger told Maurice so. He really played the violin excellently.

Tuesday January 7th

This of course was the day of *the* dance – our dance at the Palace Hotel. Although I was in the not-altogether-enviable position of hostess – one-dance-to-each sort of thing, I managed to get 4 dances & supper with Ernest, & all my other partners were very nice. I did enjoy it – & got quite a reputation for finding out sitting-out places; I also tried Turkey Trots & things much to the amusement of some of the company. Douglas Spafford & I got out on to the balcony on the top landing & had a good view of Buxton lighted up; if I don't catch something I ought to!

Wednesday January 8th

I was very tired & slept all afternoon but still was sleepy, & went feeling so to Mrs Booth's dance at 7.0 at the Buxton Hydro. I wanted to go before the end, partly because I was tired & partly as Edward had forgotten the latchkey – so like him! I managed to drag them away after a time & we went home. Alas! I fear dances have the effect of turning both Ernest's & Maurice's heads. Ernest, after several sentimental remarks, seized hold of me at my bedroom door & tried to persuade me to come with Edward & talk to them in his room while they smoked. Maurice was taken the same way last night in the coffee-room, which was dark; he murmured something that sounded like 'Darling' & tried to put his arms round my neck. Oh! they have no right to behave so to a girl much weaker & smaller than themselves. When they behave so I feel ashamed both of myself & of them.

Sunday January 12th

After receiving numerous callers at tea-time, we went over to the Ellingers for music. Mrs Ellinger looked extremely tired & depressed; could not sing, in fact, without a brandy & soda beforehand! Edward & I played the first two movements of Beethoven's No. 1 Sonata. Mrs Ellinger said great things about Edward's violin playing. Would that he could take it up & think no more of the Civil Service – but that I suppose is the unpracticalness of the 'artistic temperament'.

Monday January 13th

Too cold for words! There was about a foot of snow on the ground and of course grand tobogganing & some ski-ing. There was a mist all over the lower part of the town this morning & I thought it would be a horrible day, but walking up to the toboggan-runs I walked out of the mist into the sun & there were all the hill peaks bright & glittering. It was glorious on the track & though I am not a wildly keen tobogganer, like the natives, I enjoyed it. The hills all round were beautiful; bright & beautiful as Purity, but also as cold as Purity without the warmth of Love!

Sunday January 19th

Felt the usual sleepiness – I may say boredom – in church. Oh! 'Church of England', 'where is the *King*, that I may worship him?' After supper I read from the book Miss Heath Jones lent me, *Christ & Human Need*. In spite of its unusual sensibility & clearness in dealing with the historical Christ from the orthodox point of view, I closed it still with the same belief, namely that Christ, though among the most wonderful & the greatest – perhaps *the* greatest – that has ever lived, was man even as we are, & that his Divine nature was the same in quality – though greater in degree & realisation – as our own, & that he is Lord over our Spiritual Kingdom by his conception of it through realisation of his Divinity, & the conviction of our need of spiritual life, for which he died.

Wednesday January 22nd

I went with Mother this evening to the 2nd of the University Extension lectures given by Mr J. Marriott on the Problems of Wealth & Poverty; I couldn't go to the last one because of Mrs Booth's dance. It was extremely interesting, & I was very glad of the lessons I had on the subject my last term at St Monica's. It was dreadfully badly attended, though – unintellectual Buxton all over. The lecture this week dealt particularly with the change from the domestic to the factory system in England, & went into the Factory Acts in some detail. Most of the questions asked were stupid; no women asked any or else I would soon have followed suit, with a large risk of being squashed. The lecturer is a big fair man, somewhat like the Duke of Devonshire.

Thursday January 23rd

Edward went back to Uppingham to-day. Now the boring time begins – but I shan't let it be so this year if I can help it! Mrs Deakin called & also Gwen Spafford, who talked about nothing but her neighbours' affairs & club squabbles! Unhappy, shut up little Buxton, lying at the bottom of a basin! The people seem so short of something to do that the only way of making the time pass is by prattling about each other. Oh! to escape from it!

Saturday January 25th

This afternoon after tea Mother & Daddy started talking again about moving south, & Daddy said he had practically decided we were going to!! They began to discuss it & Daddy said he could easily arrange to go up to the works for two days every week & be with us all the rest of the time; it is absurd to think it hardly takes any longer to get to Stoke from London than from here. I sat dreaming of a home – no matter if it be small – with a garden, & a smiling warm country instead of a grey one, & as I looked out of the window I saw the sunset all red – the first colour that has broken the greyness for days, glowing like an emblem of hope in the sky!

Wednesday January 29th

Mr Risigari came this afternoon & gave me the first of this term's lessons. He was very nice and didn't look quite so ugly as usual – possibly because it was getting dark. I was very relieved to be given two new exercises, a piece by Scarlatti – a dear little Pastorale of 1690, & No. 13 of Chopin's preludes, quite the most beautiful.

Saturday February 1st

This afternoon I played Daisy Whitehead's accompaniments (very badly, but the songs were so foolish) at the Devonshire Hospital. It was quite an unusual thing to me to see all those rows of poor crippled rheumatic patients, the men all separated from the women, & all looking like so many Dickens characters. Of course they appreciated all the comic things most.

Tuesday February 4th

We had quite a gay bridge at the Whiteheads' this afternoon. I was most rash and doubled all I could and went 'no trumps' on both possible & impossible hands, but just missed the prize. I finished *Felix Holt* after dinner. How George Eliot's books do inspire me; they make all good seem worthwhile. How I long to be such a character as Felix Holt, to have no regard for failure, to hold an ideal for humanity high enough to be forever leading further onward & yet applicable to the smallest things of life! How I yearn to follow pure and heavenly aspiration, without the alloy of a desire for self-glory or of personal ambition, to heal some little part of the sore burdens of mankind!

Wednesday February 5th

The third of Mr Marriott's lectures on 'Wealth & Poverty Problems' was held at the Town Hall to-night. The lecturer was most refreshing, & very forcibly scathing, especially when he remarked that Buxton people did not strike him as being *particularly* inquisitive. The question class afterwards was much better than last week as he came down from the platform & the questioning was much more animated. When it was over I asked for my essay back, somewhat in fear & trembling as I knew how sarcastic he could be. He looked at me in surprise when I indicated which it was. I only put my initials not my name, hoping he wouldn't know the sex of the writer & perhaps he didn't. To my surprise he said 'Is *that* yours? It is a *very* good essay indeed,' & I found he had given me 'A—' at the end & had written the criticism 'This is an *excellent* piece of work. You made your points very clearly & your criticism is sober & to the point. I hope you will write regularly.' I seemed as indifferent as I could manage though the inward elation was at bursting point! Perhaps Mother & Daddy, who seemed pleased, will believe that *some* of the more complimentary of my school reports were not mere fairy stories! How a little encouragement raises one into the heights! The smallest intellectual success always brings back to me the longing for the harder, less comfortable but more idealistic life that I would choose – that I *do* choose, though circumstances seem to withhold it. The smart clothes I know I possess – the prettiness which people say is mine – what satisfaction can they give at the height compared with the slightest of intellectual achievements?

Monday February 10th
Lucky Cora! On March 9th she is going to Italy, to visit Florence, Naples, & 'the grandeur that was Rome'. I wonder if it will be always my luck to hear about these places, imagine them, hear of other people going to them & never go myself. Not that I can grumble, in this home of many comforts.

Wednesday February 12th
How terrible this news is about Captain Scott & four of his party having been dead twelve months – dying from starvation & a terrible blizzard eleven miles from food, shortly after having found the South Pole. And how grand the way they died – especially the Captain Oates who went out into the blizzard to die that his weakness might not delay his four companions, who refused to leave him. 'Greater love hath no man than this.'

Tuesday February 18th
A letter came to Daddy from Edward; something about a row with Mr Puckle. We are very differently moulded; I would have cut my hand off before writing home about any of *my* rows! But then if I had started I should always have been writing about them!

Monday February 24th
A letter came from Stella thanking me for her birthday present. It was as usual full of all the amusements with which she seems surrounded. Yet, dull as it is here, & though she finds life a bed of roses & I often find it something closely allied to a bed of thorns, not for anything would I be her! Not for anything would I change a nature that is restless with search & strife, hard & often bitter though it be, for one that is passive, complacent & easily satisfied with the small issues of life.

Tuesday March 4th
On the way to golf I induced Mother to disclose a few points on sexual matters which I thought I ought to know, though the

information is always intensely distasteful to me & most depressing – in fact it quite put me off my game! I suppose it is the spiritual-&-intellectual-development part of me that feels repugnance at being brought too closely into contact with physical 'open secrets'. Alas! Sometimes it feels sad to be a woman! Men seem to have so much more choice as to what they are intended for. Still, I suppose our position improves with the years, & I must be thankful not to have lived in Homeric Greece instead of 20th-century England!

Wednesday March 5th

I had a note from Uncle Will – who has evidently at last forgiven me for having literary aspirations – enclosing a copy of a new review, the *Poetry Review*, & particulars of the Poetry Society. He wants me to join & I rather think I shall. The magazine contained a contribution of his, *The Master*, a short poetic play, which left me with a favourable impression.

The lecture to-night was on Trade Unions, Co-operation & Profit-Sharing Societies. After the lecture I was paid quite a big compliment by Mr Marriott. On returning my essay on Chartism he said 'This is really excellent, I like your work immensely,' to which I said that I hadn't expected that one to be much good as I wrote it when I had a bilious attack! (save the mark!). He laughed & said he was very sorry but he didn't notice the essay had suffered from it, & ended up with 'You know how to *write*; that's the secret of it,' & looked at me so kindly & quite deferentially, particularly considering I am just an ex-schoolgirl with rather a full-blown opinion of my own intelligence – which however is becoming modified the more I know, since the more I know the more I realise how little I know! I was very delighted because towards the end of the lecture Mrs Harrison asked Mother if we could put Mr Marriott up next time & Mother said we could.

Saturday March 8th

I went to the Hippodrome to-night to see that extraordinary cinematograph *From Manger to Cross, or Jesus of Nazareth*. Somehow the fact of seeing it pictured – & the pictures really were beautiful, made the reality of it all seem so much nearer. What a

strange combination of mythology, travesty & history that great
story seems to be – & yet it is all so wonderful, & the *Spirit*, which
is what really matters, is so living & so embodied in all, that we
can despise none of the forms in which it is pictured, however
exaggerated or imperfect.

Monday March 10th
The most exciting thing has happened – or rather has been
promised to happen! I was only beginning to-day to feel that
things were becoming a little monotonous when a letter came
from Miss Heath Jones telling me that she & Miss Bervon have
arranged to go to the great Summer Meeting of the Oxford
University Extension Delegacy at Oxford from Aug. 1st–13th, &
asking me to go with them! Mother & Daddy were not only
quite willing, but even seemed pleased about my getting this
glorious & unique opportunity. So to-morrow a letter must go to
Miss Heath Jones telling her I will go – oh! so gladly – oh! to
have such a thing to dream about & look forward to.

Wednesday March 19th
Mr Marriott arrived at five, with golf clubs, which he very
sensibly takes round with him, & which put Daddy off when
looking for him on the station as he 'never expected a professor
to carry golf clubs'! They had an interesting but short conversation chiefly about paper-making. I always feel proud of Daddy's
conversation on his own subjects; he is really very clever in
business & a good talker, well-informed. Daddy went to the
lecture, which was on Socialism. Of course Mr M. absolutely
demolished state Socialism, but admitted it possible when *love*
was extended among men & each worked for others as he now
worked for himself, only in that case 'when Socialism becomes
possible it becomes at the same time superfluous'. Love Socialism! Ah! What a grand ideal! I told him I was going to the
Summer Meeting at Oxford, & he seemed very pleased. He
gave me two papers giving particulars about it, & also recommended me to try for one of the prize essays – an honour,
I thought, & particularly kind of him to explain all about it to
me.

Friday March 21st

Good Friday – which in spite of its solemnity brought a fresh excitement. I went first to church with Daddy & then to the first part of the three hours service with Mother, which led to one of my not-infrequent spiritual conflicts as to 'what is truth'. It would be so easy – or rather, so much easier – to accept religion in a form in which the church doles it out – beautiful enough but to me, I will by no means say incorrect, for I dare not, but not complete enough, not satisfying enough. Yet, when one cannot accept what is given only, it is hard to find fresh paths for oneself. Yet is not this very difficulty the inspiration of the determination 'to strive, to seek, to find, & not to yield'! Heaven grant me at least to be true to, honest with, myself & work from right & just motives. May it grant me also never to be self-satisfied, never to reach that pleasant state of complacency which lulls the spirit to sleep! Gladys Lathbury rang me up at the telephone while I was at church. I rang her up when I returned & learnt she wanted me to act in the play *The Amazons* which they are getting up.

Wednesday April 2nd London

We met Stella for tea at Callard's. I had on a new hat which I put on for the first time just to try it. It is just a burnt-straw French shape trimmed with a bright flame-coloured wing, & I wore a flame-coloured crêpe-de-chine tie with it & the white collar of my blouse outside. The hat is *very* smart, so smart that while Mother & I were at Dunn's we were a little worried for fear it was too much so. However it needs a little courage to be really chic, but I have no doubt Stella thought me extremely flighty.

Thursday April 3rd

After breakfast Mother had two letters explaining that Granny had been taken ill with acute inflammation of the throat & was very poorly indeed. Miss Heath Jones & Miss Bervon are worried to death & wanted Mother to stay the week-end & look after her.

Monday April 7th Buxton

There was a rush of housekeeping & spring-cleaning in the morning. I told Daddy about Mother at tea-time & he seemed quite in a temper because they were keeping her. It must be funny to be so *very* dependent on another person; I don't think I should like it. Of course I want Mother to come back as having the housekeeping to do as well as all the rehearsals makes rather a rush of life, but still I don't upset myself all that because she is delayed.

Tuesday April 8th

Mother of course found fault with everything she saw at home, & seemed to think everything a complete muddle if she was away. It is characteristic of Mother that though I always want her to come home she always upsets me when she does come; one really feels it is not worth bothering to try & keep things straight in her absence. When Mother wants to be particularly nasty to me she impresses upon me how like I am to the Brittain family; thank goodness, thank goodness I am! *They* at least have a little courage, reserve, self-control, determination & staying-power!

Friday April 11th

The first night & my first appearance on any stage. Mr Pelter said 'Splendid, Miss Brittain, excellent!' but I didn't think I believed him, even though Mr & Mrs Ellinger & Maurice & others repeated it. I drove back with the family, who called for me at the stage door; they seemed very bucked up with the whole performance & pleased with me; Daddy said he had laughed till he cried. The audience, which started being only mildly amused, were quite hysterical at the end.

Saturday April 12th

From the moment I came on everything simply *romped*. I enjoyed every moment (except the 1st song) from beginning to end. The night before, Mr Pelter asked me if I would come to a supper following the play, at the Hydro. I didn't know at all what sort of a thing it would be, this being my first appearance, but luckily, instead of possessing Mother's shrinking from the unusual, I possess a love to find out the unknown & accepted purely for the experience. I went to the Hydro with Mr Pelter & Mrs Ellinger, & while I was tidying in the cloakroom Mrs Ellinger simply raved about my frock, to my great satisfaction. Well, as for enjoying the supper – I simply *loved* it & haven't laughed so much for ages.

Thursday April 24th

I managed to drag from [Mother] a little of the closed book of her early life. It is so true that nobody's life is humdrum & everybody's life is tragic – how little everybody knows about everyone else! I have not been touched directly yet either by the thrill of joy or the darkness of tragedy; mine has been a very sheltered life, so I suppose it is all to come. We are none of us free from destiny. Poor Mother must have had a dreadful time in the midst of the poverty & struggles & inefficiency (as she tells me) of my grandfather, & too many children in the family. [Daddy] moved heaven & earth to get her; I can't imagine him passionate about anything, but no doubt he set his mind on her, wanting a wife, & as he wanted her particularly he was determined to get her. I seem to have known all along that she wasn't reconciled to it at first, but a home of her own must have attracted her & made her agree, & she probably was glad to escape from the poverty & sordidness which surrounded her for a life of steadily increasing comforts. It is not for these things that *I* should count the world well lost, I don't feel I could marry a man if there was no romance attached to him, especially if he were impatient & intolerant like Daddy was with Mother. But then I have never known the sting of poverty, so I can't imagine the great joy that release from it must be.

The history of all these things made it clear to me why Mother finds me difficult to understand & get on with, because the part that *is* understandable is like Daddy's side, which she always objected to, rather than hers. The sense of loneliness quite overpowered me; there seems so often to be *no one* here to turn to; Daddy of course is hopeless, far too shrewd, business-like & limited, & Edward is the baby that boys of seventeen nearly always are. So I began to cry weakly at first & then more miserably & entered with Mother into a variety of rather heartrending explanations concerning difference of temperament. She did seem to want me after all, & to want to make me less lonely. A few hours ago I couldn't have imagined myself either confessing my loneliness to Mother or letting her see my distress, but I am glad of it instead of sorry if only to prove how great a darling I always knew she could be.

Wednesday April 30th
Daddy upset poor Edward by wishing he had a son in the works, & E. of course began wondering if he was doing his duty by going in for what he is most fitted for, or if he ought to have ignored all the intellectual qualities which fit him at any rate to try for the Civil Service. I talked to him for some time after lunch & think I persuaded him to stick to the Civil even if he *does* fail. None of the things he is really good at would be any use to him [at the works], & none of the things which would be of use to him is he any good at. Besides, a ready-made career! It is certainly the more lucrative, but is it the highest? Surely it is better to go in for something that requires striving for, even if you do fail at the end.

Monday May 5th
I sent my essay to Oxford to-day, with an inward prayer for its success – which, however, I dare not & do not expect.

Sunday May 11th
We went to Mrs Ellinger's for tea. Professor Chapman, the Economist, & his wife, a very clever lady who doesn't wear stays & looks like it, were staying there the weekend. We got into a very animated discussion on women's suffrage; the Chapmans & I were very much in favour of it & seemed to convince everybody, though everyone else was more or less antisuffragist.

Tuesday May 27th
I heard when I got in that Mrs Harrison had rung up wanting me to play tennis so I rang her up & arranged to go at once. Between the 2nd & last sets I went to her house & had some milk & rested a bit & talked to her. She was telling me her opinion of

most of the Buxton people, with whom you never get any further though you meet them again & again, & who have so large an idea of their own importance & so little to have an idea about. She was, as she told me, blackballed when she first wanted to enter the tennis club. It is disgraceful the way people here – the snobs! – have treated her simply because she had the courage to marry Mr Harrison, who being the proprietor of St Ann's Hotel was lower in the social scale, & of course with these parvenus the fact that he is clever & well-educated doesn't count at all.

Saturday May 31st
The first thing I saw when coming downstairs was a letter from Mr Marriott & though it might have been merely information about books which I applied for on Thursday, I somehow felt it was exciting. My premonition was right enough & the first few lines drew an excited exclamation even from my self-control. For the first few lines ran 'I am very pleased indeed to tell you you have been awarded a prize' etc.! My humble essay! how glad I am I wrote it at Mr Marriott's suggestion. I didn't think I had an earthly chance; it is one thing writing the best papers in a little town like this & quite another entering for a competition open to the whole United Kingdom. Mother & Daddy were of course very bucked up & Daddy said that when Mr Marriott came here he left his Elijah's cloak behind him! Oh! I didn't know I could feel so glad. The honour & glory is the great thing, the actual prize does not matter much.

I wrote & told Miss Heath Jones & Miss Bervon & also Edward, I thought they would like to know. Mother said I ought to telephone & tell Mrs Harrison, as it is through her energy in getting up the lectures that it has all happened. Also she was kind enough to get the necessary information & recommend me, without which I could not have managed. However I refused to telephone. We met her however in the town, & Mother, to my intense confusion, insisted on telling her. I of course wanted her to know but didn't want her to be told, if that isn't double Dutch. She congratulated me & said 'I'm awfully glad' as though she really were. I have much for which to be grateful to her.

This was the 1st rehearsal of the pictures-in-dumb-show which Miss Mothersill asked me to join in. She wrote on Thursday to ask if I would take part in an SPG Exhibition that was coming to Buxton. I was not too delighted; but I couldn't very well get out of it as I promised Miss Mothersill to act next time she wanted anyone. The first scene represented a little missionary child convert inducing several of her companions to come & look at a sacred picture-book. Meanwhile 'The Sower went forth sowing' went on at the back. Next tableau showed me, the only white person (I have to be a missionary of all things!), at the dispensary. First I bind up an arm, then I rub a rheumatic knee, then I bandage someone's eyes & then rush off at an urgent call; meanwhile 'At even ere the sun was' goes on drearily at the back. The Rev. Mr Dicker, who came in towards the end, feelingly remarked 'Yes, there's something very touching about that picture; very touching.' *I* was touched with inward hysterics.

Sunday June 8th

As we passed the Slacks' house we noticed the blinds were down, & knew that poor Mr Slack after 12 days' serious illness with pneumonia was dead. I have never known such a dismal Sunday. The rain dropped off the trees with a dreary sound & the wind was cold enough for November. How everything seemed to say that we are only here for a time – a short, short time – which even to the longest-lived of us is gone like 'a watch in the night'. How the small events of our years are merged in the greater happenings of a century – merged & lost; how strange to think that the lives of those who have been around us go on even the same when our presence is departed from them.

Wednesday June 11th

The amusing-serious entertainment came off – & for this first time actually without mishap! As the missionary lady I felt inordinately good – & consequently quite incongruous. The incongruity made me want to laugh, & yet at the same time I felt the queer pricking feeling which makes you want to cry. Giving our dispensary things, tending the sick, comforting the widows (& inspecting their sewing!) & helping the neglected, did not move me, I know, because they were mission things – as in spite of the Exhibition, I remain of the same opinion – i.e. that most missions do more harm than good. No, it is simply that the fundamental springs of love & pity & gentleness towards all the world are stirred by these almost humorous representations.

Saturday June 21st

I never can understand Mrs Anderson as she is always charming to me, but has never invited me to a thing, even a game of tennis, so I suppose she dislikes me really but is good at concealing it. I wish I knew why. I always think it is more than half a person's fault when they are disliked; if only people would give one the reason *why* they do, it would so often be possible to amend the objectionable characteristic. It is quite amusing to have a nature like mine; now I am so down, life seems hardly worth living; probably before long I shall be so bubbling over with the joy of *being* that my heart will be raising itself in gratitude to Heaven simply because I am alive!

Wednesday June 25th Waterworks Cottage, Uppingham

Mother & I came here this afternoon till Monday for 'Old Boys'. Edward met us at 6.0 at the cottage & had dinner with us, & we walked about afterwards. We did not see many boys, though we met the Corps.

Thursday June 26th

I spent practically all day watching Uppingham play their 'Old Boys'. I saw quite a lot of Ernest, he came & sat beside me & stared at his toes in the usual way when all his arduous work as captain was done.

Friday June 27th

Leighton, one of the cleverest boys in Uppingham, & Carey came to lunch, & afterwards we sat for a little while in Fairfield Gardens & talked.

Sunday June 29th

Edward & Richardson came in to breakfast & we departed to chapel soon after. Ernest came in to dinner, which pleased me greatly, as I have never lost the – not exactly affection – but interest I have had for him. He seems to have grown much older; being cricket captain seems to have given him a fuller sense of his responsibilities. [Edward] brought in Leighton again to supper; I like him immensely, he seems so clever & amusing & hardly shy at all. I read Edward's poem on 'The Empire Ships', which though it might be worse is somewhat strained & weird; still, the subject is not inspiring.

Saturday October 18th Buxton

Of course I stopped writing the record just when everything most interesting was going to happen. It is reading all about the diaries of eminent men in my work for the exams that has put me on to it again. I cannot however go fully into everything that has happened since July, but must be content with a brief summary & for the rest leave the past to explain itself by the present.

In August I went with Miss Heath Jones & Miss Bervon to Oxford for the Summer Meeting. There I had heaps of lectures & saw something of Mr Marriott; I stayed behind a day after Miss H.J. & Miss B. & had dinner at his house. It was after this that I finally decided to go to Oxford & to Somerville if I can, & I got Daddy to give his permission at last. I am coaching an hour a day at Mr Lace's for Maths & Latin, so as to try & pass the Oxford Senior, which exempts one from Responsions, next July, & go to Oxford Oct. twelve months from now. I am also coaching myself for the Somerville scholarship exam. in English. I am taking the schol. on Edward's advice & by my own inclination, not because I expect to get it, but because I hate not to try.

The beginning of September I went to Byfleet for a dance, & stayed on, & then Cora came back with me to stay here a week. While she was here, Bertram Spafford, who had been following me about all the summer, started to do so more markedly than ever. One Sunday he kept meeting me on purpose all over the place, & the next day, when Cora was going, he proposed to me by letter. Cora heard all about it of course; thank goodness she was there for me to talk to. I sent back a very cold & decided refusal, calling him 'merely an acquaintance' & Daddy called it presumptuous. I was very annoyed at his daring to propose. I have not seen him since, except at a distance, & I dread meeting him as it will probably be embarrassing.

For the rest, I am working hard at Latin, Maths & English, also doing music & golf very keenly. I am beginning to be very keen about writing at once, though I suppose this should really be my receptive, not my creative, period. I want to be keenly observant of all about me, so as to get material for my Buxton story. I am also composing another story, in which the heroine is to be me, & Cora, Stella, Adrian & various friends outside Buxton to come in. That will have to wait though till I get to know more about life & particularly about London. I want to go about armed with a notebook & put down all the things, absurd, pathetic, interesting, original, humorous, satirical, that strike me as being useful for material.

I forgot to mention that Mrs Harrison has asked me to be on the University Extension Lectures local committee; it is wonderful they will deign to have anyone as young as I. I am delighted, because I hope the meetings will give me the opportunity, not only of airing some of my views, but of getting to know her better.

Tuesday October 21st
Mother had a Mothers' Union meeting at Mrs Cox's to-day, which appears to have been quite amusing. At the end of the meeting Mrs Cox suddenly said to Mother 'Is it true that Vera is going to be a lecturer?' Mother very naturally said 'What?' & Mrs Cox continued 'Why, it is all over the town that Vera Brittain is shortly going to begin lecturing!' Mother, with some dignity, drew herself up & replied to the effect that 'Vera Brittain is at present working up for two exams, one in March & another in July, after which, should she be so fortunate as to pass them, she *may* go to Oxford the following October.' 'Oh! so it's a *very* long time ahead,' says Mrs Cox, somewhat taken aback no doubt at having got the rumour so wrong. 'There is of course a chance,' continues Mother, 'that if she *should* manage to go to Oxford, she may become a lecturer in time, but the whole thing is very much of a supposition at present.' 'And what if she goes & gets married before it is all finished?' exclaims Mrs Spafford.

'In that case,' replies Mother, still with the dignity which she is able to exercise on other people's behalf but never on her own, 'not a moment of what she has done will be wasted, as what she has learnt will be of inestimable benefit to her.'

Uncle Willie is quite right; in a small narrow place like this one half thinks me too go-ahead for words, & the other absolutely mad & a perfect fool. It is so strange; if I had a talent for drawing & wished to study in Paris, or a better talent than I have for music, & wanted to take it up at the Royal College, or perhaps Berlin, everyone would think me interesting & wonderful but perfectly natural, but just because I want to go to Oxford to study the literature of my own language I am 'eccentric', 'ridiculous', a 'strong-minded woman'. It has just struck me to-day too that it is scarcely ever men who raise objections to a woman's being given what her talents deserve, but always other women. At first it seems extraordinary that women should be the retrogressive members just when the era of their true glory & justice is beginning to dawn. But I suppose it is that women are sharply divided into two classes, the old-fashioned, who can see nothing, & the new-fashioned, who see all. There seems to be no intermediate class who can sympathise with both parties. Here, for instance, one or two, like Mrs Lawson & Mrs Harrison, warmly approve & commend my trying for Oxford. On the other hand are a whole host who think it either presumption or folly. It must be that those who are blind cannot see even the merest glimmer, while the new things just at this moment of history are so very new & so very wonderful to us poor slaves of the ages, that a person who is modern at all cannot help but be very modern indeed.

Saturday October 25th
When the sky is calm & red, & the trees stand up black against it & very still, & in the distance the hills are a faint blue-grey merging into the horizon, I am forced to look up from my book & gaze until it all fades. It seems to me that the difference between the history of literature & dark motionless trees against a sunset sky is just the difference between being an Oxford student & an imaginative artist. Not that I think for a moment that the Oxford studentship is unnecessary. It is the

indispensable foundation of the imagination. The history of literature, so to speak, is necessary to a real creative appreciation of the sunset sky. 'Perfect love is the daughter of perfect knowledge,' said Leonardo da Vinci. I will add that to the list of my rules of life, & will say also that perfect freedom can only come through perfect knowledge. Only when we are thoroughly acquainted with facts can we afford to disregard them; only after a thorough understanding of technique can we dare to reach beyond it. To attempt to achieve without knowledge is like beginning a journey along an unknown road on a dark night; knowledge is God.

Saturday November 15th

This morning in the *Buxton Advertiser* was a continuation of the religious controversy started last week by Mr J. H. Ward, the new curate of Fairfield, who is a sort of Robert Elsmere. He wrote then to ask for justice with regard to a statement made at a Bible Society meeting (at which all the narrow & evangelical clergy of the district were present) that he had denied the Bible to be the Word of God. To-day there are four letters in answer, three from Fairfield men, testifying to the excellent work done by Mr Ward, & the sort of religious wave that is passing over the village; the other & longest was from a regular narrow old-fashioned evangelical parson. He condemns Mr Ward right & left as a heretic – then goes on to ask Mr Ward to answer certain statements, taken down in writing from Mr Ward's teaching – such as 'The Garden of Eden is a myth', 'There was nothing miraculous about the birth of Christ', 'I decline to believe in a God who requires me to be washed in blood', 'There is no Hell except in this life'. It rejoiced my heart to read them & to feel that there is at least one in the Church of England who is moving with the new thought & new truth of the age.

Mother & Daddy read the letters, & Mother more or less agreed, in her mild way, with Mr Ward. Daddy, somewhat to my surprise, went on like anything, saying that such men as Mr Ward were dangerous to the Church, that it would be a good thing if he were tumbled out etc. I was too indignant to speak & all my powers of argument promptly left me; I did try to argue against there being any miracle in Our Lord's life or any divinity different in kind from our own, but he seemed to think it terrible heresy, & argued on the lines of the usual threadbare superstitions & traditions – i.e. that any science or discovery that proved the Bible different from what he had always believed it must be wrong *because* it told him different from what he had always believed (not that *he* could possibly be wrong by refusing to see the Bible in the true light of modern discovery). Finally he ended up by saying that I didn't know what I was talking about, & it was ridiculous a little slip of a girl arguing with him about what I didn't understand etc.

Of course I have always known, but it is no longer doubtful to me, that it is as a plaything or a pretty toy that he spoils & pets me, not as a sensible human being who *counts*, & that he has nothing but contempt for me & my knowledge, just as he has at heart for all women, because he believes them for some unknown reason to be inferior to him, & for all learning, because it hasn't seemed necessary to him & he has never felt any desire towards it. I tried to explain what I have proved for myself, but oh! how hopeless it is to make anyone see by a few inadequate words what one has gradually proved to be truth through months of thought & hard striving. And also, it is useless trying to make people understand you unless they have in their minds beforehand a sort of instinctive comprehension of what you are trying to explain.

I do not for a moment believe that I have found the truth (what, indeed, is truth?) but I do think I have found a glimmer of it, & have entered upon a train of thought which will develop & modify as long as I have mind & spirit, but which will not alter fundamentally very much. This at least is certain, that facts proved by reason or experience or history are at least firm ground where one can stand secure. Thus I believe that the faith I hold now (which is what I have thought out for myself, certainly not what I have been taught, except in a few instances), let people call it what they like, deistic, heretical, free-thinking, even atheistic if it pleases them, is of true & lasting value to me, is, I *know*, of more real truth, is at least more able to be proved, than the dogmas of superstition & worn-out incorrect doctrine, with which the majority of Church of England parsons fill my ears every time I go to church.

Poor Mother. She *will* worry me so about remedies for my cold. I can't help getting annoyed, partly, I suppose, because I realise that I don't give her half as much attention when she is ill as she gives me when I am, but also because I get so sick of endless injunctions to get into bed quickly etc. Of course I *know* that these are what I should do, & are the most sensible instructions for me – but oh! if one was *only* sensible, would one ever rise beyond that dull level of respectable mediocrity whose meritorious shelter Mother & Daddy seemed so terribly afraid of getting away from? The daughter, I fear, in this instance is the father's living reaction!

Sunday November 16th
I started on Palgrave's *Golden Treasury* this afternoon; even if I don't pass that exam. I shall always bless it for the literary & artistic world to which it has introduced me.

Monday November 17th
I have had the most thrilling afternoon. We gave a truly fashionable bridge party, to which fifteen of the most interesting of all the people in Buxton came. Not to mention *the* one. Mrs Ellinger helped us to arrange the tables, as my original arrangement was not good. It was she, it was indeed, who got Mrs Harrison & me put at the same table; in my original arrangement, she was far enough away from me. Mrs Leigh Slater was simply screaming; she was obviously so keen to get the prize, & she talked the whole time. She insisted on telling me all about Norah Higgins, whom she met at Bournemouth, having said that when she went to St Monica's, the term after I had left, everyone was talking about Vera Brittain, & saying how I had been Head, & how popular & how clever I had been. I said I was sure it couldn't be true, & I never knew I had that reputation, as I thought they all hated me. (That to be exact is not quite true; some did hate me & others had violent adorations for me, there was very little of that half-way house of ordinary popularity.)

Going down to tea Mrs Harrison said to me how lucky we were to have such big rooms (to which I of course responded that I didn't think they were) & that she was going to try &

entertain in her little house next week & she didn't know whatever would happen. I realised that it was a sort of hinted apology for asking only Mother & not me! What really over-joyed me was, that between the hands she asked me if I would come up to her house one day & help her to send out over 200 circulars (part of the Lectures business) & stay some time. I took some of the many opportunities I had of studying her to-day. What a mixture she is of good & evil, & how strong in both! There is strength in the firmness of her chin, the uprightness of her head & whole figure, & even in its slim grace; her lips are so thin & firmly closed that they express much of hardness & cruelty & a sort of fierce, unyielding, unforgiving vigilance, yet in her eyes there are untold depths of idealism, & lovableness, intelligence, sweetness – & mockery too! Her thin sensitive hands seem to show how very much she is alive & awake to all that goes on – nothing escapes her. Oh! how what I have observed makes me long to know more!

Tuesday November 18th

I went this evening to a Progressive Bridge at Mrs Whitehead's. Crowds of people were there, many of whom I didn't know; there were eight tables, & B.S. was there! He avoided me studiously, & I tried to be as alluring as possible in order to tease him. I managed to go from table to table on small scores till I finally caught him up at the end of the evening. Poor thing! I am afraid that he was very sad & uncomfortable, as he kept turning round so that he should not have to look at me, which was rather a difficulty when he was sitting opposite. I suppose it is wrong to sear people's feelings so, but oh! the temptation!

Wednesday November 19th

Well, I am not likely to forget this afternoon; how I wish instead of its being all over, that it was all to come. I arrived at Mrs Harrison's about 2.30, & we started straight away to work, I writing addresses on envelopes & she reading out the names to me, & folding up circulars & putting them inside the envelopes. Mr Harrison also was there the first two or three minutes; they are always very sweet together. He teased me about the swiftness of my writing, & told me I could get down 'Burlington

Rd' in the same time that it took him to put a comma. Then we two were left alone, & got through simply heaps, tho' we might have got through still more if we hadn't talked hard all the time. I only wish I could remember all the conversation, it was all precious, & got more & more intimate as time went on. She said somewhat pointedly that, while you always had an antipathy to some people, there were others with whom you felt on the same plane at once, & she went on to tell me that she had noticed me first at the Hunt Ball two years ago, when Mrs Ellinger pointed me out as a débutante. I don't know whether that remark meant anything I wanted it to mean, but you don't generally trouble to think where you first met people unless they interest you a little. After tea the baby came in & played about on the hearthrug with bricks. Mrs Lawson always moves me to a sort of emotion with her affection for her children, but what she shows is not nearly so moving as Mrs Harrison's depth of joy in her child; her love for him seems somehow intoxicating & passionate, & carries one away with the idea of the most deeply felt, fully realised kind of motherhood there can be. She clasps him to her & kisses him so fervently even when playing with him most gaily, that I could scarcely bear to look.

Friday November 21st
This afternoon I saw young Mr Ward, the Fairfield curate, in the town. He has a pale, rather sad face & very thoughtful eyes, & a firm jaw. Mother was talking to old Mrs Bennett this afternoon about the letters in the paper; Mrs Bennett has great faith in Mr Ward although she is old & might have been old-fashioned, & says she heard an address of his that was most inspiring. She does not understand how any enlightened being of the present day can dare to contradict him, but said that there were so many people in the world who never troubled to think & her advice was to let them be. She says she knows from experience that a person's views may become quite unbalanced & leave them with no faith at all by a modern overthrowing of all their traditional beliefs. I can well understand this, as I remember after reading *Robert Elsmere* how desperate I used to feel, how afraid of facing the truth, which would force itself on to my reason, how desirous almost to flee from thought, & yet how

weary with thinking. I don't agree that people ought to be left alone in their blindness; I don't think one ought to *force* one's own convictions on other people, but I do firmly believe that they ought to be aroused to think things out for themselves & come to a conclusion which would be of value because of their own making.

Sunday November 23rd

To-day has been more interesting than Sundays are as a rule. We had an appallingly dull service at Burbage this morning & a prosy mission preacher, but this evening Mother & I went to Fairfield to hear Mr Ward preach. The church, which once used to be so empty, was simply packed. They were nearly all poor people & he was talking to one of them in the aisle when we got there, moving, with his pale thoughtful tired face, like a leader among them. The service was short & very simple, such a contrast with this morning, & when Mr Ward began to preach all the discomforts of our crowded pew were forgotten at once. He took as his text those most wonderful of words (which have so often served as an excuse for wearying people with all sorts of obvious & platitudinal remarks), 'I am the Light of the World.' He spoke of Christ having revealed to men their own spiritual nature, of the goal Christ gives us of help to one another – of our immortality – but it is impossible to reproduce his sermon in a few words, or to give any idea of the originality with which he treated his text. He started to speak containedly & low, & worked up to the highest pitch of fierce earnest enthusiasm when speaking of Christ as the Light of the World. You couldn't exactly have heard a pin drop while he was speaking, as a good many of the congregation were conspicuous for colds & coughs, & several brought small children (not being able to come I suppose unless they did) who were by no means silent. But he seemed to rise quite beyond the undercurrent of noise, & held everybody tense & spellbound till the burst of enthusiasm with which he ended. Afterwards he shook hands with everyone at the church door. I do hope soon to get to know him.

    Going home past the Spaffords' house, we saw B.S. without hat or coat leaning very melancholy over the gate at the end of the patch which does them for a garden. I suppose seeing me the other night must have aroused all his fervour once more. I don't feel half sorry enough, I am sure; I fear I must be a heartless little wretch!

Tuesday November 25th

Mother told me this morning that Mrs Harrison had studied music in Paris for 3 years & once could really play very well. I never guessed she was musical until the other evening, when she sang in so sweet a voice to the baby. She says I ought to give it up if I have not time, as I shall only drop it in the end as she has done, but I don't guess I shall, unless I am ever bound to by stress of other work. It is too valuable a means of self-expression, & I think everyone ought to train & use every means of self-expression that is given to them – the possession of a talent ought to be a sufficient reason for cultivating it. Almost everyone has one special means at which they excel in expression, some have only one, but others who have more than one develop their special talent all the more by the use of their lesser ones. Mrs Harrison, I am sure, like me, has several means of self-expression. No, music is too great a relief to my often overburdened feelings to give up; besides, it is my best means of keeping really intimate with Edward. That I should be good at it is necessary to his complete success; I must play his accompaniments & compositions, & the fact that he with his musical judgement thinks me good is sufficient reason for me to study for my own & art's sake!

Saturday November 29th

When we were talking about exams & fame etc. this evening, Mother told me she has always felt that I shall succeed in everything I undertake & Edward will always just miss. Well, time will show! Edward, whatever he does, has at any rate the power of making himself agreeable to anyone, which will carry him far, & keep him happy & popular. The exceptional & remarkable people seem always to be the unhappiest & the loneliest, even though theirs at times is the joy which nothing else on earth can replace.

Thursday December 11th

There was great excitement in little Buxton to-day because the Queen had to pass through on her way to lunch with Lord Newton. All the place was hung with flags & streamers. The four Royal motors, chocolate-coloured with ensigns on the back, looked the essence of wealth & pomposity & came by very quickly. The Queen & the Duchess of Devonshire were in the first. Her Majesty looked very portly in black & a sable coat; her large & rather expressionless features are not remarkable in any way for aristocratic distinction. The whole party looked very supercilious & altogether rather powdered & made up. How thankful I am I don't belong to that class of society; if I am to have any distinction, I want it to be that of intellect & talent – so far, far more worth having than the pomp & circumstance that comes from being the possessor of wealth or the product of generations of intermarriage. Expensive lunatics, that are kept in motors & sables by an industrious nation's toil!

Friday December 19th

Edward seems shocked at the idea of playing [bridge] for money, & also moralises against my love of argument. I am afraid he is much more naturally virtuous than I am. Also – thus far & no further – like the rest of the world. But I would not give up what is my own though it have to be accomplished in solitude. He forgets that his placid temper finds it easy to let an argument drop, while to my pugilistic one it is well-nigh impossible. So many people make allowances for outside circumstances & forget the difference in nature of temperament, which counts more than all.

Saturday December 20th

We went to a little dance at the Briggs'. Although I danced every dance hard & had what I suppose everyone would call a good time, it leaves me with a very unsatisfied feeling to have met so many stupid & superficial men, with whom all the girls are obviously so pleased. How I wish I could meet a good strong splendid man, full of force & enthusiasm, & in earnest about his life! There must *be* such!

Wednesday December 24th

In the evening we went to bridge at the Ellingers'. Oh! much as
I love bridge, I would not become one of those bridge-playing,
cigarette-smoking, parasitic beings for any amount of money.
There is an atmosphere of dissoluteness & slackness about the
whole place.

Friday December 26th

I am so thankful Christmas day is over; I cannot remember one
that has not depressed me. Of all events that make for
melancholy & mark the passage of time [the worst] are those
which recur at fairly long & regular intervals & are always like
each other – at least all Christmases have been alike so far to me.
I was able to start working again to-day with much thankful-
ness.

Monday December 29th

I couldn't go to bed, late as it is, without writing just a line or
two about my 20th birthday. I was awfully depressed all day
because of it, as my birthday always makes me think of all the
bad things I have done in the past year & all the nasty things
that have happened to me & none of the nice ones.

Tuesday December 30th

Alas! I fear that the year I foresaw as 'lucky' is after all ending in
gloom. Apart from the fact that I am (I suppose) a child of
worldly fortune, it doesn't seem to have brought me much
actual luck, though many more things have happened in it than
in the year I first came out. Well, I have no premonitions for
next year, though a multitude of inward prayers. After all I may
not have been wrong; it may be that in future years I shall look
back upon this one & find that it marked the beginning of
something which is to be a great joy & blessing in my life – the
significance of which I do not recognise now, but shall realise
then.

1914

Friday January 2nd

I seem to be writing to-night with hardly any of my circumstances changed from last year, when I sat here & wrote at the
same time. Mrs Harrison, B.S. & Oxford are the only really
important things that have come into my existence since last
Jan. 2nd. Otherwise – the same surroundings, the same friends,
the same hopes, the same objects in life, & perhaps a still greater
number of unfulfilled wishes! Shall I be writing here, I wonder,
next Jan. 2nd with all the circumstances still unchanged? Truly
we count time in events, not years.

    Edward came home to-day. There are rumours afloat now of
his going into the works after all – there is so much money &
promise in them that we may someday be really rich, & Daddy
naturally wants his only son to have a part in it. Mother wants it
too – even if he could get into the Civil Service, she would hate
him to go away – had I but been the boy I & my disposition
could have been much more easily spared. Poor thing! She
admitted to-day that she would much rather have an ordinary
daughter – living & sleeping & dying & leaving no impress
behind! I suppose I have all the share of enterprise & ambition.
After all I may leave no more impression behind than the most
abject parasite that ever lived on someone in this country – but I
am determined anyhow to have a good attempt, for failure will
be less ignoble than never to try. Of course E. will go to Oxford
in any case.

Sunday January 4th

E. and I went to Fairfield in the evening. The wind was blowing
great guns, & we had a splendid walk up there. Mr Ward was
most energetic; I could tell that when he read the lessons. His

sermon was even more splendid, vigorous & original than usual. It was on the text 'Arise, wake out of sleep' etc., & was a discourse of the greatest eloquence against present-day indifference both to God & to danger. He laid particular stress on the peril of sins of omission & said that virtue did not consist in church-going & 'pi-ness' but in the actual work we did every day for the sake of right. He told us that some people said he did not preach comforting sermons, but he was not here to preach comforting sermons but to arouse people from their apathy. To-night he recognised me when he shook hands at the door & gave me a very nice smile. Everyone seems to crowd to his door to get a glimpse of him.

Tuesday January 13th

We bought a *Herald* this afternoon in which both our dresses for the Cottage Hospital Ball were described. Mother's was called 'a superb toilet', & mine 'ultra fashionable'! Next to the account of the dance in the paper was a reported speech of Mr Ward's at a Fairfield meeting. The two items formed such a contrast – something like that between the idealism & frivolity in my own divided spirit!

Thursday January 15th

Quite the nicest dance of this season was given to-night by the Bowens at Corbar Hall. They have just bought the place & done it all up on a very costly scale, & the dance in elegance & ornateness certainly matched the house. Even Edward liked it. I wonder if Heaven will ever grant me the fame, the friendships or the motherhood for which I nightly pray.

Friday January 16th

Heaven, however, won't help those who don't help themselves, & as Mr Ward is one of the people I want to know I persuaded Mother to come to Fairfield with me & call upon his wife – hoping they would both be in. A little maidservant showed us in to a very small sitting-room & then left us alone for some time so I studied my surroundings. The house is quite near the church, & though tiny is much better than the places where some curates have to live. The front of the house looks on to Fairfield churchyard, but at the back & from the little windows where we were, there is a view right across the valley. It looked very dreary & miserable on such a grey foggy day as this, but sometimes must look beautiful in the brightness of our occasional clear skies. The room itself was just like the sitting-room of a lodging-house but more homely.

After we had waited some time Mrs Ward came in, obviously rather frightened of us at first & not knowing quite how to take us. She is a very small woman of the insignificant type that one would never notice out of doors, & was plainly dressed in dark blue. She is considerably older than he, & looks forty, but probably, judging from her sad expression & worn look, has grown prematurely old. She addressed us very nervously, using our names a great deal, but became much more at her ease as we explained our sympathy with Mr Ward & eulogised his teaching. She, like he, was probably one of the people, most likely a district nurse, & has not risen as far from the ranks as he. I liked her. Obviously her whole world is Mr Ward. She spoke very simply of his great gift for teaching, & with evident pride. I explained that I was not fond of church, but that Mr Ward drew me there whether I would or no. I told her I had heard many preachers, especially in the south of England, but never one to touch him. Then the letters in the paper were mentioned & we told her how thoroughly we sympathised with Mr Ward. She seemed so grateful for a little sympathy that I feel ashamed of having withheld my expression of it even until now. She recounted to us what a terrible time they have had; how Mr Ward, worn out with work & opposition, often almost despairs because his hand, that would be so liberal in its reformations, is withheld by a narrow-minded, idle, & jealous vicar. She was not sure how much longer they could stand it.

Poor souls! And all because they are progressive & try to guide men aright. Opposition & persecution seem to be a 'sine qua non' of any great & selfless work. I felt quite choky when I thought of their hard task & dreary lonely existence, & then compared it with my own pampered, sheltered, trivial life. (She seemed indeed interested to hear that I am a worker, doing my best to raise it from triviality.) I will try to get to know them well & do all I can to help them in my limited way (alas! so limited now!) & bring a little brightness to them if I may. She was interested to hear of my socialistic inclinations & said she was sure Mr Ward would be glad to know me. She came to the gate with us & seemed to like me I thought, & clasped my hand warmly & repeatedly said in her simple way that she was glad to know me. How hard it is that life should be made so difficult for pure hearts such as theirs – ardent to work, idealistic, sensitive, the very people of all others that our materialistic world so greatly needs!

Saturday January 17th
Now at last the dances are over; I have enjoyed them greatly, but am quite glad as it is very necessary to get seriously to thought & work, & leave behind me for a time that other side of myself, the frivolity so dear to me!

Tuesday January 20th
I wrote to-day for an entrance form for the much-dreaded Somerville Scholarship in March. We saw in the *Morning Post*, much to our & especially Edward's great delight, that Roland Leighton, who was up at Oxford last week, has got the first Postmastership at Merton. This information of someone else's success sends me floundering with renewed effort in the fields of scholarship.

Friday January 23rd
I thought of an idea to-day for a plot for another novel, also dealing with Buxton, in which Mr Ward will play an important part as the original of one of the characters.

Saturday January 24th
Mother & I went off to the Manchester Art Gallery. Holman Hunt does not appeal to me greatly; I am not immensely impressed with *The Light of the World*, espec. in comparison with its fame, but liked still less *The Shadow of Death*. To begin with there seems to be nothing uplifting & inspiring in the spirit of the picture, in spite of its sacred subject, & I did not care for the execution of it; everything seems to strike the eye at once, which of course is due to the fact that Hunt bestowed the same care on

the shavings which cover the floor of the carpenter's shop, as on the face of Our Lord.

We were a little tired after all this walking about, so had an early dinner at Parker's, & then went to the Free Trade Hall for the Wagner concert. Marvellous, fascinating Sir Henry Wood came down to conduct. The orchestra played all the overtures & preludes to Wagner's operas in chronological order. After the interval came *Tristan & Isolde* – that sorrowful story of love & suffering & death, combined with the ending Wagner afterwards gave it, in which the lovers, having sought in non-existence what life denied to them, are offered a glimmering promise of future redemption.

Sunday January 25th
Although it was a wet, windy morning I went alone to Fairfield to hear Mr Ward preach. The text was about overcoming the world by faith. The world does not mean this natural world, or the people in it, both of which are essentially divine, but is *convention* & *sensuality*. Convention has an atrophying & enervating effect, & we can only progress & achieve by breaking away from it. We must live in company with an ideal of immortality & must form our own Utopia – whether it be of this world or of the unknown world to come doesn't much matter – towards which we must strive. We can get an idea of immortality by gazing over a seemingly boundless ocean, & watching the waves rolling on for ever. This idea of immortality is a living for the future, which is faith. By faith we can achieve, since we can do anything if we believe we can.

Wednesday January 28th
I went to make up at Mrs Ellis's bridge this afternoon, where there was a somewhat scratch lot. Mother talked to Miss Dodd during tea; it appears Miss D. strongly disapproves of my going to Oxford as there is no *necessity* – thinks I ought to stay at home & help Mother (who needs so *much* help!). Her great idea is that girls should marry as soon as possible after leaving the schoolroom, – before they have any ideas or their minds are in the least matured. Evidently no side of the woman's movement has taken hold of her. Disapproval from such a person is almost

equivalent to encouragement. I wish she had attacked me & not Mother. The unpracticability of it too – as though marriage were to be had for the asking, & as though every chance of it was suitable to be taken!

Monday February 2nd
It appears that someone has openly declared that people may talk about Mr Ward but he has done absolutely nothing else but establish the men's class! As though *that* were nothing; it would be a great work if it were all, but he has done the greatest thing possible, he has entirely changed the spirit of all Fairfield in a year. At the men's class yesterday afternoon he almost lost control of himself, stormed & some said even swore! So Mrs Fowler expected storms in the evening & was not disappointed. All the greatest souls in all ages have had upon occasion to give rein to their passion, defend the truths they teach with fire & denounce with bitterness those who would destroy them. Mrs Fowler, who sits very near the pulpit, said he went perfectly white after his sermon was finished & seemed almost on the point of collapsing. I walked home contemplating in my spirit the glory of that rejection which is the temptation of the spiritual life. There was an influence in the air which made me feel I loved all the world & every particular person I met. I realised how much more people like Mr Ward, the strivers & strugglers of our indifferent ages, or the comparatively poor & kind & unassuming, are near to my soul than the kind of people I dance with & play bridge with. It is with those whom so-called polite society despises or laughs at that I feel I *live*, & not with polite society itself.

    Miss Dodd, part of the polite society, called when I got in. She mentioned my going to Oxford but didn't venture to raise her objections. We talked mostly about lectures; she won't bring her girls out at night to them, though she takes them to the Gardens. For her part, she says, she has been to so many lectures in her life that she has become tired of them. Personally I can't imagine anyone who pursues knowledge pursuing it with such tempered enthusiasm; I can't believe *now* when young & enthusiastic, that if I am alive in forty years' time & sane, I shall feel any different; aspiration *is* aspiration always.

Thursday February 4th

Mrs Fowler came to-night with the skirt of mine she has altered, & brought most tragic news – it is feared that Mr Ward is leaving Fairfield. She says all the Fairfield men are up in arms about it. I wonder if some of them, poor things, feel as I do, that just when a light was beginning to shine upon some of faith's dark uncertain ways, it is now to be put out & the gloom to be as thick as before. He has had more influence upon me for good & for strength than anyone I have ever met.

Monday February 9th

Mr Dodd went off, managing with great difficulty to stop talking. If his appalling piety & benevolently patronising manner towards women were not such an amusing study, it would be a distinct trial to me. As it is, it rather entertains me to be treated something like I treat my cat – as a being of utter irresponsibility & inconsequence, to whom no confidence or affairs of importance could possibly be imparted. Not that the poor man means any discourtesy, on the contrary he is all the time trying to show great deference to the 'weaker vessel' on account of its weakness! But he is one of those persons more deadly to the cause of woman's freedom & independence than its most ardent opposer, for it has never occurred to him that there is such a thing to be opposed. Woman to him has always been inferior as a matter of course & her position not even arguable! As for preaching & dictating at every moment, it seems to be a habitual affliction of his & his sanctimonious expressions beat those of any parson I know; I can't imagine Mr Ward talking of people 'going to their rest', or 'being taken to their rest'. To me it seems that the simple word 'Death' is a much grander & higher thing than any pious descriptive phrase concerning it.

Sunday February 15th

I saw a lamb to-day on the cricket-field – a tiny white thing that shivered when it felt the cold wind. The sight of small & helpless things always gives me a heartache & longing to look after them – oh! dearer than life would be anything that needed help from me.

I went to Fairfield this evening & Mr Ward preached
excellently on the text 'Prove all things, hold fast that which is
good'. I didn't ask Daddy to go with me but he decided to come
& of course he didn't like Mr Ward. He had to admit the
sermon a good one, but could say nothing else good. He called
Mr Ward 'a pleb talking to plebs', said he was not a gentleman
(in such a tone as to intimate it a *terrible* offence!), that he was
alright up at Fairfield where the people were not up to much.
He said he didn't relish sitting among servants – he felt it
derogatory! As though they were not flesh & blood like
ourselves, & had not souls equal, nay almost always perhaps
superior, to ours in God's eyes. And what are we but them – &
they but us – servants all of the Highest? 'Now at Burbage,
Marriott's a gentleman, & you sit among your own class – a
good congregation of better-class people, not these common
louts' . . . He called Mr Ward's enthusiasm & eloquence
preaching to the gallery – & if it is, then a little more preaching
to the gallery is what we want. Oh, God! What is religion? Is it
the evidence of birth & artificial polish, the obsequious submis-
sion to the patronage of wealth, of the conventional parson, dear
to the heart of Daddy & his like? Or is it a fervent soul-striving,
an aspiration towards the Highest, a steady struggle towards the
best we know, common to humanity, irrespective of the trifling
accidents of birth & wealth?

I understand now why our great religious geniuses & leaders
have been poor. How blinding & atrophying are material
possessions, the homage of custom, the paths of congenial
conventionality. Is it by attaching ourselves only to congenial
things that the world can progress? No, leadership is a solitude
& an object of persecution. Oh! may I be poor, simple in tastes,
never luxurious. May I learn to renounce all those comforts with
which I have been indulged. My sphere is among the poor &
striving & thoughtful (as I realised walking back from Fairfield
the other day). I have no part – I intend to have as little apparent
part as possible – with the opulent & luxurious, who float on the
surface of their own extreme complacency & self-satisfaction!

I have tried to hope that Daddy, even if dimly, [would] *see*
light in the end, but to-night has shown me at last that such a
desire is hopeless. Years – nay centuries – of social & spiritual

evolution intervene between him & me, & they cannot be bridged even by the utmost exertions, the most enlightening arguments. I understand now what has conventionalized, limited & checked the spiritual development of poor Mother.

Friday February 20th
I walked up to Mrs Fowler's this afternoon. Her husband was at the Institute on Sunday, where the meeting was held before Mr Ward had quite made up his mind. There was only standing room when one Godwin, a Socialist, & several other 'ists' addressed the meeting, voicing the general great appreciation of Mr Ward & his work & entreating him to stay. Poor Mr Ward, when he got up to reply, appeared to be at the last extremity of his powers of control, worn out by constant emotion & the stress of present indecision. He seemed hardly able to bring out the words. Fowler said he would not have missed it for five pounds, & certainly the sight of poor Mr Ward with the marks of his struggle upon him must have been very moving. I wonder if he realised how moving it was! I always feel that he would understand my thorough enjoyment of what in self-scorn I call playing to the gallery. I often wonder how far that trait is really the weakness it is always considered. Of course the shallow person, the gossip, who merely loves to make a sensation for the passing pleasure of seeing others surprised & the brief triumph of being the first with the news, can have no extenuating excuse. But among the natural leaders – is not the feeling such as a great actor experiences, whom the stage calls, & who, conscious of his own power & skill, enjoys the prominent position he occupies before the footlights as the very breath & soul of his being & his aspiration? The leader of men is only an actor on a larger stage, & is not the love of making an impression often indicative of his fitness to make it? Of course this trait must be allied to greater characteristics as alone it is a vice, but surely it is not blameable when it is the attendant of nobler things.

Sunday February 22nd
I had supper at the Ellingers', & put on my black dress, which Mrs Ellinger was immensely taken with. They all *would*

talk of literature & my going to Oxford. They seemed amused when I said I wasn't going to get married, & called upon Sir John Matthews, who is a lawyer, to put it down. Mrs Green said people wouldn't let me embrace a literary & virginal career. But they needn't be so confident, for it takes two to make a match, & whatever disadvantages women may have to endure in the present society, the option of refusal is always theirs. Mrs Ellinger contended a woman couldn't be a great writer unless she was married as otherwise she could never know a man properly. I said that could only apply in the case of novelists, & it was questionable if it applied then. We didn't come to any conclusion, & afterwards the conversation turned on the Woman Question, & as to whether physical force, the source of man's superiority, was not still, in spite of the veneer of civilization, the real test to-day. I sat & listened to this, saying little, as, though I have my own very decided opinions, I felt too young & that the ideas were too idealistic to be exhibited to that very worldly-wise & experienced company.

Before the men came in Mrs Ellinger & Mrs Green were talking to me in a strain that inferred that great books could only be written after great experiences by the author. Mrs Ellinger always seems to try & make me feel my own inexperience & youth, & sometimes she succeeds, but she didn't to-night. I believe I have advanced too far now to lose a certain amount of faith in myself; young & inexperienced as I am, I *have* thought & studied. I wonder if one of the consolations of increasing years is to try to crush the youth that they have lost, & to belittle it in the light of their advanced experience & ideas! But history itself often proves youth in the right, though it may be rather by instinct than reasoning. The young Wordsworth & Coleridge, when they published the *Lyrical Ballads*, though reviled by elderly & 'experienced' reviewers, were none the less the true heralds of a great & magnificent movement which was to bring a glory to English Literature such as it had not known since Shakespeare. And again & again the work of men's maturer years has proved to be, not a departure from their early ambitions & self-confidence, but the continuing & completing of their own youthful ideals.

Tuesday February 24th

I went to a bridge at Mrs Heathcote's this afternoon. No one of any interest was there – they seemed to be rather a highway-&-hedges lot. There were two appalling people, a mother & daughter, the absolute *height* of vulgarity. Both were dressed in several bright colours, with large hats overflowing with feathers. They had gold purses & card cases galore, & the mother had a gold wrist-watch studded with diamonds, & the daughter a necklace of enormous pearls. In view of such examples, one is led to hope fervently that one will never have much money.

Friday February 27th

A perfect morning, sun shining brightly at 8.30 & mist floating over everything. Directly after breakfast I couldn't resist the temptation so left my work & went into the Corbar Woods – in spite of Mother's nervous terrors of my going anywhere alone! The woods were perfectly still, wrapped in all the morning beauty; I saw not a soul except a distant workman walking along one of the paths. The birds were twittering in the trees, & the air was very warm, altogether it felt more like the end of April than February. When I got on to the heights the view was glorious. I felt like a being lifted up into some sublimer air where calm reigned supreme, while round my feet the turbulent world eddied, & I heard

> The restless sounds of man's uneasy life
> Rise muffled from below.

The hills to the west were gradually becoming clear of the mist, but still their outline seemed to melt into the sky, & Burbage village seemed to sleep behind a hazy veil. The white cottages gleaming through looked like jewels on the hillside. The sky was perfectly clear except for a few rose-coloured clouds just above Axe Edge. To the east I could see Fairfield Church like a ghost in the mist. I stood in the sunshine on the edge of the rock, alone with the world.

If I fail my exam, the reason will be 'Romantic Revival'. I know I know enough about it, but cannot stop reading about it; it interests me so intensely! So the 18th Century, which I am not too well acquainted with, gets neglected. I cannot stand Gold-smith's complacent criticisms of universal literature & Johnson's extraordinary insensibility to all kinds of art, & ignorant disparagement of it, after reading Wordsworth's spiritual reve-lation, & the imagination of Romanticism. To me he is indeed a Revelation as I knew scarcely anything of him before.

Sunday March 1st

We got into Mrs Ward's pew again. Mother's presence seemed to disturb the little woman & she would not look up. It is an amusing thing that Mother, although not a bit formidable, & I can't imagine her overawing anyone, yet manages often to make people afraid of her – I suppose by her height & her style. Whereas I, though really much more formidable & aggressive, don't inspire people with fear because I happen to be short & dainty, & I find a short & dainty person, by people who don't know her, is invariably thought to have nothing behind the smallness & daintiness.

Tuesday March 3rd

I did not do half as much work as I ought to have done this morning, as after I had read Mr Jack's essay on Wordsworth I looked on further & was arrested by his criticism of Emerson's Theory of the Infinite. This started me thinking so intensely on the subject of infinity and immortality that I could not give my attention to anything else. Our spiritual consciousness – the Oneness of that spirituality with the Soul in the Universe, the 'Oversoul' – the possibility or non-possibility of the survival of that consciousness after mortal death – these are matters that have always drawn me deeply, & have I suppose equally drawn all thinking souls since life began. And yet I realise that the possibility of immortality, by stating it as such, loses its ideality & spirituality, for when we define a thing it immediately becomes finite, & our souls, which are infinite, ask for more. I think this is what Mr Ward realised & tried to preach, when in his sermon a fortnight ago he said 'God is *beyond* proof.' Likewise therefore God is beyond statement, for statement implies proof.

Thursday March 5th
To-day was another day of deluge. Old Mottershed was very
funny when I went to pay for a pair of somewhat ancient shoes,
for which I have an affection, that he mended & patched up for
me. He regarded me with an amused smile, & then said 'Yer
ought ter be rich, bein' sa careful!' I could hardly keep my face
straight, but said the shoes did very well for 'a day like this'. He
really is a quaint old body. With his very short rotund person,
soft white hair, bright brown eyes, & smooth brown skin, just
like a piece of his own shoe-leather, he might have stepped
straight out of one of Dickens' novels.

Sunday March 8th
I got a postcard this morning from Somerville, telling me what
to do tomorrow week in connection with the exam. Such
information made it seem very close & real – as indeed it is. I
shall be so thankful to get it over; I don't remember anything
ever having been such a weight & a burden as the thought of this
exam. Of course I know perfectly well that I can still go to
college if I don't pass this exam., & also that if I don't go to
college at all it doesn't really matter, as academic knowledge is
not necessary, & is often a hindrance, to literary renown. But
though I tell myself these things, & though they will be real &
excellent consolations if I do fail, yet that doesn't prevent my
anxiety to do anything I have taken up as well as it can be done,
so I *do* mind.

Mr Ward preached on 'Not without cause have I done all that
I have done, saith the Lord' (Ezekiel). He looked at me well &
intently, though quite kindly, when I shook hands at the door –
as if it occurred to him for the first time to wonder what manner
of being I might be.

Tuesday March 10th
Surely there was seldom such barbarity as that of the Suffragette
who in the National Gallery this morning slashed & cut with a
hatchet Velasquez's famous *Venus*! They say the damage is
serious but not, they hope, irreparable. Poor artist & genius!
What has he done that the rancour & spite of a political maniac
should be vented upon his creation! It shames the glorious cause

for which the best women are fighting that *one* should act like this under cover of their standard. But I suppose every great cause, like every religion, has its fanatics, who do not stain its truth, though they may cast a shadow upon it.

Sunday March 15th

We went to Fairfield to-night & had a very good sermon from Mr Ward. It was one of his inspired nights. I was feeling very depressed before I heard it, but it quite roused me up with its 'Achieve! achieve!' & the idea, which he enlarged upon, that we do not *know* the limits of man's capacity, & that to any one of us it may be given to soar higher than man has ever reached before. What if I cannot pass this exam., – need I lose faith in my abilities, whatever other people do? Assuredly *no*!

March 16th–20th Somerville College, Oxford

I found with my very first paper that I had been working on quite wrong lines, having read more books of criticism than the works of the writers themselves, which was what they wanted. Also I found out that all the women's colleges have now entrance exams, so without this one I cannot get in at all. Of course had I known that I should have been much more careful in preparation instead of trying to do it all alone. Also, this is the worst possible year for anyone to try to get into Somerville. Last year they had forty vacancies owing to the new buildings, but this year they have only 18, & 82 people trying for them!

On the Tuesday soon after breakfast we had our first paper. The moment I read mine, I realised that I could not have any chance at all. I was so petrified by the discovery that I sat staring for half an hour at the questions without writing a word, which of course made me unable to finish the 5 questions which we had to do out of nine. However, after thinking I would ask Miss Penrose to let me go home that afternoon, I forced myself to start, & wrote an answer to a question on Thomson & Cowper very inefficiently, with only half my attention, still thinking I would go home that afternoon. However I came to the conclusion that although I knew it was hopeless it would be quite amusing to stick it out, & though it *is* useless I am glad I did, for if I had proved myself to be afraid of failing I should never have respected myself any more.

Just after my paper I had an interview with Miss Darbishire, the literature don. She has a kind & clever face & I found her delightful. She asked me whom I liked best in my period to which I of course answered Wordsworth, & she seemed pleased to think I had discovered him for myself & also that I had worked alone & against opposition.

Sunday March 22nd Buxton

[Mr Ward's] sermon was simply indescribable – perhaps the most wonderful I have ever heard him preach. But apart from his mighty gift, how the personality of the man (if it *can* be separated from his gift) influences one. At first while he is a little nervous or still conscious of himself he shows a sort of restlessness of gesture & feature, but as soon as he lets himself go he is simply on fire & never stops for a word, & he absolutely quivers all over with excitement. Not a movement or a cough was to be heard in all the big congregation. Everyone was absolutely still with their eyes fixed on him, & his Fairfield men gazed at him as upon a kind of prophet. When I get away from the sound of his voice I still remain within the magic circle of his predominating individuality. I was thinking actually to-night that it is a pity his wife is so much older than he & seems so unworthy of him. One cannot feel that she was an object of great passion to him & yet great passion he is assuredly capable of feeling. I should like to know the story of that marriage for many reasons.

Wednesday March 25th

I knew I should receive a letter from Oxford this morning & I did. I opened it; it was from Miss Penrose announcing that she had much pleasure in telling me the College has awarded me an Exhibition of £20 for 3 years. On condition, of course, of my passing the Oxford Senior in July. She hoped I would make sure of passing & also that I would try to study a little Greek before going up so as to be able to take the degree course. I was not at all disturbed by the announcement, though Mother got quite flustered in her delight & wanted to tell everyone at once & Daddy seemed quite overjoyed – though I wish they would not make demonstrations. I can hardly think it possible that it can really be mine as indeed it was no false modesty that made me think my papers were bad. Of course everyone will think me an awful fraud, but judging by my own standard, whatever Somerville's may be, I really did not think I could even get through. What they can have awarded the Exhibition on I cannot think as I finished none of the papers; it cannot have been on my knowledge for I showed none. The more I think about it the more amazed I feel.

Sunday March 29th
[Mr Ward] looked very pale & miserable, & read the lessons in that nervous way he always has when something is up, & he *read* his sermon which made the presence of that something clearer still. The text was 'The whole creation groaneth & travaileth together in pain'. The sermon was all about pain & its beneficial effect. I think he was trying to persuade himself as well as us that the blessings [of] suffering overcame its miseries. I think this because after church Mrs Ward came up to me after a little hesitation, & told me that Mr Ward was going to preach in the evening next Sunday. I then told her about Mr Ward's sermon of a fortnight ago before my exam. & all about the exam. & she promised to tell him, & walked a little way with us. Mother told her we wanted them both to come to tea, & that we would have music. I do hope we cheered her up as she seemed so despondent & there seems to be no doubt that *he* is. Oh! they will drive him away from his people – his poor & his work.

Wednesday April 1st St Monica's School, Kingswood
Miss Heath Jones & Miss Bervon were in town when I got to St Monica's so I had tea alone & had plenty of time to unpack. At dinner I was well stared at by all the girls, & afterwards was introduced to the mistresses. Everyone crowded round & congratulated me, though most of them had only a hazy idea what it was for.

Friday April 3rd
The girls gave a concert & dancing exhibition in the afternoon & about thirty people came to watch. Stella came, also Norah.

Cora was invited & told I was here, but could not come owing to some class or other in the afternoon. Of course I cannot be sure, but I think if it had been the other way round, & I had been invited to see Cora on one of the rare occasions when such a thing was possible, I would have given up whatever I was doing & gone to see her. But the position of Cora & Stella is very different from mine. They always have one another, & to see me is very pleasant, but only a variation upon seeing each other after all. But I am always alone, & they, who are used to the constant companionship of one another, cannot realise what so rare a thing as companionship means to me. It often seems to me queerly ordained that, lonely as my mental qualities make me in *any* case, I should be placed by circumstances in a physical solitude also. But solitude is a source of strength, & the strength which grows in solitude is the property of the Messiahs of this life!

Stella & her mother came fairly early & discovered me dealing out programmes. Her companionship made me warm & happy instantly & we sat at the back of the Gym. & talked. Norah and her mother arrived halfway through the concert, Norah looking very old for twenty-two. Her mother, to whom she introduced me later, seems very blasé & ineffectual, speaks in a little high whining voice & makes Norah play the doormat to her. I understood how Norah will never be able to make the use of her life that she ought to. Norah spoke very enthusiastically of my Exhibition & seemed more really interested & understanding than anyone except Miss H.J. & Miss B. who had spoken to me about it. She seemed to appreciate my ambition & object in life but to be despondent about her own. She seems to hope nothing more than merely to become a skilled artist for her own pleasure. She likes her work at the studio but all through one is impressed by the idea that she would make it her life work if she could, but that she is not allowed to do so. She said half in extenuation 'You see it isn't as if I had to make my living by it.' I replied rather sharply 'It's a great pity you haven't' & she answered very seriously 'It is indeed; the most blessed thing in the world is to be able to starve in a garret.' Norah always impresses me, though the impression this time was rather a sad one, as she seems to be a person who is greatly gifted in vain. She puzzles me a little & it seems quite certain that both she & Stella were puzzled by me.

Stella went in the middle of the dancing, which was very pretty especially when the little ones were got up in coster fancy-dress, but it all seems rather purposeless. I think they are devoting too much attention now to elegance & good manners & too little to intelligence. Miss Heath Jones always [says] she does not turn out the fashionable girl, but it seems to be just what she *is* doing.

After dinner we sat in the morning-room & nearly died with laughter while Phyllis & I recounted old rows. I told how she used to cry into her coffee cup, & she said she was always more terrified of me than of anyone else, not because of my small body which she could easily have overthrown, but because of my tongue!

Saturday April 4th
I worked matters around so as to be allowed to go to tea with Miss Fry. I found quite easily the little cottage where she stays. I sat waiting for her in a little room filled with her books when she came in, dressed in her usual beloved brown. I told her all about the scholarship & how I disliked my coaching lessons. She walked most of the way with me when I had to return to St Monica's, talking hard. I thought she looked, for her, quite strong, & the inspiring & sympathetic quality in her seems to be more vital than ever.

Tuesday April 7th
I managed to get off quite soon in the morning to go & see Miss Fry; in fact the Ladies were quite glad to get rid of me as they were writing reports. Miss Fry & I sat in her little cottage room & talked, a good deal of the time about religion. It was all very personal, especially on my side, when I discussed being ambitious & not only wanting but intending to do things.

Tuesday April 14th Buxton
This afternoon Mr & Mrs Ward came in to tea. I was very agitated inwardly about it & when they finally did arrive I felt hot & shy at once. Just at first they were both a little uncomfortable;

she, in fact, was the less nervous of the two, as she had met us before, & she walked in in her calm little way with the usual timid expression on her face. Luckily they were neither of them too shy to eat; they both enjoyed their tea, he especially. I told him I was nervous of playing because I had not practised for so long, but he said they were not critical. I mentioned as we were getting ready that Edward was very ambitious in trying to compose sonatas. 'It is a relief to find someone who is ambitious,' he said, so I replied 'We are both somewhat afflicted that way, for Edward tries to compose & I write poems, & Daddy thinks us both mad.' He roared with laughter & then said he was sure he would like both to hear the music & read the poems. I managed to play the Grieg Sonata much better than I thought I could. Somehow when he is by a kind of force *impels* one to give one's very best.

He was very pleased to hear I got my Somerville Exhibition without any coaching, & told me that he coached himself for everything except Euclid lessons, to get which he walked 7 miles there & 7 miles back. Such courage as it was – to leave his profitable business & start examinations & present himself at Cambridge at the age of 28. He told us that Fairfield suits him & he doesn't mind the struggles on account of his health; it is the restraint & the lack of independence that drive him to distraction – 'If I'd *known*,' he said, 'I'd have seen the church at Hanover before I came.' I said 'But the very fact that you're opposed shows how much you are needed here.' I looked at him very intensely, & he turned suddenly & fixed his penetrating dark eyes steadily on my face.

He is so perfectly natural & delightful & his sense of humour is very keen. There is no affected manner, no hushed voice when he speaks of things religious; religion & life are not separable to him, which is as it should be – & he does *not* wear a cross on his watch-chain. A cross on a watch-chain always typifies the effeminate & inefficient parson to me – specially when it has a text on it! He went on to say 'You see, I have thrown a good deal of the old theology overboard.' 'I shouldn't come & listen to you if you hadn't,' said I. It was so strange to be there talking to the very person I have spoken & thought so much about for six months, & formerly known only at a distance. I felt so strangely happy & content all the time he was near me. When I went downstairs to say goodbye to them as they went, we happened to mention my coming exam. & my mathematical difficulties. 'Oh! you'll do it,' he said, & half raising his hand, 'Rise,' he said to me quietly. 'Achieve.' Achieve! that is the keynote of his nature, & having thus spoken & smiled a smile of extraordinary sweetness at me, he turned & went down the drive.

Thursday April 16th

I played golf with Maurice after tea & he won by 2 up. B.S. was also playing, by himself; at the 7th I purposely made a crooked shot so as to get in his way. He had to wait for me to play my approach, which I did fairly neatly. Then I stopped to watch his drive & he actually missed it altogether. Roland Leighton came just after tea time, but I did not meet him till dinner when I arrived down late. We had to go & watch *Between the Soup & the Savoury* – Douglas Spafford induced me to promise to write an article for the *Buxton Advertiser* on the evening's performance.

Friday April 17th

I spent all morning writing the article for the *Buxton Advertiser*; Roland Leighton helped me considerably by dictating to me what I had written when I was copying it out again. Roland & I discussed various matters such as literature & religion. He is mighty intelligent, & most interesting to talk to.

Saturday April 18th

After tea Roland Leighton & I walked up to Fairfield to see Edward play the organ. We had a most interesting conversation, a good deal of which was about our ideas of immortality. He is interested in me now, though I can't make out whether he likes me very much, or dislikes me very much. After dinner I was reading Thoreau's *Walden* (Leighton told me this morning a good deal about it, having read it) which he bought in the town, & when I had finished the chapter & said I liked it he asked me to keep the book, much to my astonishment, so I did.

Sunday April 19th

E. & Leighton & I went up to Fairfield to hear Mr Ward. It was quite a good sermon & he ended it with a poem about striving 'higher still & higher' which I think was probably his own. [The sermon] was not however as good as his best; the morning ones seldom are. Leighton liked it alright, though he suggested some of the 'florid' passages would stand a little pruning. I don't think I agree about that – not in a church like Fairfield where the sermon must be suited to the understanding of the majority of the audience.

After tea we all walked round the Goyt Valley & Maurice came with us. Everything looked beautiful in its early spring freshness. Leighton is a funny boy; he was very depressed & would hardly speak a word for about half the walk. I got him to admit that there was a particular & not general cause for this, & later in the evening he refused to say that it was not due to me. I criticised him all day with most open frankness, telling him that there must be something wanting in his intellect if he could not see the intellectual beauty in music, & also accusing him of adopting an artificial instead of a spontaneous appreciation of Nature because he thought it a literary attribute. I saw him to be conceited & so determined to shake him out of some of his conceit, but did not mean to depress him.

Monday April 20th
We all spent a most lazy day, except perhaps Mother, who was dusting round. Leighton & I sat all morning on a tree stump in Corbar Woods & talked, while Edward was at his organ practice. Among other things we spoke of his mother, who seems a splendid person & who keeps the house together by her own exertions. We also talked of Edward; Leighton finds 'brick walls' in his intellect just as I do, & with me objects to the orthodoxy & general properness of his opinions. I laughed when we got in & found it a quarter to one; the time had gone so fast while we were sitting in the shade with the sun beating on the tree tops overhead. 'We have wasted the morning,' I said but he replied 'Don't say wasted; I don't consider *I* have wasted it!' There seemed to be a general concern at my departure to-morrow. Maurice bade me a regretful farewell at the door. After dinner Roland & I were examining each other's poetry most critically, and Roland wrote me out his 'Triolet' & 'Lines on a picture by Herbert Schmaltz'. I liked both,

especially the latter, which was deeper & showed more promise. Roland said to me most earnestly 'Why *are* you going to-morrow?' so evidently my presence interests him in spite of the possibility of criticism & remarks. I suggested that perhaps my departure would induce him to neglect Edward less, & he said he certainly had given up his company for mine a good deal. I copied out a two-years-old poem, 'Fragment of a Soliloquy on an Unpleasant Evening', which he liked, & gave it to him.

Thursday April 23rd Gilpin Lodge, Windermere
The day dawned with storm & wind, there was no rain but dark clouds drifted about the sky casting lovely lights & shades on the moors and mountains, which were very clear. When I came down I found a parcel awaiting me from Roland Leighton; it was Olive Schreiner's *Story of an African Farm*, which he promised me. Inside the cover he inscribed 'VMB In gratitude for much. RAL.' Queer boy! I wonder what he considers he is grateful for. He also wrote me an interesting letter, in which he said he had so immensely enjoyed his visit to *me*. He says he thinks Lyndall in *The Story of an African Farm* is like me, only 'sadder & less charmingly controversial'. He wants me to write & tell him what I think of the book. The letter ended up with a 'Till Speech-Day' – which I shall try to go to at all costs, exam., or no exam.

Sunday May 3rd Buxton
I have spent most of to-day reading *The Story of an African Farm*. It is a great book & has made my head almost ache with thinking. Religion – life – the position of women – one may contemplate them for ever. Life is very difficult & thinking is so wearying; I am very tired & yet one cannot stop & the wearier one is the more one has to think. I am lost in meditating upon the Nature of God, whether it be Law, Love, Universal Life, or all three, whether there be or be not a Hereafter. If we die utterly, is our incompleteness yet of service to the human race? – if we do not die, what is the nature of our future – shall we be units, or merged in the Universal Life? Shall we keep our spiritual consciousness, our realisation of ourselves, or shall we lose it?

What is this very consciousness? There is no answer to any of these questions, but we, poor finite mortals, must allow the imprisoned infinite to speak & to go on making answers to the questions as long as a mind exists to ask them.

Monday May 4th
Just as we were going to bed the telephone rang violently; we managed to get on after a few minutes' trouble & of course it was from Roland Leighton at Lowestoft. He rang up ostensibly to tell Edward he would meet him at Leicester on Wednesday but really to talk to me. I took the wire after he had addressed a few remarks to Edward, & when I offered to let him talk to E. again he said 'No don't, I would rather talk to you.' So we spent about ten minutes making absurd remarks through the telephone. I was cold & sleepy when I first got up to go to bed, but now I am warm and intensely conscious of life.

Wednesday May 6th
Edward went back to school to-day; no tongue can tell the difference it makes to me when he is not here; his bright sane personality makes itself felt in the atmosphere & one misses it greatly when it is gone. Even when I am not with him I feel he is there if I need him; lonely always, when he is gone I am lonelier still, & become solitary indeed. There seems nowhere any youth, vigour & enthusiasm left about me to which I can communicate my own.

Wednesday May 13th
Cora heard of a person who tells characters by handwriting & so she sent both hers and mine up & sent the result on to me. Hers is excellent, & she as well as Mother & Daddy say mine is. Cora compares mine to a stormy & strenuous night & hers to a calm sunrise over a smooth sea. All through there is nothing but reference to my strength manifesting itself in different forms – everything is '*very*'. I am supposed to have a strong and tenacious will, high ideals, acute judgement & power to take in a situation, & strong intuitive power, besides various other high-sounding things!

Wednesday May 27th

I had a violent argument with Mr Risigari this morning as I was playing the piano badly, & he complained that my 'being so mad on studying' had upset my music. I said I was sorry but much as I liked music it would have to take second place as I could not earn my living by it. He gave an exclamation of horror at my wanting to earn my living, so I said I wasn't going to live on my father all my life. He said that independence was all very well up to a point but what were fathers for? I replied very heatedly that I did not intend to be kept by mine, that I had more brains than my brother & why shouldn't I use them! He went on 'You are only going to do this because you want to, not because you have to, & so you'll be taking the place away from someone who is obliged to work.' It was the old feeble argument which economically is false, but as I could not prove it economically I said instead 'The best person always gets the place, so if I am not the best person I shall not get it & I am ready to risk that, and if I am the best person it is right that I should have it.' He looked very resigned and said 'Well, I can't argue with you about it. I see you're an idealist at a very early age!'

This afternoon Mother & I went up to tea with the Wards. Mr Ward came in after a few minutes & had scarcely been in the room a moment when he said they had laid the final trial upon him, & by his tone of finality I knew what he meant. To say I was dismayed is to speak lightly. Mr Ward showed us a photo of his men's class, 260 strong, & when Mother asked him if he did not greatly feel the responsibility of leaving them he said he did, looked sad & changed the subject. After tea while Mother talked to Mrs Ward he took me to see his novels in Mrs Ward's drawing-room, & then I went up with him to his study. Two of the walls were lined with books on shelves of his own construction, & his desk was in one corner & there was a gas-stove in the grate. I should like to have been left alone with the books for hours, some of them were poets & classics, but for the most part they were moral science and theological works. He underlines & writes over them just as I do, & pulled out ever so many for me to look at, getting quite excited in explaining the different kinds of books he would give to people at different stages of religious evolution. He gave me a book to read which he said was an excellent one for a sceptic, being modern & scientific. He was reading me a much-underlined passage about scepticism from a pamphlet when Mother & Mrs Ward came up & disturbed us. I had forgotten everything but his magnetic personality & the joy of discussing things with one so exceptionally understanding as he. He approves very much of my going to Oxford & looked pleased when I said that if I failed in this exam. I should try again until I passed. I walked away half-elated by my conversation with him, half-depressed at the thought of his departure, which is as soon as Aug. 31st. Why *is* it that the people who help & uplift us, & speak to us, not in words but in their lives, of that Best which we call God, come into our lives for a short hour & flit away like shadows? Not on systems, authorities or friends must we depend, said Mr Ward a week or two ago. We must be *self reliant*, stand *alone*. If we see too much of those who *can* help us we begin to lean upon them, & so they come out of the unknown to guide us for a few short moments & then vanish into the unknown again. They cannot give us salvation, they can only indicate the way to find it, for alas! – 'Redemption is from within, and neither from God nor man'!

Friday May 29th
As I approached the Spaffords' house I saw B.S. standing at the gate; wonderful to relate he did not go away as soon as I came near, & as I am determined somehow to stop this silly constrained business I stopped & spoke to him. He seemed as depressed as usual though he did answer; I looked at him very keenly & found that his eyes are honest & steady. Gwen appeared & spoke of tennis & asked him if we could not get some up. He became aloof at once & muttered 'Oh! I don't know –' but she insisted about it. When she asked him when it should be he said rather stiffly 'Any time Miss Brittain likes,' & we finally arranged for Thursday. Miss Brittain talked to him in a very kind voice, and smiled at him most sweetly when she said 'Good evening.' Next time the opportunity may arise for a more intimate conversation – perhaps even an explanation of sorts.

Sunday May 31st

I went up to Fairfield for the 11.0 service. There were a great many people in church for the morning, & there was a sort of electric restless atmosphere about everything. As for Mr Ward himself, I have often seen him looking miserable, but I never saw his face so tragic & full of grief as it was this morning. I thought we might get a fiery sermon but evidently he felt too down for that. All the time he seemed to need a strong self-control; I simply longed to comfort him, to give him some strength in return for some of that which he has poured out so freely for me & others. Whatever it is I feel towards him rose stronger than ever & seemed to swamp all other feelings; I don't care whether the cause of his trouble was personal loss or some less worthy motive such as wounded pride or general despondency. I would have given ever so much to have been able to remove it.

Monday June 1st

Several people have told me about the play *Raffles* which Mr Railton is getting up in aid of some special branch of the Devonshire Hospital. At the end of the afternoon he asked me if I would take a part in it. I said I could not do a large one as I was working for an exam. & could only attend four or five rehearsals. He said it was not a very large part, so I told him that if he would send it to me to look at I would decide when I had seen it. I love acting so much that I feel I must do it; it cannot really affect my work as I never do any at night, when the rehearsals are, & however excited I get, excitement cannot make me forget what I have learnt.

Thursday June 4th

After tea my tennis improved a little but not mightily. When it got too dark to see any more I walked home with B.S. He said in a very low voice that I had seemed annoyed at playing with him, & he was anxious to know if I had wanted him to ask me to play tennis. I said 'You didn't ask me; it was your sister.' So he persisted 'Would you have been annoyed if I had?' So I said 'I never say "no" to a game of tennis, whatever else I may say "no" to.' There was silence for some time after that. Then somehow the conversation got on to my usual unpopularity with committees & people in authority. He said he could well understand why the ladies didn't like me & when I asked 'Why?' quite unsuspectingly, he said 'You're too good-looking.' I got quite worked up talking of popularity; I said it was a sign of weakness, though most of the girls here couldn't understand my not seeking a cheap favour, & thought me a perfect little beast. I said I wanted to stand alone & live up to my ideals, that I did not, & never had, depended on anybody, & I added, with full regard for effect, 'Perhaps I never shall.' He suggested that I might change, but I replied that I might modify but the foundations would always remain the same. He said good-afternoon at the corner & hurried back very fast. I simply couldn't make out whether he was very upset or merely very annoyed.

Sunday June 7th
The rehearsal bored me considerably. I have come to the conclusion that I loathe my part, & that it is not worth the trouble necessary to work it in with the others. There is hardly any character to create – everything might just as well be said by someone else. Such character as there is is of the obtrusively boisterous kind, which is one thing I hate, & interprets itself mostly in slang, which is another & which I never use, finding the English language sufficiently expressive without it. Consequently I can't impart any personality to Lady Ethel, hard as I try.

Tuesday June 9th
The days are more interesting when I talk to B.S., whom I have not seen since Saturday. To fall in love with him would be a perfect impossibility, but it is very easy to be in love with love. To hear a man's voice say 'you' in a tone which he uses to no one else on earth, is in itself a gigantic temptation to make him go on saying it like that, & to go on listening. It is wrong of me to think of such things, still worse to take pleasure in them, but then I am not good, & in spite of high purposes, only a very human girl. Still, that's no excuse!

Tuesday June 16th

Oh I am so *sick* of this everlasting Latin & Mathematics – if only I could do some interesting work. I really am weary & bored with everything – strange as it is for me – but nothing seems to go very right; I have no legitimate cause for complaint, but yet life is short of something & I am miserable.

Sunday June 21st

The service at St John's was dull & the place crowded. I had my new pale blue coat & skirt on so I escaped as soon as I could into the Gardens, where I had the time of my life. We went across to talk to the Adies, & Bertram Spafford, who had been sitting with them, moved a chair for me next to his own. When I was sitting talking to him telling him I loved the play, & that acting was natural to me because I acted all my life, crowds of people came up & congratulated me on the performance, my appearance, my clothes etc. I being the centre of the circle only had to smile sweetly & say 'I'm so glad you liked it' – whatever 'it' might be.

   This evening Mother & I went to Fairfield. We met Mr Ward at the gate & Mother asked him to lunch to-morrow. He told us he had seen *Raffles* both nights & enjoyed it immensely, & thought we all wore lovely dresses. He preached a splendid sermon about will-power; the keynote of the whole was that there is no such thing as an unintentional sin, but that all wrong-doing depends on the deliberate choice of the will for evil.

Monday June 22nd

Mr Ward came to lunch & stayed all afternoon till tea. He told me, when we were having some discussion or other, that I was both artistic & scientific, & also that I was nearly as original as Maggie Tulliver in *The Mill on the Floss* as I said I had a fellow feeling for her. When Mother went out of the room for a little while he started telling me all about Mrs Ward, how she was brought up a strict Calvinist & that, though she had grown under his tuition, something that he had taken two years to build up could be knocked down in 2 minutes by an ultra-orthodox person. He told me that he felt at times very spiritually & intellectually lonely. Why he elected to tell me I can't think.

Sunday June 28th

In the course of conversation with Aunt Edith I mentioned Bertram Spafford & she appeared most anxious to have the man who wanted to marry me pointed out. We went into the Gardens after they had had the waters, & I pointed him out to Aunt Edith; at first she said he was much too solemn, but he gave me one of his semi-shy smiles as we passed him & then she said he had a 'nice, kind face'. He hovered round me all the time I was in the Gardens. Aunt Edith was extremely interested. She said he was very obviously deeply in love with me & very wretched. She did not blame me at all (though she certainly would if she knew of some of my experiments in that direction) and did not see what I could do, but said that men feel this kind of thing very much & I must be careful not to hurt him worse. I protested that it was not so certain that he felt so much about me as all that, as he never came & talked to me. She said that of course he didn't as once he had been told he wasn't wanted it would be a most ungentlemanly thing to force his presence upon me, but that he seemed to be too attracted to keep quite away. I must say that never struck me, though it ought to have done. I began to wonder if what I have been secretly despising as half-heartedness & stupidity is really a stress of emotion too great to dare to trust itself too far. If he really suffers so, I am a hard-hearted little brute to tease him as I do; I really ought to put right away from me the temptation which is brought by the power to give pain.

Wednesday July 1st

I spent a most strange & unexpected afternoon. As I was passing the Spaffords' house the thunderstorm broke which had been threatening for some time & the rains began to pour down. Mrs Spafford saw me & beckoned to me to shelter in her house. It turned out to be a terrific storm with thunder & lightning & heavy rain & instead of going home at once, as I expected, I was there for nearly 2 hours! As soon as I went in, Bertram came racing down to talk to me, and I talked to him & Mrs Spafford for some time. In the middle a very untidy-looking maid-servant burst into the room & asked if there was to be a clean cloth on the table or something of that sort. Apparently a clean cloth is rather an event, & I so nearly burst out laughing I didn't know where to look, but Mrs Spafford did not seem in the least disturbed. After a bit she went out & Gwen came in & we began a really interesting conversation. For some time we discussed books & evolution, in which Gwen more or less agreed with me, & we pretty well squashed Bertram, who seemed to think England the only country & Christianity the only religion in the world. Finally our conversation drifted as usual into the position of women, especially with regard to marriage. We – espec. I – spoke of the new era of the companionship of woman, no longer the angel, set up on a pedestal, & shut out of every-thing, & no longer the toy, the sort of soft cushion or hot-water bottle for the husband to soothe himself with after having spent the day seriously. I said that would be a veritable hell to me, but that I believed a heaven was possible even in this generation, & that I would wait for that or have nothing. I said I did not believe that the intellectual woman 'went down' except by flirting and pretending she was not clever, but Gwen said she was certain that kind of woman always found her counterpart. She talked sensibly all the time, I was very surprised, & looked pretty & intelligent too. I had to go at 7.0, though the rain was still pouring. They lent me an umbrella but would not lend me a coat as any one of theirs would trail! All the whole family (I saw Mr Spafford for a few minutes) were *most* charming to me. I am doing very wrong, yet cannot prevent myself, & fate seems to give me all the assistance in its power. I *wonder* what the result of it all will be.

Thursday July 2nd
To-night I stood by the open window & looked right out into the great wide space before me. I felt more alone than tongue can tell, but I felt a kind of bitter exaltation too, & the dreamer part of me overcame the student part. It was a very sultry night; thunderstorms had been about all day & the air was hazy with steam from the damp hot ground. The lights from the houses were mingled with the still vapour, so that everything seemed to be wrapt in a kind of luminous mist. The only impression I could gather, so far as I tried to translate it into definite ideas, was of a vague darkness, in which the trees stood out in black,

uneven groups, casting strange shadows on the ground, their outlines melting into the haze. I longed as I gazed into that dim expanse for something to worship, & respect with all my soul, something to which I can turn for counsel, before which I can kneel in reverence. I spend much time wondering whether I, who so desire to stand alone, shall ever find that something or someone the reverence of which is not dependence.

Saturday July 4th
To-day has been one of those which make one miserable, & in which everything seems to go wrong. I had a very decent game of tennis after tea with B.S. & various other people. Then I walked home with B.S. & that really depressed me more than anything; as we got into a conversation about religion which arose out of my quoting my motto from *The Story of an African Farm*, 'Redemption is from within & is neither from God nor man; it is worked out by the soul itself, with suffering & through time.' He seemed distinctly shocked by my deistic tendencies, & then insisted on trying to treat them lightly, & as phantoms of a mind either too immature to settle things definitely, or incapable of forming a true conception of facts. He said he knew I got it all from Mr Ward – a statement which I treated with the scorn it deserved, since I have only to exhibit my diary of a year ago, before ever I heard of Mr Ward, to prove that however much he has helped & comforted my loneliness, he has done little enough to alter or influence the direction of my thoughts. I started talking about my former desire to be worshipped, & said that now I had been I was no happier because of it, since I had not learnt to *love*, and that my ideal at present was something to worship. I only told him to see what he would say as I knew he would not understand, & he did not, for he asked me 'Why not God?' & was quite incapable of seeing what I meant when I said the highest expression of God was in a person & that I sought someone in whom to find it. He told me I needn't wish that as it did not bring happiness to worship someone; but I know that until I have loved someone purely, passionately & selflessly, my character-building will lack something always. Finally he got quite angry, & said that my ambition even if fulfilled would never make me any happier, and that I might

take all the honours at the University without adding to the joy of one day. I could have told *him* all that, but instead I insisted that my ambition was a spiritual ambition, & asked him very quietly what he thought it was. He said bitterly that I wanted to be famous & make a name for myself, but I should be none the better for it if I did etc. etc. I gently but firmly insisted again that I had no care for the material glory even of fame, but he did not believe it, and said that the best thing for me to do would be to learn to be a woman, as he could not see that I was acting like a woman at all at present. That really roused me, and I said that far from not being a true woman, I was essentially feminine. 'But I suppose you think that because a person wishes to stand alone, to develop her intellect & make her will strong, she is not a true woman,' I burst forth angrily. 'You don't *know*.'

He has done me great wrong, though partly my inability to express well what I felt so deeply may be a good deal responsible for the impression I left. I don't care what the people who dislike me may think, but I am sorry that one who loves me should so utterly misjudge me as to imagine me a slave to earthly ambition; I always thought love was capable of better intuitions than that. He told me this afternoon that he had already altered his opinion of me three times; well now he has probably changed it again, but I am determined to get an opportunity to put him a little less distant from the mark than he is at present. I wonder if he could *ever* understand that my search, that my object, for which I enter upon taking exams & university life, is the Beautiful & the True in every atom of created life, though most of all in men, whom I want to help with all the power that is in me, and to shield the weak, & that I learn & learn because I desire to have knowledge, believing that the more complete the knowledge, the nearer is one to Truth, my high ideal & final goal, as yet unseen but sometimes shining luminously through clouds. I wonder if he could understand how it is that I, leaning out & gazing at an earthly scene with a fierce yearning & aspiration which no friends or parents could either give or take away, feel something stir in my soul which is one with the glory, the diversity, of the world's Creator, and one with the best which is in all that is.

Friday July 10th Waterworks Cottage, Uppingham

The journey was terribly hot & the day gorgeous. Edward arrived in the midst of our unpacking muddle in the tiny bedroom, looking very tall & well. He had supper with us, & then went off to a choir & orchestra practice, while we wandered about the town buying sundry provisions. Then we went to the Lodge, Mother hoping to see the Puckles, and I to get a glimpse of the person on whose account, even more than Edward's, I must confess I have come – Roland Leighton. We became friends in the brief four or five days I was present when he stayed with us; & for my part my interest in him seems to have increased without my seeing him – & there is nothing strange in my being attracted by so marvellous an intellect & a not-easily-understandable personality. Edward said he could not take us indoors as there were boys about in various stages of untidiness, but perhaps we could speak to him through the window. Before we went he gave us a programme of to-morrow's proceedings, on which Roland is put down to receive, not only *seven* prizes, but the seven chief prizes in the school. Edward is quite depressed because he seems to be second & third in everything & will not receive a prize to-morrow. It does seem rather hard when he really is quite clever & works so thoroughly & keenly, but I suppose playing a solo on Speech Day makes up for it a little. I should feel very angry if anyone but Roland were taking off all the prizes, but as it is he I cannot be other than glad.

We went along the dark quad., past the lighted windows, until Edward tapped at Roland's & said a visitor wanted to see him. The window was opened & I leaned in. As soon as I saw his plain intelligent face & dark expressive eyes again, I knew I had not overrated their attraction for me – the call of mind to mind & sympathy to sympathy made itself felt immediately. I stood teasing & mocking him, & telling him I would look out for every atom of conceit on the morrow and squash it immediately. He said he would think of me when he went to receive his prizes & knew he would fall over the steps & make a fool of himself in some way. We only had a few moments' conversation & then Mother wanted to go. So we returned to our cottage, without having seen the Puckles, which was Mother's object, but I at least having achieved mine.

Saturday July 11th

Edward came to breakfast with us, & then we went off to chapel while he fell in with the Corps, who always give an exhibition on Speech Day. He looked very good-looking & straight & tall in his corps clothes, & is now a Lance Sergeant. At the Chapel door I saw Leighton, with his company – he looked very tired & not nearly so nice as Edward, being broad & not so tall. He is a Colour Sergeant – one or two degrees higher than Edward. We sat right in front in chapel. Richardson & then Edward led up the choir, both looking fine & impressive figures. The service was short, and as usual wonderful; when I hear the boys' voices & think of all the memories & associations connected with the school & of the thousands of boys who have sung in the Chapel, some of whom are now commemorated on its walls, I can understand perfectly why Edward regrets leaving it so much. For girls – as yet – there is nothing equivalent to public school for boys – these fine traditions & unwritten laws that turn out so many splendid characters have been withheld from them – to their detriment.

When chapel was over we all went up to the Middle Field to see the Corps reviewed. About 350 belong to it altogether; they were a fine sight as they stood for the Headmaster to inspect them. Dr Mackenzie, in spite of his contempt for women, is a splendid man – with a certain resemblance to Joseph Chamberlain. We did not wait quite till the end but hurried back to the cottage to change for the Prize-Giving. Roland did not take his place among the prize winners until the last moment; Edward said he was looking for his tie! The Headmaster stalked up the Hall very majestically & stood before the table removing his gloves with a far greater dignity than I have seen anyone remove their gloves with before. He made quite a short speech, starting with a fairly detailed mention of a school trustee who had recently died. Then he continued by giving the precepts left for boys by a great Japanese general – I forget his name, & I also forget most of the precepts, but I know the climax was that if a man could not be useful to his country he was better dead. After the Speech he gave away the prizes – most glorious books in the Uppingham binding; I envied their possessors such rewards of ability.

I forgot to mention before now that Mrs Leighton did not

come because she had to finish a book. I was very disappointed not to see her – I am a little surprised that she did not come at any cost to see Roland's great triumph, only I suppose she is so used to his doing brilliant things that she almost takes his wonderful intellect as a matter of course. Roland only received a very average amount of applause; Edward says he is not a bit popular because very few people understand him, & merely think him haughty & conceited – also he shows his feelings so little that one might imagine him to have no emotions, but I think I know better, though I have seen no other but a sort of depression which resembles my own kind very much.

We walked to the Garden Party in the Headmaster's garden. Roland appeared &, while Mother talked to Edward, I teased him about his prizes & being conceited, & then suddenly said I was very glad all the same – the change of tone seemed to disconcert him a little as he thanked me for the remark very shyly. We discussed our beloved Olive Schreiner & *The Story of an African Farm*. I asked him if he really thought me like Lyndall & why he did. He replied, in spite of my saying that the Lyndalls of this world are few & far between, that he hoped & really thought I was, & as to the reason why, he supposed he was allowed to have intuitions occasionally too. We got into deep conversation, in spite of the guests moving all about us & our proximity to the band. We started by discussing Olive Schreiner's idea of immortality; I said I was not sure I entirely agreed with her in thinking that the desire for, & in some cases belief in, conscious continuation implies pettiness or selfishness, but rather that it arose from the idea of any limit to our soul's growth being terrible to us. I said I thought that all religion arose from that fact, that it is impossible to imagine a limit set to our being. Roland said that Kant's theory was something like that, as he believed that a wise & beneficent Deity, which we must assume, would not create individuals to strive & not complete their work, & that since we cannot complete it here, there must be some state hereafter in which we can continue it.

Sunday July 12th
Roland came in to breakfast & afterwards we all three walked in Fairfield Gardens. The subject somewhat naturally turned on

friendship. I laid down the law somewhat, as is my wont, & quite thought Roland would laugh at me, but he made no sign of doing so. Instead, he listened very attentively & with rather downcast looks. I openly challenged him to tell me if he was fickle. He seemed very depressed as he answered that he could not be absolutely sure of himself, as he had taken up people, 'squeezed them like a sponge' & dropped them again, & that though he had no intention now of dropping his friends, & hoped he never would have, he could not guarantee any extreme constancy, such as Edward seems to own. I understand his feeling perfectly as it is analogous with my own. I expect he like me is constantly, if unconsciously, seeking the ideal in a person, & when he finds his idol has clay feet, becomes weary of it. I told him quite openly that I knew he was not popular – which was no disadvantage, as popularity implied mediocrity as a rule – that being an unusual person he never would have it & that therefore he ought to stick to those he possessed. E., who spoke very little, said that when he was at college he would find more people like himself. I however contradicted that & said it was an exploded fallacy that an unusual person would find friends in proportion to the crowd, because a large number only meant a greater collection of ordinary people. On the way to chapel Roland seemed depressed & said he felt we had isolated him. I remarked that I expected it would be my doing, but he said that on the contrary I had made him feel less lonely, because I had admitted to being so myself, & he felt as if I shared his isolation.

He & Edward went to the Lodge after chapel, & then both of them came to dinner again. Once more we went into Fairfield Gardens, but Roland & I were alone this time as Mother & Edward were talking together. Of course we talked of friendship again & discussed Edward; in fact we discussed him as though he were an outside person to us both & no more a relation of mine than of Roland! I laughingly reminded Roland of the fact, & he said that he had just been thinking the same thing & wondering what he had been doing. He said that he had every desire to be constant to Edward, but that he felt E. understood him so very little. I asked Roland what Mrs Leighton thought both of Edward & Richardson; he said that she had only seen

Richardson for a few minutes, & thought him rather silly. After some demur he also told me that when Edward had been with them two days his unctuous seriousness caused Mrs Leighton to say that he was cut out either for a clergyman or a clerk. I don't think I entirely agree with her, though Roland thinks a great deal of her judgement, & I have no doubt it is very penetrating, but as they are not a musical family they cannot have seen anything of E.'s artistic side, and I do not think it quite fair to judge him without taking that into consideration. I told Roland that perhaps it was just as well Mrs Leighton had not met me, as she might have said that I was cut out either for a governess or a Sunday School teacher! and be bored with me. Roland was mildly indignant & said that he thought as she did sufficiently to know that she couldn't possibly do anything of the kind, & he was absolutely certain I should never bore her. He said she was very sorry not to have seen me at Uppingham & that in fact she had suggested that Edward might bring me with him to Lowestoft in the holidays – & he asked me if I would come. I would not exactly say 'yes' as I did not want to suggest the Leightons, who are always in a state of literary poverty, should be burdened with two of us, but I did not want to say 'no' as I should like to go so *very* much, so I did not give any definite reply, but said I was sure one of us at a time was quite enough for Mrs Leighton. Roland & I talked on & on about subjects both personal & impersonal; I made him admit that he thought he was brilliant & that he would not change his opinion whatever failures he had to undergo. He asked me why I made him admit these things, & I said I supposed it was because I shared some of the feelings, & could understand them so well – in fact I held by being brilliant myself, & no failing in exams would remove the certainty though I had done nothing to prove the quality's existence. I said I was very conceited myself & I was sure he did not really mind my making him own up to things. He said that he would admit things to me much more than to most other people, & that he did not mind my knowing a bit.

I said goodbye to him with more indifference than I felt. I could not help wondering whether & when I shall see him again. He seems even in a short acquaintance to share both my faults &

my talents and my ideas in a way that I have never found anyone else do yet.

Monday July 13th Buxton
Mother & I said goodbye to [Edward] at the end of the path outside the cottage, & shortly after we bade 'farewell, a long farewell' to Uppingham also. I wonder if I shall ever see the old-world village with its long straggling street, & the romance-tinged quads & school buildings, again. I have not much respect for custom & tradition as a rule, but in Uppingham it is to be revered; all that is best & finest in the past links itself with present & future more in a boys' public school than anywhere I have yet been.

I was simply in a black mood all morning, realising how easy it will be to fail in my exam., & how ill equipped for it I am compared with what I ought to be. I suppose it will be my lot to see Edward & his friends, who are as much or more to me than my own (as I can't really stand girls), going off to the university, while I, having failed in my exam, am left here once more to toil on drearily alone.

Friday July 17th
This morning came a letter from Roland, enclosing what he calls the 'deservedly prizeless Prize poem' about 'The Crescent & the Cross'. The poem has undoubted felicity of expression – it is a blank verse fragment – but as Uncle Will pointed out, in ideas it is derivative & the personal element is somewhat lacking. This of course he put down to the writer's youth and inexperience; he is going through the imitative stage through which we all have to pass. I think the lack of personal expression is due to the strong element of reserve in his nature; he hides his deep feelings so well that certain of his friends scarcely believe he has any. In a letter I wrote him to-night I asked if he need extend that reticence to poetry.

His letter to me was brief but decisive in every sentence. He says he cannot tell me how much he enjoyed the two days I was at Uppingham, & that they stand out like an oasis in an otherwise commonplace & uninteresting term. He feels he cares still less about leaving Uppingham and its people. Edward

somewhat perturbed him by saying that talking to me seemed
to make him more isolated & exclusive than ever – thus, as
Roland suggests, implying that the more he became friends
with me the more he would drift apart from Edward. But I
cannot think that E. really feels that; it must be part of his
general depressed mood. He & I, though of such diverse
natures, have always been great friends, & I don't think there
can be a bigger difference between him & Roland than there is
between him & me.

Saturday July 25th
In spite of the showeryness of the day, we managed to have our
match against Fallowfield. We just caught the 7.25 back; it was
the usual old train that takes over an hour & a half, but the time
went very quickly, as we all discussed various things, chiefly
tennis, very animatedly. We touched cursorily on the question
of religion & the Book of Daniel, but chiefly the European crisis,
which has suddenly come nearer owing to Austria issuing what
is practically an ultimatum to Servia.

Sunday July 26th
Mother & I actually had a long & animated conversation after
supper about me, my lack of heart. I told Mother I discussed
B.S.'s affection for me quite freely with him; I hoped she was
not shocked but I wouldn't alter myself even if she were. She did
not appear shocked; she seems to grasp modern conditions quite
well, & though she said she wished she might have had a more
ordinary daughter, she managed to sympathise quite respectably with me.

Wednesday July 29th
War was declared to-day between Austria and Servia. Of
course it is feared that the whole of Europe will be involved.
This critical state seems to have arisen so suddenly out of the
long-time hostile attitude of Teuton & Slav, represented in the
feeling of Servia towards Austria-Hungary, that it is difficult to
follow each step. But Germany & Italy in case of Russia's
intervention to protect Servia are bound to assist Austria by

the Triple Alliance, while France is allied to Russia & we are connected with both by an Entente Cordiale, though without a definite alliance. The Irish question seems quite to have sunk into the background beside these momentous issues.

Saturday August 1st
According to the paper this morning, the last hope of peace is about to be abandoned, and Germany is mobilising. I went up to the tennis club, & B.S. & I walked home together as usual. I had managed to make him convulsed with laughter, without going out of my way to make any particularly witty remark, all through tea. Especially I teased him by saying I was going to write an imaginary interview with him for the paper. I don't think when he left me at the gate that he was quite sure whether I was having him on or not. Anyhow, he asked if I often took people off, & I said I did so frequently to the family when they were feeling glum, & that I took him off especially because he was so funny. Then he said I might at least have spared him, & suddenly I thought of that sentence of Nathaniel Hawthorne's in *The Marble Faun* to the effect that our greatest responsibilities in life are towards those who love us. I saw him almost in a new light, but didn't let him realise it; instead I said I could hardly spare him when he provided more copy than most people. He asked me if I ridiculed everyone & said he supposed the fact that he liked me was a great source of amusement. I asked him why he didn't take me off in return & what special disadvantage he would hit on if he did. He told me he never would want to, & could not fix on any disadvantage, though he seemed to think that he knew my character pretty thoroughly! He said that he often used to watch me & know what I was thinking in church when I was a child, & that he had always liked me. Then quite suddenly he asked me 'Were you annoyed when I told you I – liked you?' I said 'I *was*.' 'Why?' he said, and I answered just as suddenly 'Because I didn't like *you*.' There was silence for a few minutes after that & I began to feel great compunction again because I had spoken so, and because my lack of feelings leads me to be so very callous about other people's. He said sadly but somewhat ambiguously that I should realise everything some day.

Sunday August 2nd

Mother tried to get a paper when she went down to the Baths, but they were all sold up; however the Ellingers lent us theirs. But it was not so much what was in the papers that caused excitement as the rumours that were spreading about all day. It is said the Germans have declared war against Russia & that also they have attacked Luxembourg. The situation is very grave indeed.

Monday August 3rd

To-day has been far too exciting to enable me to feel at all like sleep – in fact it is one of the most thrilling I have ever lived through, though without doubt there are many more to come. That which has been so long anticipated by some & scoffed at by others has come to pass at last – Armageddon in Europe! On Saturday evening Germany declared war upon Russia & also started advancing towards the French frontier. The French, in order to make it evident that they were not the aggressors, wasted some hours & then the order to mobilise was given. Great excitement in France continued throughout the night & yesterday the Germans attacked France without declaring war. Unconfirmed rumour says that in one place they have been repulsed with heavy losses. They also broke a treaty in occupying the neutral Duchy of Luxembourg. Luxembourg's neutrality was guaranteed in 1807 by England, France & Germany, & thus Germany's attack upon it is said to be a direct challenge to Great Britain. Some of the papers seem to think that the Austrian-Servian war was only a blind & that Germany was at the bottom of the whole affair – the 'mailed fist' anxious to strike. At any rate Germany has destroyed the tottering hopes of peace and has plunged Europe into a situation the like of which, *The Times* says, has never been known since the fall of the Roman Empire. The great fear now is that our bungling Government will declare England's neutrality. If we at this critical juncture were to refuse to help our friend France, we should be guilty of the grossest treachery & sacrifice our credit for ever. Besides we should gain nothing, for if we were to stand aside & let France be wiped out, a terrible retribution would fall upon us from a strengthened & victorious Germany.

I sat this morning after breakfast reading various newspapers for about two hours. A rumour is going round to-night that England has declared to Germany that if a German sets foot in Belgian territory her (England's) navy will immediately act. There are many who think that this policy of vacillation is losing us the opportunity to strike a telling blow – that we should send troops to prevent the Germans getting into Belgium instead of waiting till they *are* in.

I should think this must be the blackest Bank Holiday within memory. Pandemonium reigned in the town. What with holiday-trippers, people struggling for papers, trying to lay in stores of food & dismayed that the price of everything had gone up, there was confusion everywhere. Mother met Mrs Whitehead in the town; she is in great anxiety because she has one son in Russia, one – Jack – in Servia, and another on his way from India. Marjorie Briggs, who was to have been married on Saturday, was married in a hurry on Friday as her husband had to have joined his regiment on Saturday. The papers are full of stories of tourists in hopeless plights trying to get back to England. Paper money is useless & the majority of the trains are cut off. It is rumoured that there is fear in Paris that a fleet of German Zeppelins are going to destroy Paris from above in the night.

Tuesday August 4th
Late as it is & almost too excited to write as I am, I must make some effort to chronicle the stupendous events of this remarkable day. The situation is absolutely unparalleled in the history of the world. Never before has the war strength of each individual nation been of such great extent, even though all the nations of Europe, the dominant continent, have been armed before. It is estimated that when the war begins *14 millions* of men will be engaged in the conflict. Attack is possible by earth, water & air, & the destruction attainable by the modern war machines used by the armies is unthinkable & past imagination.

This morning at breakfast we learnt that war is formally declared between France & Germany, that the German ambassador has left Paris & the French ambassador Berlin. Germany has declared to Belgium that if her troops are allowed to pass unmolested through Belgian territory she will protect her interests in the Treaty at the end of the war. Belgium has indignantly refused any such violation of international honour, and the King of the Belgians has appealed to King George for aid. For an hour this morning I read a fine speech of Sir Edward Grey's, in which he manages successfully to steer the middle course between the extremists who on the one hand want neutrality & on the other immediate war. His two chief statements were that the British fleet would in the event of the French coast being attacked by Germany give France all the protection in her power, and also that she would see that Belgian neutrality was preserved. Sir E. Grey's statement that 'we are prepared' evoked tremendous cheering in the House. In consequence of their disagreement with this policy, Mr John Burns, Sir John Morley & Mr Masterman have all resigned their places in the Cabinet. It is rumoured that the Secretaryship for War has been offered to Lord Kitchener.

All day long rumours kept coming that a naval engagement had been fought off the coast of Yorkshire. I went up to the tennis club this afternoon, more to see if I could hear anything than to play, as it kept on pouring with rain. No one knew any further definite news, but we all discussed the situation. I mentioned Edward's & Maurice's keenness to do something definite & Bertram Spafford said they ought either to apply to Mr Heathcote or Mr Goodman, who were the chief Territorials here, or to go to the Territorial headquarters in Manchester. I told him yesterday that the fact of a strong healthy man like himself being absolutely ignorant of military tactics was a proof that our military system was at fault somewhere. He said that at the Manchester Grammar School, where he went, they had no corps, & that many men were in the same case as himself.

The war will alter everything &, even if I pass my exam., there would probably be no means to send both Edward & me to Oxford at the same time. There is nothing to do now but wait. When I got in I found Edward had procured an evening paper with the startling news that England had sent an ultimatum to Germany, to expire at midnight to-night, demanding the immediate withdrawal of her troops from Belgium. Germany declared earlier in the day that if it became necessary to her tactics to treat Belgium as an enemy she would do so. German troops are said to have crosssed the Belgian frontier & reached Verviers. Sir E. Grey's speech has caused great satisfaction in France.

Immediately after dinner I had to go to a meeting of the University Extension Lectures Committee. Small groups of people, especially men, were standing about talking, & in front of the Town Hall was quite a large crowd, as on the door was posted up the mobilisation order, in large black letters, ordering all army recruits to take up the colours & all Territorials to go to their headquarters. Edward has been reading the papers carefully & says that at present only the trained army & the Territorials are wanted & there is no demand for untrained volunteers. Though anxious to fight he says he will wait until he hears that people like himself are needed; he is of course very young & not over-experienced. I expect Maurice will do the same, though he is longing to fight. He & Edward went off to the Hippodrome; I really do not know how they could. Mrs Ellinger, who does not seem to realise the danger of our situation at all & is no doubt perfectly well satisfied with everything so long as her pleasures are uninterrupted, asked me to go too, but I refused point blank.

I could not rest indoors so got Mother & Daddy to come out with me to look for further news. In the town the groups of people had increased, and suppressed excitement was everywhere in the air. There was a crowd round the Post Office; at first I thought they were attracted by the mobilisation order up in the window, but it turned out that Mr Heathcote & his motor car were there, with Mrs Heathcote inside driving. He was in his uniform, which looked as if he were going tonight, & was very busy sending telegrams off. We next went to the station & found there that a last edition extra of the *Chronicle* had been issued but all the copies were sold. However Smith the foreman, who told us his son had gone to the front, gave us his copy. It contained the thrilling news that Germany has formally declared war on Belgium! This looks like an answer to our ultimatum, & will perhaps free us from the necessity of waiting until midnight for our answer. Stupendous events come so thick & fast after one another that it is impossible to realise to any extent their full import. One feels as if one were dreaming, or reading a chapter out of one of H. G. Wells' books like *The War of the Worlds*. To me, who have never known the meaning of war, as I can scarcely remember the South African even, it is incredible to think that there *can* be fighting off the coast of Yorkshire.

Mrs Kay told us that her son Tom, Mrs Johnson's chauffeur, has been told he is required as he belongs to the Army Medical Corps. His wife, who had a baby only last Friday, is terribly excited because he has to leave her, as she only gets about 2/- a day when he is gone, & has three tiny children on her hands. Mrs Kay says she will have to look after them. She thinks all her four sons who are Reservists will have to go abroad as they have all volunteered for foreign service. Luckily she takes it all calmly & philosophically, though she seems to think she will never see them again.

To sum up the situation in any way is impossible, every hour brings fresh & momentous events & one must stand still & await catastrophes each even more terrible than the last. All the nations of this continent are ready with their swords drawn, & Germany the aggressor with her weaker ally Austria stands alone facing an armed Europe united against her. She has broken treaty after treaty & disregarded every honourable tie with other nations. Italy, her old ally, has reaffirmed her neutrality, & thus assists our side by remaining out of the conflict. This conflict is a mortal struggle between herself & France; life to the one will mean death to the other. Indeed this war is a matter of life & death to us, & Daddy says the key to the whole situation is the British navy & that as that stands or falls the fate of Europe will be decided.

Wednesday August 5th

All the news of last night was confirmed this morning, and it is further announced that the time limit given by Britain for an answer to her ultimatum expired without a reply coming from Germany, and that war between England & Germany is formally declared. Papers seemed to differ as to whether England must be said to have made war on Germany or Germany on England. Some say that the Germans have started hostilities against us by sinking a British mining ship and chasing a British cruiser. Thus, as the papers point out, Germany has declared war on four powers – Russia, France, Belgium and Britain, within 3 days. Nothing like it, they say, has been known since the time of Napoleon, and even Napoleon did not make war on his neighbours at so mad a rate.

The town was quite quiet when we went down, though groups of people were standing about talking & one or two Territorials were passing through the streets. Several Territorials & one or two Reservists were going off by train this morning & there was a small crowd on the station seeing them off. Close by us a Reservist got into a carriage & his father & a girl, probably his wife, came to say goodbye. The girl was crying but they were all quite calm. As we came up from the town I met Maurice and went down again with him. Though excitement & suspense are wearing, I felt I simply could not rest but must go on wandering about.

The French have sunk a German cruiser, & have seized a dreadnought and another cruiser. Heavy firing has been heard from Margate, but nothing has been seen. Mrs Kay brought the pleasing information this afternoon that Mrs Johnson is going to keep the chauffeur son's place open for him & has promised to pay the 8/- a week rent for his wife & children. All decent firms are keeping open the Reservists' places for them, & in addition to this Harrods Stores have promised 10/- each family to the families of those who have been called out from assisting in the shop.

I showed Edward an appeal in *The Times & the Chronicle* for young unmarried men between the ages of 18 & 30 to join the army. He suddenly got very keen & after dinner he & Maurice wandered all round Buxton trying to find out what to do in order to volunteer for home service. They were informed by someone at the Police Station that the best thing to do would be to telephone to the Territorial Headquarters at Chesterfield. They got on to a very interesting officer there, & told him they wanted if possible to be allowed to serve for a period as they did not want their service to interfere with their going to Oxford if it could be avoided. The officer told them to apply to an adjutant, stating their qualifications.

Thursday August 6th

To-day has principally been one of the weary waiting kind. Nothing very definite has happened. Edward & Maurice have as yet heard nothing from the adjutant at Chesterfield. Nothing very definite is known about England's policy & the papers are naturally secretive about the position of her Fleet. The chief news is that the Germans have been repulsed with heavy losses while trying to storm the Belgian fortification of Liège. The Belgians are said to have behaved magnificently & while the defenders of the forts were engaged in keeping the invaders at bay, a Belgian brigade arrived & crowned the splendid efforts of the defenders with success.

To-day I started the only work it seems possible as yet for women to do – the making of garments for the soldiers. I started knitting sleeping-helmets, and as I have forgotten how to knit, & was never very brilliant when I knew, I seemed to be an object of some amusement. But even when one is not skilful it is better to proceed slowly than to do *nothing* to help.

Friday August 7th

This morning came the somewhat depressing news that the British cruiser HMS *Amphion*, which sank the German liner *Königin Luise*, ran into a mine & was blown up. 131 men were drowned. The information cast a gloom over breakfast, during which meal Daddy worked himself into a thorough temper, raved away at us, & said he would not allow Edward to go abroad whatever happened – 'Whatever you do, don't volunteer until you're *quite* sure there's no danger,' sort of thing. Edward replied quite calmly that no one could prevent him serving his country in any way he wanted to.

The Belgian fortress of Liège is still holding out, though it is very hard pressed. 25,000 Belgians are holding it against a reinforcement of 100,000 Germans. The opposition is a serious hindrance to Germany, who reckoned on storming Liège with scarcely any trouble. All day long I knitted away. Various reports kept coming in of battles, different dreadnoughts being sunk, multitudes of Germans being killed, but none of them were confirmed.

Maurice & Edward wandered about all day waiting for an

answer & at last they got it. Just at dinner-time Mrs Goodman came to see us & said that she had heard from her husband – who is a Territorial officer at Chesterfield – that there was no room for more recruits in the 6th Derby & Notts. Regt. but that the adjutant was delighted with their letter & had selected it from many hundred other applications & sent it to the War Office. Edward's & Maurice's qualifications are considered excellent & vastly superior to the majority of those who volunteer. Daddy was quite angry about the letter being sent to the War Office, but E. said that Daddy, not being a public school man or having had any training, could not possibly understand the impossibility of his remaining in inglorious safety while others, scarcely older than he, were offering their all. E. is of course rather young to volunteer really, being only eighteen. Maurice was nineteen to-day. E. faces the prospect of whatever he may have to do with perfect tranquillity, & says that even death can only come once. We spoke of the entire absence of future prospects which war seems to produce; E. said that but for this he would have been eagerly speculating about Oxford, but now he scarcely thought of it at all. Intellect, except in very high places, seems scarcely to count at all in time of war – the ordinary average soldier fights just as well for his ignorance as any cultured man for his knowledge. And then the value of human life becomes so cheap, so that while the loss of ten men under tragic circumstances amid ordinary conditions would fill the whole country with horror, the news of the loss of thousands is now regarded with a philosophical calm and an unmoved countenance. My beloved brother! What will become of him? But as I told him this evening, dreary as life is without his presence here, dreary as are the prospects of what may lie before him, yet I would not have his decision back, or keep him here.

Saturday August 8th
No news has arrived for Edward or Maurice from the War Office, but as it is so inundated with requests, doubtless we shall not hear for several days.

Liège has kept up its gallant defence & still holds out. A rumour that arrived last night is confirmed this morning, that is, 25,000 Germans have been killed before the Liège forts. The

Germans asked for a truce so that they could bury their dead, but so far the truce has not been granted. I am incapable of feeling glad at such a wholesale slaughter of the Germans, whatever use it may be to us. I can only think of the 25,000 mothers who bore & reared those men with toil, & of the wives & families, never ardent for war or for a quarrel with us, which they leave behind them.

The two German cruisers which took refuge in Messina harbour have courageously left the neutral waters, & drew the British ships in hot pursuit. They prefer death to disarmament; it *is* a splendid instance of German patriotism.

This afternoon I went to the St John's bandaging class. Of course I have never been to one before, never having taken a real interest, but I managed to take in quite a lot & learnt how to do 3 different kinds of bandages. With the greatest industry in the world however one cannot get a certificate & therefore cannot volunteer as a nurse for six weeks.

Edward received a letter from Roland saying that he had applied for a commission in a Norfolk regiment but as yet had heard nothing. He hopes very much to get it. I cannot but think it a terrible waste of good material that such an intellect as that should put itself readily in danger, but E. says Roland has an excellent military brain, & is quite worth a commission. R. says that several timid people in Lowestoft, because they are at the nearest point to Germany in England, fear every moment to be suddenly attacked by the enemy's fleet. A good deal of excitement exists there.

Monday August 10th
No special news has come through from the front to-day. Probably momentous happenings are going on, but the blinds are drawn down and we know nothing of them as yet. Certainly great bodies of French & German troops seem to be approaching one another round about Alsace Lorraine. The Japanese are stirring themselves & there are rumours of their joining the war on the side of England.

Maurice came in this morning very excited at an announcement in the paper to the effect that 2,000 temporary commissions had been offered in the regular army. Both he & Edward tore off to see Mrs Goodman to know if they had done all possible, & tried to communicate with Mr Goodman but could not. In the end Maurice determined to tear off to Derby to see if he couldn't do something. Edward prudently refused to go & spend the railway fare for nothing as he was quite sure they had done all possible, so Maurice went off alone. In the meantime Mother & I went to a First Aid lecture class – theory – taken quite well by Dr Theobalds. Her greatest difficulty seemed to be to make her sentences sufficiently simple for the class, which consists of a great many stupidities. Mrs Ellinger sat just in front of us & was quite rude to Mother, saying she was astonished E. had not gone to Derby, that Maurice intended signing on for 3 years, that he could easily go to Oxford after, that we should give our sons to fight for their country etc. etc. Of course Maurice, having been carefully instructed by E. not to do anything rash, returned at 7.0 having spent 7/- but having done little else. He saw the adjutant about the announcement in the paper, but the adjutant said he did not know anything about it yet, but that he would by Wed. & Maurice had better call or write. Maurice also saw enough of the type that enlist as privates to make quite sure that he would not join the army in that way, which he seems to have had a mad idea of doing.

Tuesday August 11th
Very little news has come through to-day, probably owing to the censorship of the War news. This morning I practised bandaging on Betty Forsythe for some time, & in the afternoon I went to a bandaging class – though it could hardly be called a class as no one was organizing it; everyone just wandered about & did what bandages they thought they could, & most of them did it wrong. Mrs Ellinger in great form went about offering to show people how to do things which she had not learnt properly herself.

At about half-past 8 E. & I started out for a walk as I felt I had had no air all day. The evening was perfect, very still, so that no sounds could be heard except the low swishing of the grass & the cry of an occasional bird. We went right to the top of the Manchester Rd, so we were all among the hills, which looked almost black against the serene gleaming sky, in which floated

little cirrus clouds. On the way up we discussed the Leightons, &
I told E. Roland had wanted me to go there. I learnt that Mrs
Leighton usually seems very hard & unbending, but in reality is
very much the opposite.

On the way home E. explained to me how a night attack is
made. As I looked across the moor with its deep ditches &
uniform darkness, I could well understand how a multitude of
men clad inconspicuously might move across that dim surface
without being perceived. I could also imagine the eerie sensation of waiting for a silently advancing enemy – the listening to
all the varied sounds of night, & the imagining of many more –
the rippling of a brook, the cry of a startled bird, the soft swish of
the long grass in the breeze, all of which would strike with
important meaning on the ear of the listening defence.

As we came home it was almost impossible to believe war was
in the world. The peaceful sky, through which an occasional
shooting star flashed, & the sleeping hills, seemed to enshroud
our little earth in a fold of perfect peace. Yet only to-day I heard
from Cora that Adrian has probably received a commission in
the regular army & that Freke & Jack Maitland have joined the
first volunteer regiment that will be sent abroad. Even to-day it
was rumoured that 100,000 British troops are now in Belgium.

Friday August 14th
These days I seem to wake up weary; they are both long & full of
work of a somewhat tiring nature. But one must not grumble at
that; the great thing to be thankful for is the having something
to do, for without that life would be unbearable. This morning
as it happened the knitted helmets had to be given in to
Mrs Heathcote, & we have no more materials in the house at
present, so I had no sewing for the War to do at the time. I
occupied myself in learning up parts of the First Aid book, and
practising what bandages I could do single handed. This afternoon we had the bandaging class; it was very hot, but luckily not
quite such a crowd of cackling women was present.

About lunch-time Maurice rang up to say he goes to Oxford
tomorrow. He expects to have a month's drilling & then be
given a commission & go to fight. When Edward & Daddy came
in we told them about it. Edward said little, but thought a great

deal, I've no doubt; he said to me later that this Oxford business could not be entered into without the written consent of their parents. Mother in her heart of hearts does not feel altogether happy about his not going, but can do nothing when Daddy, not possessing the requisite courage, refuses to let him undertake any military duties whatsoever.

Just after dinner Eirene Dodd rang up, wanting me to go & help to move some things at the Red Cross headquarters, which is the old Royal Hotel. I walked home with Eirene & then said goodbye to Maurice – though I am going to see him off in the morning, & walked a little way down the road with Edward & him. I told him to come back 'couvert de gloire' & that then I would show him off with great pride to all the community in general.

I could have written a much more interesting account of to-day than this, but am altogether too weary for literary efforts – the war seems to swallow up even one's best gifts.

Sunday August 16th
Mother & I went up to Fairfield after tea & heard Mr Ward preach a very good sermon on 'Hitherto hath the Lord helped us'. Mother asked him at the door to come & see us before he goes.

B.S. was in the shadow of the bushes as we passed their house, but neither moved nor spoke. When I think how generously yesterday he said that though I was a flirt I had not flirted with him, and that all that had happened had been entirely his fault, I feel much more kindly towards him than I ever have before. Considering the intentional provocation I have given him, he has been remarkably patient with me. I only hope that he may some how, some day, be rewarded for the love that 'suffereth long & is kind'.

Monday August 17th
Going to the works, as he has started to do, means that E. considers himself quite grown-up & full of the sense of his importance. I foresee that to a certain extent he will be my friend but he will still more be my critic, and will judge with harshness my capacity for doing the wrong thing, & the obvious

faults to which my own fondness for particular frailties impels me. Sometimes he reminds me very much of Tom Tulliver in *The Mill on the Floss*, who thought himself unable to do anything but what was right. And I suppose I am like Maggie – who was probably George Eliot. If only I could meet George Eliot & talk long & earnestly with her, I think I should rise from that conversation much better comprehended and certainly less isolated.

Tuesday August 18th
The paper officially announces this morning that the British Army – the Expeditionary Force – has all been landed in France without a single casualty. The French seem to welcome with great joy the nation which for the first time is fighting with [them] in a European war. Meanwhile very little fresh news comes of the conflict. Japan has sent Germany an ultimatum with regard to certain territory seized by the Germans in China.

Thursday August 20th
The paper announced this morning that the British army was in the fighting line, but the statement was denied by the War Office in the evening. At night Mother, E. & I went to the Upper Circle at the Opera House to see Martin Harvey in *The Breed of the Treshams*, one of those melodramatic plays which seem to be dying out but which are rather a relief after the problem & rather plotless pieces that hold the stage just now.

Friday August 21st
After lunch I bandaged hard, and after tea had some tennis practice with Bertram Spafford. He really reminds me more every day of Gregory Rose in *The Story of an African Farm*, especially of Gregory when he first enters the story. Certainly he plays Gregory to my Lyndall. His assumption of undeniable superiority & right of criticism over any qualifications of mine would once have annoyed but now merely amuses me. The assumption is of course due to the fact that I am a girl & therefore *naturally* inferior in all respects, & especially in intellectual respects!

I heard this morning, to my joy, that Roland Leighton, owing to his defective eyesight, has not passed the necessary exam. for serving in the army, & therefore cannot go. I am glad because I did not want that brilliant intellect to be wasted, & that most promising career to be spoilt at its outset.

Saturday August 22nd
News came to-day that the Germans have pushed back the Belgians and occupied Brussels, which surrendered without resistance for the sake of the safety of its large population of unarmed civilians. The Germans appear to have entered the city in an arrogant & bullying spirit, offering the inhabitants every kind of insult imaginable. The leading article in the *Daily Mail* this morning tried to point out to us the horrors that the poor gallant little nation is undergoing. The article was entitled 'The Agony of Belgium'. It seems wrong to play tennis when such terrors are convulsing Europe – but if one is used to regular exercise, the cessation of it only leads to weariness, morbidness, and general unfitness.

Sunday August 23rd
I had a letter from Roland this morning, longer than he usually sends me, & according to him written for the pure pleasure of writing to me rather than because he had anything to say. He seems very distressed because his eyesight is keeping him out of the army.

Monday August 24th
Rather more news than usual came from the front to-day. The Russians have obtained a brilliant victory over the Germans in Eastern Prussia, & are advancing quickly in their myriads. Also the Servians have so thoroughly defeated the Austrians on the banks of the Drina that the Austrian Campaign against Servia is practically abandoned.

But, while the news from one frontier is so reassuring, the news from the other, in which we are of course most concerned, is scarcely encouraging. This evening comes the report that Namur, which was expected to hold out at least as long as Liège, has surrendered to the enemy. This is admitted to be a great

German military achievement. Some British troops were engaged all yesterday in battle. No list of casualties has appeared as yet.

Tuesday August 25th
Very grave news from the front this morning, – so much so that all faces look grave, & there are vague rumours in the paper about sudden conclaves at the War Ministry & audiences given by Lord Kitchener in the early morning. The report of the fall of Namur is confirmed; it seems to have been taken without a struggle. Without doubt, the heavy punishment inflicted on brave Liège, the fall of Brussels, & the feeling in Belgium that she has had to bear the whole shock of the war in the north without much assistance from her allies, all tended to weaken the resistance of the defenders of Namur. In consequence of this unexpected blow, the Allies have been obliged to withdraw from the Meuse towards the French frontier. At the other end of the battle the Germans in Lorraine have forced the French back, & taken Luneville, which is some miles over the French frontier. The French admit that their plan of attack has been a failure & that they were better prepared for a defensive movement. All the papers are very pessimistic & no one talks about scare-mongering *now*; the scare has become only too real, & the warning is lost in the actual.

Two British Army Corps – the 1st & the 2nd – have fought their first battle against the Germans at Mons & have held their ground. No actual casualty lists are yet issued, but the number of them this evening is estimated by Sir John French at 2,000. Eight German Zeppelins, the existence of which no one suspected, are said to be intending to sail over England, dropping dynamite on our ports & probably on our rich cities like London. Truly we of this generation are born to a youth very different from anything we ever supposed or imagined for ourselves. Trouble & disasters are menacing us the nature of which we cannot even guess at.

I had a long letter from Miss Penrose this morning which I thought would tell me about my exam. but instead it was a collection of rules with regard to men students at Oxford, which appear to be rather strict, but I suppose necessarily so.

Wednesday August 26th

To-day took place the dreadful First Aid Exam., on account of which I was not at all nervous, but at which I nevertheless did not acquit myself magnificently. The doctor was a tall fine man, with a kind manner, but plenty of sarcasm & disdainful criticism at his command. He asked me what I should do for a fish hook embedded in the skin. I answered promptly & I think correctly, but he gave me no indication, & told me to bandage Mrs Gibbons for a broken forearm. I received a small criticism for turning my back on the patient, but remembered how to do the arm, improvising with handkerchiefs as I had not sufficient bandages. Then he told me to treat another woman for a cut throat, at which I made three bad mistakes, by not finding the artery at once, forgetting to make the patient sit down, & saying a tourniquet should be put on above & below when I really knew perfectly well that no tourniquet could be applied. However he seemed better pleased when I said I would send for an assistant at once to relieve me in digital pressure.

I thought I did not care whether I passed or not, but I do very much now I have been in for the exam., not because I think I shall ever go in much for that type of study, but because of the general principle such an exam. as this involves. One of my greatest aspirations is to succeed in whatever I undertake, & to undertake nothing unless I do it well. I seem of late to be falling below this personal ideal, since I do not imagine for a moment I shall be passed in this one, & am expecting every post to hear that I have failed badly in the Oxford Senior, that therefore my Exhibition is rendered void, & my chance of Oxford postponed. I must again arise, & stir up my inexhaustible fount of enthusiasm, energy, & will once more.

Thursday August 27th

This morning to my unutterable joy & relief came a certificate from Oxford stating I had reached the 'required standard' in the Oxford Senior in Latin, French, Arithmetic & Algebra. At first my delight, which I expected to be intense, was quite spoilt by Daddy, who instead of giving me a little of the praise which I had at least some reason to expect, burst out that it was no use my thinking of going to Oxford with this war on, that I wanted to turn out my parents when they were getting on in life, that we were all robbing him etc. etc. It was a hard reward for the success of a year's steady work, & whether tactful or untactful in resenting the fact, there are some things that flesh and blood cannot stand. I rounded on him saying that if I had failed & wasted the money he spent on coaching me (which I think he must have hoped I should do) he could not reproach me more. Daddy's utter unconsciousness of my part in preparing for the exam. & of the labour & steady application worth far more than his £50, which he never missed, really roused me. He has no idea of the difficulties which I had to face, which, always considerable, become acute in such a place as Buxton, where no first-rate teaching is obtainable & one is liable to constant interruption.

Of course I am not so ignorant that I do not realise financial affairs at the works, in spite of their apparent prosperity, must be difficult to cope with, & worrying in general. It is not in the least that I resented the suggestion that there might be difficulty in sending me to Oxford – though I don't believe, & Edward agrees with me, that there is any that cannot quite easily be solved. I should not have minded being told that in the least, but what I did look for was some slight feeling of pride in my having done what I said I would do, some slight word of praise or gratification. Mother for once stood up for me warmly, & said afterwards it was abominable of Father to behave so, & that he was utterly unreasonable & did not mean what he said.

But whatever the outward acceptance of my success, I could not remain dismal long. The inward joy was too strong to be repressed. The exam., though difficult to me, is nothing to take very great credit for, but it means much to me to have passed it, because it proves that I have intelligence enough to adapt & apply myself in a short time to subjects which I have little natural aptitude for (this refers to Mathematics & the *grammar* of the languages) & use them to serve my ends. I thought of the endless coaching lessons, the unctuous facetiousness of poor Mr Lace, the utter indifference & aggravatingness of Old Cheese, & the feeling of repulsion with which he inspired me, of 'grinding at grammar' on bright sunny afternoons, when any other occupation would have been pleasanter, of struggles & despair trying to make my mathematical difficulties understood, & I felt that these were some of the things of which the chief joy was the triumph of looking back upon them & feeling they were over. There was a keener delight in dwelling on my little interview with Miss Penrose during the Summer Meeting last year, her obvious disapproval of my gay attire, & disbelief in my intellect, her advice to me not to attempt the scholarship exam. & her dismissal (mental, which I perceived) of me as an unlikely candidate. It was very pleasant to think of my three Exhibition days at Somerville, of Miss Penrose's indifference to me at the first interview, & her slight eagerness in the second, of the people I met there, & of little Miss Lloyd, who I hope has managed to get in there too. At least before me is the prospect of enthusiastic, & no longer lonely, work, & though the absence of small luxuries at Somerville, & the oppressiveness (to me) of a lot of women together, & the certain uncongeniality of some of them – I shall count these things all as jam when they are a part of the intellectual work I love, & the companionship of one or two at least with whom I can share my thoughts without dread of misunderstanding.

I wrote to Miss Penrose & told her I would endeavour 'loyally to observe' the rules & customs upon which she laid stress; my main object was of course to inform her about the exam., & I also asked her advice about Greek, which I shall have to study hard. I wrote to Roland too & returned his French books. I told him that he might see something of me at Oxford if he could face the prospect of having tea with me under the eagle eye of a chaperon, or of coming to the Principal's Saturday afternoon 'At Homes'. I am so very glad, I do not know how I should have endured to see Edward, & still more Roland, go off to Oxford in October while I was cut off for at least a year from both it & them.

Very little definite news came from the battlefield to-day. A continuous battle seems to be going on in different parts of the line, but no decisive action is reported, & no casualty list has come. It seems a crime to be at all happy when such events are happening, but it is difficult to merge the personal entirely in the general, when one feels that the personal good may turn out to be for the general good one day.

Friday August 28th

I scarcely realised till to-day what a weight is lifted off my mind by the result of my exam. To me it is hard to live without a definite object & definite means of fulfilling it in view, without a future towards which I can direct my present. I am a dreamer, but not of the useless kind which sees visions far ahead & no link with them, no germ of them, in the present things of life. Before I heard the result all was so indefinite. Edward thinks it foolish to have ever felt such anxiety as to be sensible of so much relief in its removal, but he does not understand what Oxford means to me – a breaking down of oppressive boundaries, & a step towards freedom & liberty of thought, work & endeavour.

Saturday August 29th

The exciting news came this morning of an English naval victory in the North Sea. Two German destroyers & 3 German cruisers have been sunk, but the British fleet is intact. The youngest admiral in the Fleet, Rear-Admiral Beatty, was responsible for the organisation of the engagement.

Sunday August 30th

I found a letter from Roland waiting for me, & though all his have been a strange source of comfort to me through everything, I have never received one which impressed me with quite such a sense of joy as this. He was of course writing about my exam., & begins 'I am so glad – so very glad. You do not know how wretched I should have felt if you had failed. And now we shall be able all three to be at Oxford together – you & Edward & I. For, come what may, I *will* go now. And I look forward to facing a hedge of chaperons & Principals with perfect equanimity, if I may be allowed to see something of you on the other side.'

After tea Mother & E. & I went up to Fairfield for Mr Ward's farewell sermon. Fortunately we arrived in good time, for a crowd came to hear him greater than I have seen in the church before. It will be many a long day before Fairfield sees such a congregation again. I could not help thinking of all the novels I have read dealing with clergymen, like Robert Elsmere & Richard Meynell, who rouse the minds & hearts of men &

women. Mother whispered to me 'It's just like a story book.' The service was long, but when Mr Ward came into the pulpit a sort of electric shock went through the church & he became the centre of everyone's emotions. I expected his sermon to be very personal, as I have noticed before that his chief fault is a tendency to talk about himself in a distinctly appreciative strain. But I was wrong. He made no personal reference at all except to say that he had failed in many directions in which he hoped to have succeeded there, but that no one beside himself & God knew what that failure meant to him. He had always bidden us consider three great questions – what we are, why we are here, & whither we are going. He had told us that we were not mere bundles of matter, mocked by moral insight & longing which could never attain its end, but divine spirits, full of the power to do great deeds, think great thoughts, range over spiritual worlds, & create the Kingdom of God by our Godhead – beings inspired from a source whence the supply was unfailing & inexhaustible. We were here to develop our high mental qualities, & to increase our sensibility to emotion, not to drift on idly & aimlessly but to unite our wills with the power for righteousness that runs through all things & all ages, to resist the ape & the tiger in our natures & to develop the divine. He spoke very seriously of the War, & the non-realisation, especially by the working classes, of its meaning. We did not realise, he said, that God was calling us by this terrible calamity from our life of sensation & self-indulgence. With such exhortations he impressed upon us his first great injunction – *consider* – & because these things were hard, we must *confide* – confide & trust in God, the never failing source of help & inspiration, the universal power for good, speaking through all people & all things.

Outside the church we waited a few moments for me to bid goodbye to him. He stood there in the porch, saying goodbye to each member of that large congregation, with a cheerful smile & a kind word for each, as they all came crowding out at the door where he always stands. I do not think I shall ever forget the scene – his slight figure in its white surplice showing dimly in the faint light from the church, & all his people, working men & women mostly, passing into the night, but still crowding round him & loth to leave. He must have been worn out, but stood there with his expression of gentle loving sadness, kindly patient with each one who would gladly have monopolized all his time for themselves. He gave me a moment after saying goodnight to all, in which I could only say how sorry I had been not to see him the day before. 'You shouldn't go off playing tennis,' he said smiling, half reproachful & still clasping my hands in his warm grip. Of course I wished him luck in my heart, but forgot to do so verbally in the agitation of the moment. He spoke of E. as 'Edward' & then asked him to forgive the familiarity, & told him he would write to him & said he would be able to keep in touch with me that way too. I begged him to come & see me at Somerville College if his work ever took him to Oxford – 'You will not forget that,' I said & he replied 'I will remember.' Then we had to go. All through the churchyard people were talking about him. Two women were clamouring for photographs of him to a man who evidently had been taking some. One woman, when asked if she was going to see him off next morning, replied 'Eh no! A'm not. If A' went, A' might disgrace meself by throwing me arms round his neck.'

So closes the religious & emotional movement which awoke Fairfield from its indifference & may have prevented its sinking back again for ever.

During supper Daddy & Edward read us a very dismal article in the *Sunday Times* speaking of the tremendous losses in the British Army, & the apparent invincibleness of the Germans all round. The situation seems very grave indeed. What with the terrible news from the front, & Mr Ward's farewell to Fairfield, the day has been a sad one. The only bright spot is Roland Leighton's letter – it seems a strange coincidence that in spite of all the obstacles to my going to Oxford & all his attempts to join the army, our destinies have been shaped in such a way as to bring us, or so it seems now, to Oxford together. It is as though chords begin to sound faintly which have never even vibrated before.

Monday August 31st
The news in the paper this morning was somewhat better. The Allies have indeed retreated, but only to hold a stronger position, & great as their losses are, they have inflicted casualties

out of all proportion on the enemy. Even our losses however are not so great as at first supposed, being between 5,000 & 6,000. Wounded are being landed daily at such seaside towns as Folkestone & Harwich. The evening papers implied that Kitchener has some stratagem in the background which will stagger Europe when it comes forth.

Wednesday September 2nd

After dinner we all discussed again Daddy's refusal to let Edward go into the Army, & the unmanliness of it, especially after we read in *The Times* of a mother who said to her hesitating son 'My boy I don't want you to go, but if I were you I should!' We saw Mrs Ellinger later & she seems very strongly to disapprove of Daddy. Not that other people's opinions matter to us, only they represent prestige & it is hard luck on Edward to be misjudged for what is not his fault. Mrs Ellinger however contradicts every rumour she hears unfavourable to Edward. Daddy does not care about E.'s honour or courage so long as he is safe. It is left to Edward & I to live up to our name of 'Brittain'.

Little fresh news arrived from the battlefield. The Allies are still falling back, especially on the right, towards Paris. The centre & left seem to have stood their ground. The Russians have had both a great reverse, in which three of their generals were killed, & a great victory, in which they have simply driven the Austrians before them.

Thursday September 3rd

To-day is the Kaiser's birthday, which he said he should spend in Paris. He has not done so, but at the same time he is not very far out of his calculations. The German army is now only 30 miles from the capital. One wonders if there is not some decisive plan up the sleeve of [our] Government; this gradual but decided retreat seems hardly in keeping with the brains at the head of affairs. Meanwhile Paris is preparing for siege, men & women are leaving it for small towns outside the fighting area, and the French Government has moved to Bordeaux.

With this account of British losses, & the call for 500,000 men to arms, any British subjects possibly available, should be. E. is feeling depressed & miserable because Daddy withholds him from doing his duty but being only 18 can do nothing without Daddy's consent. Mother sent a letter to Mr Haigh by E. in which she asked him to use his influence over Daddy to counteract Mr Clay's, which has been too cautious. Mr Haigh telephoned to Mother after tea to say that he had come to the same conclusion himself, before receiving Mother's letter, by reading the letters of yesterday in *The Times*, & had done his best. Edward after dinner definitely asked again if he might go & they had a conversation about it. Daddy was distinctly hostile, saying that if Edward went it would be the death of him, that he thought E. very unkind after the education he had etc. etc. Both Mother and I however talked it over & tried to make him see it from the point of view of honour. At present he is still on the refusal side, but has promised to consult Dr Hannah about Edward's health & general physical stamina.

So there is after all a chance of his going. I will not say anything but that I am glad, but I cannot pretend not to be sorry. Oxford will not be the same if he is not there. It is strange how the very fact of going to Oxford, which I thought so hard a thing to be able to do, so full of just the kind of happiness – that of work & companionship – which I most love, instead of preserving the glory that I saw in the vision of it, is transformed by the same grey despondent mist that alters everything now. 'Despondent' is not quite the word, for we are too proud to be really that. So it seems that 'that sad word, Joy' must be banished from our vocabularies, & that if it is ever reinstated it will be sadder than ever because of the toll of lives that will have been paid for it. This is no longer a time to see how much enjoyment one can get out of life, but to see how much courage & strength one can give to it. Not self-satisfaction, but self-sacrifice, is the order of the day. And I am determined to give up the now futile attempt to see what happiness I can get for myself out of Oxford, & instead to see what *use* I can be both to it & the world in general – by acting directly on behalf of war claims when I can do so, & when I cannot, by helping in the more indirect way of advising the perplexed & comforting the distressed. There are only two things possible now – to act when that can be done – & to endure – to endure grief & disappointment with patience & courage, & with a brave cheerfulness which will make other people's burdens seem more bearable to them. All this is what I say I will try to do, but as I am very selfish, & very fond of having things ordered just in the way most convenient to me, I expect there will be a great deal more resolution than success to begin with.

Roland Leighton telephoned tonight. [He] is very busy just now, having obtained the temporary post of assistant recruiting officer. I spoke to him a few minutes & he said he *would* go to Oxford, unless the unlikely happened & something military turned up in which his defective eyesight would not matter. He has done his utmost to serve his country & is really free from responsibility in that direction. I told him to-night that of the three undergraduates I expected to be specially interested in he would probably be the only one left, so that he would have to make up for the other two. I would gladly give up a good many things if he could be at Oxford at the same time as I am.

Friday September 4th

The morning opened in gloom, owing to Daddy's unconquerable aversion to Edward's doing anything for his country. He would scarcely speak, but he did inform Mother that he would put no more opposition in the way of Edward's departure, only we were going in direct opposition to his wishes. I told Mother she ought to say that *he* was going in direct opposition to *her* wishes – & though she 'didn't see why she shouldn't' I think it very unlikely that she will; she was brought up in an age which taught that a wife was *always* subservient to a husband, & must *never* disobey him even though he were in the wrong. Edward took advantage of the withdrawal of opposition, & wrote to Oxford about his joining this corps, also to Maurice, to ask assistance in getting into his camp.

Kitchener is said to be over at Ostend, with an army of 500,000 composed of the men of all nations. They are said to intend, after Germany has been gradually lured to Paris, to attack the back of the German lines. This, if only it could be true, would lead to stupendous carnage, & there might be such a battle as would practically end the war. The move is a grand one, while the very name of Kitchener, & his presence on the actual battlefield, will fill the British with courage, & strike terror into German minds.

Saturday September 5th
No very startling war news came in to-day, but everything, as the papers admit, is hidden in mystery. The Germans are said to be giving up for the present their march on Paris, & making a turning movement east & north-east. This looks as though something menaced them from that direction. The Russians have won another great victory & have captured Lemberg, the capital of Galicia. They have practically ruined the Austrian Army & comparatively little of it is left fit for military use.

First thing this morning I went with Mother to her district to carry Parish Magazines up & to bring back finished Red Cross shirts. The whole district is full of small children; indeed having children seems to be the chief occupation up there. Some are plain, miserable little wretches, but others are adorable in spite of the dirt. I saw one tiny baby of a month old, lying fast asleep in its little cradle. Its mother, a cheeky-looking red-headed girl of twenty-three, looked about 17, & had already had two children, one of whom she lost. Several of the women show possibilities of good looks, but they grow middle-aged & unshapely so fast; they pay no attention to personal appearance when their numerous children begin to come, & afterwards seem not to care at all how they look.

I went to a practical nursing class this evening, & certainly learnt a little about roller-bandaging. But the little room was full of people who prevented my seeing the demonstrations, & as they were all very noisy & the atmosphere in spite of open windows was terrible I left as soon as possible. I went on to St John's to hear Edward practise the organ. As I sat there in the dimly-lighted front row & looked at the long shadows filling the solitude & heard the organ's solemn tones echoing amidst the roof & arches, I felt a sudden acute consciousness of the sorrow of life, especially at a time like the present – felt too, almost immediately, the grand compensations of such a sorrow. To be afflicted & to endure, & to help others to courage by one's endurance, is a far greater destiny than to enjoy never-ending satisfaction or complacent supremacy, rousing others to irritation & envy, but never inspiring nobility or moving the better instincts of human nature.

Edward heard nothing definite to-day. Just before dinner he went to tell the Ellingers of his decision. Of course they were thoroughly delighted, & Mrs Ellinger informed us she really had to kiss him, though Edward of course never mentioned that!

Sunday September 6th
Edward's expected reply from Oxford came this morning. The Adjutant there enclosed one or two forms to be filled up & instructed Edward to call at his place next Friday, when he will appear before their selection & nomination committee. The Adjutant said he might have to wait some time before receiving a commission (unless he applied to a Territorial unit, which he does not want to do as he prefers Kitchener's New Army) & that also there was some doubt of his getting into Churn Camp, Didcot, where Maurice is, as it only consists of those already gazetted.

Monday September 7th
The Germans, after having so very nearly reached Paris, are turning back again – almost looping the loop – leaving the defending Allies temporarily useless under the walls of the Paris forts. The reason of this turning movement is unknown, & causes an air of mystery to shroud everything. Various solutions are attempted – either that the Germans have some new & tremendous stratagem in reserve; or else that they are becoming frightened by vague rumours of unexpected developments in their rear. In any case the situation is most thrilling.

Tuesday September 8th
Daddy went off for his holiday this morning. The maids also all went & Mrs Fowler came in to help to look after the house with Drabble, & we began the unaccustomed & very salutary task of looking after ourselves a good deal more than usual. Otherwise the day was of a type I am getting used to – a series of First Aid & nursing classes. Mrs Ellinger had a nurse in to show us bed-making etc., & took care to offer herself as the patient, & to

undress in front of the people she had asked in to watch, in order to display her expensive underclothing. To me it looked somewhat unsuitable to see so much lace & frilling when people are starving for want of peace; also I think that plain, dainty garments such as the night-gowns I am now embroidering for myself, which the wash cannot spoil, are much more appropriate for practical use than the kind of elaboration one only expects at a dance.

The news from the front is still vague, but has a more hopeful aspect. The Allies have now taken the offensive & seem to be pushing the Germans back. On the end page of the *Daily Mail* to-day were some ghastly pictures of ruined Louvain – the Oxford of Belgium – the destruction of which by the Germans is the greatest crime of the war. Even life may be more easily restored to the earth than these glorious monuments of literature & art, which the judgement of long ages has invested with a measureless distinction & value.

Wednesday September 9th
The war news is very much the same as yesterday; the outlook for the Allies seems to be gradually growing brighter. A German victory now would have no very decisive result, as long as the Allies stood fast & did not surrender, but a German defeat, with the Russians approaching from the East, would mean German disaster. There seems a chance of the German right being enveloped by Sir John French's army on one hand & a French army from Paris on the other. On the left the Germans have been pushed back 10 miles; in the centre of the vast 200-mile front, which is on the plain of Châlons, where the first Huns met their defeat, the Allies are holding their ground. Austria, the 'dupe of Germany', seems utterly shattered; not only is her army rendered unfit for military purposes, but she is full of internal discords, such as famine, mutiny, race-antagonism & mob-rioting of the unemployed.

6 Germans, with ammunition belonging to them, have been arrested in Buxton. 2 are Wenzel the hairdresser's men, one of whom is said to have cut part of a lady's hair off in vindictiveness, & to have cut a man's head with his razor. Two others belong to the town band.

Thursday September 10th

After another infinity of dusting, straightening etc. we had a second nursing lesson at Mrs Ellinger's. In the evening we had a lecture from Dr Burt; he is *so* interesting. When he was speaking about inoculation he got very worked up, & made me feel the thrill that must inspire a doctor or scientist when he is on the eve of an important discovery. The lecture was about fevers & their nature, & the means of preventing infection & contagion. He took two special kinds of inoculation for description; the first was against typhoid fever & the other against diphtheria. The former acts against the bacillus itself, & the latter, which is quite different, against the *poison* caused by the bacilli.

Several more Germans have been arrested in Buxton. Pfander the grocer in Spring Gardens was one; he has been railing for a long time against the English, & said that he hoped to see Spring Gardens red with British blood!

Friday September 11th

Edward went off this morning to Oxford to appear before the OTC nomination committee. He left himself the slightest possible margin of time for catching his train, & ran off roaring with laughter at Mother's anxiety on his behalf. We have said 'He must depart' & he has departed, leaving home laughing, with a delighted sense that he is not to be one of those men who will be branded for life because they have not taken part in the greatest struggle of modern times.

There was good news this morning of a German defeat; the enemy have been driven back twenty-five miles, & their left has been enveloped. Several Maxim guns have been taken, & thousands of prisoners captured. Our fleet have pressed right up into Heligoland Bight, but the German fleet refuses the challenge to fight.

When I went up to the Ambulance Lecture this afternoon Dr Braithwaite told me that the results of the First Aid exam. had been published. Mr Wall found my name for me among the passed, also Mother's. Not that it is a great feat as only 6 failed out of 98 who entered, but it constitutes the third exam. I have passed within six months, which is, I should think, something of a record. I spent the rest of the day chiefly in packing.

Saturday September 12th St Monica's, Kingswood

We managed to shut up the house & depart this morning without any undercurrent of trouble, contrary to my expectations. London showed very little sign of war in the parts through which we drove. The taxis with their 'Call To Arms' posters, the abundance of Union Jacks, & comparative scarceness of people in the streets, were the most significant signs. Edward met us at the door & Miss Heath Jones & Miss Bervon appeared soon after.

Edward had quite an interesting day in Oxford yesterday. The nomination board, before whom he appeared, seemed pleased to hear of his 5 years' O.T.C. training & told him that he would probably get a commission, perhaps even in the Derby & Notts. Regt, but that he would have to wait a while before hearing. He showed me a letter from Roland this evening, which R. writes chiefly to tell him to come to them at Lowestoft if his commission is not yet settled. He also says that he may follow in Edward's footsteps, as a Unionist MP friend of his, who has a good deal of influence, is trying to get the objection to his eyesight removed. If he *does* get a commission by this means I shall be desolate indeed. It is hard to smile upon Edward's going & leaving me to go to Oxford by myself, but if Roland goes it will be harder still. Roland is a unique experience in my existence; I never think definitely of him as man or boy, as older or younger, taller or shorter than I am, but always of him as a mind in tune with mine, in which many of the notes are quite different from mine but all are in the same key.

The war news was brighter still to-day – the *Daily Mail* ceased to be pessimistic & actually talked of 'Victory along the line'. The German left has been turned & enveloped, while the German centre, the most decisive part of the battle, is being driven back. The Servians too are not only beating the Austrians but pursuing them into their own territory. It seems that Austria, instead of sending a 'punitive expedition' to Servia, is having a 'punitive expedition' sent to her!

Sunday September 13th

Norah & her mother & father & a friend came to tea this afternoon. Cora proposes to share a flat with another girl, in which case Norah will be in a somewhat awkward predicament.

Cora's ambition about a flat in town seems likely to be realised sooner than mine – only when I get mine I hope to pay for it myself – else half the delight is gone. At supper Uncle Willie had a telephone message about war news from a friend of his. It is said that the Russians have smashed an army composed of the last Austrian Army Corps & some Germans, that the Germans both on the Eastern & Western frontiers are suffering terribly from lack of supplies, & have got some dreadful disease among them through eating raw beetroots with the earth on them. Uncle Willie has heard various people say that in ten days' time the Austrian Emperor will be sueing for peace, & that in a fortnight the Kaiser will be forced to flee from his people, who are already making the situation uncomfortable for him.

After they had all gone to bed Edward & I sat talking in the hall. He still has a repugnance to entering the works & wants to try the Civil Service, but as he has had so much experience of just not getting what he tried for he has rather lost confidence in himself. I tried to restore his self-confidence, telling him no one need lose faith in themselves till they know they have worked to the utmost of their powers & then still failed to get what they want. Edward knows he has never used all his powers yet, & though, as he says, he falls below the brilliant line (which he says I have not fallen below, & have never had reason to lose confidence as he has) yet it is possible for him to gain by hard work what others get by their natural & perhaps not very persevering ability. He told me as we went to bed that I had restored his confidence considerably, & he was grateful for it.

Monday September 14th
Edward & I spent a delightful lazy day, rambling about these lanes, the hedges of which are covered now with blackberries & scarlet hawthorn berries & hips & haws. Late this afternoon there was one of the loveliest skies I have ever seen – warm & glowing in the west, with tiny rosy clouds floating above the horizon, while in the east was a heavy black cloud, & just below it a long streak of the purest silvery blue, against which the tall elm trees on the sky-line stood up dark. To raise one's eyes heavenward from the cold & gloomy lane was like gazing out of earth into Paradise.

Tuesday September 15th
After lunch Edward & I went to see Miss Fry. We sat talking there for some time. I told her all about my exam.; she wondered if I should like Oxford, saying that college was rather medieval, but I thought I could stand that for eight weeks at a time provided I learnt plenty, & in any case Somerville is better than the other colleges in Oxford, & Oxford is better than Cambridge. She advised me to keep in mind all through that a secretaryship to a literary man – of course a well-known one for choice – would probably be a better way of launching myself into the literary world than any other, & it would only mean learning typewriting & shorthand after my college course. Literary secretaries are of course not mere shorthand & type-writing drudges, but have to do a considerable amount of research work, & get into the atmosphere of literary influence.

After dinner Edward & Miss Bervon played violin & piano together till bed-time, while the rest of us sat in the drawing-room & talked – chiefly Miss Heath Jones & I. We discussed Roland Leighton all evening – a subject I was very far from averse to. Miss Bervon is sure she would like him. As for me, I felt in danger of liking him too well to be altogether comfortable.

Wednesday September 16th
London, though it seems empty & not very busy, was a most inspiring sight with all its flags – British, French, Belgian, Russian, & Japanese. It is much finer to be fighting with Allies than to fight alone; to be united with so many nations is tremendously moving, & the sight of all the flags waving together on the same flagpost makes me occasionally feel cold with excitement.

The Germans are still at bay & the Crown Prince is in great difficulties. The terrible stories of German atrocities in France & Belgium continue to come.

Thursday September 17th
Edward left here this morning to stay with the Leightons at Lowestoft. Much as I enjoy being here, I envied him, partly because he was going to see Mrs Leighton, whom I am most anxious to meet, but chiefly because he is going to be with the

being who at the moment *interests* me more than anyone else does.

The German retreat has lost its panicstrickenness, & is gradually becoming a stubborn stand.

Friday September 18th

I went to tea with Miss Fry. We talked a good deal about college, & Somerville in particular. She told me about the Fabian Society of Socialists, to which both men & women belong. I found myself telling Miss Fry about Roland Leighton, though I spoke rather of him than of any connection with him, & did not make myself appear as interested in him as I really am.

I heard a rumour two or three days ago that the violinist Kreisler, who was an officer in the Austrian army, has been killed, but have not heard this rumour confirmed. Whether he be an enemy or no, I pray that after all no harm may have come to that brilliant young man. I do not think genii should be allowed in the Army. For one thing there are so few of the really great that their number could make no difference when battles are fought between millions, whereas in their own walks of life they make all the difference in the world. We do not put our kings into the field, but these, the real kings of humanity, are exposed to the multitude of dangers which come with battle. Proud though a nation may be of the genius it has produced, that genius is not a national but a universal possession & should not be made to risk itself in a national quarrel. To me the thought of Kreisler lying dead on an Austrian battlefield, perhaps with those wonderful fingers of his clasped cold & stiff round the hilt of a broken sword, is more terrible than that of five hundred slain men none of whom would have risen above mediocrity.

Saturday September 19th

Very little fresh news comes from the front; yesterday was the eighth day of the great battle of the Aisne, & the situation so far is in favour of the Allies, though no very *decisive* movement either of aggression or of retreat has yet taken place on either side.

Monday September 21st Byfleet

I arrived down to hear the tragic news that Rheims Cathedral has been shelled and burnt by the Germans – an act of Vandalism more terrible than any they have yet committed in the War. The French, hoping thereby to ensure its safety, turned it into a hospital for wounded Germans, and flew above it the Red Cross flag, but even this act of mercy towards their own countrymen could not deter these modern Huns from their fever of destruction. The whole of Europe mourns this wanton devastation of its treasure, and the feeling roused by it strengthens the repulsion felt in neutral countries towards German methods of warfare. In Italy the desire for war against her former allies is daily growing more intense.

I left St Monica's this morning & went to stay with Cora at Byfleet. The place looked as beautiful & carefully kept as ever, though numbers of their men have enlisted. I saw in to-day's casualty list that the name of 'Lieut. D. Duncan, Gloucester Regiment' is among the wounded. There is absolutely no doubt about its being Donald Duncan & Buxton will be in great excitement.

Thursday September 24th

My Greek gets on at a fine rate. I do about one sentence a day. I forgot to mention yesterday that three of our cruisers, the *Aboukir*, the *Hogue* & the *Cressy*, have been torpedoed by the Germans in the North Sea & sunk with great loss of life. This morning brought news of the further continuation of this everlasting battle of the Aisne, and also a long casualty list.

Cora & I had a long walk, talking about marriage & our ideals of it. I said that once I had thought I could not endure to marry a man unless he was older than I, but that now I felt much the most perfect thing would be to marry someone about my own age & start life together & share its development, instead of stepping into a place ready-made by a man older than me, who would only consider me an addition to, & not an integral element in, his life. Cora seemed to agree with me & happened to my surprise to mention Roland's name as though she has heard from me some time or other of him. So I told her just a very little about him & his brilliant intellect and also about the attraction I feel towards him, the extent of which I am not quite sure of myself.

In the afternoon Cora & I motored to Frimley Common, a large plateau much higher than Byfleet. At Frimley there is a camp of German prisoners, and though one feels almost mean in going to look at them as if one were going to the Zoo, yet, since it is a sight that has never been seen in England before & probably never will be again after this war, it was of too great interest to be missed. Although there is a board standing by the entrance to the camp saying that this thoroughfare is forbidden to the public, the day we were there the public were so numerous that one could hardly see the thoroughfare. Cora & I got quite close to the imprisoned Germans. They are guarded by four rows of wire entanglements – the two outer ones are fairly low & between them march the sentries keeping watch over the camp. The third wire entanglement is very high & is electrified so that none of them can attempt to touch it or injure it in any way. Inside this is another wire entanglement to protect the prisoners from the live wire. At each of the four corners of the enclosure, which looks more like a huge hen-pen than anything, are small electric power stations, to which is attached a raised platform on which a sentry always stands exercising observation over the prisoners. A regiment of National Reservists is encamped all round the imprisoning enclosure. We spoke to one Reservist about the prisoners, who are divided into two enclosures, one containing suspected civilians of alien nationality – mostly German of course – & the other soldiers taken prisoner at recent battles like the Battle of the Marne. The Reservist said that they were a decent set of men & he had no complaint to make about them; he said he preferred looking after the military half of the camp as the soldiers, who understood discipline & the principles of war, were easy to keep in order. The civilians were a ragged, unwashed, unshaven-looking lot who seemed to do nothing but crowd against the wires & gaze at the people who came to see them. One man was sitting on a log & talking to a woman, probably his wife, who had been allowed to come & see him, & stroking her hand. The soldiers appeared to have a little more energy though many among them looked utterly depressed, &

some were stretched out on the ground or at the doors of their tents with their heads on their arms as though very weary. Others were playing cards & shouting loudly over them in German, some were reading & in the distance a game of football was in progress. One or two were washing out some rather ragged garments, and others preparing tea at their tent doors. The majority were dressed in a uniform somewhat resembling our khaki but muddier in colour, and on their heads they had either kepis or nothing at all. A few were dressed in a greenish-grey uniform & wore high brass helmets, sometimes covered, sometimes uncovered; I imagined that these must be officers. They all appeared to be very well treated – better no doubt than our poor soldiers are being treated in Germany. We moved away at last, though I could have occupied myself all day looking at those unfamiliar types of face, and speculating as to what each one must have been through before getting there.

Friday September 25th Buxton
I found Edward here, not yet having received a commission; he went to Oxford yesterday on his way back from Lowestoft to wake them up & learnt that three weeks is now the usual waiting time. I talked to him nearly all afternoon & evening about the Leightons. They have the charming faculty of doing things at odd hours, which attracts me extremely as a contrast to the deadly clockwork precision of this household. Mrs Leighton is a person who seems to inspire more admiration the more one knows her; she is very high-principled & brings up her children strictly, and though she often writes till 3.0 in the morning she is always down for 8.30 breakfast. Mrs Leighton quite approved of my scheme for being secretary to a literary man, but says it would be considerably easier if I were plain as the chief disadvantage of such a course of action is the usually question- able moral character of the literary men. E. says there are not nearly so many indications of war as he expected to find, though they can see battleships out to sea, & of course all the bridges are guarded, just as they are in Surrey, where we seemed to come across sentries at every turning. Roland is still hoping to be let into the Army somehow without his shortsight mattering, but

has found nothing definite as yet, & his recruiting is practically finished.

Saturday September 26th

Maurice to my great joy came to Buxton to-day for two days' leave. I went to meet them as they came back from the station, & was delighted with Maurice's appearance in his officer's uniform. He has grown a small moustache, & looks much older & has an air of confidence & self-respect which he never seemed to trouble himself about before. He also seemed to have grown taller & held himself splendidly without any suspicion of laziness. Mother did not admit to being as much struck with his appearance as I was; I am afraid there is a little jealousy on her part, for there is no doubt that the Ellingers have gone one better than we this time, though when Edward *does* get his commission he will be even more a figure to be proud of than Maurice.

Sunday September 27th

I did not go to church this morning but instead did a little Greek & then went out with Maurice. We looked most smart together, especially as his khaki & my pale blue went excellently together. We went to the Gardens.

We went into the Ellingers' for some violin playing after supper. Maurice & Edward played Edward's own composition, a Ballade, & Mr Ellinger was delighted with it. It certainly sounds very well & has much more modernness in it than anything he has written before.

Monday September 28th

The prolongation of the battle of the Aisne – this is its 16th day – has led to very pessimistic estimates of the length of the war, but at last the Allies seem to have definitely gained ground on the centre & left. All along the line they have repulsed ferocious German attacks. All sorts of wild rumours are circulating about important people in the European mêlée; one is that both the old Emperor of Austria, Francis Joseph, who recently had a stroke, & the young Crown Prince, are dead.

Wednesday September 30th

This has been a wretched, unsettled kind of day. Edward started the feeling by his boredom & restlessness when he found the names of several ex-OTC cadets gazetted in *The Times* & still not his own. I tried to make him understand a little more fully my position at home – how it not only brings out all my bad qualities but temporarily gives me others which I don't possess by nature, & stifles all my good ones. However he did not take in much. Greatly though I long for someone to whom I could confide without having to explain every word, at present it seems that I must be completely self-contained – lonely as ever.

Thursday October 1st

I had a letter from Roland this morning, strangely enough, as I have been thinking so much about him the last day or two. He does not propose going to Oxford, at any rate for the present, & it is just possible he may not go at all. He says he could not stand a life of scholarly vegetation at such a time as this, & I am sure he could not; it will be as much as I can do, who have no call to do anything else. He says he would not regret not going to Oxford – 'except perhaps for the incidental pleasure' of meeting me. If I did not know him as well as I do, I might call that a kind of 'damning with faint praise'. Even as it is I am never quite sure where his sincerity ends, & his politeness begins. He says he has a chance of a commission in the 4th Norfolks & will know for certain in a week. I do hope he gets it; he stands the best chance of going to Oxford eventually if only he can get into the Army temporarily, while the family finances are strained.

His letter – or rather that part of it which suggested he might never go to Oxford – filled me with a kind of inexplicable mute despair – a kind of feeling which did not stop my working, but prevented me having the slightest possible enthusiasm for the work I was doing. He is certainly longing to take part in the war, considers it a fascinating thing – even finds 'something, if often horrible, yet very ennobling & very beautiful, something whose elemental reality raises it above the reach of all cold theorising'. I could have written emotion & passion into my answer, but instead I made it express tranquillity, even in complaints of women's enforced inactivity in the military part of war. There are some feelings which we dare not begin to show.

Saturday October 3rd
This is the 22nd day of the battle of the Rivers, & no decisive blow has been struck. Over 3 million men are engaged, but on the Russian frontier, in Galicia & Silesia, a great battle involving 5 millions is impending. German army corps & the wreck of the Austrian army are making their final stand. The Germans are still confident of victory but a humbler spirit is growing in Berlin, while the Kaiser, who called us 'General French's contemptible little army', has had to admit that the British forces are an important factor in the situation. The British Navy has taken the important step of sowing the North Sea with mines. As no protest was made by neutral powers against Germany's use of this condemned instrument of warfare, we have been obliged in self-defence to make use of it ourselves.

Various accounts have come through regarding people we know at the front. Donald Duncan is back again in the fighting line. His wound was only slight, & while his people were congratulating themselves on his temporary absence from the danger zone, he had once more returned to be under fire. Percy Spafford, in a letter home, says as he has not been killed so far he is sure he will not be now.

Sunday October 4th
I read an extraordinary, deeply interesting story by Tolstoi called *The Kreutzer Sonata* – the first of his works I have read. It deals with the tragedy of the position of women as mere instruments of man's pleasure, and though no doubt in Russia fifty years ago the problem was more acute, yet what he has to say on the subject is certainly often applicable to our country and time.

Tuesday October 6th
The war seems enveloped in more of a fog than ever, but there has been a terrific attack by the German right, before which in some cases we have been obliged to retreat. There has been an important Russian victory over the Germans & Austrians near

Augustow. The Czar is in the field directing operations, while
the Kaiser seems to dodge about between the Eastern &
Western frontiers of the conflict. The presence of these Sover-
eigns is thought to imply that a crisis is near. Rumours are rife in
the papers that Von Moltke, the Chief of the German General
Staff, has been dismissed from his post.

Thursday October 8th
I spent all day packing & getting ready for going to Somerville
tomorrow. Surely now, even though college life be narrow & its
seclusion, as Roland says, a vegetation, I may begin to *live* & to
find at least *one* human creature among my own sex whose spirit
can have intercourse with mine. Any life must be wider than this
lived here; Oxford I trust may lead to something, but Buxton
never will. If Roland & Maurice & Edward had been going I
should have felt quite differently about it, especially in the case
of the former, for then I should have had a certain joy to temper
the possible feelings of strangeness. Edward ought to have gone
to-day, & Roland, like me, tomorrow. We might even have met
on the journey – but now ?

Friday October 9th Somerville College, Oxford
I have scarcely had a moment to form any impressions yet &
have certainly not one in which to chronicle them. I arrived at
Oxford at 2.30 & went straight to interview Miss Penrose, who
greeted me with her strange curly smile but whom I liked again.
I discovered to my dismay – but afterwards I got used to the idea
– that I am expected to take the Degree Course, espec. as the
giving of degrees to women may not be far distant. This means
doing the Responsions Greek in Dec. This can be done if my
Latin is good enough to be more or less neglected this term – &
is it? Miss Lorimer, the Classical don, is going to set me a test
paper in Latin on Wed. If I do it respectably I shall be allowed
to take the Degree Course – if not I shall have to be content with
what they call the 'backdoor way' – starting English at once &
doing in 3 years what the majority do in 2. Pass Mods would of
course mean no English till after next June, but they say the
Classical training would be of inestimable value to me, & of
course I know it would to my English.

I interviewed Miss Lorimer, who is a small, wiry, rather astringent person, & seemed to think me lazy because I had done so little Greek. Naturally she does not realise the conditions at home, & seeing I *have* not done much Greek she has some reason for thinking me idle. She shall soon find out her mistake.

I was very sorry not to find Miss Lloyd here. I came across, however, a very interesting girl named Miss Hughes, who comes from Winchester, is in the Cathedral set, which she hates, & has been to dances, parties etc. & got tired of them, & is thought pretty mad to go to college by her associates, & altogether seems in something the same box as I am. She helped me unpack my cases from Harrods, & after dinner I talked to her all evening, sitting by the fire in the common room. We agreed about crowds of things – especially the stupidity of becoming dowdy just because you worked. She of course was well dressed, & though not exactly pretty, rather attractive.

I had a letter from Roland this morning saying he has received orders to go at once to Norwich, for though he may not be gazetted yet for two or three weeks, his application has been approved & they want him to begin to train. He has to billet himself at lodgings in Norwich & says he will be very lonely. Heaven knows when I shall see him again, but I hope Heaven will allow it to be soon.

Saturday October 10th
Being a fresher here is very comic. It is like being a new girl at school, without the terror, on an enlarged scale & with full consciousness, which you never have at school, of the humour of the situation. One 3rd year girl asked me to-day if going into meals was not an ordeal, & another whether it did not worry me to see so many strange faces. I was able to reassure both ladies as to my freedom from perturbation on that point.

Sunday October 11th
At 6.45 all the Freshers had hymn practice; we also started learning the Somerville Song. Directly after supper we had prayers, after which Miss Penrose told us something about the first Principal of Somerville, who has recently died. I am fixing

many names to faces now, but it will take longer to grasp personality.

Monday October 12th
After dinner we went to a practice of the famous Bach Choir which is doing Verdi's *Requiem* in spite of the shortage of men. The celebrated Dr Allen, its conductor, is certainly worthy of his reputation for genius, eccentricity & humour.

Antwerp, that beautiful city, alas! has fallen. It yielded at the end of last week after a gallant struggle, in spite of the fact that a large number of our marines helped to defend it. More bombs have been dropped on Paris from airships. London, in expectation of similar experiences, is now in total darkness at night.

Tuesday October 13th
Miss Hughes & I went up to the High – which is the dons' table – this morning for breakfast & sat opposite Miss Penrose. It was not so bad, as she is not nearly so condescending as one or two of the 3rd year people. I worked all morning at my Latin except for one Logic lecture, to which I went with all the Pass Mods people. Only ten men were present & about 20 women.

I went to cocoa with Miss Byrne, the little bright short-haired person with glasses, & Miss Siepmann, daughter of Siepmann's *German Grammar*. They were both amusing & instructive, especially with regard to the lighter side of college conventions. They told me about 'proposals', which seems to be a kind of ceremony you go through if you wish to call a person you have taken a fancy to by her Christian name.

Wednesday October 14th
I hardly know myself these days & yet in a way I seem to know myself too well. I live in an atmosphere of exhilaration, half delightful, half disturbing, wholly exciting. College, far from turning one out a type, seems if anything to emphasize what is individual & make one want to emphasize it one's self. I had a Lacrosse practice to-day – the first time I have played for two years. I meant to do Logic after dinner, but instead I sat in Miss Hughes' room & tried the effect on her of some of my ideas about religion. While we were discussing & I was emphasizing

various points in my customary dogmatic fashion, she let it out that by the 2nd & 3rd year people I am considered one of the 'lions' – perhaps *the* 'lion' of my year. Evidently impressions are made in a short time, but it certainly does seem short to have appeared exceptional even among the exceptional. Such a reputation requires living up to, & perhaps that is the reason for my queer exhilaration. Miss Hughes seemed to think me the kind of person whom people either adored or hated; she seemed to think I might be hated by all my year at the end of a term; I am quite indifferent to people's opinion of me, but I do not think I shall be, as people here are not jealous & resentful as they are at school; there really is not much opportunity.

Thursday October 15th

Directly after dinner Miss Lorimer told me that I am to do the Pass Mods work, as she has just glanced over my paper, though she was too busy to give it back to me. Responsions Greek at Christmas comes first & I suppose if I fail in that I shall not be allowed to do P. Mods.

Friday October 16th

Not only does college emphasize one's eccentricities, but it tends to make one underrate one's calmer & less disturbing notions & characteristics, whereas they often have greater value than the kind that show up. One is so apt to let go that which will not make an impression, & this is a mistake. Also I think college makes people selfish & self-centred; unselfishness is of course undesirable when it continually forces its service upon you & obliges you to feel grateful, but I do not think here that one *feels* enough for one's fellow creatures. I am such an egoist anyhow that I seem to take like anything to the all-for-self atmosphere.

I worked at Logic between tea & dinner, & actually managed to see a little light over contraries, contradictions, abstracts & correlatives.

Thursday October 22nd

At the Logic lecture this morning Jessop, the boy whom Edward told me has gone to Oriel, recognised me from having seen me at Uppingham, & bowed. [He] followed me in & insisted on speaking to me, though I told him I was not supposed to speak to him, & also accompanied me down the passage, in spite of my informing him that I must be treated as if I were in quarantine.

There was a very short women's suffrage meeting after dinner tonight; I joined the Oxford Society; I am very interested in it, as a small side of the enormous question of Feminism. The rest of the day I devoted thoroughly to Greek.

Friday October 23rd
Again I struggled with Greek, including my coaching this morning, but in spite of my struggles I seem only to get on very slowly & to crawl where I should like to fly. I received a letter to-day from Roland saying he had been given his commission as 2nd Lieut. in the 4th Norfolks. Miss Penrose took me in to dinner to-night. It was a little formal as of course she keeps one at arm's length, but it was not at all terrifying. She was somewhat amusing on the subject of helping Belgian Refugees to choose men's underclothing.

Saturday October 24th
This has been a bad day for me because my work overtook me instead of my keeping ahead of it, which always makes me feel depressed & unequal to being the exceptional & brilliant person I am determined to be. As a rule when I hear brilliant people like Miss Barton & Miss Rowe spoken of, I feel determined even to out-do them in glory, but on depressing days I feel I can never get to anything like their standard. But I can!

At 9.0 we had a fancy-dress dance which went on till 11.0. I went in my old Spanish peasant's dress; there really were some sights there. Miss Phillips as Plato was perhaps the most striking of anybody. I was fairly bored as it is very dull dancing with girls after having been to proper dances, & espec. as everyone danced so badly.

Sunday October 25th
As other people have said, [Miss Lorimer] is very far from being unappreciative of originality & imagination. Indeed perhaps the most wonderful thing about her is her interest in everything, which ranges from birds & plants to Classics, social service, &

poetry. She seems to stand unique & almost lonely among the other dons, set apart by her own versatility.

Monday October 26th
I do not see the papers so much as I used to or perhaps I should still feel I have no right to be happy at all; still, such war news as there is seems to be favourable, & we appear to be more than holding our own in the battle, which is now near the coast in the direction of Calais. The air was so bright & full of life, I found I was even interested in Greek Grammar & managed to learn quite an amount about verbs. I sat in the garden doing them after lunch, still feeling thoroughly happy & detached from the world, wrapped up somehow in the beauty of the day. I get to love this garden, with its vast expanse of lawn, more & more each day. This afternoon I sat & just gloried in the autumn goldness of the trees, the brown fallen leaves, the shimmering brilliance of all the green things & the clear brightness of the sky with its scattered clouds.

Tuesday October 27th
I had [an] encounter with Miss Lorimer to-day. I have definitely decided to study the lady, as I think she will make a perfectly splendid character in a novel. I am conscious of two most contradictory circumstances with regard to my dealings with her. One is that the more I try to please or at any rate not to displease her, the more antagonistic to me she becomes. The other is that the more she crushes & makes me feel small, the more interested in her I become.

On this particular occasion, I went to Miss Penrose directly after breakfast to get my form for Responsions Greek & while there happened to mention I might like Miss Sayers' room – which is next to Miss Lorimer's. Miss Penrose told me to look at the room & let her know as soon as I had made up my mind. I had wandered dreamily to Miss Lorimer's end of the passage, & was gazing at the linen cupboard at the end past it, making up my mind that it was a linen cupboard, when suddenly Miss Lorimer seemed to appear from nowhere & stood outside her room gazing at me somewhat suspiciously. I suppose I did look as if I might have been prying round or eavesdropping or at any rate as if Satan had found some mischief for my idle hands to do. Any of those things she would of course intensely abominate, so she approached me & said 'What are you doing there? Are you looking for someone?' I knew before I gave it how ridiculous the real reason would sound, but she seems to have a gift for making one do foolish things & forget all one's presence of mind, so of course I said 'I was studying the advantages of the top floor as I am thinking of changing my room.' She turned to me then with that very sweet smile which is far more withering than a frown of the utmost fury, & said 'Well that happens to be my room, so I'm afraid you can't have that, and that' (pointing to the linen cupboard at which I had most obviously been gazing) 'is the linen cupboard, so I'm afraid you can't have that either.' And with another sweet smile she went into her room & banged the door. I was so flabbergasted for the moment that I went straight downstairs without going to Miss Sayers, whose room I had really come to see. Afterwards I began to look at the incident from my favourite detached point of view, and to think with decreasing anger & increasing amusement what an utter fool I must have looked while she was addressing me.

Friday October 30th
I had a particularly pleasant Greek coaching this morning as Mr May told me that my Greek sentences were better than those of any girl he had ever had who had learnt Greek for the same time as I. Of course it is quite possible that he says the same thing to everybody, but at any rate the remark is quite encouraging. On my way to his house I met Miss Lorimer, hatless & armed with a paper. She has acquired a habit of looking through me, & did so – in strong contrast to Miss Hayes Robinson, who always meets one with a sweet smile. I might really have been late for my coaching, & loitering, instead of walking energetically & in excellent time. Miss Hughes, with whom I had a long conversation while arranging about our Hallow E'en party, says she is afraid Miss Lorimer really does hate me, & that I am one of her yearly dislikes. Miss Hughes is inclined to believe she does not think me retiring enough, but too opinionated & perhaps even conceited. I would far rather she hated me than that she was indifferent merely; there is

something very stimulating about hatred & also, if it can be
changed, it changes into strong, & not merely mediocre, liking.

Saturday October 31st

Miss Davies took me in to dinner to-night; she is absolutely
charming & I like her quite the best of the 2nd years. She talked
nearly all the time about Miss Lorimer, whom she seems greatly
interested in, & I of course was quite ready to listen. She says she
is particularly down on helpless dependent people, & on
modern people in so far as modernness implies flabbiness, as it
often does. She has a very keen Scotch brain, & has worked
extremely hard herself & so is contemptuous of people who try
to skip all the difficulties. I wonder what she would think
(supposing she thought about me at all) if she knew how greatly
I desire to stand alone, & how much I actually do. As it is she
regards me as a helpless person who always wants to be shown
things. Miss Davies went on to tell me about her favourite
brother's death in Persia. She heard the news of the tragedy on
Tuesday, & the day after, the Hon. Mods people had a class in
the morning. Miss Davies said she expected the class to be
somewhat sketchy & Miss Lorimer to be very much upset, but
instead of this Miss Lorimer took the class with her usual
thoroughness & care. Except that her usually bright hair was
quite dull & her eyes dim & tired-looking, they would never
have known anything was the matter, & she was as critical &
observant of mistakes as she had ever been. Miss Davies thinks
she cannot feel sorrow passionately as most people do, & that
the Spartanism goes all through, but I must admit I do not quite
agree, for those who show least care deepest; it is only the
shallower natures which find relief in an outburst of sorrow &
then recover.

We had Miss Chambers, Miss Barber, Miss Bedford, Miss
Kennedy, Miss Gurney & Miss Schenzinger to the party & were
extremely noisy & merry. As we were all freshers no one was shy
& everyone actually ate as much as they could possibly want.
We had an apple on a string, which they bit at till Miss Bedford
finally won the competition with the largest bite, & then after
everyone had more or less finished eating we put out the lights,
sat in front of the fire & roasted chestnuts. We were far too

merry to be in the mood for ghost stories, so we spent the evening telling tales about the Lorie instead. I told them I was going to put Miss Lorimer into a novel & asked them all to contribute stories & salient points. We then roasted chestnuts, calling them each by particular names & roasting them side by side & judging by the way they behaved of the relations of the two people. Miss Lorimer & I both split & fell into the fire, which was a distinctly exciting omen. Then we all decided to have a wish & to make an incantation of it, throwing three ash leaves into the fire as we did it, which is a Hallow E'en rite. We chose for our wish 'May the Lorie love us all', which had a particularly harmonious sound & was very appropriate for so many Classical people. We continued these stories & chestnuts & incantations till long past 11.0, thereby distinctly contravening the College rules. Finally Miss Hayes Robinson entered in a red dressing-gown & curling-pins, & told us we were keeping the whole college awake & that incidentally we were above her room. She did not however seem at all angry, & we were most thankful it was her & none other, only we did wonder how many of our numerous personal remarks, especially about the Lorie, she must have heard.

Sunday November 1st
The Oxford Council debated the other day as to whether they would not commandeer Somerville as a hospital for wounded soldiers, as not only are we healthily situated & possessed of far better sanitary arrangements than any of the nearly vacant men's colleges, but we are next to the Radcliffe Infirmary.

Thursday November 5th
I went for a long walk with Miss Scouloudi, the Greek girl. There is plenty in her & she is much more interesting than her rather heavy appearance leads one to expect. She is quite independent & not a hanger-on at all, which is all the more extraordinary as she has been educated entirely at home; she seems unselfish too, & really good & generous at heart. Miss Hughes finds me I think too much in earnest & too little on the surface to please her. Her remark yesterday about being very sorry for me having to work was very typical of her – as though

work was not the only thing worth doing, especially just now – & as though, after having had so much trouble to get this time of education, I would be willing to waste any minute of it! I discussed this afternoon with Miss Scouloudi, who agreed with me, the impossibility of forming a penetrating & critical judgement of people unless you kept yourself independent. I must never forget that this college life is only a means & not an end, & that what I came here for is to work & to study people, which I must keep myself detached in order to do. It may not be always easy or pleasant; the studies of some people, such as Miss Lorimer, may even involve me in somewhat painful situations. But that after all is the great choice – either to live for small personal aims, which have their little reward in the passing pleasantness of a smooth & easy social life, or for great impersonal aspirations which can only be rewarded by their fulfilment at whatever cost to one's self.

Friday November 6th
After dinner I went to a lecture by G. K. Chesterton on 'The War & The Class War'. The meeting was really for Socialists but was open to others & was packed; two or three other freshers & I stood the whole time, but I did not mind as I wanted to see this unique literary lion. He is so fat that it takes him quite a long time to sit down & get up again; he has several chins & fair hair turning grey, brushed straight up. He is very far from being of a prepossessing appearance, & speaks slowly in a fat wheezy voice. His speaking falls much below his writing, & I was too interested in trying to draw him to listen much to what he had to say, but apparently it was not socialistic & was distinctly displeasing to the large number of thorough Socialists that were there. One of them, a fiery-eyed young man with dark hair & the speech & manner of an orator, got up and expressed forcibly his opinion to Chesterton.

Saturday November 7th
The town was very interesting this afternoon because they were having a 'Belgian day' for the benefit of the Belgians ruined by the war, & everyone one met was covered with red, yellow & black favours. Many of the undergraduates had decorated

themselves at every possible point with these paper rosettes, including hair & shoes, and horses, bicycles, & shop windows were covered with them.

Wednesday November 11th

I got caught in the rain after Lacrosse, which made my hair pretty wet, & at tea I found Miss Davies, whose hair was in the same state, so we decided to go together to have it washed. We went to a delightful hairdresser's quite near here which is kept by two red-headed girls in brown art overalls. I love having my hair washed & thoroughly enjoyed talking to Miss Davies & the two assistants during the process.

Thursday November 12th

I have of course got my usual reputation of being insufferably conceited, hard & cold, without a scrap of sympathy or kindness. Alongside of this goes the usual interest in me, & I seem to be a much-discussed person. But if the majority do not love me, at least they cannot say I am mediocre & seem to find me original. I wonder if I shall ever have the warmth under the hard crust aroused here. I think Miss Lorimer could rouse it if she took the slightest scrap of interest in me, but doubtless she like the others thinks me insufferably conceited.

Friday November 13th

Miss Jones, the new Fellow, explained what research work meant & what methods were employed in it. It was very interesting but I found it rather hard to see what use, even from the point of view of the increase of knowledge, the very recondite information about very recondite subjects can be to the world in general – for instance what good can it do anyone to find out, after months of researching, that an obscure person called St Corin did exist but that all the information gathered about him is legendary?

Saturday November 14th

I wrestled with Logic this morning until I understood the early part of the Syllogism, & then went to the lecture. The men were asked questions on subjects we have had touched upon in almost every lecture. Of course they knew nothing at all & the most obvious answers had to be dragged from them by a kind of mental dentistry. Miss Schenzinger & I were in fits of laughter in the front row as we knew the answers to all the questions.

Sunday November 15th
Very sad news greeted us this morning in the death of our dear old Lord Roberts in France. Although he was 83 he wanted to inspect the Indian troops & had been abroad about a week. It seems so tragic that he has not lived to see how England, to which his whole life was devoted, will emerge from the struggle in which she is now engaged. Miss Wood, who is a theosophist, says he will, but I cannot make up my mind if I do believe or not in an after-existence; there is, as Olive Schreiner says, 'a veil of terrible mist over the face of the Hereafter'.

I have advanced quite far – for me – to-day in the direction of familiarity with people; I now call two individuals by their Christian names – Miss Wood, who is Katharine, & Miss Wadham, who is Dorothy.

Monday November 16th
Poor Maurice has had a nervous breakdown & is obliged to leave the Army & go home, at any rate for the present. He was threatened with one before, so I fear this will be quite serious.

Wednesday November 18th
I had a letter from Roland this evening, all about his military duties. He seems to have most of the responsibility of the company, & is doing very well, & from what I can judge seems highly thought of. He does not however think he has much chance of going to the front, on account of his eyesight.

Friday November 20th
I had rather an interesting time at tennis this afternoon, as Miss Hayes Robinson turned up just after we did, & I played with her. It is remarkable the way I am always meeting her, often doing the same things as she takes an interest in, such as Bach Choir & tennis, & she really seems to give one a personal recognition. I cannot help feeling she has somehow missed her

vocation in life all the same; she ought to have been married. I should say she is very clever indeed & self-reliant, without being either violently original or aggressively independent, & these qualities, together with the characteristic shyness which seems always to be seeking a sympathetic response, would have made her an excellent wife & really the ideal & equal companion of some brilliant man working his way from some obscure beginning to a lofty and responsible position in the world. She would have been with him at every step, & would have made a strong, sensible-minded & sweet mother to her children. She is so far from being a typical don as to be quite unrecognisable as one if you did not know it; she is very far from sharing the donnish disregard of dress, & though she is certainly plain, as most dons seem to be, the fact ceases to be obvious beneath the intelligence, humour & sympathy of her expressive face. To picture the Pen soothing the wailing of a raging infant, or the Lorie pushing a pram, is the kind of thing one could only imagine vividly in the wildest & most nonsensical dreams. But it does not seem ridiculous to imagine Miss Hayes Robinson doing any such things. Perhaps she is nearer to the ideal type of woman – to the woman we hope the future will bring – than at any rate any [other] don I have ever met. She is an instance of a woman who has spent her life in the pursuit & imparting of knowledge, & whose daily round is one purely concerned with intellect, without losing any atom of her womanliness & feminine attractiveness, without having her humaneness warped or her sympathies blunted.

Saturday November 21st
Edward was gazetted to-day; the announcement was in *The Times* this morning but no details were announced either of battalion or regiment.

To-day was marked for me by one of my rare interviews with Miss Lorimer. The chief ideas she succeeded in conveying to me were my own unimportance in the scheme of things, & the time I had wasted in the vac. She did this while smiling & being perfectly cordial, making cutting statements without seeming in the least definitely to intend to squash me, & she sat all the time with the light shining on her fair hair, calmly doing her everlasting knitting. She is a past mistress in scorn, & all the time I felt lashed & stung by her absolute indifference, & impersonal unsympathetic criticism of me, not as a person at all, but simply as a brain which only counted in so far as it was capable & no further. Yet I was immensely stimulated too, & from a keen desire to take a book off her shelf & hurl it at her I felt mightily impelled to work furiously & see what could be done even in a fortnight. It is her absolute justice which is most disconcerting because it gives her scorn such a sting & a feeling that it is merited. Though she despise you she will admit that your Logic marks are good. She seems a very part of duty & necessity; you feel she would not move an inch out of her way to help an outside person, as Miss Hayes Robinson does, or accomplish any task not strictly within her sphere. But on the other hand she would never shirk anything that came clearly on her path, however bitter she might find the doing of it, & whatever suffering it might bring her. I left her having got nothing out of her, not even the slightest interest or sympathy, feeling both depressed & stimulated. Whether I like her tremendously or loathe her intensely I do not know, but the interest deepens & grows keener every day.

Monday November 23rd
After tea Dorothy, Katharine & I & a few others had a mad stampede in the little music-room, playing on the old piano that sounds like a trumpet. Then Miss Ellis Fermor & Dorothy & I played about in the Gym. for a bit. Just at a most unpropitious moment, when I with my shoes kicked off was half-way up a rope & Dorothy with her skirt tucked up round her waist was playing about on the vaulting-horse, Miss Hayes Robinson elected to come through with two men. I was forced to remain suspended in mid-air much against my will while they walked through, & from my insecure position above I caught Miss Hayes Robinson's glance of amusement. We collapsed on the floor & laughed helplessly when they had gone through.

Friday November 27th
A somewhat gloomy letter came from Mother about Edward, who evidently is not finding being gazetted altogether a joy.

Apparently he arrived at Frensham minus most of the camp equipment he ought to have had, as he was never told what to get, and had to go straight back to London to buy the things, & stay the night there. Altogether he seems to be spending a good deal of money but apparently Father is still undisturbed over it. The 11th Battalion Sherwood Foresters is by no means a new battalion; it was formed some time ago, and started when everyone was sleeping under canvas. It is still sleeping under canvas therefore, & this is not exactly a good time of the year for Edward to begin. Also the battalion seems to be rather over-crowded with subalterns; there are 20 instead of the usual 16. The most important thing he says however is that as the battalion is not newly formed it is in fairly good working order so that he will probably go to the front much sooner than he expected – possibly about February. Naturally this information disturbs Mother very much, & indeed it seems terribly close. It is very difficult here to write about the war, as there is so much work to do that I never have time to read the papers.

Saturday November 28th
Katharine came & had cocoa with me when I had finished my work this evening. We discussed people a good deal & chiefly me. K. says that of the several people she has asked out of curiosity how they like me, most of them say they cannot make me out, & wonder if I am sincere or not. I tried to convince her that I really am, though often I deliberately act, & sometimes even deceive people. She wondered very much why I did it & I said with perfect truth that as a rule I did not know. She said I was different when I was alone from what I am with other people, & that I seem to have two personalities. I think she was fairly right there; she seems to be pretty sharp at reading character.

Sunday November 29th
Dorothy & I went this morning to the University Church where the Bishop of Oxford preached a most splendid & inspiring sermon. The chief thing I remember about it is that it was an address particularly to people like students here who are engaged in the intellectual & artistic side of life rather than the

practical. He said the great danger for such people was that they often tended to become spectators & think themselves neutral & take neither of two alternatives. But, he said, no one is meant to take no side, & we are told in the Bible that we must either serve God or Mammon; the Bible in fact did not admit the neutral person & always describes a man not so much as what he is as what he is becoming. The contemplative life, he said, is not an alternative for us to choose. Only when we have struggled & suffered & striven may we dare to view things from without as spectators & no longer as actors. He went on to say that for such as us, who could not take an active part in the war, our action was to keep up the standard of intellect & morals as high as possible, that those who fought & died for England might feel she was worth fighting & dying for. If our soldiers on battlefields abroad were fighting the enemy for the sake of ideals of honour & justice & freedom, it was our duty to see that at home we did not allow those ideals to slip.

Monday November 30th
Mr May was very pleased with the two Grammar Papers I had done & said I should easily get through on both. He also told me that he has given me the best report he has ever given any girl, so the terror of the interview with the Pen to-morrow ought to be somewhat lessened – only she is sure to find some way of squashing & not praising me – I am the kind of apparently bumptious person people in authority are fond of taking down – at any rate at first.

Tuesday December 1st
This morning was the interview with Miss Penrose, which so disturbed me that I could do nothing either before or after it for some time. She asked me one or two trivial questions about my trains & seemed quite content to let me order my own cab, & then said, with a beaming smile, 'You have a very good report, Miss Brittain. Mr May is *very* pleased with your work.' I smiled as if greatly surprised, & then just as she was about to give me the little nod of dismissal I asked her desperately if I might consult her a little about my future career, as I had no one to consult. She looked interested at once & told me I certainly

could, so I explained how I wanted to be secretary to a literary man or woman & said 'Of course my ambitions don't end there, but the achievement of them largely depends on my success in that capacity.' She smiled again as though she were pleased & I went on to say I had come to college absolutely with that end in view & to ask if she thought I was really doing the best thing taking English, or if History were not the better school. She discussed the subject with me a little & said that, as it was impossible to know what kind of writer I could get, English would give me the best general preparation as it was a history of English literature, giving practice in the English language. She said also the Classical training at the beginning was excellent drill & any University man would recognise the value of such a degree.

Katharine & I went for a short walk this afternoon & then I read her bits of my diary in the garden. After dinner I went up to the Lorie, who was seeing P. Mods people between 8.0 & 8.30. She said nothing about my report but I could tell she was in a very good temper with me. She fetched out a little volume of Homer Book VI & said she would lend it to me but I must be careful to bring it back as she had a sentimental attachment to it, since it was the first Homer she ever did. I examined it afterwards & found it full of her notes in a girlish handwriting quite different from her present one. The change in her attitude towards me is really very noticeable. From thinking me lazy and somewhat ineffectual I believe she really considers me worth something now. I certainly have worked hard to achieve this object, – & oh! if I only can get the chance, won't I just work harder still to achieve it all the more next term!

Monday December 7th
Lodz, a Russian stronghold in Poland, is reported to have fallen to the Germans. The conditions in frozen Poland are terrible just now.

Wednesday December 9th
The fateful moment arrived & I found myself seated in the Sheldonian Theatre with Miss Baker in front of me, Katharine behind me, & a grammar paper in front of me. We had a

somewhat agitated walk down from Somerville, in which we all tried to recall various bits of grammar, none of which we had in the paper. Then we waited for some time in a dark depressing cloak-room which smelt like a chair, until we were called into the room. When the papers were done I went to Mr May, who told me I was the only girl who had ever induced him to go over her papers with her. He was very pleased with the set books & said I would get practically full marks on them.

Saturday December 12th Buxton
The fateful telegram *did* arrive to-day, & late in the afternoon when I ceased to expect it. But it brought the good news I hoped for, that I had passed my Greek! So now all being well I shall attend Miss Lorimer's lectures & she will be my tutor, & I will work hard – oh! so hard & enthusiastically, both for the sake of her and of Classics. She shall not despise me or fail to receive anything that she expects from me; I will turn her scorn of me into pride of me. It is pleasing to think of having accomplished in seven weeks what people have been known to fail to accomplish in as many years. Mother & Daddy were very pleased, & Mother came slowly to the conclusion that I really must be clever & rather exceptional or so many people wouldn't say so! It is really quite impossible to talk to Mother & Daddy about Oxford, they understand the spirit of the place so little & are not even interested. It is a queer thing that it is here more than anywhere that I am least myself & most a stranger.

Monday December 14th
I went to have my photo taken this morning. I am longing for the one of Roland, about whom I think every time I see soldiers – which is nearly all day as they are stationed at the Empire [Hotel], & I cannot go out without meeting some of them. In the evenings the Park is crowded with the Tommies walking out with girls. This evening we had a variety entertainment at the theatre, the proceeds of which are going to provide comforts for the soldiers. There were classical dances, songs by Mrs Langford, the wife of the Adjutant here, comic songs by young Jellicoe, a subaltern & a very popular & jolly person, and also a sketch entitled 'Blackmail' in which Mr Railton acted. It was all

very good & went down extremely well, especially Jellicoe's songs, in the choruses of which all the Tommies, who were crowded about different parts of the building, joined in. The temporary Red Cross nurses such as Leslie Duncan & Nancy Garnett were selling programmes. It is an excellent thing for these idle people to have something as strenuous & useful to do as scrubbing floors & carrying dishes, which I saw them employed in at the Devonshire Hospital this morning. I quite envy them for the experience, for it must be both useful & interesting in spite of the hardness & monotony of the work. Now I am so busy it is quite impossible for me to do anything of the sort, especially as they have more helpers almost than they want, but if the war had come two years ago I should have been almost grateful to it for providing my unoccupied & unprofitable hours with employment.

Wednesday December 16th
News arrived this morning of an attempted raid by German ships on the East Coast. Scarborough, Whitby & Hartlepool have all been shelled. Fifty shells are said to have fallen at Scarborough, & it is reported that at Hartlepool 9 persons were killed. The cruisers were driven off, partly by the forts at the places, but presumably also by British cruisers. No doubt a naval engagement is in process off the coast of Scarborough, but the hand of the censor has obviously been at work. Probably, except for small riots & insurrections, there has been no fighting in this country for over a century.

I went shopping to Manchester to-day, & bought a little black moiré & velvet hat with red roses. Mother went with me & I quite enjoyed myself, especially when we entered a 3d. bazaar to buy toys for Mrs Kay's grandchildren, & found it a surging crowd of poor people, & an atmosphere cuttable with a knife. We departed thence armed with a red rubber ball, a scarlet & blue soldier who was also a money-box, a tin side-car & an engine.

I had a letter from Roland to-day – somewhat to my surprise, as he seemed to write for no particular reason & he wrote to me only last week. It seemed partly to insist that he has not come to regard the contemplative side of life as a waste of time, which I suggested last week that he probably had – & partly to ask what I want for my 21st birthday. He says he never considers me as 15 months older than himself & I certainly do not. It is so strange – not that I should be 21, for often I feel quite that, & sometimes, especially since June, I feel more like 100 – but that he should be barely 20. He is so old for his age, & I suppose now he is older still, with all the responsibility & anxiety he has had just lately. I suppose really I ought not to let him give me anything for my birthday, but, apart from the fact that, however much I insisted he ought not to, he would probably do it just the same, I simply *cannot* deny myself the joy of receiving a book both from him & inscribed by him. For the present I am bound to leave the feeling at that & not analyse it further lest I should discover too much. He interests me so deeply & so strangely, this serious-minded, brilliant, unusual young man who, from the frivolity & general inanity & happy-go-luckiness of the Army atmosphere, writes 'You do not know what I would not have given these last few months – what I would not give now – to meet with a little intellectuality around me or to have half-an-hour's talk with someone with some personality & temperament. Even now in wartime the Army means mental starvation. By the time the war ends, I shall have become too commonplace and orthodox for you to care to talk to.' He will certainly never be that! He says the photograph is somewhat spoilt by an incipient moustache.

Friday December 18th
The Scarborough & Hartlepool bombardment seems to be more serious than at first imagined; altogether there are over 500 casualties, of which about 100 are deaths. The leading article in *The Times* discusses & deplores this but at the same time cannot see how such attacks can be utterly guarded against, since our fleet would act neither adequately nor wisely if it spread itself out to protect every mile of the East Coast. Such contingencies as further attacks cannot fail to arise, especially as the long & dark nights favour ventures such as this, & give the aggressors time to get back again. The writer thinks they would not attempt to land troops because the difficulty of escape would be so much greater. He says that the real issues of the war would not be affected if Scarborough were now

in ashes, and that the Admiralty would not alter or modify its plans even though all the East Coast towns lay in ruins. The cheerful writer evidently does not live on the East Coast himself.

This morning Maurice rang up to say that he came home last night for Xmas, was depressed & wanted cheering. I told him to come across & we went to the town to order my photographs, none of which he liked. Maurice looks very well – almost too well, & does not show much trace of nervousness, but of course he is more natural & less shy with me, according to his own telling, than with anyone. After this short time at home he is going to a small health-resort in the South to live with a doctor. I keep trying to think of things he can do, such as playing the piano & writing stories, that he may not feel his time is wasted or he is useless.

Wednesday December 23rd
Edward came back to-night & is really here. We all went down to the station to meet the last train from London which he came by. It was 50 minutes late, so we wandered up & down the cold platform with Daddy getting more inwardly irate every moment. I did not really mind waiting at all, except that I might have finished my Homer. I always love a railway at night, the lights in the distance, the shunting & the red steam – even if it is cold & damp. At last the train came in, & he appeared, looking so fit & good-looking, in spite of having got up at 4.0 this morning. He seems so tall & absolutely grown up; I shall be proud for anyone to see him, he really is a fit object of devotion. He has never looked so well as he does in his military clothes. He told us his battalion belongs to Kitchener's 3rd Army & will probably go out in May. Apparently the French & English could drive back the Germans now if they wished & could have weeks ago, but they intend to wait until the New Armies come out so as to turn the action into a decided victory. So there is no doubt that Edward will go to the front & see fighting. When I read & read about the tragic deaths of only sons, of brothers, & husbands, I cannot think there is any reason why our one beloved representative of the Army should be spared. Christmas & the wondering where we shall all be a year hence, his accounts of their manoeuvres, his very good looks, all bring the

poignant sorrow of war nearer home. Roland too is volunteering for the front from his reserve regiment, & may be tacked on to a Territorial Regiment that will go out all too soon. He rang up tonight to speak to me when I was meeting Edward; I was dreadfully disappointed to miss him.

Thursday December 24th
The sinfully extravagant Roland rang me up this morning & spoke to me, not for 3 minutes but for six. Amid all the crowds of things I wanted to say to him I could think of nothing & my conversation was unintellectual to say the least of it. He wished to know what particular book I wanted for my birthday among the moderns but I could think of no one in particular though I mentioned Henley, Francis Thompson, Kipling & Hardy.

Friday December 25th
It was a queer sort of Christmas and as usual depressing, though in one way it was not quite as bad as it generally is because we were not supposed to be so oppressively cheerful as we usually are. It hardly seems Christmas though, with no waits nor decorations, no prospective gaieties & hardly any presents.

Saturday December 26th
Roland sent me a beautiful French hand-painted card, & wrote in French inside it. He is certainly more than a little extravagant, but he does spend his money on beautiful things, having a trustworthy taste, which is vastly better than spending it on the kind of dissipations a good many young men do.

Monday December 28th
I had a letter from Roland to-day in which he says that he is now with his mother in rooms in town & that she wants him to bring me to see her. I wrote & told him I could manage it quite easily one day, either Wed. or Thur.

Tuesday December 29th
To-day was my 21st birthday. There is nothing whatever to say about it. To be of age according to the law & to be one's own mistress does not impress me at all, nor does it fill me with grave

& sober reflections. It is having nothing definite to do that makes
another year seem a burden; when one is at least on the way
towards achieving one's object, & things are happening, one's
life is made up by events & not increasing years.

Wednesday December 30th London
This has been a day of surprising realisations and developments
– half ecstatic, wholly turbulent. I travelled down with Edward
by the 9.50; Mother & Daddy said goodbye to him quite
cheerfully, which was more than I expected. We met Aunt
Belle by the Charing Cross left-luggage office. She hadn't
changed a scrap since I last saw her, nor did she make any
observation on the alteration of my appearance, though I was
not grown up when she last saw me. We met Roland at the
Comedy Restaurant & had lunch. It seemed perfectly natural to
see Roland in khaki, I suppose because I saw him in the Corps
at Uppingham. We were perfectly incapable of saying anything
to each other during lunch.

Then I found myself in a whirl of the most surprising
proportions – I had mentioned during lunch, quite without
thinking, that I wanted to see *David Copperfield*, and nothing
would satisfy him but that he should take us to-morrow evening.
I demurred at first but Aunt Belle – who of course would have to
chaperon me – was quite ready to go & finally I consented.
Then he gave me a letter from Mrs Leighton – written in her
enormous inky writing, which almost makes a hole in the paper
& looks as if it were done with the end of a match – asking me to
tea to-morrow at the Criterion & saying she so hoped I could
come & was to answer by Roland. I told him I would go & said 'I
do hope you haven't talked about me to your mother so that she
won't expect anything.' He said 'But I have,' whereupon I
expressed my anxiety about her having a preconceived notion
of me, & my not coming up to it. I am so shy of seeing her for the
first time because from what I have heard I know she makes up
her mind & judges of people at once. If she likes me, she may be
an immense help in my future career – if she does not, well, I
dare not think of the consequences but I know it would have a
great influence on Roland's feelings, he believes so in her
judgement. Then he wanted to buy me some violets but I said

I would not have any to-day as they would only die, & I trust he will have forgotten by to-morrow. Then he wanted to take us out to lunch & I finally had to give way even to that. Aunt Belle says 'Well, he likes you, & why shouldn't he enjoy himself if he likes?' & she reminded me of what I had already thought often myself, that it might be for the last time. In this time of tragedy there can be no postponement. He said he would try to join some regiment soon going to the front. I said rather sadly that I did not know whether I most wished that he should go because he wanted to, or that he should not go because I did not want him to, and I said 'Do you want me to want you to go?' He answered 'No, I shouldn't like you to want me to go, but I want to myself.' He then asked me why I wanted to see *David Copperfield* & why I liked it, & I said the character of Steerforth had always appealed to me so much. He seemed pleased and remarked that he was just about to say Steerforth was the finest character in the book. Aunt Belle & Edward had walked conveniently in front all the way.

Aunt Belle is a splendid person to go with, she is keen about everything and took a special interest in Roland, whom she liked immensely. She came to the conclusion at once that he & I were certainly fond of each other, and seemed to encourage it, saying she approved of such things & that it was perfectly right we should feel so. While she was saying this I was wondering all the time exactly what I did feel towards him. But the evening dispelled any lingering doubts. It was just dark, and all the streets were dim, as London ever since the war began has been lighted as faintly as possible, for fear of Zeppelin raids. It was thrilling, intoxicating, to walk down dark Regent St amid the hurrying crowd. We often lost sight of Aunt Belle & Edward & lingered until on one occasion Edward came back to hurry us up. We dodged the traffic, he guiding me very carefully through it, & tentatively touching my arm now & then, as though he would have taken it & kept me more secure that way if I had given him permission. But I did not though I should have liked to. He told me during this walk that London was a very appropriate setting for me; I was so glad because I love it so dearly. We had somewhat of a rush at the end to catch our trains; in fact we missed one but found another that would do.

Roland raced round after me carrying my bag & umbrella while I went from one wrong booking-office to the other. Finally Edward found us a carriage & pushed us both into it just as the train was starting. So my farewell to him was curtailed, which was perhaps just as well. Farewells are mournful things, & this parting with my beloved brother, of whom I may see very little before he goes to France, is too sad to dwell upon.

Granny was very pleased to see us, but was a little disappointed to find we were going out tomorrow night instead of staying here to bring the New Year in. However Aunt Belle launched into an account of Roland & me containing far more definite assertions with regard to us than I should have thought of making before. 'You know, Mother, they really *like* each other,' she said. Granny seemed pleased & said 'Oh, if *that's* the case then of course it's alright,' & she came into my room & asked me 'Do you care about Roland Leighton?' so I said tentatively 'Yes'; then she insisted further & said 'But I mean do you *really* like him?' & suddenly I made up my mind in a moment, or rather, I saw that it had been made up for a long time, & I replied 'Yes, indeed I do, *really*.' 'Really' being an expressive word the meaning of which on this occasion was scarcely mistakable. The rest of the evening Aunt Belle & Granny & Uncle Billie & I discussed Edward's departure & Roland & furniture & clothes, & finally played bridge till bedtime.

Thursday December 31st
The old year departs in a whirl of the deepest & most conflicting emotions I have ever known, a tumult of love & sorrow. I went up to London to begin my shopping in a state of weariness & confused sensations, since I scarcely slept at all last night, partly because I was thinking about Roland and wondering just what I really did feel.

At lunch time Roland arrived outside D. H. Evans, where we had promised to meet him, in a taxi, & put us into it & drove off to the Florence Restaurant for lunch. In the taxi he gave me a lovely bunch of violets, sweet-smelling & fresh, very evidently proving that he had *not* forgotten my remark of yesterday. He was a little perturbed because he had not brought Aunt Belle any flowers, but she smoothed him down most tactfully & then remarked 'My dear lad, you can't be expected to have two people in your head at once!' During lunch Aunt Belle by various questionings discovered that I possessed the incongruous quality of loving children. She asked Roland if he did & he replied 'I am afraid I don't very much. In fact I would much rather have an animal than a child.' I chuckled to myself & determined to remember that remark, although when Aunt Belle was telling us how Daddy had always hated children until his experiences with us, he did say he was sure he would love a child of his own.

Next came the experience I was longing for & dreading. We drove to the Criterion (in a bus, for once, not a taxi) & waited in the entrance hall for Mrs Leighton & Roland's sister Clare. I was very thankful for Roland's moral support. I feared I should be quite overwhelmed & unable to utter a word. At last Mrs Leighton appeared & Roland went towards her to take her to us. From her appearance until the time she left me at the tailor's door I lived in a glorious dream from which I did not want to wake, the heavenly experience of the magnetism of a personality utterly in tune with my own – despite the vast difference of experience, & the less vast one of years. Marie Connor Leighton the authoress of sensational novels, & Mrs Leighton the brilliant, strong-willed, utterly lovable mother of Roland, merged in a most extraordinary way into one of the most charming & attractive personalities I have ever met. When I first saw her I decided that nothing I had heard of her unusual appearance both from Edward & Mother was at all exaggerated. She is not very tall but largely built & rather stout; she was wearing a long black velvet coat, trimmed with brown fur, & a tête-de-nègre coloured hat trimmed with feathers. Beneath this was an extremely low-necked white blouse also trimmed with fur, & a red velvet skirt. What could be seen of her hair was chiefly visible in the little yellow wisps which hung quite straight over her forehead. But when I saw her brown eyes, so like Roland's, but with a merry twinkle which his promise but have not yet acquired, I knew I should love her, & not be in the least afraid of her.

I was a little quiet at first, waiting to find my level, but Aunt

Belle as usual started the conversation going &, with her lack of shyness & Mrs Leighton's excellent & natural conversational powers, there were no possibilities of shyness though Roland & I said scarcely anything for a while. Clare arrived in a few minutes – a sixteen-year-old flapper with a plain but pleasant face, having blue eyes & very little general resemblance to Roland, and a pretty figure. Mrs Leighton put me to sit beside her & opposite Roland. In a short time we were discussing Edward. Mrs Leighton describes his character marvellously, by laying stress on detailed qualities & actions which are exactly characteristic of him. She thinks him rather prim, & wonders very much how he can be so musical & yet possess no tempera-ment at all, which is what I have often wondered myself. She was sure, she said, that he would marry & be a most admirable husband, but he would never have received a love-letter, nor would she, for he did not possess the 'touchstone' for women as Roland & Victor Richardson, their friend, do. I agreed with this & said that though Roland, the first morning he had ever stayed with us, had patronised me & condescended & spoken in the Quiet Voice, I had realised that he possessed that touchstone. She smiled over the attitude of the masculine mind to the eternal feminine, & when he protested that he was as strong a feminist as anyone could be, she agreed with me that he argued from individuals, but said she thought his feminism was a feminine quality because the individuals from whom he argued had been in his life right from the beginning. Then she smiled at Roland & said, indicating me, 'She's quite human after all; I thought she might be very academic & learned.' I refuted this accusation with vehemence, telling her how much isolated I am at college, & how little affinity I have with the typical college woman. She looked at me keenly, & so kindly that I knew she liked me.

We moved out of the tea-room & she suggested that we should sit in the lounge for a while. I asked if she were not too busy to stay, or for me to stay, & she said 'Oh no! I don't want to go yet,' & Roland remarked that his mother was busy only when she wanted to get rid of people. We sat in the lounge for about half an hour & during that time I talked freely, without restraint or shyness, to Mrs Leighton, who seemed to understand me thoroughly at once. She said she thought we should be in agreement about most things, which seemed to me a great compliment from her. We discussed Edward & one another again. Mrs Leighton said Edward understood neither Roland nor me, but that he realised the fact where I was concerned & had said to her, with some apparent respect for my incomprehensible qualities, 'She's very extraordinary; there are lots of things about her I don't understand but you might.' I said that he did not understand Roland but added 'But then I don't either.' Mrs Leighton looked at him with a half-critical, very loving expression. 'I'm not so sure that I understand him myself.' 'You do more than anyone else,' said Roland & afterwards admitted that I did also more than a good many people.

Mrs Leighton has a wonderful faculty of character-reading; I told her I had been shy of meeting her, knowing how she made up her mind at once. Aunt Belle was very interested & asked Mrs Leighton what she thought of her. Mrs Leighton gave her a short & very acute criticism, which pleased Aunt Belle immensely because she said it was so true, & I certainly should imagine it to be pretty accurate. I asked her if she had grasped mine & she smiled & said she thought she had a good deal of it pretty well, but I would not ask her to give me details. She & Roland absolutely adore each other. She said to me that he got most of his eccentricity from her & she is immensely proud of it too. Their absolute devotion & likeness to each other is almost sad in its completeness, & made him seem more dependable to me than ever, for a man who cares deeply for his mother can be trusted very far.

At last the delightful tea-party broke up, for I had to go to the tailor's, & Mrs Leighton said it was just as well I was making her go as then she might do a little work. She offered to take us to the tailor's in her taxi, but as there was one too many one of us had to sit on someone's knee. Mrs Leighton said she thought the Leighton family was hardly of the build to be supported on other people so in the end I being the smallest sat on top of Aunt Belle & Mrs Leighton combined. Mrs Leighton repeatedly said she hoped often to see me again & I said 'Oh *do* let me – of course I must.' She said also 'I am *so* glad I was able to meet you, I wanted so much to see Edward's sister,' & when I protested 'Oh! only for *that* reason,' she said 'Well, you see, dear, I had not seen you then.' We parted with much regret at the tailor's door & Roland went with them a little way & said he would return for us in twenty minutes or so. When we had finished he was waiting for us – again with a taxi – outside, & handed Aunt Belle some pale pink carnations, & me a glorious bunch of pink roses, all covered with dew & of so sweet a scent that their perfume seemed to cling to me like a benediction the whole evening.

We had a warm secluded corner at dinner just below the balcony. The table was round, & Roland sat opposite to me; I found it much easier to talk to him there than when he sat beside me. We started on a conversation which would have seemed extraordinary to any of the other people in the restaurant could they have heard it; we were discussing how we should best like to be buried. It arose from Aunt Belle telling us the story of a girl in India whose great wish when she died had been to be buried at sea. I thought I should like to be burnt on a pyre, like Achilles, with all my writings & precious possessions with me, & Roland said he would like a burial like that of the Vikings of old, & that he would like to be put in a boat & then have the boat set on fire & allowed to drift out to sea. The discussion grew more & more melancholy, though we were quite unsentimental over it, till finally I asked Roland whether he would like to be killed in action. Aunt Belle said 'My dear girl, why do you talk about such things?' but he answered quite quietly 'Yes, I should; I don't want to die, but if I must, I should like to die that way. Anyhow, I should hate to go right through this war without being wounded at all; I should want something to prove that I had been in action.' I sat looking at him with his expressive dark eyes & broad strong figure & suddenly was conscious of a deep sense of tragedy in my heart both for my sake & his; for mine because I love him & for his because it seems the greatest crime in the world that so brilliant an intellect & so promising a character should soon be exposed to danger & death. So I went on 'I know you're the kind of person who would risk your life recklessly; I was talking to someone a short time ago & I said I thought you were the kind who believes in the "one glorious hour of crowded life" theory; is it true?' He answered 'Yes I think it is,' & I said 'I know you'll offer to ride with dispatches in front of a blazing fire or something of that sort.' He thought he probably would.

His Majesty's Theatre is quite near the Florence, so we walked to it & arrived in excellent time. I told Roland I was sorry I could not put on an evening dress & really get myself up for the occasion of his taking me out, but such as I was seemed to content him perfectly. The dark crêpe-de-chine blouse I had brought to wear made a good background for the pale pink roses. One cannot tell what is going on in that deep mind of his & only his eyes ever express his thoughts, but I saw him looking at me during dinner with a look which, though by no means undisguised, was nearer admiration than anything I have ever seen from him before. I am not very well qualified to criticise the play as my interests were divided; each individual scene was excellently staged & produced & all the actors suited their parts excellently. Roland tried to avoid putting on his glasses as he did not want me to notice them, but when he found he could not see without them, he asked me if I minded his putting them on, & when I said that of course he must he did so & begged me not to look. Naturally I did look; they were not nearly as unbecoming as he thought. As the evening wore on I thought less & less of the play & more & more of his nearness to me. It was just dawning upon me that I was a different person from the one who had received his books on my 21st birthday. It seemed an age since then. Everything these two days had been dream-like & incomplete; almost everything we could have said to each other had been left unsaid, but I knew the one thing that made all the difference in the world – that the feelings which, ever since I had known him I had thought might quite possibly arise between us, were no longer a dream but a reality.

The most precious evening of my life thus far was over at last. We took a taxi from the theatre & arrived at Charing Cross with half an hour to wait for our train. He waited with us & we walked up & down the station for a while. It was a bright night with myriads of stars & a brilliant moon; the station was fairly crowded, with several soldiers & other people waiting for the New Year to come in. We were both very silent; perhaps he felt past speaking & I know I did. I had felt all along, but now I realised overwhelmingly, the imminence of our parting. I knew that this was not only a very different New Year's Eve from anything I had spent before, but that it was the best day so far of my life, not so mad or intoxicating as I had imagined it might be, but, in spite of the dream element, something deeper & more full of acute realisation. And I knew too that, as it was the first of such days, so it might be the last, that perhaps I should not look upon his face again, & that against our future communion the stern 'Nevermore' might be written in the annals of fate.

Before we got into the train he told Aunt Belle he was indebted to her for a great deal, & she thanked him profusely, saying enough for both of us, for which I was thankful as I could say nothing for myself. When Aunt Belle had got into the carriage he bent over me and said very earnestly 'Thank you ever so much.' I said I thought the gratitude ought to be all on my side, but he told me it was on his as I might never have let him know I was coming to London. Then I shook hands with him as it was just time for the train to go, & got into the carriage. But the train was late & did not go for another ten minutes. I asked him if he would be able to come & see me to say goodbye before he went to the front & he said I might be sure he would do everything possible to see me. Then we could not speak any more; I wished the train would go, for we could do nothing but look at one another with a sad, restrained expression that seemed to speak of a feeling that could find no words.

At last the train moved. He took my hand once again in a long warm grip, & once again I said 'Au revoir', for I would not say the Goodbye that I thought it might be. I leaned out of the carriage window & waved to him once & then I could not look any more, but sat silent & motionless, capable of neither words nor tears nor anything else, & yet extraordinarily conscious of that very feeling of incapability. I wondered as I sat there if in days to come I should look back on that evening as the beginning of the great glory of my life, or as an occasion which in silent remembrance I should forever mourn. Beside these newly-born dreams of a possible future my old dreams & aspirations grew pale, as would the moon's cold splendour beside the passionate flames of the sun. I felt then that I would give all I had lived or hoped for during the brief years of my existence, not to astonish the world by some brilliant & glittering achievement, but some day to be the mother of Roland Leighton's child. And yet the old dreams in themselves had not faded but were intensified for his sake. And the New Year, with all its giant possibility of grief & joy, came in while I sat motionless in the train, watching the dim railway lights in a blurred mist go swiftly by.

1915

Friday January 1st London
I travelled up to Charing Cross this morning & met Miss Heath
Jones & Miss Bervon there. Aunt Belle accompanied me to the
station, full of instructions concerning Roland, that I 'was to
stick to this one' because she thought him so dependable. I
cannot say much about this day, as it fades into the glowing
unreality of the other two. No doubt we were right, & a dubious
meeting to-day would have spoilt everything. Yet I would have
given anything to have seen him again all the same; I felt I was
just beginning – that he was allowing me to begin – to know a
little of that real self of his which puzzles even his mother. When
I did retire to bed it was not to sleep very much. Besides the
usual dreaming & thinking, in my rather worked-up state I was
suddenly seized with a creepy dread of Zeppelins, against which
the London population have been warned. I could not help
picturing to myself the close proximity of those aerial guns
beside Buckingham Palace, with their long thin funnels pointing
to the sky, which I had seen from Miss Bervon's window in the
morning. It was a perfectly clear & still night, cloudless & star-
spangled, & I finally dropped off into a very troubled sleep with
a mind confused between Roland & Zeppelins.

Saturday January 2nd Buxton
Miss Heath Jones & Miss Bervon saw me off by the 10.5 & I left
London thankful that my beloved city was still unvisited by
hostile bombs. When I got home I found a letter from Roland
waiting for me. It was one of the kind in which Mrs Leighton
would say more was written between the lines than in the lines
themselves, & it said a little of all that was left unsaid on
Thursday. He ended by saying that though meeting again

might have spoilt everything, he hated the idea that I was in London even for one day without his being able to see me – that we might not meet again for so long, & he had left unsaid most of what he wanted to say. And then 'You are a dear, you know' & his initials signed just below that unobtrusive statement. The sense of imaginative power in those few short sentences, & their restrained tenderness, were quite too much for me; I dropped my head on the bed-post & wept. Not much, however, for Mother helped me to undo my purchases & only thought my cold was a little worse. But at night Daddy started on his favourite task of railing at the war, at Edward going, at the Government – everything – showing how utterly incomprehensible everything spiritual & noble & selfless is to him. He remarked that he supposed that Roland did not think he was ever coming back. It was too cruel to be reminded of what I was determined not to let myself think about & when I had said goodnight to Mother in her room I cried in good earnest, much against my will & with a feeling of tragic inevitableness.

Sunday January 3rd
I went with Mother through all the thick snow to St John's this morning though not feeling much like church, for to-day there is a universal intercession service for peace, for favourable issues to the war & for the safety of loved ones. Probably I was in an easily movable state, but church did move me to-day for the first time in my life about; in fact during the hymns & especially Cowper's beautiful one 'God moves in a mysterious way' I felt inconveniently like crying. I could not help thinking of Roland, & praying for him despite my small belief in that kind of prayer. I did so just in case there is something in it, & after all there may be, especially when it is drawn from the pain & sincerity of sorrowful hearts as it was to-day; I could not, *dared* not, leave anything undone which there was the remotest possibility might be of some help to him even though I could not see why.

Monday January 4th
I tried to work & failed disgracefully. Miss Fry is certainly right in saying that to care for anyone at all is a serious interference to

work. It is almost a pity I could not have remained unmoved until college was over. But let my work suffer if it must! After all it is the creative artist, rather than the scholar, that I want to be.

Thursday January 7th
A dreary day, desolate with steady drizzling rain & universal greyness. Latin is not enthralling to me just at present; I hear too much of war & have it brought home all too closely to me, to appreciate reading about it in Livy. I read *Sinister Street* after dinner & on putting it down came to the conclusion that owing to the grind for Responsions my life was not nearly full enough at Oxford last term. Isolation does not matter but the exclusion of life & colour for the sake of scholarship does.

Saturday January 9th
I had a letter from Roland this morning, which at once put an end to the very slender chance there was already of my doing any work during the morning. He finds much to read in my letter which was not written in ink – says I tell him I am beginning to understand him a little but that I do not know how much it means to him to get a glimpse of the real me – since by force of circumstances & temperament I am always acting. He thinks there are few things he would rather do than write to me, but finds his spare time taken up by apparently unpleasing entertainments & functions, the result of a provincial society driven somewhat off its head by an influx of khaki. (This seems somehow remotely suggestive of Jane Austen. Even *we* in Buxton are in no wise thrilled by the presence of a thousand soldiers in our hotel-barracks.) He ends his letter with an exciting suggestion that he may be able to invent an excuse to get leave & meet me on my way to Oxford, either at London or Leicester, so that he could see me again. I got Daddy to look up trains from Leicester to Oxford, meantime inventing plausible excuses for not going round by Birmingham. We managed to find a very satisfactory train. I dare not think too much about the possibility of seeing him again so soon, lest after all it should not happen.

Thursday January 14th

I had a letter from Roland to-day saying he had managed to get his leave alright & would meet me in Leicester on Saturday. He suggests that doubtless the Colonel would be a little surprised if he knew the real reason of his wanting to go to Leicester, but says that if he had not been given leave he would have come without. Of course I ought not to let him come at all. My defiance of the conventions seems to grow daily, & leave me without any feeling of guilty conscience.

Saturday January 16th Oxford

By various judicious turnings of the conversation & by assertions that I probably should not have time to send the telegram saying I had arrived until after tea, I managed to depart from Buxton & bid a fond farewell to the family without their suspecting, or having a chance to suspect, that I was going to do anything else but catch the 1.1 train at Leicester. I did not tell many fibs either though I expected I might have to undertake a regular course of them.

Roland was waiting for me on Leicester Station. He had come up by an absurdly early train so as to arrive before me. He gave me another bunch of the pale pink roses like he gave me in London; just the colour & the kind I like best. I had not expected he would remember how I like them. He looked pale & rather plainer than usual, & said he was suffering from the regimental cold. We deposited my luggage at the other station first & then drove to the Grand Hotel, where we intended to have lunch. It was rather too early for that so we sat in the lounge & talked for some time first – chiefly about ourselves – first one & then the other – & also about intellect. Then we had lunch in a good-sized & pleasantly empty dining-room overlooking the street. When we were in the midst of it he made the astonishing suggestion of coming to Oxford with me. It appeared he had looked up all the trains with a view to accompanying me all the way & then returning to Peterborough.

I tried to dissuade him, as I felt both that he had been put to enough trouble & that I had defied conventions sufficiently already. But his mind was made up, & unless I showed that I *disliked* his accompanying me, which was quite impossible, I knew that he would come. And come he did. We travelled in empty first class carriages where no one disturbed us. He even offered to pay the difference on my 1st class ticket but I told him I was not an object of charity & could afford to pay it much better than he could. It would be difficult to reproduce our conversation at all accurately & I do not mean to try lest I should spoil the reality. It was a very sane conversation & the fascination of it lay deep & not on the surface. At Banbury we changed; the light was just going and it was cold as we walked up & down the platform. In this second train we said less than ever. But it was enough to me to see him sitting opposite me with his intent & rather sad eyes watching me. I wanted the journey to last for ever & the train not to take me to the secluded definiteness of a women's college, but to some place where I could be with him always. There was an underlying seriousness in all our conversation – partly the consciousness of the tragedies of war but chiefly because everything seemed at a standstill and there was so little chance of what we felt for one another leading to any result for some time. We were rather amused in wondering first what both my relations & his would think of the unconventional escapade, & then what the austere Edward would be likely to say – if he knew, & we wondered if anyone ever would know.

Oxford began to approach all too soon, & with it the realisation that this mad dream must come to an end. We became more & more silent. I watched the bright sunset between the grey clouds, conscious of his nearness & how I cared – conscious also of the slight & inexplicable repulsion towards him which with me seems to accompany my strong feeling for anyone. I told him he must disown me altogether when we reached the station, lest I should be seen & sent down. He demurred but finally agreed when he saw I meant it. I became more conscious than ever during the day of his extreme trustworthiness & reliability. He never deceives or forgets. He is about the only person I would trust & be sure he would do a thing as well & thoroughly for me as I could for myself. As the grey city began to surround us & the train slowed down I stood up, put out my hand & said goodbye. He took it quite collectedly & then suddenly raised it to his lips & kissed it.

Taken by surprise I resisted a little but quite unavailingly in his strong grip, & after all I did not really want to resist. I turned away from him & looked out of the window till the train stopped. I could not say any more but another brief goodbye. I even did not thank him – but hurried away to see after my luggage.

At Somerville I met several people who all congratulated me about my exam., which I had almost forgotten. I hurried up to see the Pen, who also greeted me with a radiant smile & said she had been so delighted about what she was pleased to call my most brilliant performance. She said it was a great credit both to Mr May & to me, & she hoped I had not felt it a strain & had taken a good rest & not worked too hard during the vac. This was a most unusual remark for Somerville – quite historic – & it relieved my feelings greatly as I had done nothing. The congratulatory part rather embarrassed me, so I said I thought it was sometimes easier to do things quickly. She said perhaps it was to anyone who had a power of concentration & an alert sort of brain like me. Next I interviewed Miss Lorimer, who plunged me into a long list of instructions about Pass Mods work. My interest in her was as keen as ever but seemed pale beside the greater light which still kept captive & illuminated all my thoughts. I spent the rest of the day unpacking & wandering about in the way one does at the beginning of term – chiefly between Miss Ellis Fermor's room & Katharine Wood's. At the end of the day I began to notice the usual capacity of college for making everything else seem very remote.

Tuesday January 19th
I had my first class – a Greek unseen – with Miss Lorimer to-day. The class was interesting; though I cannot imagine how the mere prospect of belonging to it ever roused me to such a pitch of enthusiasm as it did last term. In fact I feel as if nothing at Somerville could rouse me to great enthusiasm again, which is a dismal prospect now that I am in for nearly 3 years of it. I feel I care very little whether I do well or badly in my exams, whether I am considered clever or not (since after all I *know* what I am), or what Miss Lorimer thinks of me.

Wednesday January 20th
To-day was dull & the morning so depressing that I wished I
had never come, felt sure college was a mistake for me & began
to think of various excuses for going down. Still I have heard
nothing of Roland; I shall not rest until I do. There has been a
Zeppelin raid on Yarmouth, 3 people were killed & a good deal
of damage was done.

Friday January 22nd
I had a letter from Roland at last. As soon as I received it I put it
in my jersey pocket & carried it about with me all the time for
company. He apologised for not writing before, but after the
journey to Oxford his cold got so much worse that he had to stay
in bed 3 days. I thought something of the sort might happen. He
does not take nearly enough care of himself. I suppose I ought
never to have let him come with me; there were so many things
that day that I ought never to have allowed.

Sunday January 24th
I had another – a very short – letter from Roland this morning
to inform me that his regiment has been ordered to Lowestoft at
once. It must be very strange for him to be stationed in his own
town. I suppose it is because coast raids are anticipated there. I
also had a letter from Daddy. The only thing of importance he
told me was that Thomson, the boy who was head of the Lodge
when Edward first went there, had been killed in action. I
remember Edward was very fond of him. This war takes them
all, 'the eloquent, the young, the beautiful & brave', & I don't
feel as if there can be *any* justification for that.

Tuesday January 26th
This morning, for no reason whatever, I felt happy for the first
time since coming back here. The early exuberance evaporated
a little during the day; still I have proved that in spite of the war,
& of many uncongenial people, & not quite suitable surroundings, the feeling is possible – & the infrequent moments worth
living for. The Lorie was fairly merciful to me to-day in Unseens
class.
    I went to O[W]DS after dinner & was glad to have been as a

very unusual thing happened. The motion was 'That this house deplores the use of Indian native troops'. During the private business someone proposed that the subject was not one for discussion at a time when Indians are giving their lives in our cause, & that the house should adjourn. After a good deal of argument the motion was put to the meeting & was carried, so the house adjourned. I voted for it because, though it had not occurred to me before, it was my honest opinion that the motion was a very uncomfortable one, & that the only kinds of facts that could be brought to support it would be of a nature better left unexpressed at such a time as this.

Monday February 1st
There was a letter from Roland which disturbed me somewhat. He has found out that the 4th Suffolk Regt. want three more officers for the front at once. He is going – or rather has offered himself to-day – as one of them. He is so obviously anxious to go that I do not know what to think or wish. For his sake & in consideration of what I might feel if he did not want to go I am glad, but for my own sake, which is regulated by what it wants rather than by what it ought to want, I would like him to stay. Somehow I feel he may succeed this time in his attempts . . .

Thursday February 4th
After lunch E.F., Miss Barber & I went a bicycle ride through Marston village. The distant hedgerows & woods were a dreamy purple, the little stumpy willow-trees a glorious golden-brown & the streams by which they stood flowed very lively & clear.

Friday February 5th
This evening I put on my new blue & grey dress, in consideration of the fact that Miss Fry was arriving – also that there was a lecture on 'The Way to Permanent Peace' by a Mr Trevelyan whom I had not heard about before but seems a famous person. I got great satisfaction out of the dress, which seemed to ensure me a pleasant evening. Quite an embarrassing number of people came up to me specially just to say how pretty it was, so

it must really be strikingly pretty as things have to be striking here to be noticed at all.

Saturday February 6th
I had a letter from Roland telling me that his attempt to get transferred had so far been unsuccessful, & that he is to stay in the 4th Norfolks. I am so glad. But best of all he enclosed a small cutting from the paper saying that he is promoted to be 1st Lieutenant. Consequently I enjoyed my classes with Miss Lorimer & the Logic lecture more than I have enjoyed any work this term. He must be excellent to be promoted so soon in a reserve battalion.

Sunday February 7th
I heard a woman preach & take the service to-day at Manchester College Chapel – the Unitarian place. It made me wish that women were allowed to do this in other churches instead of our having the brainless & callow [curates] that are put into the Church because their parents know they will be unfit for everything else.

Monday February 8th
When I went through the hall I found a postcard for me from Edward – a tragic postcard, expressing most in what its plain unqualified assertions left unsaid. Victor Richardson is dangerously ill – perhaps dying – of cerebral spinal meningitis, & his only chance of life is to outlive the fever. Poor Edward – he must feel that disaster follows the footsteps of his friends. First there was Maurice's queer breakdown, & now this dreadful illness of Victor's.

We had a delightful Bach Choir practice to-night. It seems to me a strange but certain truth that one can enjoy the humour of things so much better when one has an underlying sadness. All through the evening, especially during the solemn words of the *Requiem*, I could not help but think of Victor near to death & Edward's & Roland's sorrow on his account, yet the humour of Dr Allen's temper in the midst of a bad cold, & of Miss Sayers gazing at him as though she were in church worshipping her only God, appealed to me immensely.

Wednesday February 10th

There was great excitement & in fact rather a 'row' at Somerville today. It appears that yesterday, before the river was by any means safe, Miss Rose took Miss Curtis & Miss Lettice Hill in a canoe down the river. Miss Rose was the only canoe-member &, as neither of the other two had had much experience in handling a canoe, practically the whole work & responsibility was hers. When they came to the weir they suddenly realised they would have some difficulty. Miss Rose tried to steer the boat to the side out of the current, and as she was doing this the current caught the boat at the side & capsized it. They all fell into the water & were shot down the weir into the rocky whirlpool beneath. As they fell they saw the waterfall above their heads & thought their last hour had come – as indeed it might have if they had not all been strong swimmers.

Poor Miss Rose is suffering innumerable things. The very last thing she could endure would be to feel she had made a fool of herself, or be obviously in the wrong, & that is exactly what has happened. She could justify her actions by talking about them – & does for almost anything, but in this one instance what she did was so obviously unjustifiable that she could not in any way possibly make things right for herself or do anything but face the music. Her real trial came as Miss Adams, the Captain, called a meeting of the Boat Club & requested everyone to attend. At the meeting she sat rigidly in a high chair well in view of everyone as though determined to face all that was to be faced. I sat on the floor opposite & watched her, admiring her courage. I believe she is suffering from a temporary loss of self-respect, which is the worst thing that can happen to anyone. Yet if people only knew the kind of things one respects them for most. Before to-day, when I looked upon Miss Rose as a hard, exclusive person whose pride it was impossible to wound, I never respected her in the least for that imperturbability & extreme self-assurance. But now I have seen the so-called weaker qualities – the sensitive emotion, the soreness, the appearance of hurt dignity & tremulous would-be affectation of amusement, I feel a respect & a warmth which her former inviolable ascendancy would never have given me. I suppose I ought to take it as a lesson for myself, and not think that it is only by hardness & aloofness that I shall win respect, & carefully keep the under-lying tendernesses & sensitiveness hidden from the eyes of the world.

Thursday February 11th
I had a pc from Edward & a letter from Roland to-day saying that Victor is much better & though the doctors will not pronounce him out of danger they have hopes of his ultimate recovery. Roland also informs me that he has alas! been interviewing the War Office again & says his hopes of going where I hope he will not go are brighter than they have ever been before.

Monday February 15th
The chief event of to-day was a glorious cycle ride of about twelve miles with Miss Schenzinger. We went first to Boars Hill & from the top we looked over a great wide plain dotted here & there with poplar trees. In the distance were gently curving blue hills. Strangely enough we could see what looked like a great white road going sheer up the side of the hill; it was too misty for us really to have been able to see a road & we were very much puzzled to think what it could be.

Friday February 19th
After dinner the Tub-Thumpers – which is the College select debating society – held an open meeting followed by coffee, to which they invited all of College who cared to come. I found that Miss Chubb was the President of the Society & Miss Rose the Secretary. I was so possessed by Miss Rose's beauty to-night that I was simply impelled to look in her direction & nothing seemed at all attractive to me in comparison. Her face was flushed & eyes very deep, & the electric light from above shone upon her hair. Nothing draws me like beauty; it exercises an almost immoral influence – especially when she got up to speak and her tall figure & rather deep gracious voice enhanced the effect of her face's loveliness.

Friday February 26th

In the evening we did our plays, in candle-light with a flickering
fire behind. I forgot myself quite soon & found *Goodnight, Babette*
easier to do than I expected, and sang rather confidently too.
There was pretty vigorous clapping when it was over & I think it
went down well, especially with some of the more artistic
people. I rushed away & changed to Victoria, to the great joy
of the audience from the point of view of my appearance. I tied
my hair with a little ribbon at the side & left it flowing. *The Dear
Departed* was a great success. The laughing was so vociferous that
we sometimes had to wait quite a long time & occasionally our
cues were drowned.

Tuesday March 2nd

Logic was boring – I wished I had cut – but we are to have a
paper on the whole of it on Saturday. I heard from Mother this
afternoon. Daddy has been going on about Edward, & Mother
wonders if I think he will really be killed when he gets out to
France, & they are both run down & altogether things are lively.
I shall have a perfectly appalling vac. Almost everyone's attitude
seems to be braver & more resigned than theirs. One must come
now to regard the sorrowful & the grievous as the matters of
course, & the pleasant ones as the exceptions, instead of, as we
did before the war, looking upon troubles as unusual &
thoroughly resentable incidents in our serene lives. I do sometimes feel – nay, am almost convinced – that once Edward has
gone to France he will never return. I don't think I shall see
much of him ever again. It is so strange that when I think of my
future life I always imagine it without his charming personality
to add to its sunnier side. I am equally certain that Roland will
come through.

Wednesday March 3rd

I couldn't help feeling that this has been a rather profitable term
from the point of view of achievement, as not only have I done a
play & the Bach Choir concert, but also got through most of my
P. Mods work. I am hoping to finish Pliny's *Letters* this week, &
do the remaining books of Homer next week; then I shall have

nothing to do but revise all the vac. & next term, & may get in some English.

Monday March 15th Buxton
I had finished my breakfast when the letters came – one from Roland which had been sent on from Somerville. He has obtained his wish at last, and is off to the front in about 10 days' time. He has been given a transfer to the 7th Worcestershire Regt. – Territorials – which is on the point of going abroad & is short of two officers. This news was not unexpected but is none the less a terrible shock to me. I can hardly realise that the moment has come at last which ends my peace of mind until the war is over – that in a few days' time the individual so very dear to me will have gone to those regions of bloodshed and death, perhaps – nay, probably – never to return. The worst of it is he wrote to me at College thinking I was going down on Monday & trying to arrange a meeting in London on that day. He says he can't possibly go to the front without seeing me, & certainly I could never let him go without saying goodbye, however sad it is to do so. But the letter was delayed & now I don't know where he is or where to write to him.

Later. I was getting ready for bed this evening when a telephone message – which with a kind of presentiment I had been half expecting all day – came for me from Roland in London. The beloved voice made me shiver with apprehension, thinking of the time when I should hear it no more. He tells me he is going to the front – not in ten days' time – but on *Saturday*. I said I supposed he wanted me to say I was glad about what had happened but I was not even going to pretend to. He only laughed. Telephoning is very unsatisfactory & there was such a noise going on I could scarcely hear anything. However I went to Mother & Daddy & announced my intention of going to London to say goodbye. They demurred a little at first but gave in sooner than I expected.

Tuesday March 16th
I talked a good deal about Roland to Mother who was quite sympathetic & seemed anxious to find out just how much he had 'made love to me' & seemed surprised to find how little he had

done so obviously. I told her about the Leicester episode on my way to Oxford last time. She did not seem at all annoyed but very amused. Nevertheless she wants to go up to town with me when I go to say goodbye – because I have not been well, not because she does not trust Roland.

Wednesday March 17th
He is coming here – *here*, to-morrow, though we have only arrived at this conclusion after long perturbation. This morning, before lunch, we heard nothing from Roland at all. But in the middle of lunch, when I was feeling very troubled from having heard nothing, a telephone message came, saying that he was in London till Friday evening. I did not think of asking him here then but arranged that I would go to London. But later in the afternoon I received a card from him, evidently written yesterday evening, saying he would be absolutely on his own in town & could meet me in Manchester or anywhere I liked. That not only made coming here seem possible but sounded as if he wanted to. So I consulted Mother & then at once dashed down to the Post Office with a wire asking if he would not prefer to spend Thursday night here. That was all very well, but evidently he was out so that at 8.15 no wire had come in reply. We telephoned to the exchange, found that no more wires could be delivered to-night and that our train left in the morning before the PO opened. I began to get in despair as we really were in a fix; there seemed a good chance of missing him altogether. However, he telephoned again, asking what he really was to do. I begged him again to come and Mother spoke to him too, saying she would be delighted to see him.

Friday March 19th
Whatever the future may bring – whether it be the sorrow I fear more than anything on earth, or the joy which now I scarce dare dream of, much less name – as long as I have memory & thought, I shall not forget to-day & yesterday. My beloved one has been here and departed again, & now indeed I may see his dear face never any more. I cannot write about it much; it is not only useless but impossible to try to record in words anything I felt so poignantly & shall always remember so vividly. When I

first came back here after saying goodbye to him – or rather, it was 'Au Revoir' that I said, because my courage would not even contemplate a *last* farewell, though I tried – I simply could not take up my pen & write; I felt paralysed. Now he has gone I can scarcely bear to think of him, & yet I cannot think of anything else.

Yesterday after lunch I went to meet his train, which arrived at about 2.20, & we drove up in a taxi. Mother met us at the door & of course Roland was very shy at first, but Mother did not trouble him to talk to her long but went upstairs, leaving us together in the morning-room. Of course I started at once on the subject uppermost in my mind; strangely enough I found my feelings much harder to keep in check than they were later on, nearer the time of his departure. I suppose it was the sudden effect of seeing him after all the agitation of mind I had had about it during the last few days, but I felt very near to tears – had even an effort at times to prevent him seeing I was, &, in fact, I believe he knew all along.

A good deal of our conversation was an argument, which I forced upon him, as to why he wanted to go; when I made him analyse his actual reasons for going out he seemed to have none that he could give. He said the vague reason of 'freedom' was hardly strong enough, he had no personal animosity against the enemy, & he certainly did not want to die himself. He has no love for the army at all & admitted that he wished he were at Oxford occupied with Classics & books. He seemed to find that part of the reason was vanity, & yet this is not enough because he does not care what people say, & certainly not enough to wish to risk his life because of it. The real reason seems to be the vague moral sense of acting up to his faith in, his highest opinion of, himself – the worship & indefinite pursuit of heroism in the abstract – oh! I know well enough really why he wants to go, why if I were a man *I* should want to go – though I cannot put into words my understanding of his own motives, ineradicable as I know them to be. After all, the most important things in life are generally those one cannot give a reason for. I told him my peace of mind was gone from now until the end of the war; he said he could not be sorry that I cared, but he did want me to approve of his going. I told him I could not pretend to be glad, that I was no heroine who could pour forth set injunctions to do deeds of daring, or wear company manners because he was going to the front. Instead of this I was only a weak imperfect being, whose only interest in the war was through individuals concerned in it, and who, since his going to the front had become certain, had begun to pray again without believing in it much, just in case it did any good. He seemed unexpectedly a little affected by this information, although I told him I prayed selfishly, not that he should do deeds of heroism, but that God might bring him back. I teased him a little – rather sadly it must be owned, because I only did it to hide my own mournful feelings; he said he knew I should tease him for that reason. I said that it was difficult to realise how utterly different everything was now from the time when he came here just a year ago, when I teased him so unmercifully and took a delight in deriding his vanity.

I asked him if he thought it better to have seen the possibility of great joy that could not be realised as yet, perhaps never, or if he thought it better to keep one's peace of mind & never see. He said he thought the first was better, & I agreed with him, agreed that it was better to suffer & try to be strong over it than never to have risen to the point where suffering becomes possible. I do feel indeed like one standing at the entrance of the Promised Land – or like one who has been permitted to gaze upon it from the mountain tops without being allowed to enter. Sometimes I have wished I had never met him – wished that he had not come to take away my impersonal attitude towards the war, and make it a cause of personal suffering to me as it is to thousands of others. But yet, if I could choose never to have met him I would not. It is better as it is, in spite of all the sorrow. I would rather be unhappy, rather be that finer person whose redemption is 'worked out by the soul itself with suffering & through time', than be able to work on calmly in complete peace of mind.

Yet I could not help speaking of the war. It seemed, I said, to have come just in time to make it possible that I should live ever after under the shadow of it, with all my future darkened by that Shadow of Death which I must always think of now as hovering close behind the footsteps of him & of Edward. 'Ah don't say that,' he said. 'Don't say it will all be spoilt; when we return, things may be just the same.' '*If* you return,' I could not help saying. ' "When", not "if",' he insisted, but I said I did not imagine for a moment he was going out without realising fully all that it might mean. He answered very gravely that he had thought many times of what the issue might be, yet he had a settled conviction that he was coming back – not quite whole perhaps, but he hoped I should not like him less if he was, say, minus an arm. He said he had had his hand read once by someone supposed to be very good, who had told him to follow up all his military opportunities, that he would be in danger of death many times but would always just escape. But he continued that someone had told him that the only thing that kept an army together was that each man individually believed that he personally would return. I told him of my conviction that of him & Edward one of them would return, but not both. It seemed to distress him. Certainly I exercised no tact in mentioning death, but it seemed so vain to refrain from doing so when it was uppermost in both our thoughts. There are two kinds of people, who have two different ways of facing probable trouble; one kind put the thought of it firmly aside & refuse to think of it until it actually comes; the other kind will not blind themselves to the very worst that may happen and act as if it were going to in case it does. I said I was of the second kind, & that I was making myself feel I should never see him again in case I did not. He said he thought on the whole that I was right – that it was the braver way. Then I spoke to him about his mother, saying how hard I thought it must be for her. He did not say much about her, only I gathered that her attitude is rather one of negative acquiescence than anything else.

We had tea with Mother, who seemed to admire him in his uniform & could not agree that he looked at all plain. Not that I would wish him to be any less plain & broad & big; it would not be he if he were. After tea we decided to go for a walk. There had been a snow storm, which kept continuing on & off, but we did not mind that & went out into it. We walked right round Green Lane, with a blizzard driving part of the time into our faces. We spoke of much the same things as we did before tea; when two people's minds are full of one subject it is impossible not to talk about it, & perhaps after all it is better to speak of

Death than to think about it in silence. I made him promise that if he met his death on the fields of France he would if possible come back from the Other Side & tell me that the grave is not the end of our apparently ironical existence here. As we came home I thought how speedily the precious moments were passing and how soon this time to-morrow, with its bitter recollection of parting, would be here. When we arrived in it was nearly dinner-time, so I changed into my pretty blue & grey dress which everyone says I look so nice in, hoping he would think so too, & I believe he did.

Dinner was quite a success; Daddy was very affable & kept Roland smoking after dinner a little longer than I cared about. But he came up soon and Mother went away & left us in the drawing-room, sitting together on the sofa in the dim lamplight, with the fire flickering cheerfully in the grate. We remained there very close together until 12.0, he with his arm along the back of the sofa nearly round my shoulders. He looked at me the whole time with an expression which meant so much that I could hardly bear to raise my eyes & meet his. Never before have I experienced such a feeling as seemed to fill that quiet room with such an intensity of emotion that everything grew quite dim. I can scarcely recall our conversation, & indeed it could hardly be called such, & any listener would doubtless have thought it absurd. Occasionally we lapsed into long emotional silences.

We spoke again for a while about a Hereafter; both inclined to believe there could not be, both wishing – oh! so much – that we could believe that there was. I reminded him how he had spoken at Uppingham of Kant's theory that a beneficent Deity could not make us end with our aspirations unfulfilled & our work undone. Roland said he had sometimes felt a desire just to become nothing and leave everything off in the middle, but when I asked if he really meant that he would wish never to taste a possible joy, never to continue a work or a happiness which he had just begun, or just begun to realise, he said he certainly did not mean that. We tried to examine what it is in us which may live again, and did indeed come to the conclusion that there is something beyond our physical & mental selves, something neither intellect nor vanity, which impels us to do right without witness & without reward just because it is right, and that this part of us, this strange inexplicable moral sense, may continue to endure. Yet, as we both admitted, we did not wish to find one another again without our physical attributes – did not wish in another life to dispense with material characteristics which mean so much to us both, but this at least we know will have to be. For me Roland would not be Roland if I could not see with my earthly eyes that strong frame so expressive of his personality, if, still more, I could not look into those dark eyes of his, or hear his voice, the sound of which I never can recall when he is absent. To feel I may never again hear that voice fills me with a greater despair than when I think I may not again look on his face; yet, after all, these things are not Roland; it is the personality behind which makes them to me so essentially expressive of him.

We sat on there while the fire died down, after everyone else had gone to bed. I knew he would say nothing definite about any possible future, being too honourable to commit either himself or me to anything while he is so young & poor, & I would not wish him to because if he made a thousand promises I could not trust him more than I do or be more sure of him than I am. But we did speak of marriage a little; I said Mother was afraid I should become just an intellectual old maid, & that indeed was probably what I should become. 'I don't see why,' he said. 'Simply because there will be no one left for me to marry after the war,' I answered. 'Not even me?' he asked in a very low voice. He said he was sorry to have destroyed my peace of mind by making me fond of him; I would not admit that I cared for him at first, but the sudden poignant stab of recollection that I might never have him with me again to tell him how much I really did, made me admit it then. But it is useless to try to write about a fragmentary conversation which was really not a conversation at all but a fitful expression of emotions made up of a strange mixture of sorrow & the saddest kind of joy. At last I felt I could stand it no longer; when one is but prolonging something that must in any case end soon, the sudden need comes to end it quickly. I saw he was looking tired & rather worn, though I think he would have stayed up all night if I had let him, so I made him put the lamp out. He took my hand and kissed it again as he did in the train once before – but this time there was no glove upon it.

There is not after all much more to be said. I was tired & slept but my night was restless & disturbed with dreams, & so, as he told me in the morning, was his. We had breakfast alone together as previously arranged, and had no time to be long over it. We neither of us said more than a word or two. I could not realise that goodbye was actually so imminent. On the ground the snow was lying very thick & the air was icy cold, but the sun was shining brightly overhead, and everything all round looked dazzling & white. All the way to the station we scarcely spoke a word. I only looked at him once or twice; his face was set & his eyes very sad. I hate his expression of silent emotion; it hurts me. It was just like the expression he wore at the Prize-Giving at Uppingham, but greatly intensified.

I shall never forget the look of the station so early on that cold bright March morning. The train did not go from the usual platform but from the one opposite, on the darker side of the station, and a train filling the line beside it made it seem gloomier than ever, and cold with the chillness of a wintry morning in places where the sun has not yet penetrated. In the distance the railway bridge & the snow-covered signal boxes gleamed in the brilliant light. On the chill station the air was crisp & quite windless. As the train was almost due to start I got up into the railway carriage to say goodbye to him. He held my hand a long time & looked at me in complete silence so sorrowfully that I wished I could have cried to ease the pain in my heart. I felt spiritually sick but as far from tears as I have ever been in my life; I did not feel in the least choked, and there was no mist in my eyes to dim the pitiless cold brightness of the morning. I did not wish him glory or honour or triumph; in comparison with seeing him again I cared about none of those things. So all I could say was just 'I hope Heaven will be kind to me & bring you back.' He held my hand & looked at me without a word. For a moment I wished he would have kissed me; many men would have done so and it would hardly have been a liberty at that solemn moment. But afterwards I was glad that he had not done so, but had remained characteristic of himself up to the last; the reservation of his emotion is somehow so much more expressive than the expression of it would be; he is so incapable of anything so light as flirtation, or of taking any liberty beyond what his own uprightness assures him he has the right to. So I got down from the carriage with the fact that we were more than just friends still unrecognised by everything but our spiritual consciousness. Then there was a slight bustling on the platform & the train began to move. We clasped hands once more as it was going &, though I was trying to train my mind into realising that probably this was indeed a final farewell, at the last I could only bring myself to say 'Au revoir.' He said it too & dropped my hand, then remained leaning out of the window looking sadly at me as I stood motionless watching the train until it disappeared altogether and where it had been there was nothing but the merciless sunlight shining on the rails. I hate public exhibitions of emotion, but if I could have burst into tears then & there I should have been glad, I felt so stunned & cold as I turned & walked slowly out of the station.

When I got in I still felt cold & sick, partly perhaps because I had had hardly anything to eat, but I did not want anything more. I picked up the paper & glanced at the casualties; I was thankful there were only a few instead of the very many there have been these last few days. Then I was so cold that I went into the morning-room & crouched beside the fire, with my eyes burning by that time with a few difficult tears. I stayed there scarcely moving for an hour, wrapped in a spiritual anguish like nothing I have ever known before. On every side there seemed to be despair & no way out. Still as I was, there was all the feeling in my heart which makes people wring their hands & beat their brows in agony; every thought brought nothing but darkness & pain. I felt I could not bear it, & wished I had never been born to suffer as human beings must suffer when they love. I ached for a cold heart & a passionless indifference. I felt I would give all I possessed in the world if I could see his face again just for one little minute – only that I need not feel I had seen him for the last time before he enters that Valley of the Shadow of Death. Then again I felt that I could not bear to be with him again or hear his voice, that I could not endure another goodbye, that if I were offered the opportunity of seeing him once more I should refuse. I tried not to think because I writhed in mental pain whenever I did think; I tried to imagine a future in which he had no part, & could only visualise a blank despair.

I was so tired with going to bed so late & getting up so early that I lay down on a chair & through sheer mental weariness went half asleep for some minutes. When I woke up again I somehow felt different. Hope springs anew in the human heart – I suppose because physical existence would be impossible without it. I began to feel that after all he might come through, that he might be wounded – not too badly – & come back not having to fight any more. I even began to dream as I often have done before I knew he was going – those dreams of the future in which he & I are together in some intellectual & spiritual unity undimmed by the dark wings of the Angel of Death, 'when the war-drum throbs no longer, & the battle flag is furled'. I felt a weak & cowardly person after all to shrink from my share in the Universal Sorrow. After all it was only right that I should have to suffer too, that I had no longer an impersonal indifference to set me apart from the thousands of breaking hearts in England to-day. In this dawn of brighter feelings I was able to fetch my Shelley & read *Adonais*, which with *The Story of an African Farm* plays the part of a Bible with me. And when I went to bed, I prayed, as I had promised, that God might bring him back.

Saturday March 20th
There was another terrible long list – 40 officer casualties added to the already large number which have resulted from the awful battle, the dearly-bought victory, of Neuve Chapelle last Thursday & Friday week. The fettered Press kept the world in the dark about it, & it is only through the long casualty lists that we are beginning to realise what it must have been. There are rumours that our losses there amount to 12,000 – & the Germans' to about 20,000. Our dear ones are going out in time to be in the thick of it all.

I also heard to-day that the 6th Sherwood Foresters went out about three weeks ago – which means that Mr Goodman, Mr Heathcote, Mr Saxby & the two Johnsons are all at the front or near it. This information, this ever-present reminder that 'the air is full of farewells to the dying. And mournings for the dead', brought back partially the feeling of despair about Roland. But I shook it nearly off again, determining to work hard & plan out my joys so that each moment is filled up. Hard manual labour would be easier; truly my sort of work is difficult now, when so much of intellectual life seems at a standstill and the war cry drowns the purer voices of the upper air. But that intellectual life & none other is the work for which I was made, & I must not shirk it & forget how urgently it is always needed, just because the fact that the intellectual and spiritual life reigns supreme above the strife of nations is for the time being unrecognised & unremembered. It is for such as I to uphold & invigorate that life. I will even permit myself the comfort of the thought that maybe I am preparing myself thereby to be a fitter companion for *him* one day – since whether or no there be any difference between our intellectual capacities, he at any rate has much more knowledge than I.

Sunday March 21st
I am slowly trying to readjust my point of view to things as they are for me now, and to make myself realise that things I valued before are still none the less valuable now because yet greater things, sorrow & love and hope, have entered my existence. It is strange how different Roland's impending departure makes everything appear. Nor do I think they will ever look quite the same again. Never before have I had any real trouble, though I have often imagined one. I wanted anything to wake up life from stagnation, anything to change the order of things, but I never imagined that it would be like this.

I had such a sweet letter from him to-day – written as soon as he got to Maldon, on the night of the day he said goodbye to me. 'I *am* coming back, dear. Let it always be "when" & not "if". The day will come when we shall live our roseate poem through – as we have dreamt it.' I was afraid he might after all not let me know what he wanted for his birthday, but he says he wants a self-filling fountain pen which I am glad to know of. It seems a somewhat appropriate gift for one would-be scribbler to give another. He actually ends his letter with 'much love' which he has never done before. I answered it in certainly no colder a strain. I let him set the note of our correspondence always & am quite ready to echo it if it is a deep one. I suppose he is right – & the only thing, which is the hardest thing, is to work & wait – certainly to hope, which one must do or die. So to-morrow I will take up my neglected Plato again. I fear there has been some danger of me, who always preached to others about courage & self-reliance, going under a little in the sadness of farewell. But if he can face death, let me show that I can face the fear of death, and work steadfastly with a tormented mind, as thousands of my countrywomen are brave enough to do.

Monday March 22nd
When I arrived down this morning I found a registered envelope on my plate, addressed in Roland's writing. I quietly moved it to my knee at the time and opened it when I was by myself. It contained a brooch – just the kind I like best & should have expected him to choose. It was made of one large amethyst – my favourite stone – set in gold & surrounded by tiny pearls. I like them best because they are full of depth and light and a soft purple intensity so that they almost seem to have a soul. The stone from its white case winked in the light – I looked at it till tears came into my eyes. With it he had enclosed a card with his name on it, & written on the back 'In Memoriam. March 18th 1915.' Both the words & the colour of the stone were symbolic of mourning – & yet, like a good omen, the amethyst was full of light. I held it up in front of the fire for a moment & the red glow reflected in it made it look like a great drop of blood.

I bought him his fountain pen this morning – I only wished it could have been something better, but I suppose anything not merely useful would be little to the purpose in the place where *he* is going. Then I started to write him what will probably be the final letter before he leaves England. I told him I could not bid him Godspeed on any but a note of hope. I wonder how much there is of resignation about his attitude – him whom I must leave now to Time & whatever is God. I trusted, I told him, that from the ruins of nations a brighter future might dawn even for such as him & me, when the shadows have fallen away. I said I would not, could not, say goodbye – since I believed that 'through much tribulation we come into the Kingdom'. I sent him all that was most precious

to me too – the best of love & hope – and so – until we meet
again – bade him 'au revoir'.

I tried to work to-day, & with some success, realising that if I
could not feel interested in my work I must do it without feeling
interested. Such is the only form of courage I can practise.

Our housemaid is very troubled about her young man who is
at the front in the 1st Sherwood Foresters. She has not heard
anything of him for three weeks, & to-day a parcel she sent him
was returned – without however any intimation of his death.
They may of course merely have lost sight of him for the time
being but it does look rather bad; if anything like that happened
to me with regard to Roland I don't know what I should do. At
least my own trouble makes me feel more acutely for these other
poor people who are anxious too. It only means more personal
sorrow of course but I do not regret it – I think it must be better
so. I should never spiritually progress if everything always went
right for me & I never had to suffer, never had to work out my
own soul's redemption 'with suffering & through time'.

News of casualties continues to pour in – still the results of
Neuve Chapelle & St Eloi. The lists seem to grow longer every
day; it feels impossible to believe that anyone who goes out there
can ever return. And yet I suppose one must do the hard thing –
not give way to despair & try to hope for the best.

Tuesday March 23rd
At last after six months' siege the great Austrian fortress of
Przemysl has fallen to the Russians. (It is a good thing it has, as
now people need not try to pronounce & spell it any more.) This
is a great victory for the Allies & ought to advance the Russian
cause tremendously. There are also rumours of Italy joining in
before very long – perhaps if we get through the Dardanelles she
will. At all events goods traffic has been stopped between
Germany and Italy, and all Germans have been ordered out of
Italy.

Wednesday March 24th
After tea a sort of restlessness came over me which urged me to
go into Corbar Woods & stand by the tree beneath which
Roland & I sat nearly a year ago, & where first we began to feel

that interest in each other which has led to so much. As I stood there, the place was hallowed by the memory of his presence, so that even the bareness of the tree-trunks & the greyness of the distance which showed between them could not prevent my soul from making itself felt in a vague aspiring, and an intense spiritual consciousness of love & vital inner life striving for self-expression. I felt again keenly the desire to be able to stand alone – the longing for a fuller realisation of my spiritual being & for the perfecting of the intellectual instrument through which it expresses and reveals itself. So strongly, as I gazed at the lonely hills behind me & the faint gleam of red sunset sky in the greyness above, did I feel the element of Unity in me & in that upon which I was looking that I knelt on the damp ground beneath the tree and prayed to that omnipotent Being that Roland might return. Then I walked slowly away, intending on April 20th to revisit the place.

Thursday March 25th
I made my head ache thinking out spiritual & intellectual problems all day. There is light – but so much darkness is all round that only a very little of the path is illuminated. I longed passionately for intercourse with the only mind that has ever been in harmony with my mind, with the only spirit that has ever walked with mine – Roland's. I thought all day about him too, wondering if he has really departed & England holds him no more. To-night, even while dreaming all the time of his departure, I fetched down *The Story of an African Farm* – that book which he & I both love so well & accept in equal measure its philosophy – & read it feverishly, that my desolate soul, striving to know & find itself & to be self-reliant, might not be quite alone.

Friday March 26th
More thinking – more wrestling with ideas, till my mind whirls with the force of the thoughts that crowd upon it. Olive Schreiner says somewhere that with a certain order of minds loss & sorrow induce them to search feverishly into the deep things of life. I think mine must be of that order, for ever since Roland departed & the first real trouble I have known dawned

upon me, I have done nothing but think & think & think, often sitting motionless & seeing nothing beneath the oppression of my struggling thought. To-day I worked out the problem of suffering & the soul. 'Redemption . . . is worked out by the soul itself with suffering.' For when the soul – the Perfect – grows, the Imperfect through which it expresses itself suffers & is rent with the anguish of its limitation, and when the Imperfect suffers the soul grows. For suffering is the most elemental thing in the world, having the elementality of our imperfection. And when the individual suffers, then only is he alone. Then all the veneer of everyday life in which others have been able to share drops away & he stands face to face with his own naked self. He strives to find means to comfort himself, seeks for help from without – but help is only obtainable from within, for he is alone now, quite alone. Then in that darkness he must either sink beneath his burden or rise above it. Only the soul, the Eternal Element diffused through all his being, is of avail; he must help himself by means of it alone. It is his soul that makes him strong, on his own soul's strength he must rely – for it is God, that Universal Unity which pervades all things & of which he is a part – which both contains him & is contained in him.

I envy people who nurse now – surely truth is to be found in such experience, even as it is embodied in all elemental things. I would like the stern labour for love's sake, for surely the soul grows thereby. I wish in the summer vacation I could somehow combine nursing & college work. I think I shall try if the war is not over.

I met Mrs Goodman in the town; Colonel Goodman & his regiment were reserve troops at the Battle of Neuve Chapelle but were not needed. Out there he says they prefer these sharp engagements where the struggle is fierce but soon over, to those long & slow ones where a small advance takes months. They seem more terrible to us because we get the casualties all at once instead of their being spread gradually over a long time – but the result is the same in the end, and has the advantage of being quicker. Colonel Goodman says that some of the men out there say the war will be over in June, & that the Generals, though they do not quite think that, have every hope that it will be over before very long.

Saturday March 27th

Edward came this evening by the late train; I went alone to meet him. Roland sent the telegram saying when he would arrive, thereby informing us that Roland was still in England & Edward had been to see him. Edward told us that after spending last night with another lieutenant, Thurlow, near town, he shopped all this morning & then went down to Maldon to see Roland. It must be trying work to wait in suspense; I am sure Roland's imaginative temperament will find it so.

Sunday March 28th

Edward & I went for a long walk in the afternoon. I talked first about the war & the way our souls grow by it, then about Roland. Roland was wrong in thinking that Edward did not approve of him; Edward feels an affection & admiration for him which he has never realised. He says Roland is a person one can be quite sure of, and trust absolutely. He was glad of what had arisen between Roland & me – partly for its own sake – partly because it would assist him in keeping Roland's friendship. He said he always had foreseen we might care for one another ever since we first met & had been so interested in one another – in fact he had hoped it might happen.

I had a letter from Roland this morning – written on Friday evening. He thinks they may go to-night – or rather Monday morning about 2.0 – in small boats of about 200 men each, under cover of darkness. They go to Southampton during the day & are kept more or less in hiding. They are landed at Le Havre, though he is not supposed to tell me that, & from there go into the fighting line. He has to censor the letters of his own platoon, & his are censored by his company commander & then all the lot by headquarters. So his letters will probably only be scrappy. Mine will not be tampered with. He has written to his mother asking her to let me know what happens to him & begs me to write too. He says he has just had a letter from her largely about me. I would give a good deal to see the contents of that letter, but at least it leads him to tell me that I can be as frank as I like with her – she will understand.

Monday March 29th

I cannot describe the impression left to-day or why I feel the conflicting torture of hours of thought has found relief in a conclusion – one embracing but a small amount of truth but I hope that truth will grow.

All that man *must* have is that compelling force – the soul's impulse of growth, which is called enthusiasm, aspiration, idealism. When one is weak, to look at life now, & see the shadow of death on all sides – death to those one loves, death to one's hopes founded on those loved ones, and to the dreams founded on those hopes – to be able to see no future, to have nothing sure in one's grasp by which a future could be built up in the mind – to be obliged to live on from day to day – in all this the soul's impulse of growth may become clouded & even fade – if one is weak. But if one is strong – if one looks deep into one's soul & finds there God, the Eternal Life – and leans on that, the most Essential of one's self – then it seems that the best future one can build for one's self either in times of sorrow or of joy is one founded not on events & circumstances, but on the growth of the soul itself. That impulse of growth which is due to the Eternal Spirit in the soul expresses itself in the soul's search for the Truth in itself, by the finding of which the soul grows. And the soul, inasmuch as it has grown great & expresses the Eternal Life within it, can by being & expressing itself help others – not by giving them something ready-made but by helping them to help themselves, to search for themselves, to accept only Truth & to stand alone, able to find in themselves the utmost source of Power – the Infinite, God. For me at present that search lies in Books – so large a part of the field of experience. In the Accumulated Knowledge of the centuries – of all Times, Peoples, Places, must be my seeking Without, wherein lies also the Seeking Within. But every other branch of experience that comes to me I must embrace. So, searching for Truth *with* Truth, that vast complex Being I call my soul will grow, & be strong, supreme over circumstance & suffering & Time & Age & Death – & by it the whole Universe shall rise.

I wonder if I have really learnt something, by these thoughts which the great new element in my life has stirred in me. If I have learnt anything it is love of Roland Leighton that has taught it to me. Strange – what it may be, this sexual love, of which – in its highest forms – the physical element is only the external sign of that which runs through soul & spirit too – part of the Everlasting Truth itself. I must learn to love more & more – I can never love enough.

Tuesday March 30th
Chiefly spent with Plato. He & Socrates & Logic seem to have given me my present impulse towards definition of everything. The *Apology* is one of the grandest things I have ever read – the final expression of a life which had triumphed over time.

Wednesday March 31st
I went for a long bicycle ride this morning all alone. I had done no work but was seized with the wandering spirit. I rode down Ashwood Dale as far as Topley Pike, & then round King Sterndale, where I paused for a moment or two inside the quaint little church on the top of the hill. As I rode I went on thinking, thinking, about the soul and suffering & power, & about both the absolutism & yet negativeness of Evil – then about the transmuting power of Good, that all true victory meant not annihilation but transmutation of the conquered. Among my other thoughts one stood out very clear – that there was only one person I would rather be with in such a mood & on such a morning than be solitary as I was – and he I may never more have again to be with me. It was such a morning as he would have loved. The shadows were very blue lying across the clear river bed, and the sound of the waters in the valley vibrated with all the living harmony of spring.

At 4.0 I had a short letter from Roland. They have received their final orders now, & left Maldon at 6.30. They may either wait in the docks a day or two or cross over to France to-night. He says he cannot realise that he may be in a trench in a very few hours, & gives me as a parting injunction 'Think of me to-morrow night – & after.' Need he have told me!

I went to St John's Church to-night to hear Stainer's *Crucifixion* given by the choir. I did not much notice whether they did it well or badly, for the music took my thoughts far away into Uppingham Chapel. I could almost hear that multi-

tude of boys singing their Founder's Hymn 'O Merciful &
Holy', which always gave me a queer choked feeling as if I
wanted to cry. Then I thought of last summer when on the
Sunday morning we sat almost alone after chapel was over,
listening to the organ recital, & Roland came down from the
choir-stalls & sat beside me. I thought of the stern Headmaster
standing in the chancel – of his last speech to his boys before the
War, undreamed of then but impending – 'If a man is of no use
to his country, he is better dead.' I saw again the stone
memorials on the chapel walls, commemorating those who *had*
been of use to their country, & had fallen in South Africa or
other less noted fields, and thought how many more I should see
if ever I enter that Chapel again. I wonder where they will
inscribe Roland's name, if . . . Think of him to-night & after! –
Yes, & forever more!

Thursday April 1st
Just after breakfast a telegram arrived for me. It simply said 'Just
on point of crossing. Roland.' It was just like Roland to remember to send the telegram he promised in spite of the hurry &
confusion and responsibilities he must have been involved in.
What a strain that journey must have been for him with that
imagination of his – to remain motionless there in the darkness
& silence, alone with his thoughts, knowing what he was leaving,
picturing the Unknown he has to face. So he has really gone. I
cannot lull my fears to sleep any longer with the hope that he
may be in safety after all – his path now will be from one danger
to another, with the Shadow of Death beside him every hour.

Friday April 2nd
When Daddy opened *The Times* to-day he said 'I wonder what
we would give for a glance at *The Times* of April 2nd 1916.' I
don't think I would look at it even if I had the chance. But I
wonder what next April 2nd *will* bring. I wonder if my hopes
will be approaching some glorious fulfilment, or still be in their
present state of anxious uncertainty, or be lying crushed &
broken, buried with the dead in the fields of France. Perhaps
even now Roland is in the trenches – perhaps under fire. All day
long, although somehow or other I got through a good deal of

Plato, I have dreamed, both about what will happen if he lives, & what will happen if he dies.

Saturday April 3rd
Mother went to decorate at Burbage to-day & was annoyed by Mrs Whitehead on account of me. She mentioned how Leslie Duncan & Hilda Cox were going to France nursing & then said she wondered Vera hadn't taken up work of that kind; so many people had given up what they were doing etc. As there has been no great call for nurses – voluntary & half-trained I mean – her remark is hardly true. The need is still present, & will be greater after the war, of highly-trained people to do important intellectual work – teaching, writing, secretarial or Government work. In a year or two many of those who were capable of undertaking it will be dead – others will require fresh training to revive the knowledge of it in their minds – some will not come back to it, others who are in the midst of training for it will have to complete their training. Where will the supply exist to satisfy the demand except largely among those women whose training is in the process during the War? But it *is* hard to realise this; I often feel I would rather do anything else. I suppose I cannot expect Mrs Whitehead to realise it, especially as ever since I talked of going to college she has thought of plenty of things which I ought to do instead. The only reason why this remark should impress me is simply because it bears upon what have been my own thoughts. Just lately there has been an appeal in the papers to women who are willing to work – clerical, armament or agricultural – & thus can set free a man to fight, to register either at the Head Labour Exchange or local ones. This set me wondering, as college work does not take up nearly all my time, since I can generally keep ahead of other people with doing half the amount of work they do. The Long Vac. consists of 3 months. Four hours a day is the most I need do. Could I not do war work *also* during those 3 months?

I had a letter from Mrs Leighton to-day, expressive of her strong personality entirely. One suffers so much less, she says, by doing than just by waiting. She ends by saying that she was very very glad to get my letter. When I had read hers I felt that I could kneel down before that loftiness of soul – before the strong unconquerable spirit which her son well-nigh worships & to which he owes so much of his own. Mighty sister mind! What wouldn't I give to be with her, talk with her, know her still better!

Sunday April 4th
Easter Sunday. I woke feeling sad & unrested, but with the words so clearly stamped upon my mind that almost someone might have just spoken them close beside me, 'And the Echoes of Despair slunk away, for the laugh of a brave, strong heart is as a death-blow to them.' So I arose & went to the Early Service, resolving I would not despair, though to-day has been one of the days when I have felt he can never return. The worst of it is that the more I feel that, the more I picture to myself all that might happen if only he did return.

After church we spoke to Miss Hyland, & I offered to do some work for the Hospital as college things did not take up all my time. I said I was willing to scrub floors or anything else, but she said there was no necessity for that if I could darn, as other people could do floors who could only cobble stockings. She said she would give me some work. I was very glad, especially as I can do some now, without waiting till the Long Vacation. The more I have to do the better I shall be able to endure life, especially if I am able to do work directly useful in the War.

Tuesday April 6th Byfleet
I went to Byfleet by the 9.50 to stay with Cora. She seemed very anxious to hear all about Roland, and as there are so few people to whom I can speak about him, I was quite glad to talk to her. At night she came to sleep in my room & we remained awake talking about the horrors of war, & the problems of truth raised by them. Even after we ceased I spent a weary wakeful night, thinking of all the terrible things Roland may have to suffer & all the horrors he will be bound to see.

Friday April 9th
I got a short letter from Mother this morning enclosing one of Roland's, the first from France. He says it is all as yet unrealisable as they seem far enough from death & horror &

fighting; nothing proclaims the presence of war except bursts of flame & smoke on the horizon at night, occasional patrols of soldiers passing, & the distant booming of heavy artillery guns.

Cora & I discussed sex questions – I propounding my theory, which dawned upon me when first I knew I loved, that sex attraction has a threefold nature of spirit, mind & body just like our whole being, & that we ought not to despise the physical attraction, so long as it is the symbol of a spiritual union also, just because we have it in common with all creation. Rather, because it is elemental & fundamental, we should reverence it as one of the laws of God. This of course is Olive Schreiner's theory but I did not realise it till just lately.

Saturday April 10th Buxton
I left Byfleet this morning in spite of urgent invitations on Cora's part to spend all next week at her flat, where she will be alone. I told her to look out for Roland's name on the casualty lists, because I have a strange feeling he will be wounded, & soon. Once in London I went off for the first time on my own account. I realise that, unless I first do things without asking permission & then say I have already done them once when I want to be allowed to do them again, I shall never be permitted to do anything.

When I arrived in I found a typed letter from Somerville, containing information about our 'emergency migration'. 'In response to an urgent appeal, the Council of Somerville College has agreed to allow the War Office the use of the College as a military hospital for the duration of the War.' Through 'the generosity of the Provost & Fellows of Oriel College' we are to have the use of their buildings in the St Mary Hall Quadrangle of Oriel College.

Sunday April 11th
I told [Roland] about the possibility of my nursing, & that if he *must* get wounded he might postpone it till August, by which time I might be efficient enough to help in looking after him. That is one dream of mine – that he should come home wounded not too seriously, & that I should have had a little

practice in nursing first, & be able to look after him & thoroughly spoil him.

Monday April 12th
Janet Adie came to tea to help me learn to typewrite. She is feeling very busy because she now has the secretaryship of one of those soup-kitchen affairs on her shoulders. It does not sound a very strenuous occupation; these people who never had anything to do before don't know the meaning of work. They are actually trying to get up what they call a women's volunteer corps in Buxton – which seems to consist in marching about & drilling, with what object they do not know. I was told I ought to join this & that & the other. Everyone seems to be *so* keen for me to give up one kind of work for another, & that less useful, but more understandable by them. The general idea seems to be that college is a kind of pleasant occupation which leads to nothing – least of all anything that might be useful when the results of war will cause even graver economic problems than the war itself. If only I can get some work at the Hospital in the summer. I wonder what they will say when they see me doing the nursing which seems to exhaust them all so utterly, & my college work as well! I always come out top in the end, & I always shall.

Tuesday April 13th
Still Roland's letter has not arrived. A thousand times more than work, it is this anxiety & suspense that wears one out, & God knows how long it is to last, or how soon it may not end for individuals in an anguish far more terrible than the longest period of uncertainty. Miss Hughes was quite wrong when she said at college that the anxiety of those at home became less acute when their people had been out a fortnight. For me this short period has brought not a cessation of anxiety but an increase. Even when letters come, it only informs one of the state of affairs about four days ago, & the writer since then has undergone infinite perils & had time to die many times. I dare not think too vividly of him just now. I don't think even when he was here for the last time I realised how much I love him as I have realised it since he went to France. The chief joy I have

now is to write to him; I feel I am writing to someone who is my very own, who will understand me as I understand myself, but whose comprehension is worth more than mine because it brings to what it reads the element of another personality, so like & yet different. If he dies I shall sign on as a Red Cross Nurse for a year, say I am twenty-three & do real hard dirty work. No object then in finishing my college course as soon as possible. When there was no joy to follow it I should be indifferent as to whether it ended sooner or later . . .

Certainly, little as I owe to heredity, I do inherit the melancholy pessimistic strain in the Brittain family – the strain that makes Daddy worry everybody else about Edward, who is not yet out, & me wear out my own soul about Roland, who at least *is* out. What would *he* think if he saw how weak & incapable of endurance I am! It must somehow be overcome – by very love itself – shall!

Wednesday April 14th
After a morning of utter boredom with Latin I went to the Devonshire Hospital with Mother to do mending. Miss Hyland was away, but I saw the assistant matron, Miss Jones. She seemed to think I could practically be assured of a nursing place there in the Long Vac. so I shall make up my mind to that. She is a very small & cheerful person between 30 & 35, not at all bustling or aggressive & disposed to be kind & encouraging. One other quite insignificant person was there darning, who seemed to think that to work hard all the term & then give up one's vacation to nursing was quite noble. Women so underrate their own sex's power to work. If only I could do more & yet more. There were simply piles of socks this afternoon, & there was certainly no mistaking the holes; never in my life have I darned anything so large. People who know me best would have been amused to see me seated in the vaccine room surrounded by wools of diverse colours, & working at socks as though they were my sole object in life.

Still I have heard nothing from Roland. Unless the worst happens to him I suppose this sort of wearing suspense will occur over & over again. Morning creeps on into afternoon, & afternoon passes into evening, while I go from one occupation to another in apparent unconcern – but all the time this quaking anxiety beneath it all – 'Lord, how long?' He went just a fortnight ago to-night. He must have been in the trenches – even under fire – by now. Waiting is terrible to those whose chief task is to wait. Centuries ago – before the war started, I was always wishing my heart could be moved & aroused, which seemed to me hard & cold, difficult to touch. I little thought its awakening would cost me so dear!

Thursday April 15th
The longed-for letter has arrived at last. It is extremely interesting & describes almost everything he has done since landing in France. He wrote at night in the kitchen of a French farmhouse, where he was billeted with three other officers. They had their meals there & slept on straw on the floor. The house is about 3 miles south of B—, wherever that is – about 5 miles from the nearest point of the firing line. They were out of range of the guns but could hear the reports of heavy artillery & see the sky lighted up at night with flares from the German trenches. They were warned to look out for German snipers but had not come across any then. They expected to be moved on in about four days & then go into the trenches.

His letter filled me with a queer exultation & yet anxiety & dread. If only I could share those experiences with him I should glory in them; as it is, the thought of all those guns he heard fills me with apprehension. Now, even now, he may be under their fire.

The repairs to my teeth were not very serious, so I discussed the war with Mr Elmitt. He sympathised with Edward's contempt for the officers in K.'s army & said Edward seemed to him highly intellectual. He also said E. might never get out at all as he was convinced the War would end by the autumn. We also discussed Neuve Chapelle. The dispatches about it were published to-day. That awful disaster was no *victory*! It was the result of a terrible blunder. The object was to get into Lille; there was nothing to stop them & the cavalry were ready, only the infantry did not join them because – they were being fired upon by our *own* guns. Either the mistake was not discovered till too late or it was impossible to get a message through. But we were responsible for over 4,000 of our own casualties. It is too terrible – this reckless waste of life, the only thing worth having in the universe. Naturally this horrible truth does not come out in the dispatch – it would undoubtedly stop recruiting if men thought they were to enlist only to be shot down by their own guns. Roland is dreadfully near Lille.

Friday April 16th
I mended at the Hospital again this afternoon. I talked to Mother about Roland too, instead of going straight to work after dinner. I like talking about him sometimes, & I may as well take the chance of doing so now – in case he is killed. I don't think I could talk about him if he were dead – except perhaps to his mother.

Saturday April 17th
I received two letters from Roland this morning – consequently I did nothing much but think of him & them all day. They were both interesting – oh! terribly interesting. He says he has not yet been afraid – although he has now been under fire. I can understand that well enough. He is afraid of his imagination, afraid of being afraid – so am I. That is why he in the midst of the actual dangers fears & dreads nothing, while I far away from all sign of active warfare read of the perils he is undergoing, & shudder & tremble.

The first letter, which was the shorter, was written, as I discovered by our dot-code, from Armentières, a fairly large town on the borders of France & Belgium, not very far from Lille. I shall describe his letter fully, as nothing I have ever heard or read has given me so definite an impression of the real meaning of war. From Armentières he wrote last Sunday morning that he was now actually in the firing line & was to take his platoon in the trenches at 7.0 that evening. The trenches run right into the town & he could hear the rifle-fire as he lay in bed. The Germans had been shelling the town two days before, but he saw nothing of it except one shrapnel that burst on their right as they marched in. The walls showed signs of former bombardment & were riddled with bullet-holes. (It has of course been the scene of a great deal of fighting ever since the war began.) He & another subaltern were billeted in a small house on the outskirts of the town facing a square called the Place République. It seems incongruous, he says, to find good shops & buildings & beds half an hour's walk from the trenches. They are to go in to-night & stay till Tuesday night – 48 hours – after which they will be relieved. An inexperienced regiment does not hold part of the line on its own at first, but is initiated by more experienced people into the mysteries of dug-outs, listening posts etc. 'It is a beautiful sunny day to-day,' he says, 'and it seems a pity there should be such a thing as war. Summer & trenches don't go together somehow.' A very characteristic remark. Sometimes I have feared that even if he gets through, what he has experienced out there may change his ideas & tastes utterly. But I don't think I need be afraid – not as long as he can write things like that, anyway. His essential characteristics & aspirations are too deeply rooted for even war to take them away.

The second letter was written on Monday April 12th – from the trenches. It is written in pencil, & there are very slight stains of mud on both the paper & envelope. He was sitting on the edge of his bunk in the dug-out which he was sharing with another officer. Firing was quiet as he wrote, but a German sniper was having chance shots at a traverse a few yards to the right of them. Some of the bullets skimmed over their roof, but these dug-outs are well covered with sandbags so that the danger inside is greatly minimised. The British artillery had been shelling a disused brewery behind the German lines all morning. The shells come straight over the trenches, & he describes them as a dull boom from the gun's mouth, a scream as they pass overhead & a crash when they burst. Of course you cannot put your head for a second over the parapet of the trench or you would get potted at once. But peering round the corner or through a periscope he watched the brewery. The smoke of the shells is mostly green from lyddite, but sometimes black, from howitzers, sometimes also tinged with red from falling brickwork. The regiment had just been ordered by telephone to keep under cover & so Roland was in the dug-out, which is a hut built into the rear part of the trench, about 7 ft. square & 5 ft. high, containing bunks for sleeping, shelves, a table & two chairs. For some unknown reason it was called 'Le Château Germaine', & had a weathercock of wood & tin, fixed there by the bravado of a former occupant.

He continued at 4 p.m. on the same day. The guns had been at it again & the Germans in return shelling our communication trenches. The continual noise gave him a headache. I don't wonder! The artillery fire had stopped as he wrote but he says 'some damned German keeps on sniping at the top of a small wooden post' a few feet to the left of the hut with 'a persistence worthy of a better object'. He evidently mistook it for a periscope. Stray bullets are always flying about their heads, but no one minds them, he says. They can look over the parapet at night as even with flares it is too dark for the Germans to aim, & they are fairly safe by day if they keep their heads down. Of course the chief danger is getting in & out of the trenches. At that point the Germans have the advantage of several buildings to snipe them from, although most of the moving is done at dark. Snipers seem to be their chief trial.

There is not much to do in the trenches, but officers have to go round every now & then to see that the men & sentries are in their places. They go round at night too, so don't get much sleep. They are not allowed to take their clothes off, & have to scrape as much mud as possible off their boots with a bayonet, tie up each foot in a sack so as to keep the mud out of their sleeping bags, & get in boots & all. They seldom have time to wash or shave properly. How I should like to see Roland in an unshaved & more or less unwashed condition. I should scarcely know him; it is hardly possible to think of him so. 'I am learning a great deal here,' he says. If only he gets through, how valuable this experience will be to him whatever he does – if he writes, especially so. He will learn & see so much more than the unobservant majority.

The whole place is like a small town honeycombed with passages & dug-outs (nicknamed 'bug-hutches') with most amusing names like 'Ludgate Hill', 'The Bridge of Size & Tiers', 'The Junior Carlton' etc. The British have held the line where they are since the beginning of Nov., when they turned the Germans out. A little further down along the trench were three graves, marked only with a piece of board on which was scrawled 'German grave. RIP'. Roland, 80 yards from the enemy & in danger of death from their bullets, at the sight of their graves is inspired by no bitterer thought than that 'Somebody once loved the man lying there'. On their way to the trenches they passed about thirty graves by the roadside – all of men of one regiment killed in these trenches. He tells me that he has received my second letter, & that this one to me will have been carried under fire by the time it reaches me.

All these accounts of danger I can stand – with an aching apprehensive heart it is true, but all the time I feel I would rather know. But my courage gave way a little when he ended 'Do not worry on my account. Goodnight & much love. I have just been kissing your photograph.' My eyes filled with most stinging tears, although I bit my lip to try & keep them back. Sometimes I think it is less the thought of his danger than the ardent desire for his presence which makes me so sorrowful, & when he writes such things as this – & he has never admitted so much before – I want him terribly badly, & the thought of what it may be if he returns, but is so likely never to be, is almost more than I can bear. At such moments I feel as if I were shut in a trap from which there is no escape, & that I am vainly beating my hands against the walls – a kind of fierce desperation, which renders me incapable of doing anything but feeling acutely conscious of inward suffering. Well, I asked for the big things of life & now I am up against them. As I said to Roland in a letter I wrote to him immediately I had read his, I think any number of weary apprehensive nights & days are not too high a price to pay for the happenings which had led to my being able to feel the anxiety I do.

I never thought I should ever say to anyone such things as I write to Roland. I suppose the nearness of death breaks down the reserves & conventions, which are seen to matter so little in the light of elemental things. Certainly I have never been so conscious of my love for Roland as I have to-day. I don't know if it is that I have really grown to caring more & more every day of the last month, or if I am only realising now how much I loved him when I said goodbye a month ago. One is often a little stunned at first by the sharpness of such an ordeal as that. Either way, the result is much the same; it means that my need of him, of seeing & hearing & talking to him, is so great that the longing for his presence drives me nearly desperate; I can scarcely keep it in check, much less face the thought that I may have to do without it for ever more. Thinking about that makes me feel utterly heart-sick & almost physically faint. Oh! my endurance is weak, & my courage fails! Now, as I write, my head aches & my eyes are tired with the tears I shed on his account – tears of weakness, which I should conquer, & have, until to-day. But when just a few words at the end of such a letter tell me how much he cares himself – it is even more unbearable than feeling how much *I* do. It is this separation that is so hard, so bitter. I should not fear the danger for him if I could share it – much less for myself.

There have been several Zeppelin raids all over the country. At Lowestoft the backs of some houses in the town were blown in, & one or two horses & dogs killed.

Sunday April 18th
To-day I finished Turgenev's *On the Eve* – one of the books Roland gave me for my 21st birthday. In the part I read to-day came the love scenes between Elena & Dmitri Insarov. They made me think of Roland & me – not what we have ever risen to in one another's presence, but what I believe we are both capable of rising to. All the rest of the day I felt wild with desire for him. Why despise physical longings & necessities just because they are physical? While we are in this world we are governed by physical laws, which are no less a part of the Deity than the spiritual & mental laws which can only express themselves here through the physical & with it form one great unity. The physical desire is after all but the outward & visible sign of the inward & spiritual necessity. So I admit, it is not enough to know that I am one with him in mind & spirit; I want his physical presence, I need to feel him near me & be able to touch him before this pain at my heart will cease to torment & drive me desperate.

Monday April 19th
To-day being Primrose Day, primroses were sold all over the country for the Red Cross. A girl named Miss Froude accom-

panied me in selling round the Park. We made about £1 between us. It was somewhat tiring work but quite amusing. People always treat you, when you go round collecting on behalf of something, as if you were begging for yourself.

I had another violent fit of desperation this morning. I suppose I must get used to them, but they alarm me a little & make me wonder what I may do if Roland dies. At present my one desire in life is to see him again. I think of how little there is of any tendency for the war to end, of how he is in the trenches day in & day out in momently danger, of the long long weary months ahead, & wonder how I shall ever bear them & get through them without any light, anything to look forward to, to carry me along. O glorious time of youth indeed! This is the part of my life when I ought to be living every moment to the full, tasting the sweetness of every joy, full of love & life & aspiration & hope, exulting in my own existence. Instead, I can only think how weary are the heavy hours, wonder how I can get through their aching suspense, wonder when they will end – & how. Ah! those who are old & think this war so terrible do not know what it means to us who are young. They at least have had their joy, have it now to think of & look back on; for us the chief part of our lives, the part which makes all the rest worth while, has either never dawned, or else we have for a moment seen what is possible only to have it snatched from our eyes.

Tuesday April 20th
I had another letter from him to-day – written on April 14th. He had then just returned from the trenches. All his men came back safe, but two of the other regiment's men had been wounded by a rifle grenade, & one of their subalterns had been shot through the wrist – nothing very serious, Roland says, but he will have to go home for a time. How I wish it had been Roland; it sounds horrible to say it, but that is such a satisfactory sort of wound to receive compared with some. I can't help the feeling that he is going to get wounded & soon. Every ring at the door startles me lest it may be a telegram. I only hope he may not be wounded while I am at Oxford, but in the vacation when I can be with him a little. He says he was quite sorry to leave the trenches, as it is all so interesting at first, though he can quite believe the

sameness gets boring after a time. On the Monday night, he &
two sergeants went out in front of their trenches to inspect a sap-
trench that the British had been pushing out towards the
Germans. From about 60 yards they could hear them calling
to each other, & he was struck with the very youthful sound of
their voices. They got in again alright, though the Germans sent
up a flare right over their heads as they were climbing over the
parapet. How I shudder to think about it!

I went to the place in Corbar Woods where he & I sat &
talked the whole morning last April 20th, just a year ago to-day.
Then, there were leaves on the trees, the sun beat down through
the branches, & we sat on the dry ground talking about his
mother, his future & Edward. To-day everything was grey &
damp; scarcely a sign of spring had yet appeared. Above my
head the tree-tops tossed & moaned; water dripped from the
leafless boughs with a dismal sound. There was a blight on the
place, which was covered with the dead leaves of last year. I
stood there thinking & thinking, wondering how I was going to
bear it all – the long weary days of suspense. Suddenly, thinking
of Lyndall's desperate prayers – sometimes I feel I *am* her – I
knelt on the wet ground, overcome by a fierce appeal for
Roland's safety to – I don't quite know what.

Vague rumours are circling round of a British victory. As
Neuve Chapelle seems to be a good example of our 'victories',
there is scarcely cause for exultation. But we are said to have
taken a hill near Ypres which is important from a strategic point
of view.

I don't want to go back at all. Everything has changed so
much since I was at college six weeks ago. On reading parts of
my diary from the beginning of the year just now it struck me as
curious how very little I said about Roland during last term,
though he was in my mind so much. I think I loved him then,
but it was nothing to what I do now. The development of my
feelings towards him has been rapid & quite carried me away; it
is almost terrible. When one loves deeply, it is almost impossible
to remember what the time was like before one did. Yet I must
go on trying to work – thinking that he may never read the letter
I have so loved writing to him, or that the one I have received
from him may be the last. I wrote him a long one to-day telling

him much the same things as I have been writing just now. How I love writing to him!

Wednesday April 21st
Sometimes I can hardly believe I am I. I feel as if I were writing a novel about someone else, & not myself at all, so mighty are the things happening just now. If, that summer just after I came out & things seemed as though they would always be stagnant & dull, someone had said to me 'Before three years are over you will not only have fallen deeply in love with someone, but that very person will be fighting on the battlefields of France in the greatest war ever known to man. And your anguish of anxiety on his account will be greater than anything you have dreamed possible,' I should not have believed it could really ever happen. To-night – not only when I heard from Roland but before – I have been full of a queer excitement – almost exultation. There has been no apparent reason for it, so I very much wonder why.

Apparently the hill we have taken near Ypres is a real advantage to us, but our losses are reported to be heavy. That means terrible long casualty lists within the next few days.

Thursday April 22nd
Mrs Harrison called this afternoon; she was as attractive as ever but looks older & more lined since the baby came. We talked chiefly about Oxford & the war. She said she supposed I should find a little time for tennis even if I was nursing, & reminded me with amusement how we had all pressed her to play so eagerly last year, & she had had to make up excuses.

Friday April 23rd
Chiefly occupied with packing & mending. There were more females than usual to-day; Mother, Mrs Whitehead & Miss Adie got together, and after discussing various people they knew who were nursing, they talked at length of cooks, & then entered on a long & deep conversation on the subject of combinations & pyjamas. I felt as if I were looking on at some amateur theatricals, & did not join in, but silently increased my knowledge of pants & vests & men's clothes in general. Finally Sister Jones came in & told us all about some very bad cases of

wounded from Neuve Chapelle she had seen in a hospital in the south of England. After that the ladies seemed to try & outdo each other in telling stories of war-horrors. I don't think they could have known or loved anyone in the trenches. They made me feel absolutely cold, & I saw in imagination the shattered bodies of those poor wounded men. But it was better than talking about cooks; at least it brought us nearer to those realities which are the things that count most just at present & *must* be faced – by women as well as men. As we left the Hospital we spoke a few words to a wounded private – a little elderly man who had been at Neuve Chapelle. I was very much impressed by his appearance. He did not look unnerved or even painfully ill – but very, very sad.

I wrote to Roland this evening, also sent him *Punch* & the *Times Weekly*. I wonder greatly about the battle at Ypres. The paper said this morning that the fight for Hill 60 is turning into a second battle of Ypres, with a front along a ridge of 15 miles. I wonder which way the 15 miles extends. Roland is only about 10 or 12 miles from Ypres.

I go back to Oxford to-morrow. Strange how the irony of fate so arranges circumstances that when it was most irksome to be here I had to, & now I should prefer to remain here I am obliged to go away. I love Oxford, but I hate Somerville. This term I mean to keep more or less aloof & work hard. It will perhaps be easier to keep this resolve now that we are all divided. If I feel lonely I can bear it; the thought that if he dies I must carry on his work with mine, & if he lives I shall share it, will bear me up.

Saturday April 24th Oxford
I returned here to-day, with Mother, who came for the weekend on her way to London. I would have given anything not to have had to come back; if it had not been for P. Mods, I would have started nursing at once. On the way Mother told me that when Daddy was at Folkestone Edward had spoken to him on the subject of Roland. Edward said to him 'What is your opinion of Roland?' & when Daddy replied that he didn't know him enough to say, but what money did he propose to have as anyone who married Vera would have to keep her (as if they will have to!), Edward said Daddy need not worry about that as

Roland's intellect would always enable him to look after himself & other people, & that he was of a most honourable nature & there was no one he would rather see Vera married to. Such is Edward's influence upon Daddy that he has been quite different about Roland ever since. That is well – & yet what is the use of it all! I dare not think even thus far of the possibility of his coming back, lest the blow should fall & I be unready & unable to face it.

There is terribly depressing news to-day; we still hold Hill 60, but north of Ypres the Germans have started to make another violent effort to reach Calais; they have broken another rule of the Hague Convention & have used bombs made of asphyxiating gas; they have also fought with a courage & fury never surpassed in the war. The French & British have been obliged to fall back just where their lines join. This evening's paper said that the Canadians had won back the four guns we lost, & that the lost ground had been regained, but that may be only the optimism of our censored & deluded press.

When I arrived here of course I found everything utterly changed, but somehow nothing surprised or excited me. I went through it as through something in a dream. I am at Micklem Hall – usually men's chambers – with six other people. The society is not exactly enlivening, but there is an advantage in being under Miss Darbishire; I am glad of the opportunity of getting to know my tutor. The house is down a little side street. It is very old & somewhat dingy-looking; my room has oak-beams, a floor that goes up & down, & dark corners & dingy draperies suggestive of spiders, blackbeetles & suchlike abominations. The house however has a garden & shady trees, which will be a great advantage in the summer; none of the other people either at Oriel or in rooms have a garden. Of course I went over to Oriel to see E.F. & Schen; there is an extreme glamour & beauty about it, but I saw clearly that even that will soon be pervaded by a feminine atmosphere. I was glad of my exclusion in spite of the society; E.F. & Schen will not desert me, & the prevailing dullness is better to my sore & anxious spirit than a crowd of ostentatiously cheerful young females. It is not the things that happen in Oxford that count now but those that happen in Flanders.

This morning before I started I received a very short letter from Roland. He was in the trenches in a wood just over the Belgian border & had been under heavy shell fire for about 2½ hours. He was then quite safe, & nothing much of damage had been done by the shells. I shiver to think of it; it is terrible. I wish I could be enduring with him, instead of waiting in suspense in 'soft' surroundings. If only this term will go quickly! – because I suffer myself, I long to alleviate, even indirectly, the sufferings of others.

Sunday April 25th
I urged Mother to do all she could about my nursing, either at the Hospital in Buxton or elsewhere. In her rooms I read Roland's letter. He was writing on a warm summer day, with primroses on the grass beside him & a bee humming round them, almost as though war did not exist. He was in the support trenches (which are the 2nd row) in a thick wood of tall thin trees, held by the British since November. It is a maze of small paths, huts & breastworks. His own dug-out is about 180 to 200 yards behind the fire trenches. Half his platoon is in the fire & half in the support trenches so he spends his time in between the two. He has his meals in the support trench, which is under cover but not free from exposure to fire; two of their men were hit by snipers as far back as the third line. A bullet whistled past his head as he was shaving. Yesterday they had their first man killed – shot through the head. The part of the line they are holding is very well known & too strong to be retaken by the Germans. His regiment may remain there two months.

Every four days they are relieved by the 8th Worcesters & go back to billets some miles away. They went out last Wednesday evening. He says 'It is very nice sitting here now. At [times] I can quite forget danger & war & death, & think only of the beauty of life, & love – and you.' But there are grim contrasts there. Yesterday morning, going through to the fire trench through the sunlit wood, he found the body of a dead British soldier hidden in the undergrowth a few yards from the path. He must have been shot there during the wood-fighting in the early part of the War. The body had sunk down into the marshy ground so that only the tops of the boots stuck up above the soil.

His cap & equipment beside him were half-buried & rotting away. Roland ordered a mound of earth to be thrown over him, to make one grave more among the many in the wood. He writes 'You do not mind my telling you these gruesome things, do you? You asked me to tell you everything. It is of such things that my new life is made.'

He finished the letter next day. They were going out of the trenches that evening, April 21st. He says he will be glad of the rest, as the four days had been very tiring. He was up nearly all the night before, mending the barbed-wire entanglements in front of the trenches. 'There is nothing glorious in trench warfare,' he says. 'It is all a waiting & a waiting & a taking of petty advantages – & those who can wait longest win. And it is all for nothing – for an empty name, for an ideal perhaps – after all.' I wonder if he really thinks that, & if he would agree with my non-militarism now. I am not sure that I agree with myself in all I said to him.

When he wrote, he had just received the letter I wrote after he told me he had been kissing my photograph. He ends up by saying 'When all is finished & I am with her again, the original shall not envy the photograph. The barrier which She seems to have found was not of reserve but rather of reverence. But may it not be better that such sweet sacrilege should be an anticipation rather than a memory?'

Ah! he speaks of anticipation as though confident of a future for us. I wonder whether now he still earnestly believes he will come back. I asked him this afternoon if he did. I wrote a long letter between lunch & tea, telling him of my desire to nurse, of my wish that he should tell me of the horrors he sees because 'women are no longer the sheltered darlings of men's playtime, fit only for the nursery or the drawing-room', certainly no woman *he* was interested in would ever be just that. I also said that I was not implying a reproach when I spoke of the barrier between us – that none could realise better than I the true value of reverence & reserve – but that what he called sacrilege was in its right time rather the culminating point of reverence & reserve, & that my letter expressed a passionate regret, not that we might have acted differently, but that everything had to cease (I pray temporarily –) in the middle with the culminating point still unreached.

The battle in the North of Belgium still rages; the Allies have fallen back 1½ miles, & the Germans in their second desperate rush on Calais seem to be having it all their own way. The fumes from their asphyxiating bombs are felt nearly 2 miles away. It is all terribly serious & said to be the most important conflict of the War so far. I was made rather anxious because the paper says that as long as the Germans hold Menin they can pour as many troops as they like between Ypres & Armentières & thus extend the battle-front.

We had prayers at Oriel to-night & afterwards Miss Penrose spoke to us very finely of the relinquishment of Somerville as our opportunity of helping in this dreadful war, & said she knew we would none of us grudge any discomfort in such a cause. There had been criticism passed upon the action of Somerville & Oriel. Therefore it was the part of every individual member of Somerville to try to avoid conspicuousness & to exercise self-restraint. She said she had no doubt that both past & future Somervillians would envy the present students their share in this picturesque & historic episode in the College's career. We all felt very moved & lifted up by her speech, & capable of putting up with anything. Of course it was splendid of Oriel, & what is more it shows immense progress in the way in which women students are regarded.

Monday April 26th
E.F. & I went for a walk this afternoon round Port Meadow; we talked chiefly of the War & women's changed attitude towards it; also of the change it had made in College, which is decidedly for the better; there is something much more elevated & less petty about it. I had a letter from Cora to-day, asking if I fully realised what probationer work at a Hospital meant. Of course I know; I shall hate it, but I will be all the more ready to do it on that account. *He* has to face far worse things than any sight or act I could come across; he can bear it – & so can I.

Tuesday April 27th
When I went to Oriel to look for letters this morning I found one from Daddy. As his are usually unexciting I opened it without misgiving. There I found written quite casually 'Maurice E.

shot himself in the head, end of last week. He was still alive last
Sat. but it is serious; he did it in the train between London &
Reading, so I am told.'

Poor, poor Maurice! Somehow I feared that this would one
day happen, & now I keep on wondering if I could not have
done more to help him. What a world of misery must have been
there! Suicide is so obviously the last resort of the utterly
desperate; sorrowful as I often am now, I yet cannot realise
such utter depths of despair. I wish I were [in Buxton] to defend
him with all my might. One does not love people only because
they are good, & Maurice is still my friend whatever he has
done. Edward's & my days of sheltered & protected ease are
over, & the time of sorrows is upon us. Victor's illness –
Roland's departure – Maurice's self-sought death – all our
friends seem to be drifting away from Edward & me, leaving
us alone together. Even he will go & I shall be quite solitary. I
wish I could nurse at once, & try by hard physical labour to
come through these troubles with strength. This evening I
looked up at Christ Church tower against the dark blue sky, &
somehow it seemed to speak of the soul's power of rising to
heaven strong & free, transcendent over all the things of earth.

Wednesday April 28th
I don't know how I am going to stand these rooms as to-night I
saw a blackbeetle scuttling across the floor. I can stand everything else but these fill me with a quite unendurable physical
repulsion. It is really the last straw – the final thing which might
almost break my already-strained nerves – oh! I wish I hadn't
any nerves, sometimes almost wish I had physical courage &
stolidness, instead of intellect, as the two seem incompatible.

Thursday April 29th
Maurice is still alive and has intervals of complete consciousness, in which he suffers terrible pain. In one of them he asked
after me so his mother begs me to write him a short note. He is at
a nursing home in Reading. Of course the news is all over
Buxton; it was in the paper last Thursday – it is strange none of
us saw it.

Mother has got my nursing at the Devonshire definitely fixed up for me. I shall have to [wear a] uniform – grey print, apron, & cap.

Friday April 30th

A letter from Roland came at last. It was sent in the new kind of green envelope, the contents of which have not to be censored as the writer swears on the outside that there is nothing inside but 'private & family matters'. He wrote last Sunday & had just been four days in billets. He took great delight in getting a hot bath in the vats of a disused factory. One night they went to a concert given by amateurs at a Red Cross Hospital. It was only a sort of sea-side pierrette performance, but a refreshingly English interlude, he says, all the same. He finished the letter in the trenches, sitting outside his dug-out, like Waldo in his shirt-sleeves – only Waldo hadn't picked up two pieces of shrapnel a few yards away. But Waldo was thinking of Lyndall, – who would have gone to our corner of the wood just as I did. He enclosed some violets, which he had just picked from the roof of his dug-out.

Saturday May 1st

I was up at 3.45 this morning for the famous Oxford May Morning ceremony. Magdalen Bridge was quickly crowded with townspeople, women students, the remaining under-graduates, & bicycles, while the river below was covered with punts & sculling boats. When the clock struck five everyone became suddenly silent, and then, just as the sun was rising, the Magdalen choir from the top of Magdalen tower sang the May Morning hymn. As they sang the sun gradually rose higher & threw a golden glow over the slender grey tower. The voices of the singers sounded very pure & sweet in the clear morning air. I had a choked feeling in my throat; I was thinking how Roland & Edward had meant to be here & how they would have loved it.

I had words with the Lorie at my class with her as she insisted that I worked in a slack & careless way because I happened to have forgotten the derivation of just one word. This was so obviously unjust that I assumed as haughty an air as was consonant with politeness & said I was not in the habit of taking words out of the crib. Then she tried to propitiate me. Next I went to Miss Darbishire's lecture on Milton at the Ashmolean; I thought she seemed a little nervous but did not know till afterwards that this was the first University lecture she had given & that she is only the second woman to give lectures for the University.

Sunday May 2nd
After breakfast E.F. & I walked to a field a short distance from Oxford, where we sat under a bush & read Milton. The grey spires & towers, dreamy in the Sunday calm, rose out of masses of trees clothed in their first spring freshness. It was an hour in which it was easy to understand all the adoration paid to the old city by her worshippers. Marjorie, E.F. & I went to evensong at the Cathedral, followed by an organ-recital. I sat listening to the glorious music with my eyes closed in a kind of dreamy sadness. To think of war! – with these grey walls slumbering peacefully in the afternoon sunshine, & the light through the stained-glass windows glowing purple & red on the ancient stone. O my beloved! He was meant to be here, in this city of beauty & intellect & ideals, not to be exposed thus all too soon in his brilliant life to the Death & Horror that stalks abroad.

Monday May 3rd
I had another letter from Roland this morning. They have now moved from their wood to some more conventional trenches about 1½ miles further south, to take the place of a Regular Brigade which has been sent to Hill 60. He was writing at 4.0 in the morning, just after dawn, as he was the officer in charge from about 3.30 till 8.0. Behind him the sun was shining on a field of clover & in the distance was a glimpse of white road. There were no violets & primroses there, but ordinary boarded trenches, with sandbag parapets & yellow clay. They go to sleep mostly at intervals during the day, as they do not get much rest at night. He continued after going his rounds. He had just been watching a French aeroplane circling over the German lines. A Maxim Gun & two anti-aircraft guns were trying to hit him. Every minute there was a muffled report like the drawing of a cork magnified & a fluffy ball of cotton-wool suddenly appeared

in the air beside him. 'You think how pretty it is – white bird, white puffs of smoke, & the brilliant blue of the sky. It is hard to realise that there is danger up there, & daring, & the calculated courage that is [true] heroism.' He says he is taking as much care of himself as he can & does not put his head above the parapet. Only the day before a man in the regiment they relieved got killed through doing that. 'It was his own fault, though, poor devil.'

Tuesday May 4th

I went to the cooking class in the afternoon; a most queer mixture was there – the Lorie in a very voluminous overall, Miss Farnell, a Miss Sidgwick, Miss Underhill from the Bodleian & myself. They all knew even less about it than I. We boiled some mutton, & prepared the potatoes, carrots, onions & parsley sauce. The Lorie remarked that potatoes were difficult to peel, they had so many facets! She also weighed her butter wrong, & she stirred her parsley sauce with such vigour that we got most of it. I liked the woman very much who was teaching; she made us do things instead of doing it all herself.

We had an amusing Chaucer class after tea. Miss Moore remarked 'People do such different things in dreams from what they do when awake.' Miss Darbishire replied 'Yes – fortunately.' When we got in Marjorie & I had a long talk about nursing; she says she admires me immensely for the way I go about things & for my intellect, but I feel all the time how short I am of deserving admiration when I don't know what I am going to do. She says I am different this term. I may well be – I feel centuries older.

Wednesday May 5th

I went to see Maurice at Reading to-day. A nurse took me up to Maurice's room, which was quite small & furnished in the usual bare style. It looked out on a green park opposite, but the blinds were drawn down as the sun hurt his eyes. Maurice was lying in bed, not looking ill at all, but his left eye was very bloodshot. There was just a little mark at the side of his head where the bullet had gone in. I felt very nervous at first but soon overcame that when I found his manner just the same as usual – except perhaps less reserved. He says his head hurts him all the time but more so when he sits or stands up.

I heard at last all about what has been called his 'nervous breakdown'. It appears that he is suffering from what is really a form of insanity – suicidal mania, which however is not inherited, & which the doctors hope he will grow out of in about a year. Maurice knows perfectly well that he has these fits; they come on him in a kind of deep depression, which at present nothing can keep off. In his normal moments he does not want to commit suicide at all & is in absolute dread of one of these fits coming on. He told me in very great confidence that it was one of these 'fits' which led to his removal from the army, & that it was his attempt at suicide then which had made him ill. Now he will have a man with him always until he is cured of this tendency – probably about a year. The man who is to be his attendant was in the room all the time I was with Maurice. He did not trouble us much & I quite forgot he was there, but it suddenly struck me how strange must be a profession in which you have to be always with a person; not as a companion, but utterly subordinating your personality to theirs.

Maurice remembers all important things & is quite ready to talk about people & the war. Rather to my surprise he remembered Roland, so I told him that R. had gone out to the front. He was very interested to hear that, & we discussed Roland for some time. Of course Maurice has no idea that it matters to me whether Roland is at the front or not. It was strange to talk about him quite impersonally & to call him 'Leighton'. Maurice told me all about his life with the doctor he lives with & likes. He spends most of his time working at law. He has also done a good deal of writing, & has had stories & a poem accepted by an agent. He asked me why I had not done any writing lately. I said I had done a little. But in my heart I said 'Life's too real just now.' In fact all my creativeness at present goes into this diary & into my letters to Roland. But naturally I said nothing to M. to bring him again into contact with the sadness & pain of the world just now.

I found a train at 4.25 back to Oxford. I left Maurice promising to write to him & expressing as many hopes for the future as I could manage. He seemed really pleased to have seen me. One view I saw out of the train window as I was coming back was so beautiful it almost hurt me. It was more like a scene from France in spring. Tall thin poplar trees stood up dark green against a background of low hills of a deep misty blue. In the foreground were fields of the freshest green, & thick luxurious bushes of pink & white may. Overhead the sky was calm & untroubled except for little fluffy masses of soft white cloud. The whole landscape seemed to shimmer in the afternoon sunlight. Life will always be worth living when such as this remains. Nature somehow seems to speak to us more clearly when we are sad than when there are earthly pleasures & contentments to occupy our minds.

Still Roland's letter promised for the day after the last one has not come. Sometimes I feel I must make up my mind absolutely to a future without joy, & that what I dread, whether it comes soon or late, must come at last. If only I could see him once again – that is all I ask at present. It is hard to know things have progressed so since our last meeting & that yet we may never meet again to have the joy of seeing that it is so. I don't think if we met now that either of us would hesitate through shyness or diffidence to say 'I love you'. It is the thought that we may never say these words to one another that makes my heart ache more & more.

The news too is bad to-day. The casualty lists are terrible – over 200 officers. German official communications are pitched in a highly triumphant key. College, pleasant – all too pleasant – as it is, will be intolerable after this term until the war ends. I am even contemplating provisional notice in case I want to go down for a year & nurse. I had some hopes of joining in the French or Belgian repatriation schemes, but Marjorie, who went to the meeting this afternoon, tells me they will have no workers under 24. So the French Red Cross remains my only hope; & perhaps I shall turn out too young for that & have to stay at the Devonshire Hospital, which will at least be better than college trivialities – or rather they are not trivialities, but I estimate the sort of work I am doing here so highly that I want to be able to give it more than a quarter of my attention as I am doing now. This kind of thing is of course my real work, & I am under no illusion as to my nursing being anything but temporary, but I do want & feel I ought to do it for the present. There are so many things one can do in the war if only one is old enough, but I seem to be too young for most. How intensely & terribly full & complicated life is at present. Roland – Maurice – Edward – college – nursing – to say nothing of such trifles as Pass Mods – why, any one of them would have been considered by me enough to fill my life, a year ago.

Friday May 7th
This has been about the worst day since the beginning of the war – at least it seems to me that it has; horror piled on horror, until one feels that the world can scarcely go on any longer. First you open *The Times* & see that the Russians are in retreat, the Germans owing to their use of poisonous gas have got Hill 60 back from the British, that the line at Ypres has had to be readjusted owing to an 'enforced retirement'. Then you open a letter from the person you love best in the world at the front. You find he has been hastily rushed off to support trenches where he is within sound of the guns at Ypres, that he has been under shell fire, & that it is a 'nerve-racking job'. And every line somehow informs you that even on so keen an intellect & so strong a will the strain is beginning to tell – as it must, more & more – either shattered nerves or death, must it be? And last thing at night you see by the stop press edition that the *Lusitania*, carrying over 1,000 passengers & crew, has been sunk by a torpedo, & that there is no word with regard to survivors. I felt so overcome by the horror that I could do no work or anything but think about it. 'Always darkest before dawn' – how much darker is it to get than this? Does it mean that the black anguish of further personal loss must be added to all this before the dawn comes – & will the dawn ever come?

Roland's letter opened quite hopefully; he was then in a farmhouse for five days' rest. It was started on May Day. As he came back across the fields in the starlight a little poem of W. E. Henley's came into his head. I shall love & cherish this poem now as long as I live.

Goodnight, sweet friend, goodnight!
Till life & all take flight
Never goodbye.

He says my letter made him very sad, both for Maurice's sake & mine. He begs me to go & see Maurice if I can. Some people would not have been generous enough to say that. It is good to be loved by someone who is far too sure to feel the slightest suspicion, & intuitive enough to give me credit for being as wholly his, & as trustworthy, as I am. He also says 'What this refuse heap of a country will be like when it gets really hot is beyond my imagination.'

The letter did not continue till May 3rd. On the 2nd – when I was dreaming about him beneath the stained-glass windows of the Cathedral – they were suddenly rushed off to occupy a line of support trenches, where they had to stay till 3.30 the next morning. They had to hold them again until the next evening – which meant sitting in the rain with nothing to do. There, in the support trenches, they could listen to the undulating roar of a distant bombardment from the direction of Ypres, 'not with equanimity, but with a certain tremulous gratitude that it is no nearer. Someone is getting hell, but it isn't you – yet.' That last sentence rang in my head all day, & is still not to be got out. Something dark is gradually coming to him & to me – God grant it may not be death. Rather suffering – suspense, anything. And in each striking of the clock, each shutting of a door, each letter I receive, especially in such sentences as that, I feel it coming nearer, nearer . . .

On the morning of May 2nd he took a digging party of fifty men to the other side of their wood to deepen a support trench on the slope of a hill. The buildings near, though out of range of rifle fire, had suffered badly from shells, & most were mere ruins. Just after he had returned to the trench a German howitzer battery caught sight of them & sent over 38 '3.5' shells, which dropped within 30 or 40 yards of them, fortunately killing no one. When the shell hits the ground it makes a circular depression like a pudding basin about 1½ yds across by 18 inches deep, burying itself at the bottom. 'Luckily you can always hear this sort coming, & we had time to crouch down in

Vera Brittain at the front window of Melrose, Buxton, about 1913

Mr and Mrs Brittain outside Melrose, Buxton, about 1913

Vera Brittain in Buxton

Vera Brittain as a V.A.D. Nurse

(*left*) Roland Leighton: the portrait he sent to Vera Brittain in December 1914

(*below*) Ploegsteert Wood: a photograph taken by Roland Leighton

(*right*) Vera Brittain: the portrait she sent to Roland Leighton in December 1914

(*below*) The Three Musketeers – Edward Brittain, Roland Leighton and Victor Richardson: the enlargement from a photograph taken at Uppingham School O.T.C. Camp in July 1914

Geoffrey Thurlow

Edward Brittain

Vera Brittain (third from left) with fellow nurses below St. George's Hospital, Malta, about 1917

(*right*) Vera Brittain
outside Nurses'
Quarters,
St. George's Hospital,
Malta, about 1916

(*below*) Vera Brittain
with some of her
patients at
St. George's Hospital,
Malta, in 1916

MALTA . 1916

Friday March 19th.

Whatever the future may bring — whether it be
the sorrow I fear more than anything on
earth, or the joy which now I scarce dare dream
of, much less name — as long as I have
memory & thought, I shall not forget to-day &
yesterday — My beloved one has been here and
departed again, & now indeed I may see his
dear face never any more. I cannot write
about it much; it is not only useless but
impossible to try to record in words anything
I felt so poignantly &shall always remember
so vividly. When I first came back here after
saying good-bye to him — or rather, it was
"Au Revoir" that I said; because my courage
would not even contemplate a last farewell,
though I tried — I simply could not take up
my pen & write; I felt paralysed. Now
he has gone I can scarcely bear to think
of him, & yet I cannot think of anything
else. For the time being all people, all ideas
all interests have set, and sunk below the

A page from Vera Brittain's diary

the bottom of the trench, which is the safest place in these circumstances . . . The explosion blows a cloud of earth & splinters of shell into the air, so that when they fire a salvo (all four guns together) the effect is rather terrifying & you wonder if the next one will come a yard or two nearer & burst right in the trench on top of you. I do not mind rifle fire so much, but to be under heavy shell fire is a most nerve-racking job.'

I answered his letter at once. I had work to do, but none of that seemed to matter, so I wrote till 12.0. I told him a little how his letter made me feel, & how I always wrote with the fear that that into which I put so much of myself might never be read by him for whom it was meant; then I described my visit to Maurice. I also mentioned my ideas about the French Red Cross. I ended by saying how I had thought of him in the dark garden under the stars, & how I had longed for him, & do long – if only I could see him but once again, I might face the future more courageously. Somewhere Lyndall says that there is an hour which 'blots out wisdom, & is sweet with the sweetness of life, & bitter with the bitterness of death, but it is worth having lived a whole life for that hour'.

I was put into the first couple of the Somerville tennis six to-day. It seemed easy to get into the team, because I did not care. I practised tennis this afternoon, but it made me feel very tired; all the time the words sounded in my mind 'Someone is getting hell, but it isn't you – yet.'

At night I was so tired & full of despair I didn't know what to do. I tried to find a little comfort from Wordsworth, & almost the first thing I opened him at was

> Surprised by joy, impatient as the wind,
> I turned to share the rapture – ah! with whom
> But thee, deep buried in the silent tomb . . .

Saturday May 8th
The loss of the *Lusitania* is confirmed, & the whole affair is worse than we thought. There were over 2,000 passengers on board, 1,500 of whom are lost. It is not yet certain how long the ship was afloat after being torpedoed but it cannot have been long, as she carried more than enough boats to save all on board.

The Lorie saw I was somewhat distressed about the war, & was very kind; she says she doesn't think the military authorities feel as badly as we do about the Allies' apparent defeat; because they know Germany is putting forth all her reserves as they expected, & has no more, while we have not sent ours yet. She also has a brother in Kitchener's Army, she told me; it was quite a tremendous confidence from her.

I had a letter from Mother agreeing with me that provisional notice was a good idea, but they don't seem to take to the suggestion of my going to France!

Sunday May 9th

I had a short letter from Mrs Leighton this morning. I felt quite sick when I saw it because I suddenly thought that if he were killed or wounded she might have written instead of telegraphing. She said very little but the Leighton family have a habit of writing so that one can read between the lines, & she is obviously in a very great state about him. 'I suppose one cannot expect much in the way of letters now he is in the thick of the actual fighting, as I am sure he is. Only – I hate the thought of that poisonous gas.'

Monday May 10th

I went to the Pen somewhat in fear & trembling soon after breakfast & opened the subject of provisional notice. She was very kind and sympathetic & asked me at once if it was for Red Cross work. I said it was; that it was really very unlikely that I should have to go down & I certainly didn't want to have to, but I rather felt I ought to. She said that was of course a question everyone had to decide for themselves, & that decision was very difficult for everyone just now. She quite understood all the reasons for my indecision. But I need do nothing till the middle of July, & a great deal may have happened by then – oh! so much!

When we got in & had to work, I said most emphatically on the stairs that I hated Chaucer. The Darb overheard me & came out saying she was very sorry! Marjorie & I laughed over it afterwards. I wonder why I laugh when I feel so sad.

There has been a large air-raid on Southend & Westcliff;

several injured, one killed & great damage done. It gets nearer & nearer London. Great indignation with America over her indecisiveness is gradually growing.

It is time for another letter from Roland. I have been suffering to-day from one of my frantic desires to see him & speak to him again. Oh! for 'the hour which blots out wisdom, sweet with the sweetness of life & bitter with the bitterness of death'.

Tuesday May 11th
Edward is now at Maidstone & when he eventually goes it will probably be to the Dardanelles. Oh! I wish it might not be; it seems to make things ever so much worse. Somehow I feel all these depressing things are leading up to something big; something which is coming soon – soon. I cannot work or do anything but wait in a kind of suspense which expects It to come any moment.

Wednesday May 12th
A letter came from Roland this morning. He is terribly busy & has no time for more than a few lines. He had no sleep at all the previous night & had been making wire 'cradles' for entanglements & cutting loopholes in his parapet all morning. He tells me I should be very amused if I could see 'the dirty-looking figure that is writing you this. I am largely caked in yellowish mud & have a promising young beard that has gone unshaved for four days.' There had been a lot of firing from Hill 60 direction again that morning.

At 12.0 Marjorie & I went out to buy cakes as we were having the Lorie to tea. [The Lorie] was very interested indeed about my nursing – became quite moral in fact. She said she thought I was quite right, & that I could not see a hospital needing people & not go, even if I did have to go down for a year or take an extra one. She was also *quite* sympathetic when I mentioned that my brother was going soon to the Dardanelles, & that I had a great friend in Flanders. I had no idea she would get so thrilled as she seemed about the nursing. She seemed to put it quite on the level of a man's deed by agreeing with me that I ought not to put the speedy starting of my career forward as an excuse, any more than a man should against enlisting.

We were quite quiet over dinner, but afterwards had cake in Marjorie's room & tried on each other's hats quite uproariously. When they had all gone & we were meditating putting away the things, a knock came at the door & Miss Darbishire's voice said 'Have you got a fire in there?' – it was a cold night. We said we hadn't, wondering what she wanted & if we had been disturbing her. Then she said 'Won't you come & enjoy mine for a little.' This was an immense privilege. We both went into her sitting-room; Marjorie sat on the floor in front of the fire & I in a large armchair. There we talked to her for some time, & she became quite confidential over interviews with scholarship candidates, especially when I reminded her how I had 'put my foot in it' with regard to Blake's Prophetic Books. As I sat there looking at her fair hair burnished by the firelight, & her calm & gracious expression, I was reminded of Miss Barton's description 'The Golden Goddess'. Then she read us, at my request, five sonnets by Rupert Brooke, the most promising poet of the younger generation, who enlisted in the Navy when the war broke out & died at Lemnos a week or two ago – to the great loss & mourning of all modern writers & literature. The sonnets were all sad & moving, in spite of their spirit of courage & hope, & through them all ran a strangely prophetic note, a premonition of early death. I should not have asked her to read them if I had known, they were so sad that I could scarcely keep back tears from my eyes. I believe she noticed something was up, too. She gave me the impression all the time that she wanted to speak seriously & couldn't come to the point. After the sonnets she showed us her facsimiles of Milton's manuscripts, & then we retired to bed – I sorrowful & heavy-laden with the thoughts of Roland & Rupert Brooke's sonnets mingled in my mind.

Thursday May 13th

Another letter from Roland came this morning. It was a very sad letter. One of his men had just been killed – the first. He was shot through the temple while firing over the parapet. 'I did not actually see it, thank Heaven,' he says. 'I only found him lying very still at the bottom of the trench with a tiny stream of red trickling down his cheek on to his coat.' Roland had just taken the things out of his pockets & tied them round in his handkerchief to send back somewhere 'to someone who will see more than a torn letter, & a pencil, & a knife, & a piece of shell'. He goes on 'He had just been carried away. I cannot help thinking how ridiculous it is that so small a thing should make such a change. He could have walked down the trench himself an hour ago. I was talking to him only a few minutes before . . . It is cruel of me to tell you this. Why should you have the horrors of war brought any nearer to you? And you have more time to think of them than I. At least, try not to remember: as I do.' The letter stops there & goes on some hours later. 'A glorious summer day, which helps one to forget many things.' All through those letters of his I can see so plainly the artist & the soldier alternating – the innate artist always rising to the surface through the necessary but less personal military veneer.

The day he wrote they had been instructed to give a demonstration of 'frightfulness' – i.e. to make themselves as generally objectionable as possible. (Heaven knows if this is a prelude to their taking the offensive, from which so few return.) They had begun at 4.30 a.m. by exploding 1,000 lbs of guncotton under a German trench, & were continuing with the help of machine guns, rifle grenades & trench mortars. They have been shelled a little by the enemy, & have been served out with goggles & respirators as a protection in case the poisonous gas is used, which he greatly hopes will not happen.

I hate to think of him seeing the dead man & feeling as he did. I would rather do it myself. I wonder, if ever I see him again, if he will wear the same sort of look as the little private from Neuve Chapelle that I saw at the Hospital. As if his look wasn't sad & serious enough before – as though he felt the world's griefs and responsibilities more than most people.

I had a letter from Stella. Only 3 officers are left in Jack's regiment, & 150 men out of 5,000. On the day he was wounded – May 3rd – he had had next to no sleep for 24 days & had not taken off his clothes for all that time, or had any food except biscuits & jam & water out of the ground – *that* ground. Then they were attacked & their trenches were taken; Jack had to be left behind when his men retired, & saw the Germans 15 yds away bayoneting the wounded, many of whom were his friends. He determined to make a desperate effort & crawl through an open space where everyone passing was shot at. Although he was hit once in the arm & 3 times through his cap he got through. He is now in a hospital in Park Lane, & is somewhat tried by people enquiring – poor things! – after their missing relatives. He doesn't like to talk about all his friends when he is practically certain they have been bayoneted by Germans.

Friday May 14th
News this morning reports a French victory in the taking of a village. It also says that on Sunday an unsuccessful attack was made by the British troops 20 miles south of Ypres on the Aubers Ridges near Lille, resulting in great loss of life. That is where I think Roland is. Comment is useless. I am now waiting for news in great anxiety. *The Times* leading article was very pessimistic to-day, & says we may have to give up everything in the world before our object can be achieved.

Saturday May 15th
I had quite a thrilling coaching with the Lorie. We discussed nursing a little before the class began; she became very interested in my attempts. Then we discussed the different qualities of poetry & philosophy – that philosophy supplies the intervening steps which poetry misses out. Added to this we got through a great deal of the *Apology*, which she was very pleased with, & even kept me at the end. She seemed not to want me to go! This class prepared me very well for a most magnificent lecture on Milton by Miss Darbishire. It had that quality, usually at present only found in lectures by men, of getting a very great deal into a few words & yet telling you all you want to know about a subject. I almost worship expressed & powerful intellect, especially when I find it in women, because circumstances have made so many intellectual women academic.

Sunday May 16th
After prayers we went to the Organ Recital at New College Chapel; four are being given, with a collection in aid of the Red Cross. A large crowd was there, & we had to stand in a long queue. The service was very beautiful; each organ piece was

followed by an unaccompanied Motet from the choir, who were in the antechapel. I was very much impressed by the first organ piece, which was an overture to an occasional Oratorio of Handel's. It had 3 movements: (1) Mustering of troops for battle, (2) Lament for the fallen, (3) Triumphant return of the victors. As I listened to the organ swelling forth into a final triumphant burst in the song of victory, after the solemn & mournful dirge over the dead, I thought with what mockery & irony the jubilant celebrations which will hail the coming of peace will fall upon the ears of those to whom their best will never return, upon whose sorrow victory is built, who have paid with their mourning for the others' joy. I wonder if I shall be one of those who will take a happy part in the triumph – or if I shall listen to the merriment with a heart that breaks & ears that try to keep out the mirthful sounds. I don't think I shall ever be one of the first kind; even if I do not lose directly, my heart will be too full of what others have lost to rejoice unrestrainedly.

Oh! these Sundays – I almost wish they need not come, they are so full of bitterness. Never do I think so poignantly & sorrowfully of Roland as when listening to music, & yet the music is so beautiful that when I know it is there I cannot refrain from listening. To-night as I stood in New College Quad. & watched the undergraduates both from that college & others all talking together, I was forced to visualise all that ought to have been – all that we planned so carefully with such toil, all that was so cruelly frustrated through no fault of our own. The Quad. in the twilight, the rooms with their many dark windows, the brilliantly-lighted Chapel, seemed peopled with ghosts – ghosts everywhere. With my eyes half closed I could almost believe I saw Edward, tall, healthy, good-looking, the typical undergraduate in the commoner's gown which he ought to have worn & which would have become him so well. And I imagined there too another plainer, but still dearer, face, & a strong broad figure with its scholar's gown – and dreamed how their faces would have shown pleasure at the sight of me, of our occasional unexpected meetings, & how I should have greeted them in delight. Shall I ever see them here, I wonder, in the university gowns they ought to have worn? 'So answered, nevermore!'

Monday May 17th

The news was rather better this morning, the Allies seem to have advanced about a mile & taken a few trenches, which means more than it sounds when the line they are attacking is so strong & well-defended. But the length of the casualty list is terrible – it again breaks the record – over 400 officers & 2,000 men. Of course the majority of these are wounded, still the proportion of killed is very high. At our drama lecture to-day I saw the Miss Frampton from St Hilda's whose brother has been killed.

I really am getting anxious about Roland now. No letter since Thursday, & no news of him since last Sunday, which was the first day of a week of tremendous fighting.

Tuesday May 18th

Roland's letter came this morning at last. I was relieved to see he was in billets. Most of the letter was taken up with a technical explanation of his position – his battalion is on the at-present-quiescent part of the front, between the battles of the North & South. But it is just possible that they may be sent to Ypres or some other danger-spot to take the place of one of the war-worn battalions enduring the hell of action there now. The night before he wrote he was kept awake by the firing of heavy guns – he supposed again from Ypres, but they sounded nearer. The London riots on account of the *Lusitania* made him angry. Why not all this before? he says. They are rioting now because the war has come a little nearer to them than Flanders, where men have been suffering & dying for their sake for nearly a year.

I had a pleasant class with Miss Lorimer; she told me I could take P. Mods as often as I like so this is not my only chance. But she hopes I shall get through this time, as my work, besides having frequent bad mistakes, has also frequent brilliances which she thinks will neutralise the mistakes. She says my work is promising & encouraging – and examiners are inclined to be kind to that sort of work.

I wrote to Roland, telling him about New College Chapel on Sunday. At the end of the letter I quoted four of Rupert Brooke's sonnets. He will like them I know. Somehow I think Rupert Brooke must have been rather like Roland.

Thursday May 20th
More long casualty lists. There is a political crisis now – a
national non-party government is to be formed for the duration
of the war. Racing has also been stopped for the duration of the
war. There is a lull on the Flanders front just at present. The
Russians are still retiring.

Saturday May 22nd
Roland's promised letter came this morning. He had just been
to the trenches of another regiment – Regulars – a little further
down the line. At one point these held a forward barricade 40
yds from the Germans in front of a ruined house. 'From here
they sapped out & made a mine a little time back. A few days
ago they heard the Germans mining towards them on a slightly
higher level. Two officers and two men went down their own
trench and found the Germans just breaking into a small gallery
on the right.' There, in that small space, they had a fight &
drove the Germans back, then they fired our mine, which blew
up the German one above. The explosion made a large crater in
the ground between the two lines of trenches. The next night the
Germans crept out to the hole & began firing at the British
parapet, killing the senior major. 'Another small party of 5 men
and an officer crept nearer and began throwing bombs into our
trench,' but they all fled, routed by bombs & grenades. The day
before Roland went there, an Engineer Officer and two men
went down the mine tunnel to explore before it was properly
free of gas. All three were overcome by the fumes, and a third
man went down, brought up the officer and one man, and going
down for the third was asphyxiated himself. The two brought up
recovered but the others had to be left down there; Roland
describes the recovery of the two men's bodies. 'This afternoon
when I got there they had just let a canary down in a cage to
make sure that the air was pure enough, & then with some
difficulty they brought up what looked like a long rigid mass of
clay – the remains of a man who deserved the VC if ever anyone
did. It was all rather gruesome to see – the mine & the way
they had to haul the men up with ropes – but it was intensely
interesting. In the front barricade you cannot talk above a
whisper because if the Germans hear you they send a bomb or

two or a rifle grenade on top of you. But one learns that here too in the perhaps monotonous round of trench warfare there is latent the opportunity for heroism – and in this case a heroism the more real because without glamour & even without light.'

There has been a terrible train disaster on the Great Western, near Carlisle. Three trains collided & caught fire. Of course one had to be a troop-train & most of the dead are from this. Not many details are yet forthcoming but it is the worst accident in railway history. When *will* these tribulations come to an end? At the very least 50 are killed & 300 injured – some of them with more injuries than people get at the front.

Sunday May 23rd
After prayers I went again to the New College organ recital. I have come to the conclusion that music awakens the usually dormant physical side of my emotions. When I am listening to music it is always the touch, the voice, the physical embrace of the beloved that I long for. I ache more then for the feel of his hand over mine and the glance of his eyes when I look into his, than at any other time. And I dream of my imagined children . . .

Monday May 24th
I saw in the casualty list that young Railton of Buxton was killed in action on May 9th. He got leave only a short time before I came back here & was in church with his somewhat depressed-looking family – poor things! – and a girl who I suppose was his fiancée. It is horrible when people get killed soon after having leave, as so many do.

Sometimes I want to see Roland so badly I feel I would give anything for him to have leave – at others like to-day I don't want to see him again till the war is over; I couldn't bear to.

The Whit-Monday Spirit was in the air; what with that & the depression caused by *The Times* I hated to-day. There were 316 officers in the casualty list.

Italy has formally declared war. I do pray it will hasten the end. She has about 3 million men & a good navy.

Wednesday May 26th

I may well dread to open *The Times*. To-day, both in the obituary notices and the biographies of fallen officers, I saw the name of R. P. Garrod, late scholar of Uppingham & intended scholar of Clare College, Cambridge. It was a very great shock to me. He was killed in the artillery engagement near Festubert on Saturday. He was an intelligent-looking dark-haired boy, & was killed within a week of his 20th birthday. I never actually spoke to him but he was so closely connected with Edward & Roland that I feel his loss almost as a personal one. He was second in the school, coming after Roland, and with Roland was joint editor of the school magazine. He was also very musical; I can see him now playing the 'cello at the Speech Day concert. The fact that he was more an equal of Roland's than anyone at Uppingham, that he & Roland both took prizes at Speech Day last year (their names are down together both as scholars & prizemen on the Speech Day programme which I have just been looking at) & even that both their first names are the same, all these make me realise the war even more than Roland's letters, & make me feel how near death & peril is to him.

I had a letter – such a sweet one – from the Beloved this morning. He wrote to me perched on the top of an iron roller, feeling very lazy '& rather pleased with the world, except that my pipe has gone out & I've left the matches in the house, & this seat's rather uncomfortable, & there's a war on'. He had just re-read my letter of the previous night. 'I am getting quite a pile of them now,' he says. 'You have written me sixteen since I have been out here, & the little case I keep them in won't hold more than one or two more.' He liked the Sonnets, & the nearness of two graves, a private's & a Major's, made the ones on 'The Dead' seem more real. 'I cannot help thinking of the two together & of the greater value of the one. What a pity it is that the same little piece of lead takes away as easily a brilliant life & one that is merely vegetation. The democracy of war!' He had to finish & go off to make his men practise hand grenades etc. since they were inclined to be lazy & prefer flirtation with a pretty girl in a cottage near by.

I wrote him a long letter this afternoon, enclosing the notices about Garrod and writing about him. I also talked about our present life – its agony & absence of ornamentation – its bareness of all but the few great things which are all we have to cling to now – honour & love and heroism & sacrifice.

I played some half-hearted tennis this evening. I also wrote to Mother enclosing the measurements for my nurse's dress. Mother said she noticed one or two of the Buxtonians were dumbfounded at hearing that I was going to nurse. They have evidently been criticising me rather unfavourably & are quite sorry not to be able to any more.

Thursday May 27th
The Coalition Cabinet is formed. I haven't been able to follow all through its intricacies, but those are things which will be in all the History books of the future & need no diary to record them. Lloyd George is Minister of Munitions, which everyone seems glad of.

Friday May 28th
I felt depressed all day & rather bad-tempered. Every day the estimate of the length of the war both by *The Times* & other people seems to get longer, while as it is I feel I can't stand much more of it sometimes. The Darb reproached me after breakfast for going out to dinner without asking her; I believe she was a little scared of doing it, & anyhow she reproves in rather a foolish fashion.

We gave our little concert to the patients at Somerville in the Garden this afternoon. A lot of them were sitting outside & others were in beds all round or sitting in the windows in their pyjamas. The combination of the lovely garden, the music & the wounded soldiers made me feel about as sad as I could feel. Men are so pathetic when they are weak & ill, & I think it hurts more to see them trying to hobble about than before they can walk at all. It all seemed so terribly wrong – to see these fine well-built men crippled & invalided, their strong capable bodies rendered temporarily, at least, useless, all for the sake of no one quite knows what. A little distance off three young officers were sitting in deck-chairs talking to friends. Others were strolling about the grounds in dressing-gowns. One of the three near us had a girl about my own age with him; she must have been either his sister or his fiancée, she seemed so glad to have him there. The worst of it was that, as officers & even Tommies at a distance give something of the same impression, every soldier I saw reminded me of *one*. As I stood watching them & observing their different injuries, I could imagine *him* with a wrecked & broken body struggling to walk with the help of a padded stick. And one tall thin officer in pyjamas & a long coat made me think very much of Edward. They all looked quite cheerful, especially those in the windows round. But I was thinking of all who never come back, whose crushed & broken bodies lie lifeless on the fields of Flanders, past all the loving redemption which is given to these & such as these at Somerville.

Monday May 31st
This has been a vile day – a suitable ending to a dreadful month. First of all, Miss Darbishire burst in & demanded to see me as if I were a little school-girl. She spoke to me about going to New College last night without permission – which I expected. Then she spoke to me at length about my work, seeming to think I was doing too much in the cooking line. So I asked if Miss Lorimer had complained about my work. She said 'Oh no! She was going on what she had noticed herself.' I then asked if *she* had noticed that my work was bad. She said again 'Oh no! She didn't mean that at all.' So I said 'Then well –?' She hastily assured me that it was entirely for my own sake that she was calling my attention to all this, as I seemed to have to work at unusual hours, getting up early and going to bed late. I said I liked working at odd times. After a good deal more conversation I explained that I mightn't come up next term if I wanted to stay nursing. She seemed quite distressed to hear that. Altogether I don't think she came off very well, and I departed to the amused Marjorie feeling I had really got out of it best.

I am always impressing on people that one must be self-sufficient and strong enough to stand alone, because when life is most bitter is just the time one has to. One's friends always fail when one needs them most. The only friend who understands & does not fail is now a target for the German guns. I haven't heard from him for almost a week; it isn't Roland's habit to refrain from writing for so long. This is the bitterest thing of all; it is well to keep it for the last.

Tuesday June 1st

There were rumours, increasing all day in alarm, of a Zeppelin Raid on London. Altogether 90 bombs were dropped & four people killed.

    I am longing for this term to end & let me begin nursing.

Thursday June 3rd

I had a letter from Roland this morning. He was very sorry to hear of Garrod's death. Poor Garrod – for, as Roland says, 'It is part of the irony of life that one could not find anyone less of a born soldier than he. A scholar, & a musician, & above all a peace-lover.' Roland had just written to his mother; 'but there is so little that one can say.' They were going into the trenches & were to instruct some of the Highland Brigades of Kitchener's Army in the art of trench warfare. 'We have only been out here two months but we feel quite war-worn veterans already in comparison with troops that have just come over. But even two months is a considerable time out here.' I don't know what 2 months may feel like out there, but here it feels like 2 years. I simply ached to see him to-day. It is hard always to be separated from the person you love best, harder still if you don't know definitely when you will meet again, but there is no agony in the world quite like that of knowing that there may be no meeting again. Sorrow is so different when experienced from when dreamed of. Whatever compensations there may be in it here or hereafter, these are only apparent from the distance, never when you are in it.

Sunday June 6th

A letter – such a nice one – came from Roland this morning. This is his third month out there and he wonders 'if I shall still be Somewhere in Flanders when July comes, & memories of Speech Day & all that I had hoped of Oxford'. He recalls the Sunday that we walked up & down Fairfield Gardens together & wouldn't come in out of the rain, and continues 'And I couldn't keep the tears out of my eyes afterwards when Sterndale Bennett played Karg-Elert's "Clair de Lune" in the Chapel. You were sitting at the back near the door, & I couldn't see you without looking round, I remember. It all seems so very far away now. I sometimes think I must have exchanged my life for someone else's.' He thinks it would be very nice if he could get wounded & get sent to Somerville & lie in a deck-chair & talk to me. He wonders what I will look like in a nurse's uniform – supposes it can't be very becoming to anybody – thinks it a pity to have to wear a horrid stiff collar when you have such a very nice neck to cover up in it! This & the suggestion that I must look very charming in a green overall are about the first compliments he has ever paid me. I wonder if he really thinks I am pretty. I should like to know – it would be just like him to say so the less the more he thought so.

The men of Kitchener's Army whom Roland's regiment were instructing in trench work went out again the day before he wrote. He thought them quite a fine lot of men, but having officers too old – two of the 2nd Lieuts were over 30, & were being instructed by subalterns ten years younger. 'I cannot help thinking,' he says, 'that enthusiasm is more valuable than experience in a war like this.'

After supper I went to Miss Darbishire to talk about my plans – or rather, lack of plans – for the future. She & Miss Penrose both wanted to know as definitely as possible what I meant to do. I told them as much as I know myself & promised to work all I could. Miss Darbishire was very anxious to know if I found the work a strain. She was very sympathetic & I think guesses that I have something more than just the war in general on my mind, for she told me that her sister was very ill the whole of her first year at Oxford, which made her work seem very unimportant & necessitated its being done at odd times. It amuses me that these dons, in trying to dive down into the depths of one's soul, are rather apt to reveal a little of their own at the same time.

Monday June 7th

To my great surprise & joy I got another letter from Roland. He thought he was enclosing a newspaper cutting about Ploegsteert Wood, but either he forgot or the Censor took it out. He speaks of 'the sheer delight' of standing in that wood in the early morning & listening to the waking song 'of what seemed all the birds in the world'. His company had been withdrawn into farm-houses just behind the line & he had a farm almost to himself – one still occupied, however, by the owners, who seemed indifferent to German shells. The woman was most attentive & kept on sending him up small bowls of fresh milk by his servant – 'I don't know,' he says, 'if she expects me to wash in it or what.' That morning he went to his first funeral at their little cemetery on the road to the trenches. A shell fell among a group of their signallers two days ago, killing one & wounding others. One young lance-corporal had died of his wounds that morning & they buried him hurriedly at 12.30 sewn up in his blanket, because the grave & little cluster of men round it formed a distant target for the German guns. It was all very simple – no flag-covered coffin, no firing party. The man was recommended for the D.C.M. a short time ago for laying telephone wires under fire. 'It is a pity he could not live to wear it,' Roland says. A few days ago he actually got up a concert for his company & sang duets with a French girl. He says I should be amused to see him doing this sort of thing, his last experience of which was as President of the Union at Uppingham. I doubtless should!

I worked hard all day. It is getting abominably near Pass Mods – but near my nursing too.

Tuesday June 8th

Still more to my surprise & joy I received two more communications from Roland. He described a manhunt they had early that morning, trying to find a sniper who was lying just behind their lines. He had six shots at an Artillery Officer in the morning, two at their Signalling Officer, three at Roland, & several at odd ration parties during the evening. They sent out search parties to poke around in the ditches & long grass where the rifle reports seemed to come from, but had to give it up at 2.0 a.m. as it was getting light. 'I wish we could have found him,' Roland wrote. 'It would have given me much pleasure to have caught him red-handed & shot him on the spot.' It makes me feel nearly mad to think of him shooting like that at Roland, trying to destroy not only his poor body but the happiness of at least two people in the world – his mother's & mine. I too could have inflicted almost any punishment upon him – but not death. I should have felt that perhaps he too had a mother at home who was hiding an aching heart beneath a brave face, or some girl who loved him & shuddered & felt chilled whenever a particularly loud ring came at the door-bell.

Roland said he had been looking through the letters I had written him since he went out, & doesn't think he can carry them all about with him, as apart from any question of room they are liable to get lost, for which he would never forgive himself. 'There is only one person to whom I could trust them. May I send them to you to keep for me until you can give them back to me again yourself one day & levy for such sweet guardianship what price you will?' I told him I would certainly keep the letters for him, but knowing my capacity for doing the unexpected it was rash of him to say I could exact what price I would.

Wednesday June 9th
Operations of immense importance are said to be developing on three fronts – the Italian, the Dardanelles & the French front near Arras. I only hope they will give Flanders a rest; it has had more than its share of the scourge during the last few weeks.

Thursday June 10th
I saw in *The Times* obituary notices this morning the death from wounds of Murray Drummond-Fraser. He was only 21, I always imagined him more. I have often played tennis or bridge with him, & always liked him very much. So they are all departing; fulfilling, like the Achaeans of Homer's *Iliad*, a cruel fate – 'the eloquent, the young, the beautiful & brave'. Words of grief become almost meaningless in these days, they have to be used so frequently. But one does not feel any the less. Sorrows do not grow lighter because they are many.

I had another short letter from Roland this morning. They had been shelled a good deal & had sent the men into a hollow in the field but no damage was done. He had just been to mass in a very small chapel in the village. The congregation consisted mostly of old men & women, typical stolid Flemish peasants.

There are rumours that they are going to a different line of trenches, though not out of their divisional area. 'This,' he says, 'will not mean Ypres; only a little change of scene.' Still, I am anxious. They would hardly move into a *less* dangerous place.

Saturday June 12th
Edward arrived at 5.30. We talked all evening both before dinner & afterwards, sitting in the garden until it was almost dark. We talked of course about the war, which Edward thinks may last for years almost, and about my nursing, which he approves of very much & thinks it would be quite a good thing for me to go down for a year. Of course, as he says, even if there are enough nurses in France now, or in England, there soon will not be, as in a short time our army out there will be about double what it is now. I had not thought of that before, and it makes the need all the more urgent for people to be trained ready for them. We talked a great deal about Roland & Richardson, whom Edward saw the other day. Mentally the illness seems to have left very little mark on him, all his ideas are the same about everything, and though physically he is still somewhat weak, he will be able to go back into the army shortly though probably never to the front. He like Edward has the fixed conviction that Roland will return. He says Roland is the kind of person who always gets what he wants. Edward says Victor doesn't quite like to admit it but he does not feel that Edward will come back. Edward himself seems to have a queer sort of premonition that he will fall – he says it will be part of the irony of life if he does, because he so loves peace. He says that he dreads death for purely egotistical reasons, as he feels very ambitious sometimes, but really it has not any very great terrors for him.

I sat listening to all this feeling rather chilled. Every time I see the dear lad I seem to love him better; he is growing into so much finer a person than I ever supposed he would be. He talks about Roland & he going along different paths & about Roland probably having altered very much since enduring at the front all he has had to endure – but still the rather wide gulf between them seems to me to be growing narrower rather than wider. It is curious how his feelings about himself, & Victor's, correspond to my own sorrowful predictions. In fact to-night, sitting beneath the trees in the gathering twilight, the feeling was so strong as to be almost a conviction that once Edward gets out he will never come back. I showed him some of Roland's letters & read him Rupert Brooke's War Sonnets, which seemed to stir him very deeply.

Monday June 14th

I saw in the casualty list to-day that a Lieut. F. Helm, of the 8th Manchester Regt., was killed in the Dardanelles. I think it must be Frank Helm, with whom I acted in *The Amazons* and *Raffles*. I begin to feel I shall soon have no male acquaintances left – to say nothing of friends. Poor Miss Kessler heard to-day that her brother has been killed in the Dardanelles. She is going home to-morrow. The Dardanelles is a regular death-trap, & most of the Lancashire & Manchester Regiments, in which I have so many acquaintances, seem to be there. The time has passed for commenting on these swiftly-accumulating tragedies. One can only feel a dull agonising ache, worse than a sharp & startling pain. It cannot find expression, & gives one no rest – ah! if it is really to go on for years, what shall we do? I wonder if courage & endurance will bear the strain. They must – helped by the inspiration of direct usefulness & constructiveness. To-night there is news of a new battle on the Yser. I wonder where Roland is now, & where his change of scene has taken him. Schen & I at Oriel, where I went to dinner to-night, arranged provisionally to share a sitting-room – if I come back. I told her my future arrangements depended entirely on the casualty list. She is a very dear child. There are vague rumours that we are near victory in the Dardanelles. It is probably untrue – but even if true we have had to pay a terribly high price.

Tuesday June 15th

I went over Somerville Hospital this afternoon. It is really splendid – much better as a Hospital than a College. The Hall & the JCR make fine wards, and it is all so sweet & clean & fresh that it must be quite a joy to be convalescent here. Nearly everyone was in the garden. One poor man lay in a tent some little distance apart from the others; the Matron said they were

afraid he would not recover. Most of those in bed were asleep.
Others were lying about in chairs or on their beds, & all looked
very pathetic. The ones suffering from shock go into the little
rooms, where there are only two people & sometimes only one.
One poor man had his hand, with a long healed-up scar across
it – looking like a bayonet wound, swollen to double the size. I
think the wound must have been poisoned. The man looked
rather depressed though he tried to be cheerful. The matron
said to him 'How's the poor hand getting on?' & he replied
'Quite well, but I don't care so long as it doesn't have to hold a
rifle again.' Judging by the look of him & his hand, I should
wonder if it ever will. Oh! they are all so, so pathetic! Seeing
them filled me with a longing to begin nursing right away. I
know I shall get to love them, & like to hear them telling me all
about it.

Miss Hughes & I went on the river this evening & took dinner
out. I like her ever so much better than I ever have before; I
suppose with one's friends it is the same as I am finding it with
Oxford – that everything seems so much more precious when
there is a possibility of leaving it. We punted home as the sun
was setting – or rather I lay in the punt, exulting in the golden
light of the sunset on the water, while she worked the pole. I
would have liked to stay out for hours more.

Wednesday June 16th
We had a gathering of the clan this afternoon; Schen, Miss
Hughes, E.F. & Marjorie came to tea with me in Micklem
garden for a sort of farewell party in case Miss Hughes & I go
down – for a year or more. Miss Hughes, Schen & I walked
round the Quad. in the twilight just as all the lights were
beginning to come at the windows. We became quite sentimental.

Thursday June 17th
I had a letter from Roland at last. The Germans had been very
quiet all night, & seemed to be mending their wire most of the
time. There is a field of tall grass now between the trenches,
which has its disadvantages as you are apt unexpectedly to come
across unburied remains of long deceased Germans; 'which,

without going into further details, is decidedly unpleasant.'
They have been shelled a bit lately, both in their last farm,
where Roland had his suspicions of the owner, & in his section
of the trench two days ago. Three of the company were
wounded & another knocked down & bruised. Some children
playing in the road were killed & wounded also. 'It's not so bad
when you know you're in for it,' he says, 'but it gets on your
nerves rather wondering whether the next one is going to drop
on your farm or not.' He is getting quite skilled in the nuances of
shell sounds.

Pass Mods began to-day. There are about 50 men & only 4
women.

Friday June 18th
I had another letter from Roland. He had just been investigat-
ing a new kind of hand grenade 'with discretion & a penknife'.
He found it a fascinating toy. They have had an epidemic of
mine explosions in their part of the world the last few days.
Theirs seem to have gone off where they were intended to & the
Germans' where they were not, & none of them in his trench.
He asked me to send him a rattle, telling me not to laugh at the
infantile sound of the request; it was to be a loud one so as to call
the attention of respirator-swathed men to the fact that he
would like to give an order if he could only speak intelligibly
through a smoke helmet. There he had to stop. *And* – he adds a
postscript which he says is a feminine peculiarity I have
remarked on before – 'It is possible that I may be able to get 6
days' leave in the near future.'

My mind suddenly felt confused & the approaching Plato
paper went right out of it. Oh! when is 'the near future'? If it can
only be soon – if it can only really happen. To look into those
dark eyes, after all they have seen & I have felt – ah! no one can
know what it would mean. Sometimes I have felt that I would
forgive the future if it would only bring him to me once again –
give me one hour to blot out wisdom. At other times I have
thought I couldn't bear to see him till the war is over, that
though I am out for hard things there is just one I could not
endure, & that is to live over again the early morning of March
19th on Buxton Station. But now that there is a chance I may

have to do it, I know it is worthwhile. One is willing to pay the bitterness of death for the sweetness of life.

I went to Plato feeling that this paper could be what it liked. As it happened it was a splendid one. I absolutely dreaded Unseens this afternoon; but I could do nearly all the Greek one & the whole of the Latin.

After dinner came the Going-Down Play. It was as usual a sort of pantomime, representing expeditions of various Oxford celebrities to the Never-Never Land, & of course bringing in topical events. As Miss Rowe was stage-managing & Miss Sayers a leading light, I heard that it was unusually good even for a going-down play. The definite 'take-offs' were simply excellent. Miss Sayers with her chorus became Dr Allen to the life; she had even borrowed his robes for the purpose, & had all the tricks off pat. There were some very clever songs with topical allusions. I think the one I liked best of all was the one they all sang together at the very end about Oxford. It was written by Miss Rowe to the tune of 'John Peel'. The last verse ended

> For we've had a good time,
> And there's more ahead.
> And we're all going down in the morning.

Afterwards as Schen & I walked around the dark Quad. we couldn't get it out of our heads. It would be useless to deny that we both felt rather sad; she knew as well as I that I may be bidding both her & Oxford a longer au revoir than just the vacation. Schen doesn't want Miss Hughes & I to go & leave her the odd one of our clan, and just because it has been hard to work this term and I have felt about things as I have & realised that I may have to go down for a time, I have learnt to love Oxford very dearly. Even if I do come back next October in the ordinary way, Oxford will always mean more to me because I have felt about it as I have this term.

Sunday June 20th
I spent most of the morning & afternoon on the river with Miss Hughes in a punt. All the way along the river was fringed with bushes of wild roses. Lovely dragon-flies darted across the

water, both the more ordinary kind with brown wings & thin blue bodies, & the more rare ones with wings of a deep sapphire that gleams in the sun. Miss Hughes also taught me to punt a little, with some success. Several times I nearly fell in, but just managed to avoid doing so!

My year at Oxford – how much I have learnt in it! How I love 'old Oxford, with its spires so grey'! And yet – apparently at least – I have by no means done all that I meant to do. I am going down this year conspicuous for scarcely anything – unless it be for prettiness & athletics, which are the two things I care about least of all. Only a very few – my friends, the literary nucleus of our year, of which I am one – are at all aware that I have an intellect or a character. Scarcely anyone knows of my literary attempts & ambitions. I have no reputation whatsoever for the things I am best at & care for most. It is perhaps my fault; I haven't tried to have. When I know a thing is there, I mind so little whether people think it is or not. And yet – somehow I feel the reputation will be mine some day, even at College.

When I got in I went to the Cathedral, for perhaps the last occasion for a very long time. There I looked at the crimson & purple reflections of the stained-glass windows on the grey stone, listened to the music & thought about Roland, with vague scraps of poetry running through my mind, wakened by the day's emotions to creativeness. The anthem was glorious. I did not hear the words of it till right at the end, & then it seemed to me significant that what I was regarding as my hymn of Au Revoir to Oxford should close with the words 'And sorrow, and sorrow, shall flee away'.

Friday June 25th Buxton

I spent the morning unpacking. Again there was nothing from Roland. This is the longest interval there has ever been. But at mid-day came from Mrs Leighton the packet of letters returned by Roland to me, and also a long letter from her – the longest she has ever sent me – written by her at 1.0 in the morning on four sheets of wove paper. It was a quaint mixture of strength & humour, & passionate love and agony, on account of that dearly-adored son of hers. When I realise the deep anguish that *will* express itself in these letters of hers, courageously as she tries to hide it, I feel a weak & cowardly person beside her. 'I meant to have written you a very long letter, but I am restless to-night and cannot settle myself mentally to do anything thoroughly. I am glad you are going to work in a hospital. Roland says that you hope after a time to get out to France. I am sure you know, as well as I do, that if one has an original mind & something of ambition, it is not by poring over books that one grows & develops. I send you a slip from a paper with a few quotations from the poems of Rupert Brooke. Will you let me have them back when you have read them? Because I cannot do without them, until I get the book. For they are Roland all over. They are just what he might have written. The last lines in particular' – they were from 'The Soldier', 'If I should die, think only this of me' – 'cut through me like so many knife-stabs with their truth in the matter of likeness to him.' This alliance of her thought & mine makes me feel I know Roland better than I thought I did. I sat up till 1.30 reading my own letters. It was so interesting reading side by side mine & the answers to them from him. There is first-rate material there for an autobiographical novel!

Saturday June 26th
I had a letter from him – at last. I am afraid after all his possible leave is something very indefinite & unsettled. He only says 'I ought to get it before the end of summer, with luck.' So I must go on disciplining myself to work without hope. Leave even in a month may mean never. A month is such years now, & so much can happen in it.

He tells me they have just taken over some fresh trenches, about 300 yards from the German lines. At that distance they are fairly safe from rifle grenades & suchlike annoyances, but are much more likely to be shelled. 'There are trees, hedges & growing corn which prevent one side seeing very much of the other. So much so that the other afternoon I crawled with two men up to within about 70 yards of their trenches, completely hidden in the long grass.' Oh! I wish he wouldn't do that. It makes me feel more sick and apprehensive than anything. I wonder why they have to do it. For if they were once seen they would never return again. 'Everything,' he says, 'goes on much the same. It is all most unmeteoric, anyhow.' He had heard from Mrs Garrod, to whom he wrote when Garrod was killed. She says that he was killed during an artillery bombardment. A shell struck him full on the head as he was standing in the trench talking to his sergeant. 'It was at any rate a painless death "and no one knew what it had lived & worked for".' He asks if I ever knew a boy called J. S. Martin at Uppingham. He was killed out there a few weeks ago. He was in the Royal Irish Rifles &, 'though not intellectually brilliant, one of the most charming persons I have known. I came back from camp with him the many years ago that make last year, when War was a newly-discovered toy which both of us hungered to play with. I was growing to have quite an affection for him. The second of my year now.'

He says of his possible leave 'It depends on whether we are in for anything exciting, I suppose . . . It will be so unreal to come back to England for a few hours. Perhaps after all it would be better not. But I don't think so. I shall have changed so much & you perhaps as well; & I shall have forgotten the Quiet Voice and you the charming art of rebuking it. And everything will hurt because it can only be so ephemeral . . .' He stopped there. It would be daylight, he said, by the time he had finished seeing about a wiring party & could go to bed.

In answer I wrote the longest letter I have ever sent him. I told him about many things, at first treating him as if he were a public meeting & giving my views about personality being greater than war & impossible to be buried by that which was weaker than it. I said I didn't believe Olive Schreiner really meant 'no one knew what it had lived & worked for'. The whole of *The Story of an African Farm* is such a contradiction of that sentence, even though she does prefix it to the second half of her story. I bade him when thinking of Martin & Garrod to say, not those words, but these which Francis Thompson said of the great Victorian dead—

> They passed, they passed, but cannot pass away,
> For England feels them in her blood like wine.

I quoted also from 'The Ode to the Setting Sun'

> . . . birth hath in itself the germ of death,
> But death hath in itself the germ of birth.

I spent most of this morning in the attic looking through old Uppingham magazines for the poem inspired by 'Clair de Lune' which Edward told me he wrote. It was so strange looking through those magazines, especially the ones Roland and Garrod edited. It made me feel that either then or now was utterly a dream. I easily recognised Roland's editorials by the prevalence of his favourite adjectives – 'ephemeral', for instance. I found, too, the résumé of the Headmaster's speech at Speech Day last year. 'Every man ought to be of use to his country. If he can't be that, he's better dead.' I came across the poem at last.

Clair de Lune

Soft with the breath of flowers
And laughter of dead showers,
The passionate pale-lit hours
　　Encompass wood and lea;
And down the whispering river
The moon-bright dimples quiver
On waves that start and shiver
　　For fear to join the sea.

But when Night's veil grows older,
Her subtle silence colder,
The poplar's blackness bolder
　　Against the dawning sky,
New day's renascent embers
Make June's dear dreams December's;
And no one else remembers
　　Except the moon and I.

Sunday June 27th

Behold, a new experience beginneth!

I got up at 6.30 & went to the Devonshire Hospital. The Devonshire is a convalescent hospital, chiefly for rheumatism resulting from wounds. I ran round the Men's Day-Room,

where meals for the soldiers are served, putting out forks &
spoons which seem to be permanently greasy. After that I took
trays to patients still in bed. Another nurse & I have three wards
to look after, numbers 5, 6, & 7. There were three men in bed in
7, all dears. Two of them were about thirty, & both very anxious
to talk & tell me how they got here. Neither of them could walk.
One had been 3 months in France in hospital, 12 weeks at
Sheffield & 19 in Buxton! The third man was younger than the
other two, dark & good-looking. He was very quiet and read, or
pretended to read, a magazine while I was talking to the other
two. He speaks in a perfectly refined voice & when I afterwards
cleared up the table by his bed, he apologised for making such a
mess. I rather suspect he is a gentleman ranker. There were
three men in Ward 5 and four in Ward 6. These latter were
singing 'Killarney' in harmony. One in Ward 5 was pretty ill,
though very cheerful, & could not get up; I straightened his bed
for him; I didn't have to make the other beds until they were up.
This man asked me if I had come on here from another hospital,
which I thought one of the nicest compliments I had ever been
paid! It is very nice to be addressed as 'Nurse' and 'Sister'. After
breakfasts & beds I had to dust the wards, wash the doctors'
tables, and put hot water in the jugs. One man told me that it
hadn't had such a dusting for weeks! All this means a considerable amount of running about, as the Hospital is a huge place. I
managed to find out where were the kitchen, the sink, & the
rubbish baskets, which are the things chiefly used in my work.
The military nurses are all quite young & very kind, and showed
me everything. At 10.30 one of them took me round to give me
instructions in how to hand out the milk to those that have it – a
job I have to do every day. Afterwards I collected the mugs, put
them back in the day-room & put one or two things ready for
dinner. This was all very strenuous, & after it I had nothing
particular to do until dinner-time.

I talked to a Scotch soldier they called 'Jock', who had been
there ever since Christmas, when he was sent back from the
front after a month with frost-bitten feet. This man told me he
had frequently stood up to his waist in water in mid-winter,
and hadn't had any hot meals either. He also told me how
many young officers & men had been shot soon after going out

through over-carelessness about putting their heads above the parapet of the trench. The men are keen to have a look at the battlefield, put up their heads to see, – and it is all over with them. He told me how they had lost one of their officers in this way – a Capt. MacGregor, who was a splendid officer & greatly loved by all his men. The first day they went in the trenches he exhorted his men all the time to keep their heads below, but was not at all careful of himself; he said it was only his men that mattered. He was a big man & used to walk upright in his trench, so that his head was visible above the parapet. The first day shells fell all around him but nothing touched him. But the second day through not stooping down he was shot through the head by a rifle 10 minutes after they went into the trenches.

I hear dozens of war stories and if I wished could hear hundreds. The men like to talk about their experiences, and a new person to tell their stories to is quite enough to start any of them off. I had the dinner to see to, and to take to patients still in bed – three upstairs this time – and then was off duty for the rest of the day. I am only going in the mornings to begin with, but when they get a little busier & I am a little more experienced I shall go in the evenings as well. Oh! I love the British Tommy! I shall get so fond of these men, I know. And when I look after any one of them, it is like nursing Roland by proxy. Oh! if only one of them could be the Beloved One!

Monday June 28th
We heard from Edward to-night that he will probably go out in 2 months' time. He thinks it will be to Malta or the Dardanelles – that death-trap. He says Smith-Dorrien dined with his CO last week & told him that he was at home because of some disagreement at the front with French. It is rumoured that French has not the same theories as Kitchener & Smith-Dorrien, & will perhaps have to go. I suppose we are approaching our lowest ebb now – the Russians quite beaten, the Dardanelles nearly hopeless, France & Belgium almost entirely occupied by the enemy, Calais not far from his possession. Yet 'it's always darkest before dawn'. Perhaps the dawn will come quicker than we expect, now that we have ceased to anticipate it.

Tuesday June 29th
I liked nursing even better this morning. Always there are practically the same things to be done but to-day I never had an idle moment. Miss Cookson was also there as a V.A. nurse. I was quite glad to see another uniform the same as mine. She looked so well in hers that I began to think mine can't appear as bad as I think.

Wednesday June 30th
I actually had too much to do this morning – an occurrence which is quite ideal as it gives one no time to feel tired. Besides my usual work I had to get Johnson up single-handed as everyone else was very busy also. I had to rub his heels with methylated spirit & bandage his leg again – to prevent bed sores. I am getting tremendously interested in all this medical business. I think there is a good deal of the rolling stone in my composition – the rolling stone with a thread of consistency running all through it.

Friday July 2nd
The same as usual – even in its disappointments. There must be some important reason for the long intervals between Roland's letters. And to-night I feel so strongly my knowledge of his intangible nature, which is always accompanied by the insistent desire to know him tangibly too. Oh! just to feel again that he is a reality. I think the waiting & not knowing is more tiring even than walking miles over the stone floor of the Hospital or practising for the nursing examination to-morrow.

Saturday July 3rd
The letter from Roland was just a short note written at his dictation by his servant to say that he had cut his fingers a little. I suppose he did it with those beastly wire entanglements or something of that sort. They are being sent down south, presumably somewhere about the place where Garrod died – Festubert. In consequence all their leave has been cancelled. This is a very bitter blow. I had hoped to see him just once more before he went into the thick of the fighting – but now – Well, I suppose it was not to be. Perhaps those are given most to endure

who are most capable of endurance, & it is like being paid a
compliment by Fate. But I didn't want her compliments, I
wanted Roland. He ends 'Very much love, dear. R.'

Sunday July 4th

At dinner-time I found a letter awaiting me from Mrs Leighton
– and such a dear letter too. Herself & her letters are an
unexpected consolation – one I never dreamed of possessing a
year ago, when I missed seeing her at Uppingham. 'If it would
give you real pleasure – & I think it would – to send me your
copy of Rupert Brooke's poems I may confess that I shall be very
very glad to have it, just because it had been yours. But if this
particular copy has associations for you that another would not
have then you must not hold yourself bound by your impulsive
& sweet offer of it to me. Write to me about Roland whenever
you like & at as great length as you like. I may not always answer
quickly but you will know that this is only because I have so
many letters to write.'

Monday July 5th

I have just been looking at myself in the glass; tiredness makes
one positively ugly. As I have got to be continuously tired for
many days to come I fear at this rate all I ever had of beauty will
come to be a thing of the past. Such is war! Even attractiveness
must be sacrificed to usefulness. I told Roland the other day that
my roughened hands are not worth kissing now!

Evening work at this hospital does not involve so much
walking about as the morning & includes one or two really
interesting things. I had to rub one man's back, & paint another's
frost-bitten foot with a strong-smelling mixture of some sort.
Preparing the suppers is quite strenuous as every one of those in
bed has something different. I had to make cocoa, bovril, hot
milk & toast, & did not leave till 9.0. It is splendid having so
much to do.

I had a letter from Miss Lorimer in most cordial terms,
congratulating me on my 'well-deserved success'. She says she
is glad I like my new job, & puts also 'Do spare yourself all you
can for the first month until you are trained in a little; it would

be such a pity to break down.' I wonder what she will do herself.
Something remarkable, I know.

Tuesday July 6th
I met the postman on my way to the hospital; he had two letters
from Roland for me & one for Daddy. I took the two letters &
put them in my pocket, & there they tantalised me the whole
morning. For I never had a moment to look at them.

The first, written on July 2nd, told me that he was writing in a
little room which overlooked grey-green cornfields, red-tiled
houses, & a wooded ridge in the distance. The district was a
colliery kind, and miners' cottages dotted the road. He frequently sees the men going home. He is billeted in a house on
top of a hill, where he is quite comfortable & has a real bed to
sleep in. The proprietor is a small farmer 'and Madame is the
sage-femme of the village and announces it on an unnecessarily
large brass plate on the door. She spends a large part of the time
chasing Marie-Louise, aged 4, whose ideas of discipline are
somewhat lax.' They have been there 2 days & probably stay
another week. They are at the back of Festubert, Givenchy & La
Bassée. He doesn't know where they are going next. Just now
they are about 10 miles from the firing line & are said to have
been brought there to be used as a flying column & rushed off
wherever they are wanted. At present they are resting. But he
tells Daddy – not me – that he thinks they will be in for
'something exciting' before long. Alas! . . .

He wonders if one can be a soldier & an artist as well. 'I often
think how strange it is that no one here knows me in any other
than my present role. Someone once called me a chameleon,
long ago.

> Oh damn! I know it! And I know
> How the May fields . . .

and, knowing, still go on inspecting rifles & seeing that men
wash their feet; and you meanwhile make beds & wash up
greasy knives & forks: and both perhaps do it a lot better, if only
because it is the last thing we should have imagined ourselves
doing a year ago.'

Friday July 9th

Nursing is a great rest to my brain, which has consistently been thinking & pondering for the last five or six years. As I went home at dusk to-day in the cool evening air beneath a clear sky which still showed traces of sunset, I began to ask myself 'What *do* I think about when I am doing my work at the hospital?' I came to the conclusion that I thought of nothing at all except the thing I was going to do next. I couldn't do college work now before the ending of the war. I realise now how very depressing it was. This kind of thing enables one to keep more cheerful & therefore more brave. I crossed the Rubicon to-day by writing and telling Miss Penrose that as far as I could tell I meant to go down for a year. But it was not really such a very mighty step, only the outward sign of one, as I had made up my mind about it really for some time.

Saturday July 10th

The news of the surrender of German S. West Africa was confirmed this morning. It was our first complete victory. Tremendous operations seem to be impending on the West.

Nursing was again very interesting, especially this evening. I had to paint & bandage an amputated finger among other things. There was a concert going on a great part of the evening given by Miss Sharp's band, & Mrs Ellinger, dressed up very much & most unsuitably, sang some very inappropriate songs. I found a very nice letter from Miss Penrose when I got in, wishing me good luck in my Red Cross work, saying of course they would miss me next year but she quite appreciated & understood my desire to help with nursing & thought my work would benefit greatly in the end from this experience of the deeper & more serious side of life. Miss Hyland caught me this morning, told me to be careful not to overwork (people always seem afraid of that with me −) & insisted that I take to-morrow morning off & do not go till 5.0.

Sunday July 11th

I took my half-day off this morning − with the result, as I afterwards heard, that considerable muddle reigned in the wards where I usually go. I actually quite enjoyed church, because I cannot as a rule go if I want to, I suppose. I felt very sad all the same, for music in church always makes me think especially of Roland. Canon Scott-Moncrieff, whose brother, Brigadier-General Scott-Moncrieff, was killed in the Dardanelles a few days ago, looked very worn & grief-stricken. I felt so dreadfully sorry.

Tuesday July 13th

I had more rubbing than usual to do this evening, which I always like. Nursing was very interesting to-day altogether. I always get Johnson up & put him to bed now & it is a treat to do anything for him, he is such a dear boy. I went out for a short bicycle ride this afternoon. This evening Nurse Carter asked me if I had been out during the afternoon; I said I had, in a red jersey, & on a bicycle, & asked if she had seen me. She said she had but thought it couldn't be me as I looked so young. I told her the nurse's dress made me look much older, which was perhaps just as well as the soldiers might not respect me enough if they knew my real age.

Wednesday July 14th

Nurse Vaughan is too ill to take duty, so I have the three wards to do in the morning & only just manage to get them through in time. Some of the soldiers' remarks are most amusing; as I was dusting Ward 5 this morning, Sergeant Bishop said to me, in the tone of one making a remark & not the least familiarly or trying to pay a compliment, 'Well Nurse, I've noticed many faces but I've never seen a pair of eyes like yours.' I said of course that I wasn't aware there was anything particular about them & he said 'Well you've got a look in them different from anything I've ever seen, though I can't explain what it is quite.'

This evening I had an extremely vigorous time. Eleven new patients suddenly arrived; Nurse Robson & Nurse Cornell had to look after & arrange about them, & it was Nurse Bailey's afternoon off, so Miss Windsor & I were left to deal with the evening patients in the Laboratory. We got through them somehow & of course as we were short-handed there was an unusually large number. Besides the incidental & continual occupations of fetching basins, clearing away cups & filling hot-water bottles, I had to rub a new patient's chest, rub Hopkins' back & bandage it, paint & bandage Hibbert's foot, paint & bandage Hill's ankles & legs, put Johnson to bed & bandage him to his splint, collect & wash the cups, & rub the chest of the man I always go to last thing at night.

It is delightful getting to know these people, which I never should if I had always remained Miss Brittain & never 'Nurse'. They look upon me here from quite a different point of view. I get nearer to 'the people' & find them so immensely interesting & intelligent. And I couldn't be treated more thoroughly as a nurse if I had been nursing for years. Of course the patients see very little difference between a V.A. Nurse & an ordinary hospital nurse.

I am coming to the conclusion that practical ability is of much less importance in a nurse than psychological fitness. Adaptability, sympathy & magnetism of temperament count for more than the ability to bandage or make foods.

Thursday July 15th

I came home to-night more weary & footsore than I have been since I started nursing. This is all the fault of one charming Sister who this morning had me on the run & besides my ordinary work made me follow her round cutting people's toe-nails & washing their hands & feet. This afternoon besides my ordinary work she gave me a whole stack of flowers to do for the day-room, so I did not get away till past nine.

Still I have heard nothing from Roland. There has never been so long an interval as this – it will be a fortnight on Sunday since I heard anything about him. To-day I watched every post with great eagerness, only to be disappointed. Oh Roland, Roland! Where are you now?

Friday July 16th

Still no news of Roland. If it were not for the nursing I don't know how I could bear this – but nursing takes all one's energy and occupies a great deal of the time that would otherwise have been spent on sad thought. In between my duties I can scarcely bear thinking about him. Something has happened I am sure. He would never willingly keep me so long without a word, as if

one has no time for letters there are always Field Service
Postcards. I feel as if I couldn't go on much longer without
news of some sort, & yet it is no good feeling like that because
one *has* to go on, come what may. Fortunately during my two
hours of rest I half involuntarily went to sleep, I was so tired.
Otherwise I should have thought & thought – for I find it very
difficult to read just now, especially fiction; the immense
realities of the present crowd in upon my mind, making
concentration almost impossible & fictitious events quite trivial.
I have not written to Roland for a week myself; I have a horror
of pouring out my heart to someone who may never read it – of
writing letters which will be officially returned unread by the
person for whom they were intended. So I am waiting to hear
either from or of him. I often wonder just how I should take it if I
heard he was dead. Sometimes my heart feels very tumultuous,
full of passion & fierce desire; at others it is possessed by a sort
of blank & despairing resignation to what one feels must be
inevitable. But enough of this; writing about it only makes it
worse.

I had very hard work to do to-day as I had Miss Windsor's to
do as well as my own, as she has calmly gone away. I have never
worked so hard in my life; it gives me a little insight into the lives
of those who have always to work like this. I wonder what it is
all for – what it will lead to. One does not mind how long one
walks along a steep & toilsome path so long as one knows there
are pleasant & restful fields at the end. Yet that is a coward's
thought after all; the brave do not ask for respite during toil or
compensation at the end. That service which is in itself noble is
almost insulted by definite & formal recognition – 'Honour has
come back as a King to earth.' To work towards the best that
one knows, whatever the past may have been or future may be –
that is all one can do.

Saturday July 17th
Still no news either of or from him – though I watched for each
post with a feverish impatience that was agony. Something
really *must* have happened this time. If it is the worst, may God –
if there is a God – help Mrs Leighton & me! If only it could
mean that he is wounded! I, last of all people, want him to suffer,

but suffering can change to health, while nothing can change Death to Life. And if he were to suffer physically, I should at any rate equal the agony mentally.

Sunday July 18th
Still I have had no news. But I couldn't wait any longer but had to write him a short letter to-day – just in case he is really alright & wondering why he does not hear from me. But I wrote it with the feeling that he would not read it. I wonder if it will be officially returned. I think that is about the most horrible way of learning about casualties that there is.

Tonight I sat alone beside the morning-room fire, with aching head & heart. And while part of the time I gazed into the glowing coals & part I buried my head in my hands, a series of memory pictures passed through my mind, of events that happened during the few occasions I have been with Roland in the flesh. Buxton – Uppingham – London – Oxford & the journey thereto! Strangely enough, though I have seen him so little he is intimately connected with all the places with which I am most closely associated. I can scarcely bear to think about all this because it only makes more manifest to me what I may have lost.

Monday July 19th
There was at last some slight news of Roland – though nothing more than information of his existence on July 14th. He just sent a picture postcard of Lillers to Daddy. 'I will write as soon as I have time. I am very hurried at present.' But that at all events was better than nothing.

Tuesday July 20th
I had a short letter from Roland at last this morning, written in a great hurry. He says he is at present leading 'too peripatetic an existence' for letter-writing.

Thursday July 22nd
The Russian retreat still continues. The Germans are only 5 miles from Warsaw. There are vague – very vague – rumours that Turkey wants to sue for a separate peace. I wish she would

– before Edward gets sent to the Dardanelles. I saw in a paper to-day that the total estimate of dead in Europe in this war exceeds 5 millions! – & the wounded exceed 7 millions.

Friday July 23rd
Another strenuous day. The man in 5 requires a great deal of my attention. It is impossible almost to go into his room & get away without his wanting something & he is always pealing away at bells. He is very impolite & never grateful for anything that is done for him; he is of course unable to move. Nurse Olive thinks he may die; he has complications with his sciatica and looks very ill & unhealthy. Still no letter has come from Roland. I am aching for a long intimate letter from him.

Saturday July 24th
I received the long & intimate letter from Roland which I so much desired & also another little one besides. Both came by the same post first thing this morning, but I had no time to read them until 2.0. This has happened more than once & is very tantalising, though I rather like it in one way. Having an unopened letter of his in my pocket gives me the same sort of stirred-up anticipatory feeling that I get before meeting a person I care for greatly & haven't seen for a long time, or an exam., or an occasion like Speech Day.

  Just after lunch I opened them both. 'I have just been reading your last letters over again. There is so much in them that I read & then forget – so much both written & unwritten. Mother was very right (she usually is in those sort of things) when she said that you would be able to write the best possible love-letters. Your letters to me are like an interrupted conversation; and I remember afterwards in odd moments what you said, and wonder sometimes if you get tired of talking to a phantom in the void who does not answer or show that he has understood.'

On this day (18th) they were back at the mining village of Burbure, though they were further south a few days ago at the junction of the French & British lines. 'I went up to the trenches and through our lines to the French, passing a sentry in khaki on one side of a small traverse and another in sky-blue two yards further on.' He says he 'found everybody very enthusiastic and loquacious & unshaven. I had quite a long talk with two or three of the men. They seemed less inclined to grumble than ours, more resigned to the inevitable perhaps, as men who had well counted the cost of such a war, conscious that they were fighting on French soil still for very national existence.'

He wrote the next little paragraph in the train, going much further south to a district where no British troops have yet been. 'There are French soldiers at all the stations who cheer us as we pass. It is a glorious day & very hot.' He continued a little later the same day. They had just arrived in billets, very hot & dusty after a few miles' march from the station. Their destination was a sleepy little village of poverty-stricken old women who had never seen khaki before. And amid all the heat & dust of the march it occurred to him to wonder why sunsets are always more beautiful than sunrise.

The next part of the letter was not written until the 21st. On that same Monday night that he mentioned in the last paragraph he was wakened at 1.30 in the morning by an orderly with a note from headquarters ordering him to pack up all his things and take a party of 50 men off to report to the Headquarters of the VIIth Army Corps at M— at 8.0 a.m. – a place 3 miles from where he was then. 'On arriving I found a very charming château which the headquarters were to move into that evening. My job was to help the Camp Commandant get everything ready. I had a very busy day yesterday as a sort of Assistant Chamberlain of the Household, and the same to-day. This morning another 50 men arrived for me, and I have risen to being temporarily attached to the Staff of the VIIth Corps here as Officer Commanding the Headquarters Company.' He, the Camp Commandant ('a very charming & dandified Major') and the General ADC are the only officers there out of 16 who have not got 'red hats'. He has been given a small room in the château and is, he says, getting quite used to meeting Generals and Staff Colonels round every corner. 'There are 5 generals in the house now and heaps of people hanging around with enigmatical appellations such as "The DDMS" (Deputy Director of Medical Services).' He doesn't know how long he will stop there but appears to like temporary Staff appointments. I don't know quite what the Staff appointment means – perhaps it is that they have discovered how intelligent he is. I wish they would keep him there till the end of the war; and for himself, capable as he is at anything, military science would just suit him, and it seems a pity to run the risk of wasting a brain like his on the dirty work.

I had another strenuous night to-night. I heard that Dr Sawdon said Johnson would never be able to walk again (though he does not know this yet) as the muscle of his right leg was shot right through & will never knit. I felt dreadfully depressed by this; his desire to make efforts to walk is so pathetic. I do hope there may be some faint chance for him still.

Monday July 26th

I had another letter from Roland. He was rather less busy when he wrote but finds telling people to do things is very tiring. He does not quite know what he is going to do next. 'My CO came round yesterday & wanted to have me back again with the battalion. The Camp Commandant wants to keep me here. I prefer this to wandering over France doing nothing in particular, but on the other hand don't want to miss any real fighting.' He now has the use of a motor-car which he shares with the Field Cashier and the Assistant Director of Postal Services. These are the advantages of being at Headquarters! He continues 'I have heard no more about leave yet, but still have not given up hope.'

Tuesday July 27th

A letter came from Cora with the information that the best thing to do in order to get into the Camberwell Hospital was to apply for a Special Service form through Devonshire House. I know one has to be inoculated for this hospital, which is called No. 1 London General. So I got Friday off for it.

Wednesday July 28th

Nursing seemed rather lighter altogether to-day. I seemed to get things done quicker. I also began to feel less antipathy to Smith, the man in 5, who has had his great shaggy moustache shaved off, and now looks quite a young man (which he is, only 27) and one who would be very good-looking if he were well. I feel sorry for him now in spite of his incessant ingratitude & grumbling; after all one doesn't know what he may have been through. I helped Nurse Olive to wash him again to-night.

Friday July 30th
I went with the motor to meet Edward at 6.25. He appeared looking very big and extraordinarily healthy; his face and hands are very tanned by the sun. I almost wished he had not come. I can regard his going almost with equanimity except when he is here & then I feel how indispensable he is. Daddy insists on asking him his opinion about parts of the general situation – which he never seems to think of – and treating his answers as words of wisdom. Edward however did just say that soldiers did not bother themselves much about the general situation, their chief object was to get trained and be ready to do their part, whatever it was; they did not trouble their heads to carp and criticise; only civilians had time for such things.

Saturday July 31st
I got my communication from the Red Cross this morning, telling me to send in my name through my own Commandant & County Director, saying that they noted I wanted to go to No. 1 London General but could not promise I should get there even if I were selected. They also enclosed terms of service.
    Miss Heath Jones & Miss Bervon arrived at 2.30. Miss H.J. is mad to do some war-work – munitions, nursing or motor-driving, none of which she would be any use at.

Sunday August 1st
I was back at the Hospital this morning. There was a good deal of work to do. Smith is very ill now & is thought to be dying so cannot be left. I had to leave my work & sit with him for about an hour this morning. Had anyone told me a month ago that I should sit by a dying man, lift him when he choked and constantly turn him over, I should have been terrified at the idea. Now I do it – not with equanimity, for I cannot think with equanimity of anyone's dying – but with calm.

Tuesday August 3rd

Roland is – alas for me! – back in the trenches. 'I have been back with the Battalion a day now. My little experience with Corps Headquarters was most interesting, though short-lived.' They went back into the trenches 3 days from when the letter was written – to-day; 'which was chiefly why I and the 100 men I had with me were recalled. Also two of the officers in my Company are away – one with a badly sprained ankle, and the other, I am afraid, dying of appendicitis in a Military Hospital a few miles away.' He is now acting junior Captain. Edward thinks he has a chance of promotion. He continues 'While I was at Corps Headquarters I didn't have any real Staff work to do, or much chance of showing that Roland Leighton has any more ability than the average subaltern. I think they were very pleased with me, though, as the ADMS asked the General specially whether I could not be kept there permanently. The General said that was impossible in the circumstances, but that if he got together a permanent Headquarters Company, as he intended to do soon, he would offer me the command of it.' Meanwhile he has learnt a good deal and enjoyed himself. He got a glimpse of civilisation one afternoon by motoring into Amiens, which was 'filled with French officers & very gay & unwarlike'.

Wednesday August 4th

The anniversary of our declaration of War on Germany. There is nothing to be said about this New Year of War, for it is so obvious that a year ago no one expected a second year of it that disquisitions on the subject take the form of mere truisms. There is more to be done than there is to be said – the renewal of our determination & our vows in a cause which now is much more obviously that of justice and freedom than it was a year ago. Whatever the papers may say, the majority of us have passed beyond our blatant loud-voiced 'patriotism', our want of realisation, our irresponsibility, our inappropriate indifference, and are quiet & resolute, weary but still tenacious, confident of the issue and determined that come what may, it *shall* be.

It was an appropriate day, perhaps, for Edward's last with us. He is typical, in some ways, of England's best spirit at the present moment; confident & tranquil, ready for death if it must be, anxious to possess a thorough knowledge of the part demanded of him and not over-troubled about the rest of events which he cannot affect. He never worries and is never sentimental; never even emotional.

I had an unsatisfactory sort of letter from the Red Cross, talking vaguely of delays and numerous interviews. British authorities & their Red Tape are distinctly depressing. Strange that they should plead for volunteers and then make it as unpleasant as possible for you when you have volunteered.

Being the anniversary of the war, there were special intercession services and prayers for the renewal of vows. There was a service at 7.0 and both Mother & Daddy were anxious that Edward & I should go, though we should both have preferred to stop away. Neither the Church of England nor one's relations allow themselves to think for a moment that one can renew one's vows much better in a private place, in resolutions not put into elegant clerical language by other people. God – if there be a God – is much nearer to one on the night-enshrouded moorlands than in a crowded & stuffy church. The only part of the service I liked was Cowper's hymn 'God moves in a mysterious way', which I am always very fond of.

Edward & I walked up the Manchester Road right as far as the turning down to the Goyt Valley. The night wind blew fresh in our faces, and all around us lay the hills and moorlands, dark and silent. In the distance the lights from the town gleamed faintly & now & again a dim glow shone out from the window of some solitary cottage on the hillside. We talked for a long time & very seriously – much of it was about Roland & much of course about the war. Edward expressed again, as he did that evening in the garden at Oxford, the half-haunting instinct that he may not return. He says it is not as if he were a full-fledged & well-known composer; he cannot see that his life at present is much use to anyone; he is not even sure that it is much good to himself. We walked back the last part of the way almost in silence. There was so much to think – so little to be said. Afterwards he & Mother sat up talking in his room till a quarter to 12.0.

When I said good-night to Roland's photograph I realised that I owed him an apology. This afternoon I showed it to Miss

Bervon & she exclaimed with great enthusiasm '*What* a nice straight face.' I was seized with a sudden embarrassment & said hastily & quite irrelevantly 'Yes, he *is* very plain, isn't he!' My dear love! Even if he has hair like a brush & a mouth too resolute for the smallest degree of beauty, no one could be plain with such dark well-defined eyebrows & deep intelligent eyes. His photograph reminds me so much of that first parting – the worst. For to lose Edward, though he seems to take many of my pleasant recollections with him – does not, cannot, mean the same to me as it meant to lose Roland. What does happen is that the remembrance of that morning's agony, all too intense before, is now intensified. My future, my work, and above all Roland, are all – for the time being at least – gone from me.

Thursday August 5th

I said goodbye to Miss Heath Jones & Miss Bervon before going to the Hospital; they are departing even before Edward. I said one goodbye to him at the bathroom door; he seemed cheerful enough but his eyes looked very sad. But I managed to get 10 minutes' respite from the Hospital a little later to see him off by the 9.50. We all assembled there on the station, Edward & I, soldier & nurse, & Mother & Daddy. Fortunately we had not long to wait. We were all calm & cheerful and talked of nothing in particular. I looked long & carefully at Edward as he stood there, tall & sunburnt, the typical soldier; I was committing his image to my mind. I wish I had done the same with Roland, but I felt too half-crazed the morning he went away to have presence of mind for any such thing. As the train went out I stood & waved to him, with a sick sense that it was perhaps for the last time in these our short years. So we have seen him off – to France, the Dardanelles, the Persian Gulf? What matter which. In all these stricken countries there are thousands of British graves, and there is so little reason to hope that what one loves best may not make one more. Fortunately the station had not the desolate look it wore when Roland departed. There was no icy stillness, no snowy roofs, no pitiless gleaming rails, to make matters worse. Edward just went, that was all. And I said 'Au Revoir,' but he said 'Goodbye.'

There was no time for grief. I went back to the Hospital

straight away. All day long the house – as much as I saw of it – was very depressed. Mother was quiet & quite sensible but Daddy too mournful for words, constantly saying that all his interest in life is gone & we may as well put him in the churchyard, etc. etc. I was sorry for him of course; for I know what it means, even to a less selfish person than he, to see the light of one's eyes depart. But I wonder if it ever strikes him that I too may any moment lose my heart's desire, that I have in fact stood to lose him all these months, and that the hour of darkness, if it comes, will be all the harder to bear because it has been so long delayed.

I received a letter from him just before I went back to the Hospital this evening. 'Dear Child – I have always liked this name for you, though I ought not to call you "child" ought I? – thank you so much for Rupert Brooke. It came this morning, and I have just read it straight through. It makes me feel as if I want to sit down and write things myself instead of doing what I have to do here. I used to talk of the Beauty of War; but it is only War in the abstract that is beautiful. Modern warfare is merely a trade, and it is only a matter of taste whether one is a soldier or a greengrocer, as far as I can see. Sometimes by dint of an opportunity a single man may rise from [the] sordidness to a deed of beauty: that is all.' They were going into the trenches the next day & were then in a village just behind the line. 'Much troubled by flies but otherwise nothing to report, as the newspapers say.' The officer Roland mentioned in his last letter died of appendicitis last Friday. Roland went to the funeral on Sunday. 'Such a waste of life! It is a pity he did not die like a soldier when he had lived as one.' He goes on 'Please don't do too much work at the Hospital, will you? You seem to, dear, by your letters.' He adds a ps asking for socks if Mother is making any, and says he is 'still trying to get leave but with no result.' I feel inclined to say with the Psalmist 'Lord, how long?'

Friday August 6th
I had an unsatisfactory interview with Dr Sawdon about the British Red Cross 6 months' sign-on business. It seems to mean a long delay & the chance of getting to London is the very

remotest, and there is practically none of working with Cora or Stella. I think I shall try the French Red Cross.

Saturday August 7th

I had all sorts of queer dreams about hostile armies fighting one another on our own English fields beneath my very eyes. The rain poured down all day – drearily, drearily. Warsaw, the Polish capital, has fallen to the Germans. There are great rejoicings in Berlin over the achievement. As one paper says, 'Hours graver than any of the War have arrived,' but though we do not underrate our Enemy's success, we still look to the future with courage & hope.

Sunday August 8th

Nothing much happened until the evening. Then Lieut. & Mrs La Page came to say goodbye (Lieut. La Page was told on Thursday he had to leave for the front to-night) and stayed to supper. Lieut. La Page is quite a small man, scarcely any taller than his wife. He is bronzed & good-looking, with clean-cut resolute features and deep-set, straightforward and rather beautiful blue eyes. Mrs La Page can't be much older than I. She looked very pretty when she took off her wet hat, but very pale. They have only been married five weeks. Three companies of the Royal Engineers (in which he is) were going off to-night at about 1.0, he told us. Mother said we should like to come too & he immediately took up the idea & said he would get us on to the station. I think he was glad to think that someone would be with his poor little wife (though she is not the feeble sort of girl one can pity) after he had gone, so late at night.

Then began an experience one of the most interesting I have ever had, though I don't think I should care to have it repeated. The La Pages left soon after supper and we met them again outside the Hydro at a quarter to 11.0. They looked pathetically young and sad. There we were joined by two extremely uninteresting and plain women in black – the mother & sister of Lieut. La Page's Captain, who turned out to be an extremely objectionable person with no chin & none of the manners of a gentleman. We all went up to the Market Place to see Lieut. La Page's and the other two companies gather together & parade.

The night was dark & very damp; a light misty rain was falling most of the time. Almost all the town lights were out except the two tall lamps in the middle of the square. I remember watching myriads of great moths beating themselves high up against the glass, & thinking vaguely how many dead moths must be found at the foot of the lamps in the morning. In a few minutes the market place was seething with mules, transport wagons, an unruly crowd, and Tommies loudly singing drunken songs. The majority of the men could scarcely walk; they had been making a night of it – starting early in the afternoon.

When they had all been collected & were marching about to cool their brains, we escaped from the crowd & went down to the station, Mrs La Page & her husband arm-in-arm in front. When we got outside the station one company was already there. We passed through them with difficulty & Lieut. La Page conducted us on to the platform. Soon after, the men of one company came lurching on to the station just as though their packs were top-heavy. Most of them were dancing, singing or swearing, and the air was heavily perfumed with a mixed odour of beer & whisky. The objectionable Captain rushed about in a very excitable fashion, and swore at the station master; there was very little doubt that he was not far from being liable to the same accusation as his men. The calm, self-controlled behaviour of the two lieutenants – Lieut. La Page & the Junior Subaltern, a quiet-faced boy with a very nice smile, was in very great contrast. Of course Mother & the Captain's relations were very horrified – and the officers for the sake of appearances tried to make light of it. I did neither; I was feeling very sad & pitiful and a little ashamed. Probably the majority of them – all decent men really – had never done such a thing before, & probably never will again in the serious time that is before them. It seems such a pity that on this perhaps only occasion of their lives when they are conspicuous, they should allow themselves to be conspicuous in such an unhappy state. The band, although half-seas over, was vainly endeavouring to produce some tune or other, and after a great deal of effort did manage to achieve a slight & wheezy resemblance to 'Auld Lang Syne' & 'Tipperary'. I think I shall always remember the scene – I had such a very strange sense that it was all unreal – just the disorderly crowd scene in a play. The pitch darkness of the night, the half-sober crowd of men, the unusualness of the hour & the wet and shiny platform all contributed to the idea, which grew stronger as the night went on.

The train was supposed to go at 12.45 but owing to misman-agement on the Captain's part (he had put horses in with mules & none of the transport wagons were ready) it did not leave till 1.30. So we were on the station for nearly 2 hours, during which time the noise & the crowd increased. It was somewhat difficult to get the men in, both because there was insufficient room in the train & because they were in an uproarious condition. At last they were all in and, after a little more delay, at 1.30 the whistle went. Lieut. La Page & his wife both behaved admir-ably. They did not kiss or utter any last words on the station. He just gave her a quick hand-clasp & a 'Goodbye' & turned away – in great contrast to the objectionable Captain, who was giving sloppy kisses to his mother & sister, who in their turn were saying 'Oh darling!' or the like. Mrs La Page watched her husband get in & mingle with the crowd of officers, & they did not look at one another again. She was white & very still, but quite composed, as an English girl should be. I admired her very much. Little though she suspected it, I understood. I *knew* what it meant just to shake hands with the best beloved, & make no sign – but to turn away feeling as if the sun had gone out for ever. As soon as the train began to move we hurried out of the station to escape the crowd. After all we did not accompany Mrs La Page home as a very nice young officer waited to escort her. I said good-night to her with an aching heart, for in that parting of theirs both my own sad partings seemed to be repeated & included. It was pitch dark as we walked home.

Monday August 9th
I was paid a little reward to-day for all the work I have done at the Hospital. When Nurse Olive & I were doing Smith she said she had saved him up for me to help her because she likes me to help her best. She then said 'We do miss you when you go off, it's just like one of us. No other V.A.D. has been much use to us before! In fact we could get on much better without the majority of those who have been here!' I was pleased, naturally, as I

suppose it shows a certain amount of adaptability and is at any rate getting near a proof of my dictum that a person of real intellect can do anything he or she chooses.

This evening when I came in from work I found a very interesting post. One letter was from Schen, giving [a] most entertaining account of her work in the aeroplane workshop, also of her intimacy with the queer artisans who make munitions and who regard her quite as one of themselves. The other letter was from Mrs Leighton. 'I was so very glad to get your letter this evening, Vera dear,' she says. 'It is I who have been neglecting you. So many things crowded upon me, and so much work went wrong, and so many letters of sympathy had to be written! One of the hardest to write was called for by the death of the son of Mr Hornung the novelist (the author of *The Amateur Cracksman* – dramatised as *Raffles*). I had been subconsciously hoping that Roland would not see or hear too much about the Rupert Brooke poems because I knew all that they would make him feel. He could do as good work himself – and though I would not draw him back now if I could, yet when I think of his abilities and possibilities and of how his wonderful youth and life and personality may be shot into nothingness any day, any hour, I get fiercely angry at the waste of it. It is true that this kind of machine war is a trade.'

Friday August 13th

Mother & I went to London for the day – and I was very lucky all through, in spite of the unpropitious date. Cora met us at St Pancras, and after a short conversation we decided that the best thing for me to do was to try & join the same VAD as she has. It is about the best in England, as the Commandant is on the VAD Selection Board; if they approve of you it does not take more than 10 minutes to be enrolled, but they have to see you before they will do anything. I found out that if you go to a good VAD they will do all the wire-pulling for you and all you have to do is to volunteer. So I joined this VAD and they will send me a Special Service form which when I have filled it up I shall return to them, volunteering to serve as a VAD for 6 months either at home or abroad, wherever they want to send me. Cora & I asked if it were any good saying where we preferred to go, and if it were any use saying who we wanted to join with when we were sent. She & I of course want to go together, and Stella. The Secretary said she wouldn't advise us to ask to be sent to any special place as they might keep us much longer and then not send us there in the end, but she said it was almost certain that we could all go together as VADs are sent out in batches, and she promised to write a note herself to the Commandant, asking if we could be together. We enquired if there was any likelihood of our going abroad and she said there was a possibility but that it was more probable we should get somewhere in England, as for one thing nurses are more wanted in England just now and, for another, they usually send out abroad people more experienced than we are. Though we should of course prefer to be in London it doesn't much matter where we go so long as we go together, and I don't much mind about not going abroad if I am wanted more in England; the chief point is to do what is needed. The Secretary told us we are not likely to be called up till October as the demand for nurses follows the fighting, and as there has been a lull lately the length of the nursing waiting-list corresponds.

Saturday August 14th
I was not so tired as I expected at the Hospital this morning. When I went into Smith's ward I got quite a fright as he had a screen round him and was lying on his back with his eyes closed and hands crossed in front of him. I thought he was dead, he was such a ghastly colour; I only wish he had been, poor creature, for his life is nothing but a dreadful misery both to him & everyone else. The end is not far away now; he keeps trying to pull the bed-clothes off him, which is often a sign of death approaching. He was more troublesome than usual this morning, and it is difficult now to understand what he says.

I found a letter from Roland when I got in, not a long one but very significant. 'It is just possible that I may manage to get leave soon, after all, if I am tactful and have my – dare I say, usual? – luck.' They have been in some horrible trenches lately – once German, recently French and now taken over by the 7th Worcesters. Roland describes them as 'Nothing but 2–3 feet of water, and mud and fleas etc. Not at all nice. I do like to be able to get clean and dry. Nothing is more horrible than the feeling that never, never will one be able to get free from mud & wet again.'

Monday August 16th
Sapper Smith died at a quarter to 7.0 this evening. It is a merciful release for him as well as for us. Nothing could have looked more dreadful than he did this morning. It quite made me shudder to see his great bony hands at the end of his thin skeleton arms. I pray that when I come to die it may not be like that. We ought to pray in our litany for deliverance from a lingering as well as from a sudden death. It is not death itself that presents such terrors to the mind, but dissolution, and when that begins before death . . . I was not actually with him when he died. Nurse Olive said that after he was dead he looked exactly the same as he did this morning. I should like to have seen him dead as I have never seen death except in a two-day-old baby, and I should like to have seen it for the first time and faced and got it over.

Tuesday August 17th
Mother had a letter from Edward in which he said he had heard from Roland, who really seemed to think he might get away on Aug. 25th. I still won't think that it could be as near as a week to-morrow. If it is true, this diary will be quite inadequate to express what I shall feel. Sorrow is hard to describe, joy still harder, but the queer mixture of intense happiness with piercing agony practically impossible. If he comes it will be worse than ever after he has gone. And yet – 'one is willing to pay the bitterness of death for the sweetness of life.'

Wednesday August 18th
Never, never have I been in such agitation before. He has got leave; he is in England now. This morning as I was dusting bedsteads at the hospital Mother came with a wire from Mrs Leighton to say 'Roland comes home to-day.' Then at 1.0 came a wire from Roland himself handed in at Folkestone Pier at 12.29 to say 'Just arrived.' Mother asked leave off for me from Miss Hyland, who was very kind, & I wired at once 'Please tell

me how to see you.' The reason for agitation is that since then I have heard nothing at all, neither by telephone nor telegraph.

Thursday August 19th
This has been another day of agitation and misery and suspense. I waited all morning in vain to hear something of Roland, till at last at about 12.30 he telephoned from Lowestoft. I could hardly hear anything he said and there was such a noise going on that I could scarcely recognise his voice. The only thing characteristic of him that I could really hear was his laugh – that laugh which I expected never to hear again. Even after telephoning nothing was satisfactorily arranged; we left it quite indefinite whether he would try to come here to-night or meet me in London to-morrow.

Friday August 20th
I am bringing myself some time after to write about these next few days. I attempted to do it just after they were over, but each time I took up the pen & book & tried to write, it was with such a feeling of anguish that I could not help giving up the attempt. It is hard enough to do it now, but if I do not the so-far-most-important days of my life will go quite unrecorded. As it is I have forgotten many precious details which I can ill afford to lose when every little thing meant so much.

On this Friday I went to town by the early train, feeling horribly stirred up inside and finding it very difficult to realise that I was actually doing what I had dreamed of for months. Just before I started, a delayed letter, written last Sunday, came from Roland, which would have saved me much mental disturbance if I had only received it within a reasonable time. 'Am writing this in my notebook sitting on a couple of rather wet sandbags at the door of my dug-out. I am on duty till stand-to at 2.30 a.m. The night is very quiet; not a sound from the German lines. It is raining very slightly, but the sky is deep blue and the stars magnificent. And what do you think? I am coming home on leave on Wednesday – in three days' time. I did not know definitely till this morning and only had time to scribble a very hurried few lines to Mother, telling her to let you know too.

I cannot realise that I am coming at last, dear . . . I shall have about 6½ days in England.'

I tried to keep calm, but it was no good. I kept watching the country fly past, and wondered what he would be like and if his personality would be changed at all. (Oh! how it hurts to write all this, – after.) When I reached St Pancras & waited in the Waiting Room till he came, I tried to make myself look as nice as possible. But it wasn't much good, as the train had made me hot & untidy, & flushed with inward excitement. I couldn't keep still but paced about, now in the Waiting Room, now on the platform. At last, on one of my marches over the platform, I saw a figure I thought I knew go up & speak to a porter. I say 'thought' because since I saw it last that figure had acquired a maturity and a premature air of having knocked about the world which made me feel quite sad. If anyone had told me he was thirty I should not have been surprised. He seemed rather thinner too, and wore his clothes as if a military uniform & he had grown into one another. The next moment I was meeting him face to face. Partly owing to his short-sightedness and partly to his inward abstraction he would have passed me by quite calmly if I had not asked him in an effort at amused scornfulness if he failed to recognise me. Then he stopped and we shook hands without any sign of emotion except his usual paleness in tense moments. We stood looking at each other for quite a minute without moving. I scarcely realised where I was or what I was doing. It was difficult even to realise it was he. I felt as if the intervening months had never existed & that he had never been to the Front at all.

At the Florence we seated ourselves at the same table as we went to last Christmas just before *David Copperfield*, when the possibility of his going soon to the Front seemed then very remote and I asked him how he would like to be killed in action. It seemed so strange to see him sit there with his nerves quite unharmed after 5 months' daily peril and hear him, knowing what the dangers are, still speak so confidently.

He asked me if he was only going to see me for to-day. After considerable argument we arranged that he should come to Buxton with me for the night & then I should go back with him to Lowestoft for the week-end! What the world would say did not then enter into our calculations! I told him I had to interview the Matron at Camberwell, – which would have seemed so important if I were doing nothing else, but was on this day just a mere incident. We drove there in a taxi directly after lunch. I stood all through the interview, and know now just how a servant feels when she is being engaged. I told her quite unflinchingly that I was 23. She appeared quite favourably impressed & upon my assuring her that I did not mind hard work at all, or even long bus drives in the cold of a winter's morning, she promised to apply for me when their new huts were ready but said it would not be until about October.

Roland found a toy-shop where we went in to buy some mouth-organs for his men. I had had no experience of him when shopping & was very greatly amused – though anyone without plenty of time to spare might even be annoyed! I never saw anyone play so much in all my life! He took up first one mouth-organ & then another, & incidentally let the man at the shop know that he was no amateur officer but had been five months at the front. He was rather fond of proclaiming this at all the shops he went into & was very proud of the extra attention this distinction gained him. And very right, poor darling, that he should be too. He ought to get all the service he can when he has risked everything he possesses. But I couldn't help smiling a little, though really it was rather pathetic. Poor things! It is well that there can be *some* advantage from having been at the Front – even so small a one as this.

Before tea we sent off wires home to say Roland was coming, & to Edward & Victor to ask them to meet us at lunch in town to-morrow. Then Roland went off to telephone to Mrs Leighton to ask her to ask Mother & Daddy if I could go to Lowestoft, as under the circumstances it was a little strange for Roland to ask me, & I to go, without further consultation of anyone else. Roland told me at tea that his mother was rather startled by the various things he proposed to do & said 'Really, Roland! What does it all mean?' After that the world's point of view suddenly struck us both & we felt a little subdued. Roland said his mother was the freest & easiest person in the world, & would have no objection herself to unconventional behaviour, but she realised well enough that society would not stop at calling us unconventional, & that relations which could be carried on quite easily away from society (like Waldo's & Lyndall's in *The Story of an African Farm*) would hardly do in the midst of it. This attitude really hadn't struck us before, but when I came to think of it, it certainly occurred to me that if I saw another girl as intimate with a man as I was with him I should think – well, a great deal. In fact I should have hesitated very much to have the same relation to any [other] man as I had to him. Only he is such an utterly reliable person & has become so much part of my life, that I had taken the whole relation as a matter of course, without seeing at all how it would appear to other people.

During dinner in the train we discussed the world's attitude, & railed against society & its habit of rudely awakening one out of one's dreams. After dinner we went back to our carriage & went on thrashing out the same subject in low voices, & inwardly cursed the man who occupied the seat opposite & prevented our conversation from being as free as we should have liked. Finally at Derby the man got out. Strangely enough, when the train began to move on through the darkness – it was now about 9.0 – & we were left alone, I began to feel a kind of dread & an awkwardness at being left there with him – especially when he got up from the other end of the carriage & came & sat close beside me – and I almost wished someone else had got in. I tried not to think how much he thrilled me, though his presence was so magnetic I could scarcely bear it, and I turned from looking at him to watching the lights rush past through a chink of the down-drawn blind. I felt – not exactly sleepy – but dreamy and almost unreal. Only three days before, he had been at the Front, & now we were sitting close together in a dim, swiftly-moving railway carriage & I was feeling almost afraid . . . In a few minutes I looked round & saw the quiet, half-cynical smile upon his face that I have grown to associate with his more serious feelings.

'Why do you smile?' I said to him.

He did not look at me & answered quietly 'Only an idea.'

'What is it?' I asked.

He did not reply for a moment & then said in perfect calm 'Would it make things any better if we were properly engaged?'

'Roland!' I said, & continued somewhat unnecessarily 'What do you mean?'

'That,' he answered. 'Shall we be?'

I knew well enough what I wanted to say, but I thought of his youth and the brilliant career which if he comes through this war will undoubtedly be his. I wondered if, even though I would never marry any man until I could prevent myself from being a financial burden to him, I should hinder that brilliant career – or stand in his light in any way. I wondered if, though he is so old for his years, & the war has made him older still, he really knew his own mind, or if by waiting he would find someone who would suit him better & he would care for more. Yet I knew he wasn't the sort of person to love quickly or lightly – but I felt I couldn't let him say anything to my people without first hearing the version of his Mother, who loves him so passionately & understands him so well, & would not advise anything not for his best. I wanted to do – not what I should have liked, but what was right. If it were better for him I could renounce him – simply because I love him enough for that.

I leaned my head on my hands, looking away from him, & said 'Oh Roland! You said there was nothing in it.'

He took me up quickly – 'You know I didn't mean *nothing*, in that sense.'

'Oh! why did you say that & spoil everything?' I asked him.

'It hasn't spoilt everything, dear, has it?' he said quite gently, but a little anxiously.

I thought I would test him by using a little scorn & so I said as contemptuously as I knew how 'My dear *child*, you don't know—'

'What don't I know?' he asked.

'Your own mind,' I answered.

'Perhaps if I were twenty-*three*, I might,' he said very promptly. I laughed & felt inwardly delighted at the quick-wittedness of the reply.

We argued on in much the same strain. I can't put it all down here, for it was so precious & so painful, because of my inward confusion & turmoil. He was obviously puzzled, & didn't know how to take me; in the end he became quite angry, though very quietly so, & he was so tired too – an accumulated weariness from lack of sleep. As for me, I scarcely knew what I did or said. I wanted so much to do the right thing & yet didn't seem able to. Only I made him promise he wouldn't say anything to Mother or Father without my permission.

Mother met us at Buxton and said Father would have come only there was a wire from Mrs Leighton saying something about telephoning, so he had waited behind in case she did. Roland & I hardly spoke to one another again during that evening. We both felt embarrassed, as I had given him no definite answer, and refused to say whether I would go to Lowestoft or not. Daddy welcomed him very cordially and was obviously waiting for him to speak about me, which he would have done had it not been for my prohibition. Towards 11.0 Mrs Leighton rang up & asked if I could come. Mother answered it & as I would not decide said to Roland 'Is she to come or not, Roland?' He answered rather diffidently 'Yes, I think she is.' I said nothing, so Mother told Mrs Leighton I could go.

Roland was so tired he could not keep awake, so we all went to bed. I let him go without glancing in his direction & without saying good-night to him. I think he rather felt the apparent coldness – if his answer was true when I said to him in the train 'You know how much being engaged means. Do you really care for me like that?' and he replied 'Yes, like that.'

Often since I have felt repentant about refusing to say good-night, or treating him with even assumed indifference after all he had been through. I have often thought since how strange it was that the war seemed to have gone very far from the thoughts of us both, and we spoke of it scarcely at all, though our whole future is entirely concerned with it.

Mother seemed most anxious to know if we were engaged. I told her quite cheerfully that he wanted us to be, but I could not make up my mind. She little knew the real reason I had for hesitation, & thought that I did not know whether I liked him well enough or not, and was quite indignant. I heard her the next morning holding forth to Father about it in the bathroom, though she afterwards swore she had not mentioned the subject to him at all! 'She says she can't make up her mind, the little fool! That's just like Vera. You never know where you are with her.'

Saturday August 21st

Breakfast – for which I was careful to arrive in time & Roland came down late – was a somewhat embarrassing meal. Last night I had teased him about the letters I was keeping for him & said I would either not give them back or else ask something so impossible that he would have to let me keep them rather than give it. I had been thinking everything over the night before – I did not go to bed till about 1.0 – and many of the objections to our engagement which I had first seen & tormented him over seemed to have faded away. I wanted to tell him this, and to give him back my letters, but felt shy, and didn't quite know how to do it. I waited about & put it off till a few minutes before we had to go to the station. Then I called him into the drawing-room and we both stood by the window, I with the letters in my hands. At last I said abruptly 'Here you are; take them. You can have them after all. I don't want anything for them.' I knew what I *did* want, but all through me we weren't engaged & I did not dare to ask for it.

Then I said vaguely 'What we were talking about last night . . . I didn't know what to do, but I do want to do the right thing, but if you still want me to . . .'

'Well?' he said.

'Alright,' I answered.

'Oh!' he said coldly & a little ironically. 'Do you really think it necessary?'

I didn't know how to take him nor he how to take me. We stood looking at each other for a minute or two. Mother began to call for us to get ready to go to the station. I wanted him so much to speak to them before he left, perhaps never to see them again, but I didn't know how to ask him to. I put the letters into his hand and simply said abruptly 'Take them.' So we went away without his having said a word to [Mother & Father] about me or the future, & I felt a very bitter regret, not alleviated by the fact that it was all my fault.

Once on the London train the same embarrassment & intermittent sparring as on the previous evening began again. I kept reading my own letters, chiefly to myself, but now & then out loud to him. I asked him if he was surprised that I had taken his 'proposal' in the way I had. He said he was certainly a little astonished at first, though if he had thought about it beforehand he would probably have known that I should take it just exactly as I did. We were getting a little more in touch with one another & he was condescending to move a little from his distant seat by the other window when a somewhat inquisitive young officer came & shared our carriage, and by the time Leicester came & he got out, the freezing process had proceeded some way again. But this time we talked on the subject of an engagement without much ado and he kept urging me to say *something*, whatever it was. 'Say what you *want*, whether right or not,' he said.

If it had not been for shyness I should have capitulated quite. After some more vague discussion, I finally said 'Very well, I will show what I should have said last night if I had said what I really wanted to say.'

'Well?' he said. 'What is it?'

I took out of the packet one of the letters I had written him when he first went to the Front – the one I wrote to answer that in which he said he had been kissing my photograph. At the end of my own letter I had said 'I envy the photograph. It is more fortunate than its original; *she* has never quite been able to break through your reserve . . .' I smiled half-cynically to myself as I read this. With him there beside me it was so difficult to believe that I could ever have brought myself to put it. He seized hold of the letter & tried to take it away, & after a little resistance I gave it up to him, pointing to the momentous words. He read it in silence, & then looked at me, & I back at him, still with the very cynical expression. Suddenly he came over from his window & kissed me – with such a boyish shyness & awkwardness that I could have laughed – only I shivered instead. He had so obviously never kissed any other girl before me. I wonder how many young men of his age could say the same. I drew away from him and said rather mockingly 'Oh, you needn't be in a hurry. You certainly haven't had much practice at this!'

Again there was silence & then I began to talk again, seriously this time & on a difficult subject – which however I had to touch upon in order to explain my somewhat strange attitude. I spoke of the lack of faith I had in men & their love – & expressed my doubts whether the intellectual & spiritual in love could rise & live untarnished in spite of its constant association with the physical that is in us all. I told him how I had hated the idea of marriage & how I had determined before meeting him that I never would marry anyone . . . I told him all about B.S. 'He didn't want a *companion*,' I said, rather fiercely. 'He just wanted a wife.'

'I'm not like that,' said Roland in the gentle, considerate voice I have learnt to associate with the rousing of his emotion. 'In fact, rather the opposite.'

'I know,' I said. 'I wouldn't stop in this carriage another minute if I thought you were.'

He laughed – a little bitterly, and his eyes looked rather distressed.

'Forgive me for seeming to doubt you like this,' I said. 'I do trust you more than anyone in the world. But I have thought on this subject & got so angry about it that all my views have grown a little distorted. The iron has entered into my soul & I can't get it out. You do understand, don't you?'

'Yes,' he said sadly, 'I do understand.'

'And are you angry with me,' I asked, 'for talking like this?'

'No, dear – of course I'm not,' he said, still very gravely.

'I will try & trust in you,' I said. 'And learn to believe in you these few days.'

So, without any actual question and answer, but more through a mutual arrangement founded on a mutual under-standing, we agreed to consider ourselves engaged. We admitted too that, much as we would have liked to keep it to ourselves, the world for convenience' sake would have to know. We decided with some amusement that we would tell Mrs Leighton we were engaged for three years or the duration of the war. The originality of the notion seemed to please Roland, even though the reservation had no foundation in fact. So the conversation lost its previous tone of seriousness & almost gloom, though Roland remained rather distant & grave all through the day.

Edward & Victor were on St Pancras Station waiting for us. Roland, not quite so tall & much broader, seeming much older, in the tunic he had slept in many times & a very worn & dirty-looking Sam Browne belt, presented a very marked contrast to the other two. (Really I think he was rather proud to emphasize his negligé & war-worn 'Front' appearance.)

So the Three Musketeers, as Mrs Leighton calls them, met together for the first time since the War began. From their calm greeting you would never have guessed that in the meantime Victor had almost passed through the gates of Death, that Roland had had five months of the possibility of coming to them, face to face, that Edward had overcome various difficulties placed in his way of being a soldier, or that Roland had fallen in love with me. I thought I might be in the way, & had made plans to leave the three alone but in the end none of them came off. However I managed to give them a short interval to themselves during the afternoon & otherwise played the part of a very interested spectator without seeming to be in the way at all.

During a long & somewhat elaborate lunch Roland did most of the talking, which to me who am used to his saying very little, appeared somewhat unusual. I can easily understand that at school he must have been the acknowledged leader of the three. The great idea of the two was to ask him questions about things at the Front – technical details & problems of all kind – & then let him expound them at length, which he did quite readily. I listened with great interest, as I had never been given such a good idea of the Front before. It isn't every man that has enough reverence for women to speak without reserve – as he does, the dear Feminist – of the business side of his life. But he knows that a woman – at any rate this particular woman – could understand very well indeed. He went into all sorts of technical details about trenches, barbed-wire entanglements, positions etc. He dealt too with many of the usually unmentioned & more unpleasant aspects of the war, such as the condition of the charnel-house trenches, or the shooting of sentries who go to sleep on duty & are described in the casualty list as 'Died'. Military discipline I suppose – but all the same it makes me feel sick to hear about it; no man can quite understand what it means to a woman, who knows the trouble & pain the production of an individual costs, to hear of this light destruction of a human creature for what may be simply the result of physical overstrain. But I suppose it might have such serious consequences that this cruel stringency is imperative. Roland told us how he saved the life of one such man – a very decent person

– by waking him up before the Corporal who was with him came on the scene & also saw the man asleep. The man of course could not be punished, for, Roland says, the word of only one man, even though he be an officer, is insufficient to condemn anyone to death. Roland turned to me & asked me to excuse him for the technical details he was going into. I told him with some scorn that I was as much interested in them as anyone else. He smiled & continued & did not apologise again.

Soon it was time for the train again (Roland says he never sees me except either in the train or at meals!). Liverpool St had a dirty & very bustling appearance on that afternoon, chiefly due to the very small platforms & the very large number of people either going by train or seeing someone off. We only had just a moment or two to say goodbye to Edward and Victor before the train went. I did not know if I should see Edward again, as he thought he was going to the front the next week & was making all preparations for departure. The train moved off & they both saluted gravely.

I was interested in the country we passed through as I had never been anywhere near the East Coast before. We passed by the Norfolk Broads, & all the way along the scenery was flat & watery. At the end of dinner Roland produced a little bottle of chlorodyne; I meant no curiosity, but I suppose my eye, which has become trained to the sight of medicines & drugs, looked at it a little enquiringly. He informed me rather diffidently that he had had a slight attack of dysentery while in France but was quite alright again now. So there was some reason for his paleness besides insufficiency of sleep. This same lack of sleep began to tell on him before the end of the journey, and I sat, feeling extremely wide awake myself, watching the long eye-lashes droop slowly over his rather white cheek. I wanted to hug him but fortunately – or unfortunately as the case may be – a certain cold reticence always comes & checks me before I put these warm impulses into action.

He roused up a little when we arrived & got into the taxi that was waiting for us. I was thinking somewhat apprehensively of meeting all the other Leightons at once, & two of them unknown to me, but managed to take quite an intelligent interest in the position of the sea when he indicated it to me. The taxi stopped before a rather tall and round-looking house, something like a large turret with a small piece of garden in front. I could not distinguish anything very clearly as the light was fading fast.

Roland & I walked up the little path to the house; he opened the door & I stepped into a darkness much more complete & baffling than that outside. Several vague figures promptly emerged from a lighted room in what looked to me the distance. A dim white-robed figure whom I knew by the voice to be Mrs Leighton came up to me, took both my hands & greeted me so warmly that almost all my shyness disappeared. She explained – as I had already gathered – that the house was darkened owing to the prevalence of Zeppelin raids. All Lowestoft suffered in the same way, but they especially because the house had so many windows, & standing by itself right at one end of the town was a landmark far out to sea. They were only allowed to have lights in two rooms – the dining-room & Roland's bedroom, because they faced the back, & even in these the electric lights had to have brown paper shades & the windows thick dark curtains to cover them entirely. She then introduced me to Mr Leighton & Evelyn, & Clare, whom I had of course met in London.

Then Mrs Leighton took me by the hand & led me with great care into the room I was to have. She explained as she piloted me along that she was putting me into Roland's room because, as my family *had* allowed me to come & face the Zeppelins, she was determined I should be in the safest place possible. Roland had been turned out to share a bed with Evelyn in his room on the top floor. I told her it was a shame to turn him out & I was not the least afraid of Zeppelins, but she said he wouldn't mind at all. By this time she had put the light up & I had a full view of the strange, eccentric-looking but inexplicably attractive woman who was Roland's mother. For the moment, although I knew well enough what she would look like, I had the same feeling of startled petrifaction that seized me – for a second only – when I saw her before in London. She was wearing a white muslin dress of no particular shape, with a wide sash in which the predominating colour was pink. Her hair – I had never seen her without a hat before – was a pure corn-coloured gold slightly touched with grey; it could hardly be called dressed, but was fastened up indiscriminately all round with very apparent hairpins. She seemed very large by the side of me, but was neither quite so stout nor so tall as I had pictured her in my recollection. In that moment of observation I took in some of the resemblances & also the differences between her & her beloved son, who is like her in so much. Her complexion is coarser than his & less pale but equally clear, and whereas his brows are very dark & rather arched, hers, though distinctly marked, are more in accordance with the general fairness of her colouring. Then more distinctive than all were her eyes – so much the same as his & yet again so subtly different. Hers have not the long curly lashes nor yet the slight short-sightedness which give his an occasional sleepy appearance. In hers is a kindly humour which his so far lack and, serious though they can be, they never have the look of almost tragic sadness so characteristic of his when he is thinking or feeling deeply. In both their eyes is the same expression of vivid intellectuality, the same infinite trustworthiness, the same indication of a capacity for, not the superficial & apparent, but the real & intrinsic, unselfishness.

'I *am* so glad to see you, dear,' she said, still holding my hands, & impulsively drew me close to her & kissed me very tenderly. She stood away from me a moment, looking at me meditatively and still very kindly. I felt subconsciously amazed at the love & generosity which welcomed me so warmly – I who had come to share with her the place in her boy's heart which she alone used to occupy. Apparently in her short scrutiny she had discovered signs of weariness in my untidy & much-travelled appearance. 'Aren't you very tired?' she asked.

'Not very,' I replied.

'Not after all your hard work – & these journeys?' she said. 'Why, dear, you must be worn out!' With that she kissed me again, said she would leave me to myself to take my things off, & that Robert had been wanting very much to see what I was like. 'I feel as if you will take some knowing again,' she said. 'You write very charming letters, dear.' I wondered to myself whether the letters had had a charm for her as authoress or as woman – the Mother of Roland. I hoped both. With that she left me, telling me to come to the dining-room as soon as I was ready & not to hurry.

My hair very much needed tidying, & I looked about for my case, which Roland in the confusion of arriving had left in the darkened hall. All the Leighton family seemed anxious to look after me, & by my bedroom door I came across Clare, who had been hovering in the distant background while her mother was talking to me. She is not much taller than I but plumper, & has a healthy though not over-bright colour, clear candid grey-green eyes, & two great plaits of dark brown hair, tied up in the middle with wide ribbons. She said Evelyn should find my [suitcase] & promptly disappeared.

Evelyn with the case was the next person to appear in the limelight. I had quite expected to dislike or at least be annoyed by him, as I have a prejudice against boys between the ages of nine & sixteen. But this particular fourteen-year-old delighted me; he gazed at me very attentively, but with a frank & charming interest instead of the usual furtive inquisitiveness of the small boy. He was tall for his age – almost as tall as Roland, but very slender and wiry looking, & was dressed in the dark blue uniform of a naval cadet. The likeness to Mrs Leighton was slight compared with Roland's resemblance to her.

I washed & tidied as best I could in a few minutes, & then went into the dining-room, where Roland already was with the others. I sat beside him in the place left for me, next to Mr Leighton & opposite Clare. I felt a little shy, though not unpleasantly so, beneath Mrs Leighton's critical & affectionate gaze from the other end of the table. Mr Leighton is fifteen years older than Mrs Leighton – who ran away with him when she was eighteen – but somehow did not *look* much older. His hair & moustache, which are both abundant, were quite frankly red. His eyes were blue & quite small, and in figure he was slim & of medium height. I have always known he was very deaf – a result of which is that the family since they have to speak so loud seldom address him at all, and he himself only volunteers remarks occasionally, either to enquire what the conversation is about or to make some statement quite irrelevant to it. There was a keen observation beneath all his quietness, & I could see he was studying me even anxiously.

Everything was done in a free & easy manner, in great & pleasing contrast to the ceremony & fussiness at home. They all have a quite unblushing habit of discussing one's personal appearance in front of one. This is a little disconcerting at first but one soon gets used to it. During this particular meal Mrs Leighton remarked to the company in general 'Have you noticed how Vera's eyes look straight *through* you as well as at you?'

'Yes,' said Clare. 'Isn't it awful!'

I smiled & said I had not been aware I was so rude, but Mrs Leighton said she didn't mean that, but she had particularly noticed the straightness & directness of my look. Incidentally she also discussed & admired my complexion, and remarked that there were several notes in my voice the same as in Clare's. After dinner she insisted on turning my face to the light to see exactly what colour my eyes were. This – since they are a mixture of green & grey & a sort of amber colour – is always somewhat difficult to determine. Roland said they were hazel as far as he could tell.

After dinner I was carefully piloted all over the house by the family to see as much as the darkness would reveal. I was particularly struck by a large room on the first floor, three walls of which consist almost entirely of windows, fronting the sea. The room now is a jumble of displaced furniture, half-packed trunks & books, and some artistic materials belonging to Clare, who paints there in the day-time. The Leightons are always in a state of semi-preparation for departure, in case the Zeppelin raids become too disturbing for work.

Roland seemed restless & wandered about a good deal & it was to Mrs Leighton alone that I talked during the earlier part of the evening. We went downstairs & sat in the dark drawing-room, where I could distinguish very little beyond the white gleam of her dress. It is very easy to talk intimately to her (for me, at least) at any time, but under such circumstances especially so. Roland kept wandering in & out but never became a permanency. I wondered if Mrs Leighton wanted to write but she told me she wanted to talk to me & had in any case made up her mind that she would do no more work during Roland's leave. Mrs Leighton told me the Zeppelin raids never came after 2.0 as after that they had not sufficient time to get back before daylight. The only warning given was the sudden putting-out of the electric light; this was not much help to people who went to bed at early hours, but her habit of regularly going to bed at 2.0 was very useful now as she was able to give the alarm if any raid did come. In fact the family, with the exception of Clare & Evelyn, seemed to have acquired a habit of all staying up until Zeppelin hours are nearly over. I quite hoped a raid would come while I was there, as I have always since the war began been anxious to see a Zeppelin, and I knew I should not be afraid, for so long as the being who is the source of all my hopes & fears, & I, were together, it did not seem to matter very much what happened.

Mrs Leighton & I talked for a long time. She told me various details about publishers & their annoying habits, to all of which I listened with of course immense interest. Then she led me on to nursing & strangely enough seemed as interested in my experiences as I in hers. She has an immense capacity for being really & genuinely interested in everything. She was the most sympathetic listener I have ever had, & seemed to under-stand everything without explanations being necessary. All the time I talked with her I kept being impressed by the resem-blances to Roland – & again the differences, which were all the more emphasized because the resemblances are so strong. In certain tones of the voice, in points of view, & their way of putting things, they are so very alike. The chief difference of course is her lack of shyness & unnecessary reserve in contrast with his extreme reticence. Consequently she talks much more & is much less afraid of showing her thoughts & feelings to someone in sympathy with her. And then of course she has all those qualities which he lacks through the mercilessness of youth – humour & kindness & tolerance & genuine sympathy. She is such a very hopeful augury of what Roland if he is spared will become & may even surpass.

She took me to see her temporary bedroom, where only a candle, which she only lit for a moment, was allowed, and which seemed to be almost entirely filled by a very huge bed. Roland followed us in, and in a very few minutes we had all established ourselves on the bed, where we stayed talking for at least an hour. Roland lolled on the pillow end of the bed, & Mrs Leighton on the other, while I sat on the edge of it with my feet dangling down a long way from the ground. Mrs Leighton talked a great deal about Roland, & told me all about his childhood, knowing I suppose how I should love to hear. Roland lay on the pillows without making any comment, listening quite contentedly & as if it were all as a matter of course (which I suppose it has become to him) her telling me how she had always worshipped & adored him from his very earliest years. From what I observed myself & from what Edward told me – how all the family look up to & adore him, how he has always had everything he wanted that it was possible to give him, and how all the little spare money there has been has always been his, I wonder he is not more autocratic & spoilt than he is. But she told me that never from his earliest childhood had he once attempted to take advantage of her worship of him. This is so completely the Roland that I know. He never would take advantage of anyone, strong or weak.

After telling me about his childhood Mrs Leighton got me to talk about myself and the great contrast between my life's desires & the small opportunities in my previous life for their fulfilment. I said just a very little about the way every aspiration *might*, had it not been so strong, have been nipped in the bud by the frantic attempts to turn me into an uninteresting, conventional, ordinary person. Mrs Leighton needed no more than a little telling to make her understand. She was very interested in the incongruity between my parents & me, and wanted to meet them, especially Father.

When we had been there about an hour she suddenly asked me if I was hungry, & when I confessed I was rather, we roused ourselves from the bed & went back into the dining-room, where she produced a large tin of freshly-made buns. Mr Leighton was still there & we all started munching buns while she & Roland produced the gramophone & some records. I do not remember everything that it played but I know Braga's 'Serenata' which I have so often heard on Edward's violin. Last of all Mrs Leighton put on that glorious & very moving love-song 'Ich liebe dich'. I half-suspect she did it as a little experiment to see how I should be affected by it. I sat quite quiet & as apparently unaffected by it as possible, but I could not, though I tried, avoid gradually turning my eyes to where

Roland was standing near the gramophone. Ever since we went into the dining-room he appeared to wrap himself in a kind of aloofness, not so much from the others as from me. His face when I looked at it now was as nearly expressionless as he can ever make it; for all he seemed to be aware of it I might not have been there at all, & I need not have troubled to try & hide the fact that I was looking at him, as he did not take the least notice of where I was looking or what I was thinking. And yet he says music affects him deeply! But just so he looked in Uppingham Chapel when Mr Sterndale Bennett played Karg-Elert's 'Clair de Lune'. I did not understand him at Uppingham, & I could not make him out that night at Lowestoft. I can't now.

The gramophone at last was stopped & we decided to go to bed (as Mrs Leighton said Zeppelin hours were over for that night at any rate). Roland had put the records away & disappeared without saying anything to me or attempting to say good-night. Mrs Leighton came with me into my room, talking again about Roland; how she was going soon to tuck him up in bed, which she had done ever since he was a baby. She told me that the first night of his leave, when he had come in so tired from his journeyings & an accumulated insufficiency of sleep that he could scarcely stand, he was just like a child, and nestled down into the bed saying how lovely it was to have sheets & pillows again. Something hurt at the back of my eyes like tears.

She then looked at the bed & asked me if I was sure I should be warm enough. I said I knew I should because I never wanted many bedclothes. 'Why, you little thing!' she said in her impulsive way. 'You never seem to want anything!' I fancy, I don't know why, that the look she gave me was almost sad. I told her that I was nearly impervious to the influence of comforts & luxuries & that I was trying to break myself of those which still had a hold on me. She kept on looking at me meditatively as if she were studying me again. Then she kissed me again & left me – left me thinking as I have never thought of anyone before in my life, of how I worshipped Roland & adored his Mother. One can trace in his character those high influences of hers which have been his from his earliest years.

Sunday August 22nd

I shall never forget this day. It will shine out in my memory like a beacon long after nearly all else has passed into oblivion.

I don't remember exactly how I spent the first part of the morning, but it was chiefly in wandering about & getting acquainted with the lie of the land which I had seen so dimly last night. The day was showery & rather cold but there were fitful gleams of sunshine between dark clouds. Heather Cliff stands in a position which its name exactly describes; it is almost on the edge of a low cliff which at the back is covered with gorse & heather & in front slopes gently down towards the sea. Between the foot of the cliff, along the top of which runs the promenade, and the sea, is a small flat plain of grass & sand – just the spot for landing & mustering a surprise party of hostile troops. Lowestoft has indeed been afraid of both invasion & bombardment ever since the war began. As a guard against both these two dangers the plain between the cliff & the sea has been thoroughly entrenched & defended with wire entanglements, and on top of the cliff along the front are several machine-gun stations. On this particular Sunday morning the sea, though grey, was calm, and on the horizon a few trawlers were drifting lazily to & fro; it was almost impossible to believe that there was a war on & that this was one of the towns in England compelled to realise it most clearly.

Clare & Evelyn decided to support the myth of family respectability (they are the only ones who ever do) by going to church. I never had much opportunity for conversation with Clare, but from various remarks dropped by the family I gathered that her mind is at present largely occupied by religious doubts & difficulties both imaginary and real – a mixture of the kind which beset me at the age of fifteen & laid the foundations of my present agnostic tendencies.

Soon after breakfast Mrs Leighton took me into the drawing-room & showed me her collection of old photographs – chiefly of her children when they were small. Even in those childish photographs of Roland there was more than a hint of the almost tragic sadness which so often comes into his eyes now. And even in those days he had a very marked air of arrogance – that self-confident assurance of being something above the ordinary –

which is so characteristic of him to-day. There were very few portraits of Mrs Leighton; she said she did not take well. The best one was a snapshot of her talking to George Meredith in his garden. When she showed it to me she told me how she used to spend days with George Meredith – who seems to have taken rather a fancy to her – during the last years of his life. He liked to have her talk to him or listen to him talking; this became rather a trial as he was so very deaf and somewhat crotchety.

I found Roland playing about with his papers in my room. I had previously asked him if I might be graciously permitted to see the poem his Mother had told me about. When I came in he handed me the notebook he always carries about with him & pointing to a particular page said 'This is the Villanelle you wanted to see.' The poem was dated April 25th, 1915, and was called 'Violets'. I remembered how on that day he had written me a letter – he was then in Ploegsteert Wood – enclosing some violets from the top of his dug-out which he said he had just picked for me. With this recollection in my mind I read the poem.

> Violets from Plug Street Wood,
> Sweet, I send you oversea.
> (It is strange they should be blue,
> Blue, when his soaked blood was red,
> For they grew around his head;
> It is strange they should be blue.)
> Violets from Plug Street Wood,
> Think what they have meant to me—
> Life and Hope and Love and You—
> (And you did not see them grow
> Where his mangled body lay,
> Hiding horror from the day;
> Sweetest, it was better so.)
> Violets from oversea,
> To your dear, far, forgetting land
> These I send in memory,
> Knowing You will understand.

I handed it back to him without criticism. I could not have made any; the union of brilliance of intellect with personal love closed my lips quite effectually. Not until after I had parted from him & he sent me the poem enclosed in a letter did I dare to say how perfect I thought this small literary gem of his. I only said 'Why didn't you send me this at the same time as the violets?' 'Oh, I don't know,' he said. 'It wasn't finished for one thing.'

I looked out of the window to the sea below and asked him to take me down to it. We walked across the grass plain & along the sand to the water's edge. The sea means less to him than it does to me because he has lived close to it on & off all his life, but to me it always speaks of infinite aspirations & dreams & longings. It was just like a dream to stand with him beside me, & gaze out across the water & feel the breeze from the North Sea against my face. Far away along the coast to the north I could see Yarmouth Pier, like a black sea-monster rising out of the waves, and on the horizon the trawlers were still steaming lazily to & fro. It all felt so ephemeral; I could not believe I had been at my prosaic Buxton home only two days ago. It seemed as if either that or this must be unreal; they did not both feel able to fit into the same life. We walked along the beach & sat down on the end of a breakwater a few yards away from where the waves were breaking on the sand. For a while I said nothing, but looked out across the water and listened to the soothing lullaby of its eternal song. I felt then that I could ask for nothing better of life than to sit there for ever with the sound of the sea in my ears and Roland standing on the beach by my side.

At last we began to talk a little – quite tentatively – about the engagement. He told me his mother had been rather bewildered by the 'three years or duration of the War' limitation until he had explained that it was scarcely to be taken seriously. I had told him the day before that I wanted to talk it all over with Mrs Leighton & he said she was going to speak to me about it sometime to-day. I asked him how he really thought she liked me & said I believed she looked upon me in almost the same light as he did.

'Well,' he said. 'She can't see you from quite the point of view that I do.'

'Why not?' I asked.

'Well,' he said again. 'Obviously she can't be in love with you, can she?'

'Are you?' I enquired, looking at him very straight.

'Yes, of course,' he said, but regarded me with the rather cold & puzzled air I had noticed the evening before. If I can't make him out, I think that sometimes he cannot understand me either.

In a minute or two he offered to show me the trenches on the grass plain & we went along in that direction. We had to pass by one or two rows of wire entanglements, which he said were very bad because they could be penetrated quite easily when only one or two strands of wire had been cut. The long rows of stakes & tangled wires extended right from the foot of the promenade wall to the sea, but in one or two places they were not quite joined together, so as to enable people to get through. Roland took me down into the trenches, which he told me were just the same as those at the front. The parapet was well above his head, & the ground all boarded. He explained to me various technical details, such as the use of periscopes, ways of taking cover from shells, the difference between fire trenches & reserve & communication trenches etc. He told me that the French had a habit of burying a dead man in his dug-out by just putting him inside and blocking up the entrance. The chief disadvantage of this was a consequent shortage of dug-outs. We began to talk about the more gruesome aspects of the trenches & to discuss callousness. He said one began to take horrors as a matter of course so soon, & I said one found that even in a hospital, where the tending of suffering soon became a mere matter of business, & the sight of pain just an element in the day's work. Why, even the gentle soothing touch with which one learns to raise a head or smooth a pillow or bandage a limb is only something acquired by practice and only in very rare cases inspired by pity. Roland told me that every day in his trenches he was accustomed to pass by the foot of a dead man who had been buried in the parapet. By this time the foot had become quite black, but he saw it every day & thought nothing of it. I asked him if he thought this callousness was a permanent thing & meant a loss of sensitiveness ever after. He said he did not think so; it was an acquired necessity in war, but he thought that if he left the trenches for a long time & then went back, what he had to do & see would give him the same feelings of horror as they did at first. I said I didn't think I could ever grow callous about the suffering of someone I loved, especially if that someone were he. Somehow this conversation made me feel very like crying. It seemed so dreadful that anyone could grow callous about the things we had been speaking of – especially such hypersensitive people as he & I.

[After lunch] we intended going for a walk & went through the gate out on to the heath behind the house, but there were so many nurses and prams on the more public parts, & so many couples 'Sunday afternooning' on the less, that we soon gave it up as impossible and returned to the garden. He fetched two chairs out of the summer-house & put them very close together at one end of the tennis court, where though right in the open we were quite hidden by the surrounding bushes from both the road & the house. But in spite of the nearness of our chairs he attempted no form of caress except to put back the hair from my eyes with a very gentle hand when the wind blew it over my face.

It was enough to be near him – in fact that means so much that any further sign of demonstrativeness hurts me and I could not bear it to happen often. I suppose anyone who had seen us sitting there would have thought we were exchanging endearments quite foolish & meaningless to anyone but ourselves, but as a matter of fact we were talking quite impersonally on our old subject of the possibility of a future life. We keep on discussing it & never get any further, and that afternoon was no exception to the rule. We were still more inclined to think that there was not than that there was, Roland arguing that we were probably entirely physical after all, & that our personality depended in no more than the more or less of grey matter that composed the human brain. But he again confessed that this explanation could not be made to fit the soul's striving after impersonal aims, or that strange thing called duty which made one unhappy if the right but unpleasant thing was not done, or, more than all, that human idealism & heroism which deliberately chose something to its own material disadvantage because it instinctively felt that this was best. We puzzled on over the question – which in spite of its attractiveness is so very unprofitable, since no one in this world can come to any definite conclusion however much discussion takes place. And in any case the spiritual evolution of the human race now & here, independently of the fact whether it continues in another state of existence or not, is our concern here, since in this alone we have something not utterly unknown or impossible to strive for, & can feel the ground firm beneath our feet. Yet it is only in human nature to hope for a Hereafter, to wish that this vital sensitive thing that is one's self may not cease to be – still more that what it loves may continue also.

I sometimes feel that if only I could know that

> Hand in hand, just as we used to do,
> We two shall live our passionate poem through
> In some serene to-morrow,

I should not be troubled much by an absolute certain denial of the immortality of the soul. After all, most of my ideals are independent of whether it is immortal or not – as all ideals, to be of any value, should be. And yet – if he never came back to be part of my life – with what anguish I should seek to believe that 'there are no dead'. As for Roland himself, his thoughts of death seem to be associated very little with either hope or fear. He looks upon the ending of life as a terrible & indescribable thing, but five months at the Front seem to have taught him to look upon actual death itself as something inconsiderable & small. In consequence he seems to combine a passionate love of life with an indifference to death quite remarkable even in a soldier. One sees the artist in his keen enjoyment & appreciation of life itself & all things vital & living; the soldier in his resolute schooling of his artistic imagination, the keeping it strictly apart from fear, either of danger or of death. At times again he paradoxically drops both these points of view at once & says that the idea of being nothing at all has an irresistible attraction for him. Into that phase of his nature I cannot enter, for in all my changes of mood I never feel that. I may worship him but – no, I don't understand him. It is the fact that I long so much to understand him thoroughly – which would take years – & may never even get the chance to understand him at all, which makes the possibility – I suppose I should say the probability – of losing him so terrible to me, & the thought of life without him so infinitely empty.

The conclusion definitely unreached, we rose up, reluctantly rather, & went in to tea, which we were again late for. After it Mrs Leighton strolled round the garden, I think with Roland, & Mr Leighton, Clare, Evelyn & I went down to the sea again. Mr Leighton kept with me all the way down to the beach, without saying much. Whether due to Roland's connection with me, or to something in my own personality, I seem for some reason to have pleased & even touched this silent man, who shows his fondness for me in quite small & very tactful attentions. This morning, for instance, he was out before breakfast to pick me a rose which he presented to me without a word when I came into the dining-room.

Clare conversed with me on the way up from the sea, more personally than she had ever done before. In many ways she reminds me of myself at the same age – not so long ago, but I seem to have learnt a tremendous amount since then. Only she is much more sensible than I was – in fact I think she will always have more of this quality than I shall at any age. She has the same characteristic as I had of obvious introspection & the same fondness of talking to other people about themselves, & herself.

'You know, you're a cynic,' she said to me. 'And I think I know what has made you one. It was reading that dreadful book *The Story of an African Farm.*'

'Yes,' I said, 'perhaps it was. But you're a cynic too. Was it that book?'

'Yes,' she said, 'I adored it, but it has made me cynical. It seems fated to have an influence on our family.'

Once her reserve was broken she talked without further restraint. 'Do you ever feel that things puzzle you & you don't know what to do, & you are miserable because nothing you want ever goes right?' she asked me.

'Yes,' I said, 'I do, and did – I think I am very like you in many ways.'

'Yes, you are,' she agreed. 'And like us, there's one thing you're not – you're not a scrap sentimental – but I think you have lots of emotion in you, & you might have a bad temper.'

I began to think the penetration of the 'Bystander', as her

family calls her, a little uncanny. 'All of you have heaps of emotion too,' I said. She admitted that they all had. 'Perhaps Roland most of all,' I went on, 'though he is so clever at hiding it.'

'Oh yes – *he* has. But I expect,' she said humbly, 'that you know him much better than I do.'

I smiled at this. 'I don't think I do,' I said. 'I really know him very little indeed.'

When we got back to the house we found Mrs Leighton & Roland wandering about in the garden. Roland asked me to come for a walk again. When we had gone some way along the road, we turned off into a rough path past a thicket to the edge of the cliff. Then he said to me 'Let's sit down here for a little while.' So we sat down there on a soft dry bed of heather, and were very silent for a few moments. Immediately beneath our feet the cliff, still covered with gorse & heather, sloped down to the shore. The sea, as calm as the sound of it was scarcely noticeable, was a vast grey shadow, joining indistinguishably with the sky, over which a thin filmy veil of sombre mistiness seemed to be drawn. Through this shone the faint steady gleams of a pale moon, disclosing but blurring the outlines of all things round, and making the whole world grey.

Then, as I sat there gazing, Roland suddenly put his arm round me and drew me close to him – closer than I had ever been before. At first I half-resisted a little, but in the darkness it seemed absurd to be so shy, so I did not resist long but gave way to him & said half-mournfully, half-playfully, 'Well, Roland, I suppose it may as well be now – since afterwards perhaps it will be nevermore.'

'Now or nevermore?' he said dreamily. 'Well, perhaps, but I don't think so, dear.'

I had taken off my hat because I loved the soft sea-breeze to blow over my face & hair. His arm was round me still & with his other hand he gently played with the little wisps of hair that the wind blew over my face. After a time he rested his head against my shoulder & we became quite silent . . . I never thought that anything would ever happen to me like this. They say every woman has her hour. I don't quite believe that, for I fear that some have none, & most of the others are lucky enough to have more than one. This at all events was one of mine. I knew I worshipped – and I came very near to believing – what is hardest of everything for me to believe – that I *was* worshipped – worshipped by this brilliant, strong, unsensual being, whose head was so close to mine, bent low with emotion & a kind of awe. As far as I had then lived, it was the sweetest hour of my life.

But in being there, knowing we had been together in life so little, & were so soon to part again, there was such a painful joy & a joyful pain that I could scarcely bear it, & suddenly wanting to come back to earth again for a moment I said 'What's the time?' He laughed at the abrupt & intentional bathos, & produced his watch. 'Twenty-five to nine,' he said. 'We needn't go yet.'

It all seems so unreal when I think of it now, that it is sometimes hard to believe that it really happened. Yet it is one of the few things the memory of which will go with me to life's end, be that soon or late.

Again I felt his fingers playing caressingly with my hair, and then 'You are a dear,' he said, and gently drew my face down to him & kissed me.

Oh! I am glad his kisses come so seldom, for they mean so much that I could not bear the agonising joy of them often. They give me a thrill & a shock; they stir me in a way that the easy voluptuous oft-repeated kisses of a sensuous man would never have power to do. There, on that dark heather-covered cliff beside the sea, I realised the depth & strength of my own passion – realised it & was afraid.

At last he sighed, looked at his watch, & rose, & I too. It was over; the spell was broken. 'We ought to be going now,' he said reluctantly, and we turned back along the rough path.

Supper was rather a quiet meal. Roland & I were a little subdued by the recollection of the last few hours. I hoped after supper I might get a chance of seeing Mrs Leighton alone, but Mr Leighton insisted on sitting with us until a very late hour. While we talked Mr Leighton sat at the other end of the table and reconstructed in matches the formation of the various armies in different battles. Occasionally he broke into our conversation with remarks on the situation in France, and once asked us to come & see the strategy of the Retreat from Mons, as depicted in matches on the tablecloth. He demands so little of anyone that it seems to be an invariable rule of the household to do whatever he asks immediately. At last however he did go. Roland quietly but firmly said *he* was going and, departing ostensibly to bed, left me alone with his mother almost before I realised he had gone.

We were both standing, and remained in absolute silence for about a minute. Mrs Leighton was looking at me very earnestly and there were tears in her eyes. Then she sat down on the edge of the table and said to me half-crying 'You do love him, don't you? This isn't at all what I meant to say to you, dear, but you must forgive me, for though I have always tried to treat them all alike, none of the others have been like him; he has been my Prince, and I've always worshipped and adored him so . . .'

'How you must detest *me*,' I said quickly.

'I don't indeed, dear,' she said. 'I am very fond of you, but I *do* want any woman that gets him to care for him so very much – just as I have done; it means so much to me . . .'

'I do, Mrs Leighton,' I said, with a half-angry consciousness that I could not make my voice anything but chill & emotionless. 'But I am quite incapable of saying anything that will show you how much. You see, I have never really loved anyone before.'

She regarded me through her tears with that warm glance of sweet consideration that always moves me so much. Then she put her arms round me and said 'We will love him together, dear.' I gently disengaged myself & sat down on a high wooden chair in what was I am sure a very stiff & distant attitude. Inwardly I cursed myself for the absurd reserve which would not let me respond, as I wished to do, with a warmth equal to hers. I felt all through the conversation that I was hopelessly inadequate and unresponsive and cold, which tormented me greatly when I would have given anything to show to her of all people what I really felt. I don't suppose, even though her intuition is really remarkable, that she will ever know this, unless she happens to get hold of this book one day, and realises not only what is here, but all that even this means of self-expression leaves unexpressed.

I said to her when we had talked for some time that I was

afraid she had not got much out of me, because the more I felt the more I kept it to myself. She said she had thought that perhaps in this week-end she might get to know me really well, but she felt that after all the writer of the letters was the person she knew best. She said she had known as long ago as last summer that I meant something of importance to Roland & it had certainly been a shock to her then. So much so that when Victor was staying with them she took him aside one day & made him tell her all he knew about me. He did not of course know me very well, but told her I was very good-looking; only I had a cynical mouth, and was in fact rather cynical altogether. 'She rather despised me, I think,' he said. 'But then you see I'm not clever, & I expect she would look down on me rather.' I think it was Richardson who told her Roland had given me *The Story of an African Farm*. At any rate, when she knew that she felt instinctively that our fate was decided. That book, she said, had had such an immense influence on her life, but she never had thought it was going to be the same to us. She even told him a day or two ago that she was sure that book of Olive Schreiner's was responsible for all that had happened. Well, it may be. The Lyndalls of this world are few and far between, and if Roland made her his ideal woman, & then when he met me felt, even after five days' acquaintance, that he had met her in real life . . . I should like to meet Olive Schreiner and tell her about it.

She talked a great deal to me about Roland and herself, of how much he had meant to her always, & how even when he was a tiny child she had felt so lonely when he went away. And all through everything there was never the slightest suggestion of the mother-in-lawish resentful attitude of 'You have taken him away from me'. No, there was nothing but a sweet & open generosity, which treated me unreservedly as an equal who shared with her her love for Roland, and there was never the least hint that she thought she was being generous. I could have fallen down & worshipped her.

She said she thought that where Roland's chief fascination lay was the fact that he was that rare combination, an artist and a gentleman. I loved this description of him, for it is so true & in all its briefness so exact. She said however that if he came through the War and I did marry him she expected that I should often find him very trying, and that it was quite probable she would sometimes be taking my part against him – the woman on the woman's side. She said I had no idea how much, being a woman, she had realised & sympathised with my woman's point of view during the last few months.

All through this conversation she wept intermittently and kept dabbing her eyes with her handkerchief till it was wet, after which she borrowed mine. When she had recovered a little she subconsciously fluttered the latter about till it was dry. I couldn't help feeling all the time what an unmoved little iceberg I was. I really ought to have been the one to do all the talking, and instead of that it was she who did it.

It must have been quite 3.0, and long past the hour of the Zeppelins we had completely forgotten, when we heard steps on the stairs & a noise in the hall, and who should walk in but his lordship, whom we supposed to have gone to bed long ago. Difficult as I find it to visualise him when he is gone, I can always see him vaguely as he came into the room with his tunic crumpled & his dear eyes half-closed & very sleepy. He said in an indignant but very drowsy voice 'What *are* you two doing?' In fact he dusted us round like anything, & Mrs Leighton teased him the next day about this assumption of authority over 'his womankind'. In fact Roland the Feminist wanted to go to bed but was unable to do so while two disturbing women downstairs would insist on discussing matters intimately concerned with himself.

When we left the dining-room Mrs Leighton seemed to disappear, and this time, perhaps too moved by the sight of the intimate connection of two people so dear to him, or possibly too sleepy to feel shy, he actually kissed me good-night. The silkiness of his fair moustache is a great contrast to the stiff bristliness of his close-cropped head!

Monday August 23rd
We got up early, though I felt anything but like it. In fact I was tired & sleepy all day. It was a glorious hot morning and I stood by the gate for some moments looking at the sea, radiant with sunshine. Mr Leighton came out and joined me. He addressed a few commonplace remarks to me to which I endeavoured to

make him hear the answers. Had he not been deaf or had we not been obliged to go in to breakfast I think he would have spoken to me more confidentially. As it was he never mentioned to me either Roland or the engagement – but he showed me very plainly by his manner that he understood it all.

We had breakfast quickly & the taxi seemed to come round very soon. Mrs Leighton, a vision in a large hat with nodding black daisies & an unseasonable blue serge creation with white fur on it, appeared quite unaffected by the proceedings of the night before. I however was very conscious that insufficiency of sleep had made me extremely plain. Even Roland, accustomed as he was to the sleeplessness of trench life, was very drowsy at times during the day.

As we got into the taxi Evelyn and Clare hovered round the steps saying goodbye to us, & especially to Roland, with that cheerful assumption of indifference which brothers & sisters always seem to think it right to display towards one another. But Clare is extremely fond of Roland; she is a dear girl, for she does not seem in the slightest to resent my monopolization of Roland. She has her full share of the Leighton generosity and under-standing of someone else's point of view. Mr Leighton came with us in the taxi. We drove down to the station in rather melancholy mood. While Mrs Leighton & I settled ourselves in a carriage, Mr Leighton and Roland walked up & down the platform more or less in silence, Mr Leighton looking crushed & rather old, Roland with his cap on the back of his head and an air of complete indifference. When the train was due to depart Roland shook hands with his father and got in. I leant down to say goodbye to Mr Leighton & to my surprise he held the hand I had put out and kissed me. Mrs Leighton watched the small scene, looking herself surprised and pleased and a little sad, and as the train moved off she exclaimed, half to Roland, half to herself 'Well! I never knew Father do a thing like that before. Vera must have impressed him. He wants to show her she's one of the family now.'

We arrived in London between 11.0 and 12.0. The Howard Hotel turned out to be a peaceful-looking grey building with window-boxes of pink flowers, in a rather sloping street. The Leightons engaged their two rooms and then we separated for the time being, Mrs Leighton to interview her publishers & Roland & I to do some shopping. He & I went off both rather subdued. It was almost painful to be alone together when the knowledge of the impending parting lay like a cloud upon us. With the memory of the previous evening at Lowestoft in our minds, I think we both felt that the only satisfactory way to spend those few last hours would be in some quiet solitary place, where love could ease its desperate pain a little by expressing itself, and perhaps break through that foolish shyness of ours, which even these days had not been able to dispel, once and for all. The knowledge that we had only such a short time left, and even that had to be spent in the publicity of London shops and streets, had a tantalising effect that was irritating & jarring. I had that desperate feeling of wishing it were all over and done with that always enters the present for me when something I hate is going to happen in the near future. I find it hard enough to learn to live for the day, as one must in these times; I find it quite impossible to live for the hour.

Roland went to various shops making small purchases while I waited for him in the taxi. Then I had my V.A.D. coat measured at Hobson's, where he bought a few more things. I let him choose a pipe for himself at Dunlop's, so that he would be sure to get one he really liked, & then to his complete surprise insisted on giving it to him with a small brown suede case to keep it in. Next we wandered round looking for a periscope for Edward, and finally landed at a shop where we abandoned the search for periscopes and Roland bought a vicious-looking short steel dagger – in case of – accidents. He handled it with great deliberation, and professional interest, wondering whether it would do for getting between someone's ribs or not. To see the thing in cold blood & think of its use made me shudder. I talked to him afterwards of the horrible wound it would make and the unpleasant sound of its being drawn out, and though he took an almost morbid delight in playing with it, he admitted that he thought he could not use it himself except under the fierce excitement & madness of hand-to-hand fighting. The sight of this dagger in the hand of one of the most civilized people of these ironically-named civilized times depressed me to morbidness also, and half for professional, half for purely morbid reasons, I made him promise if he got wounded to let me see the wound. I watched him write out the cheque for the weapon & said to him rather sadly that it was very incongruous that a person with such artistic handwriting should have use for a thing like that.

During the afternoon he bought me some red roses to wear. I felt half-peevish with tiredness & sadness & self-restraint & said I would not have them, but I wore them in the end after all, and kept one afterwards in the drawer where I put my few treasures connected with the one person on earth that I love as I love him. But I told him emphatically that I would not be labelled, and he comprehending said he hated the obvious too. I have deep-rooted objections to wearing an engagement ring which there is no need to go into very deeply here. Certainly I have, owing to unfortunate heredity, a trace of conventional social instinct which makes me understand a certain amount of pleasure in wearing such a ring. But my best self refutes this instinct, for it recognises the custom as a survival of those days when woman was the possession of man, and the ring was the token of this. It is the symbol of the old inequality & therefore hateful to me. A wedding ring is different because the man can wear it too & it is recognisable as such. The old idea that a woman ought to wear a ring in order to warn other men that she is appropriated is absolute nonsense. There is just as much reason – more – for a man to wear a ring to show other women that he is appro-priated. But society does not think *this* necessary! Besides, in ordinary loveless 'arrangements' it is as much the custom to wear a ring as in real love-affairs. So the only way left to prove that yours is a real love-affair is *not* to wear a ring. The non-possession of one is the symbol of the freedom which I should lose by being engaged to any of a thousand men, but shall never lose with Roland, since he considers it as precious as I do. His sharing of my point of view is just another proof of the many he is always giving of his complete trust in me. It is an additional reason for the trust which I cannot feel for men in general, but really am beginning to feel for him.

We went back to the Hotel, and waited in the lounge till tea-time still in the same state of almost sullen subduedness. A gloom seemed to have settled upon us more deadly than actual sharp pain. Finally Mrs Leighton came in, and we were soon joined by Mr Burgin, the author, with whom we had arranged to have tea. Mrs Leighton informed him I was 'serving my King & country' by giving up college, & nursing in a Buxton hospital. I was grateful to her for implying the value she recognised in my humble & glamourless work. Tea dragged on, with Mrs Leighton & Mr Burgin holding the conversation. Roland played absently with his dagger, but he spoke very little, and I still less. I had to catch the 6.30 from St Pancras and at last got up to depart. Mrs Leighton came to the door with Roland & me. She told me in the passage she didn't feel he would be killed, but perhaps would get wounded – some little wound, she hoped, that would bring him back to England for a time. He got into the taxi while I said goodbye to his Mother on the steps of the hotel. She told me that if I had any stories or articles any time that I wanted to try & publish, I was to send them to her, and she would give me all the help she could. Then she kissed me goodbye &, holding my hand, told me again in her sweet impulsive way that she liked me very much – *really*.

I felt as if I wanted to cry. So much I had meant to say to him was unsaid, and yet it seemed, as he agreed, to be no good saying any more. He said very bitterly that he didn't *want* to go back to the front, and this glimpse of England and real life had made him hate France more than ever. I couldn't believe I was really going to part from him; it was so queer to look at him with an earnestness that tried to commit to vivid memory his features, and to think that in little more than a few minutes they would only be an image in my mind.

At St Pancras he wanted to pay for my ticket, but I wouldn't let him, saying I must assert my independence more than ever now. Again I wished desperately it was over, and yet felt at the same time that for him to go away from me was quite impossible. Conversation was difficult & in jerks. I said I wondered if I should ever overcome my dislike of railway stations & he said decidedly 'I *never* shall.'

It was difficult to realise that what I had thought about so much – the possibility of finding a man whom I could love, which seemed so impossible – had really happened. 'Roland, am I *really* engaged to you?' I said.

He looked down at me, his face very pale and a kind of quiet blaze in his dark eyes. 'Yes' he said, in the low and rather musical tone of his deepest emotion.

We tried to be brave & hopeful of course. I reminded him of the verse of Browning, a mutual love of ours—

For what is our failure here but a triumph's evidence
Of the fullness of the days? Have we withered or agonized?
Why else was the pause prolonged but that singing might issue
    thence?
Why rushed the discords in but that harmony should be
    prized?

But when the time for getting into the train came near, the crowd of people round my carriage was very depressing. He said angrily he wished there weren't other people in the world. I reminded him sadly of a sentence in the first letter he wrote me after we parted before. 'Someday we shall live our roseate poem through – as we have dreamt it.' A little wistfully I said that it seemed further away now than ever. He only said 'We must – we *shall.*'

A stir in the crowd indicated the train's imminent departure. I had made up my mind before that I would not kiss him on a crowded station, but the misery of farewell put that all out of my head and he at any rate was in a sort of despair, quite oblivious of the crowd. He stooped & kissed me passionately almost before I realised he had done it. I got up on the step of the carriage & he stood as near me as he could. He looked away from me a moment & dragging out his handkerchief furtively drew it across his eyes. I hadn't realised until then that this quiet & self-contained person was suffering so much. It was a revelation I would have given a great deal to have had before of his real feeling, & my own value to him. And I felt very sorry for him too, for I had not the least inclination to cry myself. To me it seems that while women make a great fuss about little things, when something happens that really matters we have absolute control of our emotions, but with men it is the other way about.

The whistle sounded & the crowd moved a little away from the door. But he still stood close to me and as the train began to move he pressed my hand almost violently, and, drawing my face down to his, kissed me again, more passionately than ever. And I kissed him, which I had never done before, and just managed to make myself whisper 'Goodbye.' He said nothing at all, but turned quickly from me and began to walk rapidly down the platform. Although I had said I would not, I stood by the door as the train moved out of the station and watched him walking away through the crowd. But he never turned again. What I could see of his face was set and pale. It was over . . .

I sat very still watching the growing darkness. I still did not want to cry though sometimes the landscape looked a little blurred. And when the Derbyshire hills came they looked quite different from what they had seemed when I passed them before. Apart from the formal bond of engagement, Roland and I were somehow more closely united than we had ever been before. Roland was mine and I was his; nothing could alter this fact, though the sea divided us, and the cruelty of war might soon part us for ever. The world was different for always. When on Miller's Dale Station I looked up at the white moon shining above the deep blue mountain, it seemed to pierce my heart and say to me 'Changed. Changed. Changed.'

At home I found an upset which I would gladly have dispensed with that evening. The parlourmaid met me at the station & told me that Mother & Daddy had had a wire to say Edward's battalion was ordered to France that night, and they had gone off to Farnham to say goodbye to him. So, with weariness gone into oblivion, I sat up till about 1.30, thinking of the hateful, depressing house, my farewell to Roland, & Edward gone. There seemed to be nothing left, for I felt that Roland was taking with him all my future, and Edward all my past.

Tuesday August 24th
I went back to the Hospital, and because all interest in it had gone, tried all the harder to think it was interesting. At 6.0 Mother & Father came home, having been on a wild goose chase. Edward's battalion had certainly gone out, but he himself, to his great disgust, had been left behind with 8 other subalterns including Thurlow to be attached to the 13th Sherwood Foresters (which is the reserve battalion at Lichfield). The reason for

this was that the 11th had 38 officers and 8 had to be left behind. These were not necessarily the least competent or the youngest, but the ones the CO liked least. Edward has never been able to get on with him, and Thurlow has had this dislike reflected on him. Both Edward & the CO are probably to blame. Edward says he is shifty & not a gentleman, and probably shows he thinks so rather more than discipline admits as wise. He means to try for the Artillery again but I do not suppose that will be much good & he will just have to wait till they send him somewhere, whether he waits six weeks or six months.

When we were going to bed I told the family I was engaged to Roland. They received it first as unsympathetically as I expected; I don't mean this was because of Roland as they both like him as well as they could like anyone so completely above their understanding. But they would have adopted the same attitude towards my engagement to whoever it had been. Father with his usual tactfulness said it seemed very ridiculous because of course Roland wouldn't come back. I felt inwardly very angry indeed but merely said I thought that all the more reason for being engaged to him while he *did* exist.

But it is a consolation to me to think that I am privileged beyond anything they have ever known, in loving Roland & being loved. Neither of them has the vaguest notion of the love of man and woman & its glory & inspiration and sacrifice.

Wednesday August 25th
The day, in nursing & talking, passed like a vague unprofitable dream. Mother kept telling me rather querulously that it would have been so much better if Roland had said something to Father, who expected him to, and gave him every opportunity. I tried to make Mother understand my reasons for refusing to allow him to say anything to Father, but of course quite without success. But she had at least the grace to tell Father to be thankful that a straightforward honourable boy was the one to want me. His intellect is neither here nor there of course!

Friday August 27th
I had both a letter & a wire from him to-day. The wire simply said 'Till we may live our roseate poem through.' The letter was

quite brief. 'Nearly at Folkestone now. I am trying not to think of it, but the thought will come. Oh damn, I know it—

> Goodnight, sweet friend, goodnight,
> Till life and all take flight
> Never goodbye.'

Saturday August 28th

To-day has been much the same as all the days – and all will be like one another, I suppose, until he is either killed or comes home again. Oh! if he could only be wounded just a little!

Sunday August 29th

Roland's letter was short but very comprehensive. 'I got back here this morning after a rather tiring journey by train and motor. Did we dream it after all, dearest? No; for if we had it would not have hurt so much. I am feeling very weary and very very triste – rather like (as is said of Lyndall) "a child whom a long day's play has saddened". And it is all so unreal – even the moon and the sea last night. All is unreal but the memory and the pain and the insatiable longing for Something which one has loved. I feel as if someone had uprooted my heart to see how it was growing.'

Monday August 30th

Nursing as usual. A letter from Roland came at tea-time, enclosing his perfect little Villanelle. And the letter was so – oh so sweet! 'I am very glad that neither you nor Mother were at Victoria to see me off. It was very sad. The men were boisterously cheerful in a way that deceived no one; the officers walked up and down the platform or stood in little groups, all very quiet and self-restrained. There were not very many women there, but there was a look in their eyes that made one turn one's face away in reverence. "It would be so much better if they would not come," I heard one weather-beaten major saying. "It only makes it harder." They stood very still as the train moved out, each as unconscious of the rest as if she were in a separate world. Only one actually cried – a young girl of about twenty. I thought of you & I turned my face away again. It hurt so.'

He is quite uncanny with his ability not only to sympathise with, but to see from, a woman's point of view. Quite apart from my personal standpoint, it will be a terrible tragedy if he gets killed – with all this rare fullness of promise.

Tuesday August 31st
Much the same. I had a short letter from Roland, written in a wood. 'I have brought the company out wood-cutting this morning, and am writing this sitting on a tree-trunk in a clearing. It is a glorious morning – very hot outside; but in this world of green and brown it is a sheer delight. The wood is about 3 miles long and covers two little hills and a valley between. Someone has just begun to whistle part of the Over-ture to *William Tell* and it sounds so appropriate here among the aisles of trees with the ring of axes as a background. And this is war!'

Wednesday September 1st
Hospital work makes me so weary, although for some unknown reason they all seem very fond of me. Miss Windsor said to-night that she had been telling Mrs Ellinger how good I was as a nurse though she did think me too young, & Mrs Ellinger said I was good at whatever I took up.

Thursday September 2nd
I had a letter from him. 'Everything is the same here. Still the same old billets at St L— and the same fleas to make a nuisance of themselves. We ought to be going back into the trenches to-morrow, but it has been postponed a few days in order to enable another brigade to fit themselves in. I am going to play in a Cricket Match this evening – Married vs. Single, got up by my platoon. I am playing for the Married – merely to equalise the sides of course!'

I saw in *The Times* that my second cousin Frank Marrable, whom I have never seen, has died of wounds in the Dardanelles. He was twenty-eight & I believe very handsome, and was engaged to a girl in Ireland.

Friday September 3rd

Edward turned up this evening for the week-end, after a brief telephone message. Apparently Lichfield is a sort of depot of reserve officers – there are over a hundred of them – who are doing nothing in particular but wait to be drafted out to whatsoever regiment needs them. There seems to be a good deal of refuse there from various battalions. His best though slender chance now is to get into the Artillery & even so it will mean the waste of a year's training. It is all so unsatisfactory.

Disquieting thoughts troubled me this morning concerning the position of women, especially nurses, who toil and give up everything in life worth having for £20 or £30 a year.

Saturday September 4th

A letter came from Roland which was rather bitter and cynical. He must be catching it from me.

'It is not good for autocratic persons always to get what they want from other people,' he says. 'I should of course love a letter each day, but only on condition that you really have time to write it. It hurt me to hear of your going to sleep the other night with all your clothes on out of sheer weariness. Please promise that you will never stay up late when you are tired, just for the purpose of writing to spoiled & selfish autocrats. You know, dear, I would rather not get a letter for weeks than that you should not get enough sleep. I believe you work yourself too hard as it is at that wretched hospital.

'Poor diary! Don't let it get behindhand if you can help it; though it must be very difficult to write in it – afterwards – what one really felt so long ago. (To me it seems months ago already.) But think how useful it may be some day, when I have forgotten you and you have forgotten me; you might find it hidden away somewhere, and read it through again and laugh a little over it and perhaps cry a little too, and in the end find it very useful to make a novel out of. Such things have happened before . . . But I must not be cynical.

'This afternoon we are going to practise an attack – possibly but not at all probably in preparation for a real one. I am gradually getting back my old interest in what happens out here. I will not say "Out of sight, out of mind"; though you might think so. But it is perhaps easier to forget out here – to forget not what one has known & has felt, but the pain that accompanies the memory.'

Monday September 6th
To-day from Roland came a most adorable letter, perhaps the nicest one he has ever written me.

'It seems so long since I looked at that little bent brown head close to my own "queer bristly one" once on the edge of a cliff among the gorse & heather; and your hair would fall in wisps over your face. "These are the things I strive to capture in vain; and I have forgotten your eyes . . ." But I haven't, sweetest. They are very "wet", as Clare said, and make me think of Oscar Wilde's:

> And her eyes they were green and grey
>   Like an April day;
> But lit into amethyst
>   When I stooped and kissed.

Lyndall's eyes must have been like that.

'I do wonder if I am like my letters in the same way in which you are like yours. We both seem less reserved in letters, more like our real selves. In fact you pretend to understand my letters better than myself, don't you? Am I such a fearsome person in real life after all?'

Tuesday September 7th
Ordinary sort of day, except for R's letter, which is never ordinary.

'It is raining now & I have just had to beat a hasty retreat from the orchard where I was in the course of having a bath – an unusual thing in England at 11.45 a.m., but I have to get one when I can out here. I usually amuse other people rather with my washings, which are unnecessarily prolonged and elaborate. As it was, the rain caught me in the last stage when I was crouching in a wooden tub and receiving the somewhat icy contents of an inverted bucket in the small of the back.

'We go into the trenches to-morrow, and holding the unenviable office of Mess President I shall have to be busy this afternoon making arrangements for the feeding of six somewhat particular officers during 12 days of isolation. I have discovered incidentally that I could make quite a good cook! You will have to give me lessons.'

Back in the trenches – alas! for my peace of mind. I think that anyone who goes into the Infantry is a real altruist. It is the worst paid, least interesting and most dangerous branch of the Service.

Thursday September 9th
A letter from him this morning.

'England & you seem very far away to-day. I suppose it is because I always live for the present, and my present consists now of walking along miles (or what seem miles) of trenches mostly very muddy & dilapidated, and intermittently giving sundry instructions to unshaven and mud-bespattered followers with a view to the aforesaid ditches becoming ultimately more inhabitable. I know of nothing more melancholy & depressing than an old trench, disused and overgrown with grass, with dug-outs fallen in or wrecked by shells, and here and there a forgotten grave and a rusty bayonet. Of such is the glorious panoply of war!

'Excuse this melancholy tone. It is only temporary; and you yourself are as much given to moods as I. Please try not to be depressed, dearest, and bitter, and as cynical as when you wrote of the "kind condescension of a person with a Quiet Voice towards Someone he is supposed to love".'

This morning Miss Hyland told me the Matron of 1 London General had written for my reference. 'Of course I told her you were undesirable in every way,' she said with a sweet smile. Nurse Robson was showing me various instruments & telling me their names, after dressings had been done, & as we were going downstairs I said to her 'If only I had you to myself for a fortnight I might learn a little.' She said 'Well, you're such a dear, you know; it is so nice to teach you things.' And I wondered if she would have understood if I had tried to explain how love of learning is part of the very essence of my being. I only said 'You see, I love learning so much.'

I came in to-night very tired & with a sort of vague pain, so sat in a chair while Mother brushed and plaited my hair for me. When she had gone I felt too tired to move, and so sad, & I sat thinking how things might be if Roland and I were married, and how they are, alas! now. Almost unconsciously I acted Lyndall, for I sat gazing into the glass, not because it was the glass, but just because it happened to be in front of me. I thought & thought, and then suddenly becoming conscious saw in the glass my own reflection without the veil of self-consciousness which usually prevents one from getting a clear idea of one's self. I found myself looking into the soul in my eyes, & then I started, for it seemed to be not I but my own Sorrow that was looking me in the face with so straight & grave a gaze. There was something almost uncanny about those eyes, and I got up feeling suddenly cold all over, and was not thereafter inclined to look into the glass again. It was as though I had seen a ghost.

It is strange and agonising to think of my dearest so far away. Often I have to press my fingers tight into my hand when I recall the feel of his arm around me. Whether it is mere sex instinct to wish to feel the nearness of the beloved, to have beside one the warmth and thrill of his corporeal presence, or whether it is something more, I really do not care. It is what I want – 'the fierce insatiable desire for Something one had loved.' I wonder why when he was here I found it hard to realise that his life had been in danger many times – frequently, continuously. When he was with us & I could feel his vitality, his actuality, it was so difficult to believe in his previous peril. Yet it is easy enough now. 'Knowing not the hour of her mourning but knowing well that already it may have struck.' Oh! if I can only get him back to hold & kiss & worship once more, how tenderly, how strongly, how reverently, I shall love him!

Friday September 10th
Rather a bad Zeppelin raid happened in London on Wednesday night. A new patient at the hospital who was in the 4th London General Hospital on Wednesday night told me that all the patients sat in their windows watching one of the Zeppelins, which looked like a great silver cigar in a luminous cloud, which was the smoke of the shrapnel from our anti-

aircraft guns bursting beneath it. One of the guns was only about a mile from the hospital, and that and the bombs made a terrific noise. The streets were full of excited semi-dressed people whom a policeman was vainly trying to keep quiet. The hospital was in a turmoil all night from the patients afflicted with nerves. The paper reports 20 deaths, but rumour says 175, which is probably nearer the truth.

There is better news of the Russians. They have captured 1,700 prisoners and 60 Maxim guns. But I suppose this success is only an incident of the great retreat.

Saturday September 11th
I went this afternoon to Leek with Daddy in the motor & coming back tried to learn to drive it. The first time came off all right, but the second was distinctly disastrous. In taking a corner I did not turn the wheel sufficiently & ran into the wall. The glass screen broke into a hundred pieces, which fell in showers about us. It was a marvel that we escaped without injury of any kind. The front of the car was smashed & the mudguards crumpled up, so it will cost a good deal to put it right, but that is covered by insurance. Mother of course was terrified but neither she nor Father made as much fuss as I expected.

There was a letter for me from Roland when I came back at night. He actually seems to be thinking of staying in the Army if he is alive when the War is over! I started composing arguments against it when I went to bed.

'I wonder sometimes which I am born to be: a man of action with lapses into the artistic, or an artist with military sympathies. Mother has asked me once or twice lately whether I should like to go into the Regular Army as a profession. I say no, because I foresee the atrophy of my artistic side. On the other hand a literary life would give no scope for the adventurous & administrative facet of my temperament. What am I to do?

'I have just missed to-day's post, sworn in most undrawing-room fashion at one of my sergeants for leaving undone the things he ought to have done, have had to give away some of my men to do unnecessary work for the Engineers, and, assisted by the anticipation of having to wander round muddy trenches on a cold night for an indefinite period, am not in a fitting state of mind to write any more of a letter to you. I am apt to be cynical when annoyed, and should afterwards regret having been bitter towards Someone who has enough cause for bitterness on her own. Please forgive the interlinear acerbity of these last two pages.'

The more I transcribe these letters of his, the more I realise their literary beauty. Verily they are gifts of 'a rarer sort than gold'.

Sunday September 12th

When I got in I found a letter from the 1st London General Hospital, written on behalf of the Matron. It was to say I was selected to serve in that hospital as a V.A.D probationer about October.

I had another delightful letter from Roland – detached & slightly meditative. 'I usually write to you in the afternoon, as now, so that the letter can go with the orderly corporal at half-past four. Yesterday I was so tired that I fell asleep and did not wake up again till after tea-time. Hence you did not get even an empty envelope with nothing inside!'

I wrote him a long letter, giving the various arguments I thought of last night against his being a permanent soldier. Though it seems an absurd and ridiculously futile thing to do when there is so great a chance that he may not be alive in the distant future to meet the choice. Poor old boy. Oh! *damn* this war!

Monday September 13th

In the evening I had a long and most charming though rather sad letter from Mrs Leighton. 'I have been rather more than usually unhappy over Roland's state of mind and heart since he went back. I understand so well the "dust and ashes" feeling. I knew it would be like that. There was no help for it, because he was leaving so much behind him – everything he cares for most in life – and he had realised in those few days' leave all the colour and warmth and glory of what he might be sacrificing for ever. He wouldn't have been his own passionate, worshippable self if he hadn't realised it with all that heart-breaking keenness; but it has been hurting me just like knife-stabs to think of him out there now, facing the darkness and the danger, not with a new hope in his heart but with a new pain there because of the sweetness and dearness of all that he had torn himself away from. In a way it would have been kinder to him if that week of his leave had been less glowing, less sweet. And yet – if the very worst were to happen – which I will not let myself think of – it would be just one little scrap of comfort to tell oneself that he had known in the dreadful moments that he was very dearly cherished. But I am not going to think of this, Vera dear, as I have just said. I dare not think of it. But now, if even in spite of myself, the thought does come to me, I feel as if I were stretching out my arms to you.'

Tuesday September 14th

I have heard nothing again from the London Hospital, but had a letter from Roland, who gave me a fine if somewhat morbid description of the charnel-house condition of his present trenches – poor darling!

'This afternoon I am very sleepy – almost too sleepy to write. It is partly the warm weather and chiefly perhaps not getting more than 4 hours' sleep at night and being too busy to get any rest in the day. I have been rushing round since 4 a.m., superintending the building of dug-outs, drawing up plans for the draining of trenches, doing a little digging myself as a relaxation, and accidentally coming upon dead Germans while looting timber from what was once a German fire trench. This latter was captured by the French not so long ago and is pitted with shell-holes each big enough to bury a horse or two in. The dug-outs have been nearly all blown in, the wire entanglements are a wreck, and in among [this] chaos of twisted iron and splintered timber and shapeless earth are the fleshless, black-ened bones of simple men who poured out their red, sweet wine of youth unknowing, for nothing more tangible than Honour or their Country's Glory or another's Lust of Power. Let him who thinks that War is a glorious golden thing, who loves to roll forth stirring words of exhortation, invoking Honour and Praise and Valour and Love of Country with as thoughtless and fervid a faith as inspired the priests of Baal to call on their own slumbering deity, let him look at a little pile of sodden grey rags that cover half a skull and a shin bone and what might have been Its ribs, or at this skeleton lying on its side, resting half-crouching as it fell, supported on one arm, perfect but that it is headless, and with the tattered clothing still draped around it; and let him realise how grand & glorious a thing it is to have distilled all Youth and Joy and Life into a foetid heap of hideous putrescence. Who is there who has known and seen who can say that Victory is worth the death of even one of these?'

Thursday September 16th

Three soldiers from the Devonshire smashed up the shop belonging to the son of Wenzel the hairdresser to-day, because he was foolish enough to say he was a German and proud of it. I and everyone else sympathised very much with the soldiers, who are spending the night in the lock-up! The Wenzels, father & son, are enemy aliens, and as such ought to have been interned long ago. They would have been but for the slackness of the authorities here.

Friday September 17th

I have been able all day to do nothing but think of a very short letter from Roland this morning – short, but a letter which contained the words 'Hinc illae lacrimae.' We arranged when he was with me that he should write those words if ever they were going to make an attack or he was going to be otherwise in some special danger, for the Censor would not of course pass any precise information of that kind.

All day long I have tried to think what it will be if in a day or two I hear he is dead, & if that message he wrote me at the end of the letter is the last I shall ever have from him. I shiver every time I see a telegraph boy now-a-days. I try to steel my heart in preparation for it but I only keep realising, more & more, how deeply, how terribly I love him. The recollection of his kisses, his touch, every sweet moment that I have lately spent with him, keep coming back in a flood of memory and make my heart ache till I feel I can bear it no longer. Even as I write he may be lying dead, just one lifeless thing among thousands of others, upon the battlefield, and all that is left to us who worship him is just

> . . . some corner of a foreign field
> That is for ever England.

I sent him a brief message to-day, more than usually deeply-felt, for though I have been aware of his danger all along, this time there is cause for special apprehensiveness. 'Remember, She knows not the word "forget". Death cannot conquer some things, & over them "War knows no power".'

Saturday September 18th
I went with Mother & Edward & Miss Cookson to see *Tannhäuser* at the Opera House. The music was grand, and ordinarily I should have revelled in it, but to-day it seemed to make everything worse, and once or twice I felt so much that I could not stand it that I almost got up and went out. I kept thinking all the time how I should feel if the telegram came – kept thinking that perhaps while I was at the theatre, presumably enjoying myself though far enough from it in reality, all that was he might be lost forever, or he might be lying in agony in some far-off hospital. And the music aroused more & more, as it always does, all that I feel for him . . .

Sunday September 19th
I really meant to sit up and do some writing to-night but I am so tired & have such a headache from the day's anxiety and suspense that I feel I cannot – before I hear.

Sunday is a dreadful day; no possibility of getting news, but one has to wait and work all the same. It is extraordinary that one can go about one's business with apparent cheerfulness, knowing that all that counts in life may be gone in aeternum. I should lie awake at night thinking of it too, if it weren't that I get so tired that I sleep in spite of myself. But now – only to end each day of waiting, to bring the next with some possibility of definite news – is all that matters.

Monday September 20th
Only a short entry to-night, as I still have a bad headache from the vigils of the past three nights. For they are vigils, for even though I have not stayed up, the nights have been so disturbed

& restless, and anxiety as much present with me in sleeping as in waking, that I have not had much rest. Time seems to stand still, and I am almost afraid to hear anything relating to him at all.

I saw a case of psoriasis at the hospital to-night – all over a man's back. It was rather horrible, but interesting, as I had never seen anything like it before.

I came back at 8.30, and found a letter from Maurice, who obviously knows nothing about Roland & me. I hardly like to take the responsibility of telling him myself, yet it is impossible to write back in the same strain unless I know he knows first.

Tuesday September 21st

I scarcely thought it possible I should have no news to-day, but it is still a case of waiting, & hearing nothing. This morning as I went down to the hospital the day was beginning full of sunshine & a glorious autumn freshness, and to-night as I came back the evening sky was a deep-blue splendour, lit by a moon which tinged the clouds surrounding it with a luminous rosy brightness. I thought how he would have loved it and wondered if his eyes were closed to it forever, or if he was looking up at that same moon, far away, and thinking of me as I was thinking of him. All through the day I keep remembering various incidents when he was with me & each time I recall anything it means a sharp pain – like a knife-stab, as Mrs Leighton describes it. I have to clench my hand tight so as to bear it.

Mother took Johnson to the Gardens this morning in his bath-chair. He is such a dear gentle boy that she quite enjoyed sitting with him; he talked without shyness, although he is never in the least bit forward; he is a very pathetic person. Mother came into Ward 6 to tell me something when I was revising a very bad poem I had written called 'Waiting'. I don't know what she thought I was doing. Father went off to Brighton to-day. All these incidents just at present pass by & leave no impression. There is only room in my mind for one thought, though to think it is sorrow. I feel as if I could not bear much more suspense, though I suppose it is a case of 'needs must'. My heart aches so for him, out there in the danger & darkness.

Wednesday September 22nd

A letter came from the Red Cross saying I was to go to France at
'some future date'. As the Camberwell Matron has engaged me
& the Red Cross knows this, I thought there must be some
muddle and decided to go up to town to-morrow & see what it
all meant. Mother of course was perturbed at the idea of my
possibly going abroad with no more than Devonshire Hospital
experience. I can't say that I feel experienced enough yet to
want to go myself. Of course I shall if they need me, but it
scarcely sounds like a definite order.

I said goodbye to everyone at the Hospital. They all were so
nice & seemed so genuinely sorry to lose me, & excited at my
sudden departure. Johnson was almost in tears, poor lad! The
appearance of popularity is most disconcerting, I am not used to
it.

Half-way through the evening Mother telephoned to say a
letter had come from Roland. 'Have just come back to billets
from the trenches,' he says, 'very tired after a somewhat trying
12 days. Everything exciting that was expected failed to come off
after all. We expected an attack on the day I mentioned; they
issued minute orders as to what was to be done when it came;
parties went out to reconnoitre the German wire at night; we all
slept not only in our clothing as always but hung round with
revolvers, haversacks etc., & ready for an alarm; but it never
came. Only away to our left in the French area we could hear
what is even at a distance the most terrifying thing on earth –
the pounding of heavy guns, now fainter, now louder, but
coalescing always into one dull thundering roar. It lasted for
three days and three nights on end, lapsed for a little, & then
went on again intermittently, growing fainter & fainter. At night
the sky was lit with the flashes & flickered strangely with a
yellow, restless glow. They say that we may be in for a little more
excitement in a day or two's time, but personally I rather doubt
it. In any case, if you do not hear from me even for a week or
more, do not think that anything has happened. Whenever
there are wars and rumours of wars of any kind, however
innocent, it always means my being kept much too busy to
write letters. Meanwhile I am very glad to have a rest again.
One of our officers is away and I have been doing his work as

well as my own, and even without any rumours of attacks 12 days on end in trenches is rather trying to the nerves.'

I should think it must be. The whole tone of this letter indicates the tension of his nerves. To think that *he* should have to be wasted out there, of all people. No, perhaps not wasted. 'I have been doing his work as well as my own.' That is just like Roland – like one who knows the deeper unselfishness, & hides it beneath a cloak of apparent egotism.

Friday September 24th

I went up by the early train with Uncle Bill; he left me by the London Bridge tube, & I spent a joyous morning wandering about London by myself more freely than I ever had before. The day was fresh & invigorating, with an energy-inspiring buoyancy that only London can produce. So I walked to Hobson's, where I was going to see about some more V.A.D. things, from St Pancras. Hobson's is in Soho, in one of the little back streets behind Regent St. I had an amusing time wandering through a Jewish market trying to find it. But I managed to get there in the end by dint of various inquiries. After ordering my things I had plenty of time to spare, so wandered about Regent St for over an hour. I met Miss Heath Jones & Miss Bervon for lunch at Fuller's. They of *course* could do nothing but talk about the engagement, & how they had never thought I should meet any man who would appeal to *me*. They drove me to St Pancras in time for the 2.30, & I came home. Mother informed me that for Maurice's sake she had told Mrs Ellinger about Roland & me. She said Mrs Ellinger seemed very taken aback & looked quite crestfallen. But she said she would tell him, and I am glad I have not to do so.

I found another letter from [Roland] when I came in to-night. They seem to be on the eve of great events out in France.

'Have just had a very delightful evening,' he says. 'We have got the Transport Officer of another battalion messing with us at present. He is a very charming man and rather a friend of mine, but his greatest asset is that he possesses a very good gramophone. This I insisted he should produce to-night. It did me a lot of good as mental refreshment. Among other records he had two that Edward used to play, Raff's "Cavatina" and Saint-

Saëns' "Le Cygne". What a number of things have happened since the days when he used to condescend to fiddle at my Saturday afternoon Entertainments in the Schoolroom at Uppingham!

'We are billeted in a different village this time, a little nearer the trenches and much more comfortable. These are to be our winter quarters when out of the trenches. That is, if we are still out here through the winter. The idea now seems to be that the war will end in a great smash-up of some kind at the end of October. Personally I know nothing and don't much care. There is certainly an appearance about things as of something being about to happen soon.

'*Monday morning.* Am writing in a wood – the same wood that I mentioned before – while the men are having their interval for dinner. I am feeling very annoyed at being here at all really, as I very much wanted to go out riding with Adam. But it is my turn to-day. Yesterday morning we spent riding round the country reconnoitring roads & defences & villages in case we had to occupy them in event of an attack. It was a glorious day & I have a special weakness for long white hedgeless roads with Noah's Ark trees planted on either side. Attempted a poem this morning beginning "Broken I came from out the Ditch of Death", and produced some of the most appalling rot.

'Your adventures with the motor, if not potentially so serious, would have amused me much. I couldn't help laughing at the thought of you clinging quietly to the steering wheel and waiting for the bump. I am surprised that your Father didn't say something about "These women again!" & their traditional incompetence. But you might have been killed, you know; which would have been a sad inversion of the natural order of things, when you are at home and I am here.'

Saturday September 25th
To-day was a blessed immunity from work. Not having had a week off since the end of April I shall be glad if I can get a short holiday now – although all the time it is so strange not to be working that I can scarcely settle down. Mother had a letter from Father objecting to my nursing arrangements in general and talking about 'showing his dependents a thing or two before

long'. I'll see how long I'll be his 'dependent'. For the country's sake I deliberately postpone the intellectual independence that college would have led to, & he flings it in my face.

I had a short letter from Roland this morning. 'The posts have been rather disorganised the last few days,' he says, 'and your letters & I expect mine also have been delayed en route. There are movements of troops going on & a general subdued uneasiness. They say that we are to be shifted again in a few days – further North this time, but nothing definite known yet.'

Edward, cheerful as usual, came to spend another week-end. He seems to be able to get fairly frequent leave where he is now. He was pleased to hear I eventually shall have a chance of foreign service. A poster on the station this evening said 'Increased activity in Flanders'.

Sunday September 26th
I found two letters on my plate this morning – one from the Red Cross, the other a tiny thin envelope from Roland. I opened the Red Cross letter hastily, & found it to be a kindly-expressed information that as I wanted to go to the 1st London General Hospital they would be pleased to appoint me there if the Matron would apply to a certain address asking for me. Then I opened the one from Roland – without apprehension, though the thunder clouds have so long been gathering over the West that I might have known . . . It was a very tiny note, but God knows it said enough.

'I know nothing definite yet, but they say that all posts will be stopped very soon. Hinc illae lacrimae. "Till life and all . . ." '

The other, similar note was only the shadow cast by the coming event. This, I somehow knew at once, was It. In a way I am almost glad that the great decision is coming at last. Resignation is a horrible deadly thing – but it is not resignation that I feel. No, but my heart has been so torn & seared by anxiety & suspense that the Climax finds me ready to face it. In a few days, I suppose, I shall know whether I am condemned to the loneliness of a lifelong maidenhood, having lost all I love – or else I may have him, & all that he means for me in the future, back again to tend & serve & cherish in his helplessness & pain.

Meantime I can only wait & hope & try to keep my cursed imagination in check – think of Mrs Leighton, & try to be brave.

To him I sent a little note written straight from my heart. Ordinarily I would never have admitted so much, but Death is an excuse for anything, everything.

'If this word,' I said, 'should turn out to be a "Te moriturum saluto", perhaps it will brighten the dark moments a little to think how you have meant to Someone more than anything ever has or ever will. What you have striven for will not end in nothing, all that you have done & been will not be wasted, for it will be a part of me as long as I live, and I shall remember, always. Yes, "till life & all" . . . Au Revoir.'

He may never get that & read it. But it has been a satisfaction to me to send it all the same. —Oh! it is terrible to love someone like this. I try to be brave & calm, but I can't. It hurts me so . . . and he in danger, my darling—

Monday September 27th
Yes, it has come. The storm which has so long been threatening has burst at last over the Western Front. It is a very swift confirmation of the warning in my little message of yesterday. We got up early this morning to have breakfast with Edward, who was going by the 7.50. I, not having been woken up in time, had not even begun to dress. Edward as usual was late, & the *Daily Mail* arrived in the midst of our hurried breakfast. The paper has been for such a long time comparatively so uninteresting & always depressing that we have never been in a rush to open it immediately, and I do not know why this morning when we were all in such a hurry it should have occurred to Mother to read it at once. But when she did open it we all exclaimed, for in large headlines was the tidings 'Two Real Victories At Last. German line pierced in two places. The French & British take 20,000 unwounded prisoners & 33 guns.'

Sir John French's communiqué began: '*Sunday, 9.30 a.m.* Yesterday morning we attacked the enemy south of La Bassée Canal, to the east of Grenary & Vernelles. We captured his trenches on a front of over five miles, penetrating his line in some places to a distance of 4,000 yards. We captured the Western outskirts of Hulluch, the village of Loos (near Lens) and the mining works round it & Hill 70. Other attacks were made north of the La Bassée Canal, which drew strong reserves of the enemy towards these points of the line, where hard fighting took place throughout the day, with varying success.'

Another communiqué later in the same day says that severe fighting has taken place on the ground won by us yesterday, owing to the counter-attacks of the enemy. The result is that with one insignificant exception we hold all the ground gained. What perhaps affects me most of all is a little bit of the French communiqué, which seems to mention that part of the line where *he* was. 'Our troops, operating in combination with the British Army, delivered a vigorous attack *north of Arras* which permitted us to gain a footing at several points in the enemy lines.'

The leading article struck a note of rejoicing. But – whether I am unpatriotic or not – there was, I am afraid, very far from rejoicing in my heart. I could only remember that the 7th Worcester Regiment had been where the thick of the fighting was – and think what the price of victory might be for me.

Edward went off rather gravely, as he seems now to expect that he will be called to the Front quite shortly with reinforcements.

Victory or defeat – and neither worthy to be weighed in the balance with the one human life beside which the fate of the whole British Army appears insignificant. 'The greatest victory since the Battle of the Marne' – perhaps. And he – who represents all the light of life to me? Oh! how *can* he have escaped – how can anyone possibly come back from that hell of shells & machine guns & flying bullets & thundering cannonades which can be heard even over the Zeeland border! Perhaps even as I am writing these words he is lying cold & uncared for in the midst of a mangled heap of slain, suffering or – dead. Poor Mrs Leighton – my heart in its own anguish goes out to hers. She will be thinking of me to-night, as I am thinking about her. I wish I were with her. It might make the unendurable slowness of these awful hours a little less hard to bear.

I can't help thinking what a terrible nerve-strain it must have been for him – all the long expectation of an attack, & the waiting, waiting for it to come. I wonder how that extraordinary temperament, which paradoxically combined a passionate love of life with a remarkable indifference to death, stood him in the supreme moments that he went through. Maybe I shall never know. I only pray that if the worst has happened his Mother's love and mine went with him into the dark Valley of the Shadow and wrested a final victory even from the anguish of the grave.

Later news reports the Germans still hard pressed by the Allies, & furious fighting proceeding more or less along the line – hand-to-hand battles with the bayonet. I wonder if he ever used the dagger he bought.

It has been a dreadful day – waiting and waiting & able to settle to nothing. Ah! a year of war has taught me what these victories mean, though we certainly haven't had much experience of victory. At first it is all splendour & glory & advance & captures & wonderful achievements. And then gradually come admissions of hardly-earned triumphs being won back by the enemy, stories of horror which the papers dare not print on their principal pages, & long, long casualty lists in which each name means a home rendered desolate.

Tuesday September 28th
This has been a terrible day – a day of waiting & restlessness & anxiety, of feeling it was impossible for any news of individuals yet, but nevertheless thinking that all the time perhaps news – the worst news – might come. One simply cannot tell at all. If he were wounded or killed in the early part of the fighting we might hear by now quite well. On the other hand he may have fallen in the desperate battle that has been going on in his part of the world ever since the first attack, and had anything happened yesterday or the day before we could not know yet. And the worst of it is, that even if such a miracle should happen that he had come unscathed through this first part, he may fall any moment in the fierce fighting still raging round Hill 70. The news in the paper is much the same as that yesterday. The Allies are still advancing and in many places the Germans seem to have surrendered fairly easily. The paper says the chief advance has been made by the French, but nevertheless the worst part of the fighting seems to be where the British have extended their line south – information of which extension the paper gives us

officially for the first time but which I of course have known ever since the 7th Worcesters marched from somewhere south of Ypres to Hébuterne, which I think is near Lens.

The papers, especially the evening ones, are beginning to be full of awful personal accounts of sanguinary conflicts – details which will of course multiply and grow worse as days go on. They make one shudder & wonder how anyone at all can possibly come out alive. The wounded have already begun to come into London. I may be sent for any moment now, as they are certain to hurry in finishing the extension at Camberwell, for it will doubtless be terribly needed.

After an almost entire lack of initiative on the part of the Western Allies for a year (Neuve Chapelle & the two battles of Ypres being the disastrous exceptions) it takes one almost back to the wild excitement & impatience for news of the early part of the War. But in those days, for the majority of us in England the excitement was everything, and the apprehension which no excitement can quench or atone for was confined to the small class composing the relations of the Regular Army. We are suffering now – as no civilian population in the world's history has ever suffered before – what they did just a year ago. We know now – to as great an extent as they ever knew – the suspense, the anxiety and the pain.

Mother met several people in the town who are anxious about relations or friends. Feelings on hearing news of victory are terribly mixed – no one knows what it may have cost them individually. Class distinctions slip away & are lost in this great community of anxiety.

I was on the look-out for telegrams & telephone messages all day, but nothing came. I tried to make time pass by walking & walking & then cycling over the hills, for I could not rest. In the town this evening I met Miss Sharp & Dorothy Adie, who both congratulated me on my engagement. I could not even pretend to be pleased or that I had anything to be congratulated for; it was such irony to receive congratulations on the possession of a fiancé when I did not even know whether he was alive or dead.

There was no peace of mind to be gained from all this walking & wondering. News of further British victories in the evening papers did not seem to make matters any better. In those dreadful hours I cursed Providence because I was not a man and in it all. A woman – especially *now* – has nothing to make up to her for such anxiety and suspense as this. It seems years since Sunday – and more like centuries since I left the Devonshire Hospital, though in reality not a week ago. The day's only consolation was two letters from Mrs Leighton. If it were not that she is in the world, waiting & suffering with me, I don't know how I could bear it all. And strangely enough she seems to find comfort in me. All this dread & anxiety about the dear being so worshipped by us both seems to bring me even nearer to her. I suppose it is weakness to want to turn to anyone, but love makes one so terribly human. No, independent as I would be, I could not do without her loving strength, now. She cannot know herself how much she means to me.

Wednesday September 29th
Still no news – still waiting & weariness, & a heart growing almost numb with its pain. I suddenly realised to-night when Father was talking of the Dardanelles being better than we thought and the prospect in France being hopeful, that, selfish as it is, it matters to me personally not at all when the war ends if *his* concern with it is over. Hopeful signs hitherto have made me rejoice purely & simply because the sooner it was over the sooner he would be out of danger. But if it takes him from me the shadow of it will be over all my life and whether it is actually going on or has finished will make very little difference.

This afternoon I sorted out & went through various old papers & bits of rubbish precious for what they recall, & put them tidy, in readiness for leaving them for some months. They took me away from the present & back to the days before the War, even back to the St Monica's days, which after all were not so long ago though they seemed like centuries. I was back again once more in the dreams of those days – ardent, impersonal dreams & ideals, in which no man ever had part. The average girl may think of little else but love & marriage & a home, but I never did. Love came to me quite unbidden – unwanted almost, with all the grief & pain it has brought me. But – if I could give all else up to keep him, I would give it gladly.

I found a lot of old dance-programmes which I tied up & put

away with the sort of half-sorrowful, half-scornful indulgence a middle-aged woman might show when coming upon traces of her youthful folly. They seemed so long ago – so out-of-date. Some of the men I once danced with are dead – almost all are out where Death & Danger surround them every hour, or soon will be there. I wonder if I shall ever go to another dance. Very unlikely.

Thursday September 30th

I did expect I should at least hear something to-day but no news came. Again I wandered about but every telegraph boy I saw going in the direction of the Park made me hasten home, and every loud ring at the bell when I was in the house made my heart beat so fast that I felt choked & stifled. From all sides I heard that people had been getting news of casualties during the last few days, and *The Times* obituary list was long with the names of people who had fallen in France & Flanders, chiefly on the 25th & 26th. But in a war like this no news does not necessarily mean good news – quite the reverse. It simply means that in certain parts of the line there has been more confusion than in others. Loos is probably one of those places as the most vigorous part of our attack took place there. It makes me so angry to think that so many people are hearing news of their relations & friends – are even getting them back wounded, but *I* can hear nothing of my one dear soldier. It is impossible he can have come through unharmed; he may be flung unidentified on a pile of forgotten dead, or perhaps dying in some French hospital among strangers who know nothing about him beyond the information on his identity disc.

The Allies' advance seems to be waning somewhat in fury. Well, I wonder if yet *another* day will pass & leave me still in suspense.

Friday October 1st

No, it hasn't done. This evening I received, of all things in the world, a *letter* from him. I cannot describe quite what it made me feel – I who during these last few days had been trying to make up my mind that I might never see that handwriting any more. And after all he had not been in all the dreadful fighting of the week-end. The letter was written on Tuesday, however, & he was going into the trenches the next day; so perhaps he has been thoroughly in it by this time. His letter is short & very guarded & makes no comment on the general situation.

'It is rather cruel to disturb people with false alarms. This last one has, it would seem, been as false as the former one of a few days back. There is still time for it to materialise; but that is improbable. Three is a lucky number, & the next may be a real one. I hope so. It depends always on what the other parts of the line – British & French – are doing. One can only wait. We go into the trenches to-morrow.'

The worst of it is, when he says he hopes the next alarm may be real, I think he really means it. His is no bravado courage, proclaiming what it shrinks from performing. I believe he almost delights in danger – in the vigour & exuberance of it.

Judging by the obituary notices already in *The Times*, the list of officer casualties is going to be terrible. There were nearly 50 this morning. Among them, to the great grief of us all, is that of 2nd Lieut. Maurice Greenhalgh, who used to go to Holm Leigh with Edward, was a great friend of his, & always competing with him for the top of the form. He must have occupied much the same position with regard to Edward as Garrod did to Roland. Greenhalgh was a small, frail-looking boy whom we used to nickname Hackerschmidt – very fair, & delicate in complexion. Father was more upset about it than I have ever seen him so far over anyone, as he was very fond of Greenhalgh when he was a little lad. Edward will be very sad about it indeed.

I found to-day the photograph of the last O.T.C. Camp; taken just a few days before war broke out. The Three Musketeers are all seated in a row, Edward as a lance-sergeant, Roland in the middle as a colour-sergeant-major & Victor as a lance-corporal. It is excellent of all three. Edward looks immaculate & very cheerful, & Victor somewhat serious & meditative about nothing in particular. Roland is rather more dishabillé than the others; he has a somewhat unshaven appearance, his coat is thrown back & his shirt open at the neck. His eyes look at you out of the photograph with an almost challenging straightness; in them is that sad, intent look I have seen so often of late. Just so he might look if ordered to lead his men into battle against difficult & dangerous odds. So very like is this photograph that it makes my heart ache desperately with the longing to have him back with me again.

Sunday October 3rd
I had a somewhat bitter letter from Maurice saying that I might have known disappointment would overrule any surprise he might have felt, and so on. I attempted to answer this letter but it was difficult, as I did not know quite where I stood with regard to him. Roland does not believe in platonic friendship & it is quite possible that Maurice does not either.

Monday October 4th
I awoke out of a strange dream this morning. Roland didn't actually come into it – he was at the front but I knew I had been married to him for 'a year & a day'. In the dream I was engaged vigorously in Hospital work but nevertheless I kept coming across college people – I remember Miss Hughes in particular – all of whom I told with great eagerness that I had been married for a year – & that I had a son. Then the scene suddenly changed & I was standing (of all the absurdities) beside a large bed in which Roland's son lay sleeping tucked up in the clothes. I was showing him to somebody, & telling them that the baby was only a fortnight old, & pointing out its remarkable resemblance to Roland. Later on in the dream the baby – which was fair with blue eyes – acted as if it were much older than I said & curled its fingers into mine.

Tuesday October 5th
I am beginning to think I should like to hear from Roland again. Safety is a thing much easier to hope for than to believe in. And I know there has been more fighting the last few days. *The Times* obituary was terrible this morning – about 80 officers published as killed in action or died of wounds. The notices took two whole columns of the front page, & an entire page was filled by their biographical notes.

I wish Camberwell would send for me. This *is* the first week in October. Holidays do not suit me, least of all now. I want to work again.

I had an idea for a play to-day. There is to be a girl in it more or less like me, a young soldier very like Roland, & a doctor. The setting is to be topical but the keynote of the plot is to be the psychology of the mind of the girl, who is thrown into trouble & confusion when two alternatives, both of them pleasant, are open to her, & who, only when the opportunity for choosing seems to be over, deliberately makes her choice – makes it with a sudden revelation of how she ought to have chosen all along.

Wednesday October 6th
Simply boring. I am tired of being at home waiting for things to come off. One is always waiting, waiting, in this war. It is enough to turn one's hair grey – is a thousand times worse than hard work.

Thursday October 7th
Waiting for two things at once is really getting on my nerves – or rather it is teaching me to have 'nerves', which are things I greatly despise. Silence from Roland is worse than anything, for there may be so many reasons for it. Perhaps if I knew him better his smallest actions would puzzle me less.

Mother said to-night, when I made her go for a walk with me because I could not rest indoors, that she really thought it very rash to hurry (fancy hurry! ever since Christmas!) into an engagement like this with someone I knew so little. I amused myself for some time with pretending to share her doubts about my feelings (doubts! about the one feeling I have ever been sure of!) and by telling her that if I had to stay at home doing nothing for some months, I should probably break off my engagement, just to make a little variety! I believe she took it all as gospel! It seems to surprise her that I don't always want to be kissing him when I am with him. In fact I don't believe she thinks that what I feel for him is really love at all, & is quite sure that I don't in the least know what I am about. But in the darkness I thought of the one being on earth whose life means all the world to me, and felt like laughing & crying at the same time. Laughter for the world's ignorance of the meaning of a love like mine – tears because I am parted, perhaps for ever, from what means so much.

The news in the papers is scarcely encouraging. The trouble in the Balkans is growing enormously. Our absurd censorship allows us to know so little that probably quite the majority, & I among them, scarcely understand the situation at all, & it will no doubt break upon us in all its dreadfulness when it is just about as bad as it can be. Undoubtedly matters are going to be still more serious for us. One scarcely believes it possible that they can be until they are.

Mr Venizelos, the brilliant Greek premier who favoured the Entente, has been obliged to resign because his sovereign, King Constantine, whose wife is the Kaiser's favourite sister, refuses to approve of his policy. This means that Greece will break her word to join with Serbia against any aggressor of Serbia, & will either remain neutral or enter the war with Bulgaria on the side of Germany. The most extraordinary thing of all is that an Anglo-French force (for we are of course pledged to protect Serbia against any fresh attack on her) has landed at Salonika, which is I suppose the only way they can reach Serbia, and the Greeks appear to have agreed, even though grudgingly, to this. And thus we are starting a sixth campaign when we are unable to achieve success in one. Truly it seems a tangle which will never be unravelled. And if Greece enters the War on the side of the enemy the Anglo-French force will be in a delightful position, surrounded by enemies on all sides.

The War is like a snowball which gathers volume as it goes on rolling. Every day seems to take us further from the end. Every month introduces some new & complicating element which further involves all the elements already there. It is too gigantic for the mind to grasp. And through everything, involving things still more, run everyone's personal interests & loves & despairs, most terrible of all.

Friday October 8th
As usual no information of any kind came for me to-day, but a good deal, though vague, came for Edward – who did not return till the last train. First thing this morning came a letter marked 'Immediate' from Thurlow, to say that the CO of the 13th had sent the 1st ten names on his list (of which Edward, but not Thurlow, was one) to the War Office for 4 days' leave,

which of course means speedy departure. Later this evening a wire came from Thurlow saying the four days' leave was cancelled, he had entered Edward to return Monday noon, and there were rumours that the officers were for the 11th Battalion – which chance of course pleased Edward, who has been wanting to be with his old battalion all the time. There have been several casualties in the 11th already, though not perhaps of the most glorious kind; two certainly have been wounded, but two or three are in the hospital suffering from nerve attacks.

It looks as if he really is going this time and soon. Father of course started bemoaning that he would never come back & it was for him alone he had kept the works up, so as to have plenty of money to start him on some career etc. etc. I asked if it were not equally important that I should have a career too. He answered very decidedly 'No, Edward was the one who must be given an occupation & the means to provide for himself.' The secondary sex again! It makes me feel very angry that I, the more intellectual of the two, should be regarded in this light because I happen not to be a man. But I will show them. If Father though knowing me will not believe I have any value, the belief shall be forced upon him by facts. Hitherto, although he has after difficulty permitted such what he calls whims as going to Oxford, he has never regarded me as anything more than a plaything. Someday the plaything's intense reality & achievement will astonish him.

Saturday October 9th

Roland and the Hospital seem both to be growing mythical. I can visualize Roland's features even less than I could before, and he is such a brilliant, incomprehensible & elusive person that unless he sends letters to emphasize his humanity, he tends to become quite an abstraction. And I *want* him human. Though I cannot even in imagination see his face, the mere remembrance of his touch is enough to thrill me.

Father has been perfectly awful since he heard Edward is really going to the Front. He talks of giving up the house, the business, the motor, his railway contract, & of doing things which vary from having nothing more to do with any of us to shooting himself! He rails against the Country, the Government, the Army, Mother & the War Office. It is quite indescribable.

Thurlow is coming to-morrow, just for the night.

Sunday October 10th
This, although Edward's last day, was a very nice one. At 7.0 Edward & Father went to meet Thurlow, & I for a walk. I met them as I was coming back. Thurlow is about Edward's height & strange, though very pleasant, looking. He has a big nose, very straightforward blue eyes rather closely set, an almost invisible moustache & a very decided chin which Edward says expresses far more strength than he really has. But I was very taken with him; none of their descriptions did him justice. He was very quiet & it was hard to hear what he said sometimes, but it was possible to make him fairly at ease & amuse him. I had a vague impression all the time of there being a great deal somewhere behind – a quiet strength absolutely trustworthy. He seemed very disappointed that he will probably not go with this draft. Somehow I don't think if I hadn't been engaged to Roland that his shyness of me would have disappeared so quickly. But I suppose he felt there was safety in the fact that I could have no designs upon him!

Monday October 11th
It was a joyful morning in spite of Edward's departure, for a letter, and a very nice one, actually came from Roland.

'Although I have not answered them, your letters of the last few days have meant perhaps more than usual. Everything is so very unsettled. We may be in the middle of an attack quite suddenly, with only a few hours' notice. My company has already been under orders to take a certain position at a certain time & then had the orders cancelled again a few hours later. So far this Army has seen no fighting at all (in the present "show", I mean). In fact everything has been normal on our front. As to the present fighting, you know more than I do: for you have newspapers & time to read them. We get only a few bare facts in telegrams. Good-night. I am just going to fire a few rifle grenades at the Boche. I'll let him have an extra one – from you.'

Edward & Thurlow went off by motor, not by train, for which I was very thankful. Before they started, Thurlow in a kind of shy way tried to efface himself. He said he did not want to interrupt any sad farewells. I told him we did not have such things in this family. They departed, both looking very cheerful, & Edward sitting on the little seat at the back because there was no room for both in front. As they drove down the drive, Edward turned & waved to us with the sweet and fascinating smile which is his greatest charm. He wrote a long letter to Mrs Leighton yesterday. I hope she will not think it 'wooden', as she thought one of Victor's lately.

Friday October 15th
There was another very bad Zeppelin raid on London & district on Wednesday night. About 50 people were killed. Until to-night we had no idea where it was, but with this evening's post came a letter from Aunt Belle, to say that the Zeppelin had actually been over their house at Purley. Aunt Belle says the noise of the bombs & the aerial guns was terrific, past imagining unless heard. I wish I had been there.

Saturday October 16th
This morning when I was writing and for once really not thinking very much about the post, there came the long-anticipated letter from the Red Cross. But by the same post came a pc from Stella saying 'I've got my orders; have you?' so I felt it would be alright; and it was. The letter was a short & peremptory order to go to the 1st London General Hospital, Camberwell, on Monday next, and to wire saying I could go, when I would be given further instructions. They say London is packed with wounded now, & more keep coming every day.

Sunday October 17th
I mostly packed all day the things I have to take, and arranged for the disposal, since Mother & Father really are leaving Buxton, of what I did not want to take. I visited the spot where Roland & I sat and talked the first time he came here, and bade

it farewell, for even if he & I remain after the War is over, it
is not very likely we shall come back to Buxton again. This
evening the leaves were falling fast, and the dusk enveloped all
the glorious tints of autumn in a sad neutral shade.

Thursday November 25th 1st London General Hospital, Camberwell
Was off this morning, but did nothing in particular but write
letters and have a bath. In fact I did very little work all day, as in
the afternoon the hospital was open to visitors. So I just stood
about & watched them coming round & made many-tail
bandages. We made the ward look very nice by clearing away
all the bowls, instruments etc., & putting a table with chry-
santhemums on it in the middle. Then after tea 15 of us
V.A.D.s who came about the same time had to go to Matron's
office & talk about signing on. We were very pleased because we
were all asked to sign & no one was told she was unsatisfactory. I
had a sort of inward jubilation afterwards at having done
something so irrevocable – something which I simply cannot
get out of.

    I heard from Victor to-day that he cannot meet me next
Saturday as he is on guard at the Arsenal, but will try next week.
I had a letter from Roland too. He is staying with the Somerset
Light Infantry till Dec. 10th & is there in the capacity of
Assistant Adjutant. The letter, though short, had much more
hint of his real personality than his letters have had for a long
time.

Friday November 26th
I almost enjoyed the actual work to-day. It was a lovely
morning, bright and energy-inspiring, and all the time I thought
to myself of an expression, 'the top of the fullness of life,' which I
believe someone first used about the trenches. I was on this
afternoon with little Sister Armitage, who treated me quite as an
equal, & told me all about how nice Matron was to her when her
fiancé came on leave. Stayed for supper at the hospital because
it is such a cheerful meal.

    We heard to-day that Sister Oldfield has been warned by the
War Office that her departure is imminent. I shall so miss the
sight of her when she goes. She sat in the same pew as Stella & I

at prayers, looking, with her graceful figure & fair hair & dreamy eyes, like some sweet Abbess with a tragic & romantic past.

Saturday November 27th
Had a letter from Dorothy Grist offering somewhat belated congratulations on my engagement. And I had one from Roland – one that nearly made me cry, for it was so very Roland, and yet a Roland I had never actually come across before – someone penitent, remorseful, almost humble, with a half-fear, which I could read between the lines, of having even temporarily alienated my love for him. For it was in answer to the one I wrote when I was angry at the scarceness of his letters & the sense of personal infallibility in them.

'Dearest,' he says, 'I do deserve it, every word of it and every [sting] of it. "Most estimable, practical, unexceptional Adjutant! . . ." Oh, damn! I have been a perfect beast, a conceited, selfish, self-satisfied beast. Just because I can claim to live half my time in a trench (in very slight, temporary & much-exaggerated discomfort) and might possibly get hit by something in the process, I have felt myself justified in forgetting everything and everybody except my own Infallible Majesty. No, I don't deserve to get any letters at all – only to be ignored as completely as I have ignored you – and Mother. I don't think I have ever been so angry or despised myself so much. I feel as if I hardly dare write to you at all.'

The 'dead' Roland was only sleeping, then. But I nearly wept, and was sorry I had hurt him & wrote him a sweet letter in my off-duty time. I was nearly mad with longing for him, I wanted him so.

Sunday November 28th
Hateful Sunday – very cold, no letters, not off till 6.o. Then I went to the new VAD sitting-room to write letters, and soon began to shiver as there was no fire there – only radiators that don't radiate, & far too many windows.

Monday November 29th
Heard from Mother that the house at Buxton is in considerable upset and they will be glad to move. B.S. has got a commission – in the Staffordshire Yeomanry.

Wednesday December 1st
Roland's letters put me into the seventh heaven at once. For the later one, written on the 27th, said that he pretty definitely expected to get leave on Dec. 31st. 30 days! – if he doesn't 'get hit by something in the meanwhile' – O merciful God! And I *may* get leave too – but even if I don't I shall see something of him, & even to see him for an hour – They were such sweet letters, too. He wants to see me in the blue & white pyjamas I told him I was sitting by the fire in, and recalls a day in the drawing-room at Buxton, the first time he came, when I had been washing my hair, and afterwards played Edward's accompaniment in my dressing-gown, with my hair hanging down my back.

Thursday December 2nd–Friday December 3rd
My chief occupation is to go round at various times during the night to see if everyone is all right & to give them drinks of hot cocoa & milk, which I have to make. It was queer to move about on tip-toe in an absolutely dark ward – the only light being a much-shaded electric lamp on the Sister's table.

I had another charming letter from Roland – about the cold there, which he does not mind, about his ignorance of the Leightons' migration to Brighton & the purport of my Lowestoft visit, & about the sweet anticipation of his leave.

Sunday December 5th–Monday December 6th
Quiet night-duty. While I was away at second dinner my Sister heard the same mysterious footsteps coming up the ward as I heard the night before & looked & saw nothing. Night-duty is certainly a nerve-stirring business.

Two more letters from Roland came at supper – both delightful. He says my letter in answer to his apologetic one nearly made *him* cry, but he was glad I wrote the first one, even though it hurt him more than perhaps I thought it would, for it was good for his Infallible Majesty – and I am very adorable when angry! He says the cold out there has gone now and changed to rain, making the trenches a sea of mud – which, however, he does not seem really to mind. I don't think physical conditions can affect him as much as they do some people – or else his endurance is unusually splendid. Perhaps it is that. He wants me to leave his present for Christmas till he gets his leave – well, till then!

After supper Turner & I went to Brixton, which does not sound romantic. But it was a lovely morning of sun and wind after a very wet night, and I felt intensely thrilled to feel the freshness of the air & to see the red-brown tower of Brixton town hall, & two white spires in the distance, against a background of racing clouds in a pure rainwashed sky. It made me think of Rupert Brooke's lines—

> We have found safety in all things undying,
>   The winds, & morning, tears of men & mirth,
> The deep night, & birds singing, & clouds flying,
>   And sleep, & freedom, & the autumnal earth.

How glad I am I am not a professional nurse! One day I shall have time to contemplate and enjoy the things I love.

Tuesday December 7th–Wednesday December 8th
Out of the darkness & rain to-night a letter from Roland came for me. He has at last had mine from Lowestoft, and has a half-amused, half-resentful desire to know what conclusions we came to in our criticisms of him. After all, he thinks, even if I am an approximation to Lyndall, very often the best kind of love is that of an ideal incarnate in a person. I think that he is right. I certainly have no objection to what Mrs Leighton called a 'Lyndallesque Romanticism', and if he loves me because I am like his ideal woman found in a book – well, so much the better.

Friday December 10th–Saturday December 11th
Had rather a busy night, as a convoy arrived at 8.30, almost before we had time to get ready for it. The convoy was 46 in number & we got seven of them – five head cases, 1 foot & 1

back. None were very ill except one of the head cases, who had a very bad mastoid. The extra work kept us going in the morning too. I took about 35 temperatures & pulses in 45 minutes!

I don't get much chance to read the paper or study the war now-a-days, but judging from headlines and summaries the Allies seem to be in about as bad a position as they have ever been. Certainly in France we are holding the enemy, & that, it seems, is the most we can ever hope to do there, but the Dardanelles expedition is an acknowledged failure, the once-brilliant campaign in Mesopotamia has been spoilt, and the Salonika Expeditionary Force seems to have gone to Serbia only to be annihilated in a hopeless death-trap. If Roland should get sent there!

Sunday December 12th–Tuesday December 14th
Night-duty was much as usual, but long, because I was impatient for it to be over. Nothing occurred to prevent my going for the night off, and I had a letter from Mother in the morning to say they would be pleased to see me. So after supper I dashed off, got the 10.5 to Brighton & arrived there in no time, as I was half-asleep all the way. It was a glorious morning, and I saw again the sight I love so well – the sun shining on a wide expanse of sea. Distant piers were dim and wrapped in mist. The front was crowded with people, and there seemed to be a good many soldiers & girls about, either engaged or newly married. The Grand [Hotel] is a most imposing place with its golden & balconied front & sheltered verandah. Mother had got me a room next hers on the third floor, where I changed with great relief into mufti while Mother talked to me, telling me all about the removal from Buxton and the various difficulties of closing the house, storing the furniture & coming to the Grand.

Mother had written the previous evening to Mrs Leighton asking her either to dinner or tea, & when we arrived we had found a wire from her saying she would come to tea. After 4.0 I waited about in the lounge & on the verandah. Mother waited too; she had put on a purple velvet dress in which she looked very sweet, but seemed a little nervous at the prospect of the momentous meeting. Since their approval or disapproval of one another would, I knew, make a great difference to me, I suppose

I ought to have been nervous too, but I was so pleased at the thought of seeing Mrs Leighton that I quite forgot to be. She arrived at 4.30 – a little late as they had had to wait for the train on Hassocks Station – and brought Mr Leighton too. I introduced Mother & Daddy & we all settled down to tea in the lounge. When she saw Daddy, Mrs Leighton looked a little amazed & said incredulously 'Who's this?' & then asked if he were quite sure he was not on his honeymoon, & that Clare, who had said 'Be nice to the old man!', would get rather a shock if she saw him. This pleased him at once, and, as he had been well warned, Mrs Leighton's eccentric garments appeared not to disturb him at all. I saw she had made up her mind to be especially charming to Daddy, who, as I expected, appeared to interest her more than Mother. They talked to each other hard; Daddy was quite at his best & quite lent himself to her fascinating & warming influence, and she appeared to be quite interested in everything he talked about. They discussed Edward & she criticised him in her usual way without his minding in the least, & even asked him if Edward's lack of comprehension of women was inherited from his father.

I did not talk much, but sat opposite her & watched Roland's sweetest expression coming & going as she smiled. She told me I was looking ever so much better than when she last saw me, when she felt quite troubled about me & wrote & told Roland she was sure I was putting up with more than he was! But she said to-day that she was going to write & tell him I looked charming! She spoke to Mother & Father of her certainty that Roland & I were bound exceptionally strongly to one another, by intellectual as well as emotional ties, and that his love for me was essentially of the nature of a romance, chivalrous & loyal. She said she would not be surprised at anything he wanted to do – she said this very meaningly & smiled at me. I knew what she meant of course, & when she left & said that she hoped I didn't mean to go on nursing for the rest of the war if it were a long one, I said that only some very big thing would make me stop. When they had gone Daddy actually came up to my room & said to me 'John, you're very lucky in those people.' He confessed Mrs Leighton had charmed him absolutely, and said she was benevolence itself, while Mr Leighton was a very capable man behind all his quietness.

Tuesday December 14th–Wednesday December 15th
When I went on duty at night I heard various disquieting rumours that another big move is impending on the Western Front, & that all leave is cancelled. I felt dreary and depressed, & sick almost to despair, for I have very little hope that he will get leave now – or that he will not be mixed up in this offensive, since he missed the last. This work is almost impossible without hope, and to lose what little there is leaves life a mere grey emptiness. This wretched war is as rich in postponements & disappointments as in more tremendous calamities.

Thursday December 16th–Friday December 17th
When I came down to breakfast found a tiny note from Roland saying simply 'Leave from Dec. 24th–31st. Land on Christmas Day.' Of course I was wildly thrilled, anxious & in a turmoil, and greatly troubled lest something should happen in the meantime to stop it, as other people's leaves have been stopped.

Saturday December 18th–Sunday December 19th
In the morning I found my way to St John's Wood to see Schen. We talked about college. Somehow while I listened, although Schen herself, who has worked for the War, did not seem narrow or in a rut, all the life at college seemed suddenly to become very small, & ridiculously self-important & complacent, & remote from the War. In fact some don at Oxford, writing on the subject of Somerville at Oriel, said that these ladies, 'instead of joining the Red Cross Nurses', preferred to shut themselves up in St Mary's peaceful Quadrangle, where they could 'devote their attention to their "studies" and their games' without being perturbed by the terrible tragedies going on outside its walls. It was bitter and a little true – and yet in a way a shame, because many would like to go that cannot. But they do not honour their war-workers; men's colleges give a prominent place to the names of those who are serving their country in one way or another; women's colleges carefully refrain from all mention of such of their members. And while Schen was talking, I suddenly

knew that nothing will induce me to go back there while the War is on – and as for after, if it comes soon, whether I go back or not depends entirely on Roland. I felt for a minute or two as if I could not endure Somerville's complacent self-sufficiency in the midst of this world upheaval.

Sunday December 19th–Monday December 20th
In the morning had letters from Edward & Mrs Leighton. She likes Mother & Daddy, & was more interested in Daddy because he has greater possibilities. When she said Mother struck her as having suffered from having been too patient with him all her life I almost started at her penetration.

Thursday December 23rd–Friday December 24th
It does not feel at all like Christmas Eve on which I am writing this, although Mrs Leggatt & I spent nearly all night filling the soldiers' red bags, which we made, with crackers, sweets and nuts. But if I have not the Christmas feeling, there is at least joy in my heart; I can think of nothing else but the probability of seeing him in two days' time. For I cannot, dare not, call it certainty yet, – dare not even allow myself to feel thrilled.

In the morning I had my hair washed at a pleasant little shop near Victoria. I found by enquiring at Victoria yesterday that the only boat-train from Folkestone arrives at 7.30 p.m. As it is sure to be late and he may not even come that way, it is of no use my waiting so late on the chance of seeing him, so apparently I shall have to give up any idea I had of seeing him to-morrow. And perhaps after all his family has first right to him.

Saturday December 25th–Sunday December 26th
At 8.0 I went to the communion service in our little chapel. I had not been to such a service for ages nor had any faith in all it is supposed to imply, but I went to-day because Christmas at a hospital is an entirely new & unusual experience for me, and I felt too that I must thank whatever God there be for Roland and for all my love and joy. So I knelt in the little chapel, and looked dreamily at the Latin inscription on its walls of 'I am the Resurrection and the Life. He that believeth in Me, though he were dead, yet shall he live, and whosoever liveth and

believeth in Me shall never die.' The sweet music of the organ & the sight of the wounded men who knelt & stood with difficulty made tears come into my eyes – tears of gratitude & joy & a still further intense unnameable emotion. And I thanked God for the Beloved, and prayed for his safety and our happiness.

Directly after breakfast I went down to Brighton, sent on my way with many good wishes from the others. I walked along the promenade, and looked at the grey sea tossing rough with white surf-crested waves, and felt a little anxiety at the kind of crossing he had had. But at any rate he should be safely in England by this time, though he probably has not been able to send me any message to-day owing to the difficulties of telephones and telegrams on Sunday & Christmas Day combined, & the inaccessibility of Hassocks. So I only have to wait for the morrow with such patience as I can manage. Being a little tired with the energies of the night, I spent a good deal of the rest of the day in sleeping, thinking of the sweet anticipation of the morning and of the face and voice dearest of all to me on earth.

Monday December 27th
I had just finished dressing when a message came to say that there was a telephone message for me. I sprang up joyfully, thinking to hear in a moment the dear dreamed-of tones of the beloved voice.

But the telephone message was not from Roland but from Clare; it was not to say that Roland had arrived, but that instead had come this telegram, sent on to the Leightons by Mr Burgin, to whom for some time all correspondence sent to Lowestoft had been readdressed:

T 223. Regret to inform you that Lieut. R. A. Leighton 7th Worcesters died of wounds December 23rd. Lord Kitchener sends his sympathy.
Colonel of Territorial Force, Records, Warwick.

New Year's Eve 11.55 2 The Crescent, Keymer, Hassocks, Sussex
This time last year He was seeing me off on Charing Cross

Station after *David Copperfield* – and I had just begun to realise I loved Him. To-day He is lying in the military cemetery at Louvencourt – because a week ago He was wounded in action, and had just 24 hours of consciousness more and then went 'to sleep in France'. And I, who in impatience felt a fortnight ago that I could not wait another minute to see Him, must wait till all Eternity. All has been given me, and all taken away again – in one year.

So I wonder where we shall be – what we shall all be doing – if we all still *shall* be – this time next year.

1916

Saturday January 1st Keymer

This day last year was the first New Year's Day I had had with Him in my life. To-day is the first New Year's Day I have had with my life empty through the loss of Him. I am immeasurably richer than I was this day two years ago; I am incomparably poorer than I was this day last year.

Clare and I went over to Brighton in the morning to see about her mourning at a shop on the front. Brighton was terribly windy & garish & heartless & cold. The general air of indifference made me almost lose my temper, & I felt it would be impossible ever to go back there at all – bad enough to go to Brighton itself – but to the Grand, where we had lunch – never! But somehow I felt sadly distinguished and infinitely lofty in the midst of that overdressed chattering crowd in the hotel; they showed their vulgarity by gazing inquisitively at my mourning as I went by.

We went back by 'bus, which took quite an hour. We were glad of it, Clare & I, for we had the most intimate conversation we have ever had, and wept quite unashamedly at the beginning of it. I made her promise that if ever she wanted any help of any sort, or anything done for her, she would ask me – for I can gain nothing now in life except by giving, and, even as I would have given all to Him, would rather give to His nearest than to anyone else on earth.

Edward & Victor had already arrived when we reached the Crescent. They both looked tall and fine and knightly, with their handsome faces grave with sorrow – like courtiers without a king. Victor's manner was still shy and abrupt, but his eyes were full of a sincerity and steadiness almost disconcerting; they seemed to arrest your very soul and make you wonder if you had committed any secret sins to render you unworthy of his

scrutiny. I used to call Roland Sir Galahad, but the name suits
Victor still better, for while both have the chevalier's purity and
uprightness of heart, Roland was too much of a leader for the
rôle. Sir Galahad was like Victor – one who follows in simplicity
and humility the ideal that is set before him.

Before they went we had the 'Morning Hymn' on the
gramophone. If anyone had told me that I should ever cry
openly before two lieutenants of the British Army I should not
have believed it. But as it was, not only I but they wept quite
shamelessly as the music made more vivid our vision of how the
world ended for what was – and still is – the most terribly dear of
all things on earth. It calls up rather a different vision for me
since I learnt the details of his death. I do not so much see him
lying amid a heap of fallen soldiers with his white face upturned
to the glory of the Eastern sky, and the Archangel in the
Heavens with his wings spread protectingly over them. Now I
see a small room in a Hospital, and a bed with all that remains
of Him lying upon it; the few objects in the room are becoming
faintly visible, and gradually filtering through the window with
growing intensity the cold blue light of Dawn falls upon his dear
dead face – upon the 'queer bristly head' that rested against my
shoulder – upon the closed beautiful eyes that I loved more than
my soul – upon the firmly shut lips that I kissed in the first
agonizing awakening of passion.

> O gentle child, beautiful as thou wert,
> Why didst thou brave the trodden paths of men
> Too soon, and with weak hands though mighty heart
> Dare the unpastured Dragon in his den?

Yes, we all wept. And Victor went and stood outside before
he need have, in the wind & darkness and rain, struggling with
himself. Why, even as they two sprawled on the bed talking to
Mrs Leighton, the want of that third, who would have lain in the
middle, made that very camaraderie a grief.

Sunday January 2nd
We had more details to-day – fuller, more personal, more
interesting, & so much sadder. So the day opened once more –

it has begun so all too often this week – with our sitting round the breakfast table scarcely touching our breakfast, but trying with eyes that tears had made to ache acutely, to see to read messages sent us concerning Him. Two letters came – one from Colonel Harman, and one from the Roman Catholic Chaplain, who was with Him in the hospital at Louvencourt the afternoon of the day He died.

At midnight on Dec. 22nd his platoon was preparing to repair the wire in front of their trench, and he went out first, before allowing his men to go, to see if all was safe, and to select the spots to be wired. He was always very down on officers who wasted the lives of their men or made them take risks they themselves had not taken first, and he must have performed this same act on their behalf literally dozens of times before. He used often to say in letters to me that he was going out to mend wire, and I thought nothing of it. Evidently this time the Germans must have seen him, or else the place was a sufficiently obvious lacuna as to lead them to suspect that someone would attempt repairs at that spot, for they opened fire almost at once, with rifles previously trained on to that place. He fell, and his Company Commander, Captain Adam, and his platoon sergeant went out immediately and carried him back into the trench. The doctor was talking with the Colonel some distance off; he was sent for immediately and went to Roland as fast as he could go. He evidently did all he could, for the Colonel says he 'was splendid'. In less than 6 hours he had Roland in the Hospital Clearing Station at Louvencourt, a distance of 10 miles away. Probably he could only be carried on a stretcher; at any rate he must have been for a few miles, till they got beyond the lines of the trenches. The doctor accompanied him to the hospital, which they reached about 6.0 in the morning. At 10.0 he had a severe operation; it could not be done before because he was suffering too much from shock. But there seems to have been scarcely any hope from the first; 'his chances of recovery were very remote,' says the Chaplain. The Chaplain gave him Extreme Unction immediately after the operation while he was still unconscious – which shows that those who performed it knew that hope was practically over. He was visited twice again by the Chaplain in the afternoon, when he was recovering consciousness, made an 'act of contrition' and received absolution. The Chaplain intended to visit him again and give him Holy Communion, as the doctors said he might last another 48 hours, but he died quite peacefully at 11 p.m. Except for the time when He was actually under the operation, he was conscious from the time he was wounded right up to the very last. He kept up a conversation with the doctor and all of them until he reached the hospital. He evidently talked a good deal with Father Purdie, but on religious rather than personal topics, it seems. But I shall write & ask the Chaplain what he knows; we must have been very much in Roland's thoughts, for he was to have seen us in two days' time, and there may have been some casual mention of us.

Two sentences – one in the Colonel's letter & one in the Chaplain's – hurt me more than anything. The Colonel says 'The Boy was wonderfully brave,' and the Chaplain 'He died at 11 p.m. after a very gallant fight.' Yes, he *would* have been wonderfully brave; he would have made a gallant fight, even though unconsciously, with that marvellous vitality of his. None ever had more to live for; none could ever have wanted to live more.

'Someday we shall live our roseate poem through – as we have dreamt it.' I wonder if he thought of that. Perhaps he thought that the very pain he was suffering was a guarantee that those words were coming true very soon indeed. Will they ever, I wonder? Oh, if only we knew that, all would be well.

I am glad he died a confessed Roman Catholic. For the Roman Catholic Church holds out a fairer and surer hope of a Life hereafter than any other faith in the world. If ever I felt inclined to enter any Faith, it might well be that one – at any rate I shall certainly examine it closely as I have never done before, and shall care more for that Interpretation of Religion than any other. After all – I cannot sweepingly state that I have *no* faith – *no* hope of something more beyond this puzzling life. And even if I cannot utterly *believe* in [a Life hereafter], I would like to act as if in the hope of one – to live and act on the chance that there may be one, rather than as if I were certain there is not. It seems to be this that He did – & I can wish to do nothing better than to act as He has acted, right up to the end.

They buried Him on Sunday afternoon, Dec. 26th, in the little military cemetery at Louvencourt, the small village behind the lines, where the Clearing Station was to which they took him. Colonel Harman was at the service, the first part of which was in the church, and the last part by the grave-side. The Colonel says in his letter that as they carried His body out of the little church the sun came out & shone brilliantly. But all the same, I cannot feel He is dead – even though they talk about 'His body'. I remember I told him on the cliff at Lowestoft that if he died I should find it impossible to believe in his death. And when I remember his closeness to me that Sunday evening on the cliff – I feel as if it will be impossible always.

Mother came to tea in the afternoon; everyone seemed impressed by my nurse's dress, which I had put on at Evelyn's request, and Clare said she didn't wonder the Matron gave me extension of leave if I went about the Hospital looking like that. She ended by making a sketch of the cap. Mother was very nice – but I almost felt as if she were a stranger. One cannot pretend to live in any other than one's own atmosphere when one has reached the bed-rock of life. Edward went with Mother at 5.30 as he intended to spend the evening with Victor. Before they left we had the 'Morning Hymn' once more. And this time I thought all the while of His body being carried from the darkness of the church into the sunshine outside . . .

After supper I sat long with Mrs Leighton before the dying fire, discussing problems of the future – my future, and trying to find out how best to face the old ghostly enemies whom Roland's death has caused to rise again from the graves where His love had buried them.

January 3rd 1st London General Hospital, Camberwell
Hateful return to night-duty – all eyes on me.

January 4th
Desperately lonely – beginning to realise more than I did at Keymer. Hateful night-duty on officers' corridor.

January 9th
Wandered about Camberwell alone, extremely miserable.

[January 13th] Keymer

I arrived at a very opportune though very awful moment. All R.'s things had just been sent back from the front and they were all lying on the floor. I had no idea before of the aftermath of an officer's death, or what the returned kit, about which so many letters have been written in the papers, really meant. It was terrible. Mrs Leighton and Clare were both crying as bitterly as on the day we heard of His death. There were his clothes – the clothes in which he came home from the front last time – another set rather less worn, and underclothing & accessories of various descriptions. Everything was damp & worn & simply caked with mud. All the sepulchres and catacombs of Rome could not make me realise mortality & decay & corruption as vividly as did the smell of those clothes. I know now what he meant when he used to write 'this refuse-heap of a country' or 'a trench that is nothing but a charnel-house'. And the wonder is, not that he temporarily lost the extremest refinements of his personality, as Mrs Leighton says he did, but that he ever kept any of it at all – let alone nearly the whole. He was more marvellous than even I ever dreamed.

All that was left of his toilet luxuries came back – a regular chemist's shop – scented soap, solidified Eau-de-Cologne etc. We no longer wondered why he wanted them. One wants the most expensive things money can buy to combat that corruption. Even all the little things had the same faint smell, & were damp & mouldy. The only things untouched by damp or mud or mould were my photographs, kept carefully in an envelope, & his leather cigarette case, with a few cigarettes, a tiny photo of his Mother & George Meredith, & the three little snapshots Miss Bervon took of us, inside. He must have had those things always on him, & the warmth of his body overruled the general damp & decay. There was his haversack crammed full of letters – he seemed to keep all he received. I found the rest of mine, & also several of Edward's. There were letters from officers of the Norfolks, from Mrs Bennett at Uppingham, & one or two very pathetic & grateful epistles from the mothers of Tommies, thanking him for his sympathy & careful record of details, & hoping he would come safely through. There were letters from Tommies too – Norfolks & invalided Worcesters – letters

intimate & affectionate but always respectful, almost reveren-
tial, at the same time. Mrs Leighton remarked almost with awe
how very openly one has to live at the Front, when any moment
one's most private personal belongings become the property of
one's nearest relations & friends. No one ever needed any proof
of *his* uprightness – but if we had, here was proof irrefutable &
convincing of a purity almost awful in its completeness. The
very worst things we found were one or two quite small unpaid
bills. And we wondered as we looked through them how many
other dead officers would have things sent back to their people
such as to leave *nothing* to regret, nothing to cause tears of
bitterness as well as of grief.

Friday January 21st Camberwell
Night-duty was as loathly as usual, though not quite as bad as
some have been lately. I had a very nice letter from Daddy,
applauding my decision to leave off nursing & take a rest to
think things over. He promises to give me £50, nearly all of
which I shall not want, & most of which I probably shall not
spend, as I hope to save a little, but which I will not refuse this
time as it will be a useful stand-by to have in the background &
will save me from financial worry amid my other anxieties.
One's parents are queer people. 'Distance lends enchantment,'
says Mother, & it seems about right.

I went out with Stella this morning, but she got annoyed
because I told her she was too pleasant all round & her
character wanted trouble to give it depth. So, as she got
annoyed & walked off, I went on the top of a 'bus to Regent St
to look at mourning rings, but did not see anything that I liked. I
hate Regent St now; it is full of young officers, who all make me
think of that officer with whom I once walked in Regent St, and
who will never walk there with me again.

Saturday January 22nd
I had a very sweet & sympathetic letter from Mrs Leighton, who
seems not quite to know what to advise me to do – unless I go
home & write. But she says she is sure the light will come, if I will
only wait. I bought the *Sphere* in which Clement Shorter had
written a charming little notice of Roland in the Literary Letter

part, & had printed 'Violets'. The context sounds as if the poem was written to his Mother, but no one reading it could doubt in what relation he stood to the person to whom he wrote it, even though they did not know me.

Sunday January 23rd
Just a month ago to-day.

And we are still looking for the shattered fragments of that world which the War Office telegram smashed for us. I started to-night to write a little story about him & me. Stella & I walked in the Park after night-duty, & I mentioned some of my many perplexities.

[January]
It seems more than probable He went out of life without knowing it. He would almost certainly have sent some message had he known – and to have received some message to inspire the long dreary years ahead would of course have made it easier for us. But had he known I feel his personality would somehow have been with us that night, & we should have realised, instead of being as utterly unconscious of what was happening as we were. In view of the fact that he said he would wish to know himself if he were dying, I cannot help feeling sorry if they did not tell him; I felt it was in a way deceiving him to let him give all he had without being able to take to himself the credit of having done so – without being conscious of his own heroism in making the supreme sacrifice. Being what he was, he would have liked to have realised what he was doing, & he would not have been afraid. I always think those words describing Lyndall's death – 'The old strong soul gathered itself together for the last time; it knew where it stood' – pictures the ideal conscious passing of a Splendid Soul. And yet – he would perhaps have suffered exceedingly if he had fully realised all he would never have any more – if he had known he would never see sunset and dawn again, never go back to his Mother or Uppingham or 'Life and Love and' – me. As it was he must just have gone to sleep, glad to be at rest after the weariness of 4 months in the trenches in the worst possible weather, thinking he would wake to the light of day next morning, possibly seeing dreamily in his mind (as one

does in quiet after long stress) scenes of the past at school, or at home when he was a child, or with me in later years, & probably rejoicing that he was wounded at last as he always meant to be, & thinking he would have a long happy time at home, seeing much of the people he loved. To us at least it is heart-breaking to think he thought all this, and they around him knew it could not ever be – though if as the Chaplain suggests there were medical reasons that rendered it inadvisable to tell him, they were of course quite right not to do so. And of course it was easiest that way for him, but in view of his personality, was it best? I can scarcely think sanely about this at all, and that is just what I cannot decide.

In my mind I have lived through his death so many times that now it has really happened it seems scarcely any different from the many other occasions in which the only difference was that it was not an actual fact. In fact I don't believe even now that I have felt such an utter desperation of renouncement as I did the first time he went to the front. I think my subconscious self must have told me then that I should not have him for long, in spite of my apparent belief, originated I suppose by my desire, that I should. Into my diary of that time, and into all my letters, there seems to have crept in spite of myself a quite unmistakable prescience of death. I was always writing to him about it, & facing it with him from all points of view. I remember writing once, before he came home on leave, 'If only Fate will let me see him once again, I feel I could forgive it anything it may have in store for me.' Have I forgiven it? I wonder.

When the beauty of sunrise at the end of night-duty, or a glimpse of very pure sky behind bare tree-branches, takes me for a minute out of myself, I get sudden shocks which shake me to the very depths, of realisation that of all these things he loved so he is conscious no more. At least we do not know that he is, – though equally we do not know that he is not. But there is such an immense gulf between being conscious of them & not being so, that while still in life one feels it scarcely possible that one ever should not be. And then, although I have often wished I was dead, it seems so unfair that I should be left to enjoy these things, & he not. And I feel as if I am taking an unfair advantage of him, & can never enjoy them again because he cannot – or because *perhaps* he cannot. I wonder – when I think of that infinitely sad look in his eyes, in spite of his natural gaiety – whether he *was* one of those whom Maeterlinck writes of as (subconsciously) Prédestinés. It is strange to think that into the things we speculated about so much – he & I – he has entered, passed over what seems such an impassable barrier until it comes, and he *knows* – while I am left here, speculating still.

If only the War spares us – He shall be to men as the Arthur Hallam of Tennyson's *In Memoriam*.

Tuesday January 25th–Wednesday January 26th

On Sunday night at 11.0 – the day of the month & hour of His death – I knelt before the window in my ward & prayed, not to God but to Him. For if the Dead are their own subconscious selves they can surely hear us and know that we are thinking of them even though we cannot know that they know or are thinking of us. Always at 11 p.m. on the 23rd day of the month I mean to pause in whatever I am doing & let my spirit go out to His. Always at that hour I will turn to Him, just as the Mohammedans always turn to Mecca at sunrise.

To-night I have been very unhappy. First of all the day-nurse in my ward – quite a nice girl a year or two older than I – is going to be married next week and has invited the men who can get up in the ward to her wedding. And when I came on duty to-night the men would insist upon talking about it.

Two letters about Roland, which were great contrasts except in the sentiments they expressed, came for me to-day. The first one was from his servant. The man evidently knew all about me, by the way in which he writes; I know he often used to post Roland's letters to me. His letter is very respectful and expressed in the quaint way most of these men have. He asks me to pardon him for writing but feels obliged to in the circumstances 'inasmuchas' he was his servant all the time he was in the Worcesters & accompanied him on his travels, even to the Somerset Light Infantry. He 'must admit', he says, that Roland was the most beloved officer in the regiment, both among officers & men. He then describes to me the details of his death, much as I already know them. But in his opinion Roland ought never to have gone outside their line that night as there was bright moonlight, & the Germans, who were only 100 yards away, must have been able to see him with ease. He says, too, that it was a sniper who shot him, which hardly tallies with the Colonel's statement that the Germans fired a few rounds from fixed rifles. Perhaps Colonel Harman thought we should feel all the angrier if we knew one of those vile snipers had killed him – but certainly, the vital nature of the wound suggests a sniper's careful aim rather than an accidental bullet.

I thought of Him going out in the bright moonlight and wondered if His rashness had overcome his prudence after all – just on that one occasion, on that last day when He should have been more careful than ever before. And I ask myself in anguish of mind 'Was it heroism entirely – or was it partly folly?' Certainly at points the two qualities come close. Some people, such as Father, would call all heroism folly; and, in fact, all heroism is to a certain extent unnecessary from a purely utilitarian point of view. No one would have accused Roland of shirking if he had remained in the 4th Norfolks & been now at Lowestoft instead of in a grave in France. But heroism means something infinitely greater & finer, if less practical, than just avoiding blame, & doing one's exact stereotyped duty & no more – & 'heroism in the abstract' was His ideal. But during the night – & I scarcely think in the after-time I shall quite be able to describe just what sufferings have been mine during these dreadful nights, I thought of the Heroism, whether touched with recklessness or not, that caused Him to go out in front of the line into the bright moonlight & led to the sacrifice of all that meant so much in the world, all that was so exceptional and brilliant & fine. And I looked out of the ward window to the tall church-spire & to the dark banks of clouds with rifts between them of bright moonlit sky, & cried in the bitterness of my heart 'Dearest – oh Dearest! Why *did* you?' Ah, if he could answer – if even I could know that he hears! And I wrote to Victor asking whether he thought it *was* rashness that led to His Death, or whether it was still that uplifting quality of Heroism without which He would not have been so adored & had that immense influence over officers & men to which even His servant paid tribute.

The other letter was from a Captain Adshead of the 7th

Worcesters; he was evidently rather a friend of Roland's, as Roland told him about me once and showed him my photograph. He asked Mrs Leighton for Roland's fiancée's address, as he is engaged himself & on that account sympathises with me very deeply. His letter is long & perfectly charming; it is remarkable how it is possible to get from a stranger a kind of wonderful understanding which the people who have been one's friends appear unable to give. He also has been making enquiries about Roland's last hours, and it seems now that we have gleaned all the information there is to glean. And it is as Mrs Leighton thought – no word will come from Him to lighten the burden of the years to come, for He seems not to have had the slightest idea that He was even badly hurt, & even the doctors themselves were surprised at the suddenness with which he took the wrong turning. I lay on the bed & cried bitterly, thinking that never, never, never will there be any word or message to us from Him again. If only I could feel as dear Captain Adshead seems to feel – 'Try & be brave, just as though he were by your side now – as I know he is in spirit though for a time you cannot see him.'

Wednesday January 26th–Thursday January 27th
On Thursday morning a letter came from Mrs Leighton, saying His servant's letter had made her as bitter & sad as it made me. She also told me what would once have been a glorious piece of news but now makes tragedy a thousand times more tragic. Shortly after His death a letter arrived for Him written in the handwriting, which they knew, of an influential friend of His. This letter was sent to them from the front; Mrs Leighton would have returned it unopened, but Mr Leighton opened & read it. It was an offer to Roland to get Him a good position on the Headquarters Staff at Salonika. Just the sort of post we all said he ought to have had, rather than be risking his life in the trenches constantly, just the post where his great abilities would have had scope, & he would have been in comparatively no danger. He would have accepted it too, for He was longing to see more of the world, & sometimes even regretted not having been sent to the Dardanelles; he was just ready, too, for such an offer, for though he would have hated never to have seen active

service, he would not have hesitated to accept after 9 months in the firing line. In such a position His future would have been assured, & on a staff-captain's pay he could have married without rashness. Ah! the pity of it! How *can* one placidly assume that things happen for the best, when they so obviously take the worst turn they can. As each fresh circumstance has turned up, I have thought that nothing could magnify the bitter irony of it all. The day before his leave – his probable marriage – his ignorance of the death of which he deserved & would have wished to know the glory – the lack of fighting in general at the time – the fact of its being something he had done dozens of times before – the family drinking to the Dead & sitting up to wait for Him, when he was one of them – their expecting the fatal telegram to be from him announcing his arrival – what could, it seems, be worse? And now this new thing has come – this new big thing. Oh! if that letter had arrived a month earlier. He might have been at Salonika now, doing work after his heart's desire, & I might have been his wife . . .

Oh! if – if – if . . . !

Mrs Leighton & I at Lowestoft blamed Him for his chameleon-like characteristics, & what we thought his neglect of us. But these were mere temporary surface things, implying no inward unsoundness, & we should not have thought even of them had we realised, as we have realised since his clothes came back, the meaning of War. When we think of that distilled Death, the mud of France, of his numerous offices & absorption in & enthusiasm for his work – it is wonderful that he kept in touch with us to the great extent he did. What a marvel He was – & yet He was allowed to die. One begins to feel that if there be a God or Fate (call it what you will) It is after all not infallible & that this was one of Its mistakes. And yet – I remember in November in the garden at Lowestoft Mrs Leighton & I were discussing a possible child of Roland & me, & she said that just because we were both so brilliant we must not expect too much, as Nature never allowed anything to get too near to perfection. May not this also apply to Him? And if so, then 'Blessed art thou among women' applies both to her for having made Him happen & to me for having gained His love. For when one thinks of His strong honourable character, his influence, immense & pure, over all ranks of men, his school record, his Army record, his prizes, his poems, the many who adored him, & the fullness & crowdedness of the life that was so very brief, viewed in this light does it not seem wonderful that this Perfect thing was allowed to exist at all, rather than that it was not permitted to last? Oh! if one knew anything at all that would shed a little light on the immense Chaos of doubt & speculation.

I answered Mrs Leighton's letter, enclosing a very comforting one that I had just received from Victor. Nothing can console one for the waste of Roland's future, but Victor has at least convinced me that his life was not needlessly & recklessly thrown away. Whether the night was moonlight or not, the wire would have to be mended, as the enemy might easily make an attack when it was dim before dawn, but the men, being bitter about the death of one they loved, would naturally seize upon anything on which they could exercise their bitterness. Roland, says Victor, was not imprudent, nor Colonel Harman a fool, & it is safe to assume that the work had to be done that night. Whether it was absolutely necessary for Him to go is questionable, but He would not have been He if He had not, for not only did He like to do everything Himself to make sure it was done thoroughly, but He would never allow anyone, especially an inferior, to take a risk he would not take Himself. On Liverpool St Station that last time the Three met, He said to Victor 'The men always know when an officer's afraid. The man who doesn't care a damn they will follow anywhere, but the man who hesitates about anything will never get them to follow Him at all.'

I also sent to Mrs Leighton yesterday one of the enlargements I have had done of the Three Musketeers taken from the last O.T.C. camp group. It has enlarged excellently. Roland himself is so good that I can scarcely bear to look at it.

Oh! these dreadful nights! I did not know I could suffer so.

Friday January 28th–Saturday January 29th
I am thoroughly fed up with the way the day-people in 8, 9, & 10 *will* fuss, & interfere with me on my night-duty, which is nothing to do with them at all. They expect me to do & thoroughly finish single-handed exactly the same work as four of them on together

in the evening never by any chance get done when I arrive &
usually leave to me to finish. How *hateful* life is! I wonder if it will
ever be any better.

Saturday January 29th–Sunday January 30th
Had a pc from Edward saying he may get leave from Feb. 4th-
8th. Whether I shall be able to see him is, I suppose, a different
matter; I don't even know whether I shall be on night or day-
duty, & cannot get Miss Bickham to tell me. The way they treat
us like children here & make mysteries of trifles is too ridiculous
for words.

Sunday January 30th–Monday January 31st
Night-duty was particularly irksome again, as Clark did nothing
but call me all night, and in the morning Sister Henderson went
for me for making badly some beds I hadn't made at all, but had
left to Miss Row – whom of course I couldn't give away. I was
then informed by Miss Spurling that to-night was to be my last
night on night-duty. Detestable day-duty! Night-duty is bad
enough, but I *loathe* the thought of day, never any time to
oneself, never anywhere one can go to be alone, never the right
person to go out with on one's times off. And somehow packing
my things made me realise how utterly wretched I am – how
there is no light at all, either in present or future. Last time I was
on day-duty was when He was still in this world. I hated it badly
enough then, though nothing but His existence seemed to
matter at all. But how unspeakably I shall loathe it now! And
nearly two months have to pass before I am free – free to give
myself for a little space to thoughts of Him – nay, to Him
Himself. As I packed therefore I wept many bitter tears. I
wonder if ever, ever I shall get over this feeling of blank
hopelessness, of feeling it is cruel that I should have to suffer so,
of wishing I had never been born at all. At present it all gets
worse every day. In the utter blackness of my soul I seem to be
touching the very depths of that dull lampless anguish which we
call despair. And I don't feel as if I shall ever rise out of it again.
I am crushed – altogether crushed, by life – I have no power of
resistance left, no courage – not even any desire for courage.

Little, sweet phrases from His letters keep coming always into my mind – & I just cry & cry.

I had several letters this morning. Marjorie Barber has been telling the Lorie about me & says she is very grieved, & is going to write. Clare says she thinks I idealise Him a little, whereas she treasures Him for His faults. So do I – but I see now how small they were in comparison with His essential greatness. Victor's letter is another great consolation – he is wonderfully comforting. I know now why I felt as if I knew him well when I met him on New Year's Eve, though really I had seen very little of him at all. For Roland used to talk to him about me; He called him the 'Father Confessor' & seems to have felt he would understand even what I meant to Him. A great deal of the letter is about the dawn of His love for me. And though it hurts me terribly, partly because I did not know or realise it while He was alive, yet I must quote some of it here because it is all so infinitely precious and sweet.

'Do you remember the two Karg-Elert pieces that Sterndale Bennett played at the beginning of the service that afternoon? One of them, "Clair de Lune", seemed to have moved Him deeply. He said it reminded Him of you in its coldness & the sense of aloofness from the world. He always used to say that He was not worthy of you. Again I cannot recollect the exact words of His letter, but they were something like this: "I want very much to go to the Front and I shall go. You remember what Lyndall said about wanting a thing very much; that if you want it sufficiently you achieve it. Well, I want very much to come back, and I shall come back." '

Monday January 31st–Tuesday February 1st
There was very much of a Zeppelin scare to-night. The Hospital was in utter darkness, passages black, lamps out, blinds down. I stood at the window of my ward, feeling strangely indifferent to anything that might happen. Since He had given up all safety I was glad to be in London, which is not safe. But nothing happened.

Tuesday February 1st
I don't know why, but this afternoon I began to feel a little more strength of will & purpose than I have ever felt since His death.

Perhaps it is Victor's letter; perhaps it is that Matron was right
& night-duty is too great a strain in such circumstances after all.

Wednesday February 2nd
I had a letter from Mother to-day; she went to Keymer on
Monday & found poor Mrs Leighton in very low spirits & Clare
most depressed & in tears. Mother asked Clare to spend the day
at Brighton to-morrow, which I hope she will do as the change
may be good for her. She is really more remarkable than
anyone, even Mrs Leighton, realises; Roland always oversha-
dowed her. Mrs Leighton says she would very much like me to
be somewhere near her.

Friday February 4th
Duty was somewhat wearying to-day. There seemed to be a
great deal to do without much need for it. Sister Burdett is a
dear & very sensible, but Sister Borner has a talent for making
work. To-night when I asked if I should take the clean towels
round she exclaimed 'Oh no! no! no! I always take them round
myself, otherwise I *know* there will be a muddle.' So poor Miss
Brittain has so far fallen from her pedestal as not to have
sufficient brain to give out thirty clean towels & take thirty
dirty ones away! Such is the reputation of a VAD. No wonder I
want work in which I can exercise a *little* initiative.

   Mother came up to-day to town & I took her to see the
reproductions of Louis Raemaekers' Cartoons at the Fine Art
Galleries in New Bond Street. They are horrible & beautiful –
intellectual and extraordinary. He will live for all time as The
War Artist, just as Rupert Brooke will live as The War Poet.
Looking at these Cartoons, I realised the influence of Art –
realised how an artist like Louis Raemaekers or a poet like
Rupert Brooke may have more influence on the War than even
such a life-destroying cataclysm as the Battle of Loos – may be a
greater result of the War than any territorial acquisition at the
end of it.

   Mother & I had tea at Marshall & Snelgrove, & then I had to
return to duty & she to Brighton. They had Clare over for the
day on Thursday. Daddy is getting quite fond of her. I am
determined that I will make a great difference for good in her

life. I believe after all that perhaps in her – Bystander, appreciator, reproducer of impressions – I may find more of Roland than anywhere else. Dear dead Boy! – & yet all this afternoon & especially this evening when I came from Victoria on the top of a 'bus & the sunset was glorious, I felt that He was not dead at all, but was with me all the time, sharing my impressions, & trying as from a distance to make me feel that He was near.

Saturday February 5th
Strenuous day as there were two operations. The first was a dangerous case – an internal growth – and the man in poor health. He was at the theatre about 2 hours from 10.0, & got through the operation, apparently rather to everyone's surprise, & they said they did not know what would happen when he came round. He had not come round when I went off duty at 5.0; his mother, who had been sent for, was sitting by his bedside as he lay very pale & still. I thought of Roland lying pale & weak & unconscious after *his* operation, & I had to bend over my broom as I was sweeping the floor, so that the patients should not see the tears I couldn't keep out of my eyes.

I had another letter to-night from Roland's servant, giving a few more illuminating details of His death. It proves Him conclusively not to have thrown His life away recklessly or needlessly. He was hit because he was *last man* to leave the dangerous area for the comparative safety of the trench, and so was at the post where the Roland we worship would always have wished to be when He met Death face to face.

Sunday February 6th
I had a morning off & went alone to High Mass at the Roman Catholic Church in Spanish Place, that Roland loved. It was glorious in there, & made me feel very near to Him. There was no tawdriness in the beauty of the church, & the heavenly music seemed to struggle & aspire till it soared to the very gates of Heaven. It made one feel that it surely cannot be the grave which holds the secret of this puzzling life. I liked the incense too – only I cried and so could not smell it much. The whole service was so different from the prosaic, dull, mismanaged services of

the Church of England. It seemed to fill me with the light & softness & warmth of which I stand so much in need. After all, why should not the senses be the instruments of the soul, instead of being crushed & neglected? They were surely not given to us only to be disregarded. I thought all the time how pleased He must have been if He saw me kneeling there, in *His* church.

Tuesday February 8th
At lunch-time to-day a postcard arrived from Mother to say that Edward had a wire last night telling him to return to the camp immediately, as he is to go to the Front this week. This time I feel the alarm is real. He *would* go just now, when we all feel the dreadfulness of it most. Had he gone six months ago, it would not have seemed like it does now; because then there was someone in the world who mattered so much beyond everything. But now – he is all I have, all there is to fall back upon – all that is worthwhile in my future – and if he goes I shall have nothing left. And it is very unlikely I shall be able to see him again to say goodbye. Perhaps I shall never see him again at all. Yet I cannot feel anything but an utter, utter weariness. There comes a time when nothing has power to move one much. There are limits to one's capacity for realisation. I have reached those limits.

Thursday February 17th
It is just a week to-day since we said goodbye to Edward on Charing Cross Station. And now he is in the trenches. It is all unbelievable.

The days are *so* long, & they drag so one after another. I woke up to such a shock of despair this morning, because I had been dreaming about Roland – I don't know what it was all about, but I know in the dream I was feeling a desperate longing to see and touch him, and he came in and I did touch his hand – oh! with such a thrill of infinite joy. And afterwards I saw Him standing in a street – Regent Street, I think – in khaki, very upright and soldier-like. And then – I awoke to the reality.

Tuesday February 29th
I saw by to-day's *Times* that Lort Carey has died of wounds in France. Matters have gone beyond comment now. Not a single

friend of Edward's but has suffered somehow through the War – Roland & Carey among the dead – Thurlow and Ivan Dyer wounded – Victor almost ended by meningitis – Ernest Wynne gas-poisoned – Maurice Ellinger given over to a fate yet worse than any of those. I remember how friendly Carey used to be with Roland and Edward – and how when they were both up for the scholarship exam. at Oxford, they had dinner in his rooms at Magdalen, only a little more than two years ago. It seems impossible that it is such a short time. Of the three who went in for the scholarship, Roland, Garrod & Edward, Edward alone remains. And now Carey has gone too – and there is one more chime for the midday bell at Uppingham – one more name for the Chapel walls, where it seems all the flower of Uppingham will be.

I had another letter from Mrs Leighton continuing what Captain Adam told her about Roland's twenty minutes of agony. And Mr Leighton has drawn up a plan for me, which she has enclosed, showing accurately exactly how Roland was hit, and what followed, & the lie of the land in general – drawn up from Captain Adam's statement. It is very valuable for me – and gives things very accurately. She is going to meet Captain Adam for lunch on Wednesday. She tells me she has been very busy writing her book on Roland – even though it may not be published.

Wednesday March 1st
A few of the older V.A.D.s were told to-day that they might have to go abroad ere long. 'Ere long' of course more likely means months than weeks. But we – our lot – will be among the next. I have quite decided to stay on here, & go on foreign service when it is offered to me – especially as Miss Burdett & I were on alone to-night & she was quite encouraging. She asked me if I should like to go abroad one day, nursing. Of course I said 'Yes.' She let me do every single dressing & went round with me, showing me how, and also offered to lend me books on the subject of surgical nursing. Of course as soon as I get on to the theory of anything, I am interested at once.

Since Stella came back I can't do with her at all. She is too easily cheerful and pleased with life for words. Cheerfulness

always irritates me – there is always something self-satisfied
about it. It is very different from that gaiety and wit which, as
Roland said, is always sad at heart.

Thursday March 2nd
I met Mother this afternoon; she seemed to be astonished at my
decision to stay on here when I hate it so much, but seemed
vaguely to understand what I meant when I said that I couldn't
leave because to leave would mean defeat.

We went to Fishmonger's Hall Hospital to see Geoffrey
Thurlow. He was sitting up in a large easy-chair, wrapped in a
green dressing-gown, with a brown rug on his knees. He seemed
to feel cold – still, of course, from the effects of shock – and kept
close to a small gas stove that was lighted beside him. Somehow
he looked very attractive; in his strong-featured face his blue
eyes with their long brown lashes looked beautiful. His hair was
quite thick & soft – not close-cropped, like Roland's. He talked
much more to-day, & more intimately – all about Edward & the
Front, & his own fear of being afraid. He was wounded in the
front-line trench during the bombardment. He talks so quietly
that it is a little difficult to understand all he says when he is
telling a story, but as far as I could make out he stayed in the
front-line trench after being wounded, rallying his men &
ordering them to 'rapid fire' to try & keep the Germans off,
until they were nearly surrounded & only one or two besides
himself were left, and then he ordered them to get away. Even
then he wondered if he ought to have gone or stayed for certain
death. He perfectly realised all the time what was happening &
was never worked up at all. Edward is right when he says
Thurlow understands himself. I could only think of the courage
which even after he was wounded & shaken made him stay &
rally his men till staying was useless any more. It is all the more
remarkable when one remembers that he is a non-militarist at
heart but put aside his personal objections to War for Patriotism's sake. His manner was very serious, & he worked his
fingers nervously & looked terribly sad when talking about the
front. He showed us gas and steel helmets that he had, & said he
was quite certain a steel waistcoat could not have saved Roland.
When we were going he admitted he was afraid of me the first

time he met me, but actually asked me to come & see him again before he leaves the hospital on two months' leave.

Saturday March 4th

Went to Oxford by the 1.45, after being allowed off early. Marjorie Barber met me at the station & took me to her room looking out over the High. I sat for quite a long time looking at the High and feeling that I never appreciated it properly in the days when I could walk in it often. 'Nessun maggior dolore . . .'

In a few minutes Schen came in, & they made tea. Then came a knock at the door and Miss Lorimer walked in. She seemed very delighted to see me, and strangely moved by the sight of me in mourning; the reason of which she of course knew, even if my ring hadn't told her. She was wearing the usual brown jersey and skirt, and so far as appearance went it might have been only yesterday that I said goodbye to her on Oriel staircase and she quite unexpectedly told me to take care of myself. After tea we began to talk about my hospital, and I told her lots of my experiences, including the arrival of the convoy at night. She spoke of others who were nursing and she said that she hoped they would come back, and hoped very much that I should.

Then we began to talk about the War, and about those who went out – and those who died. The Lorie put her arms over her head, let herself go and talked her own philosophy. Marjorie & Schen were quite amazed; I daresay I should have been in the old Oxford days, but now even for the Lorie to break through her time-honoured reserve & cast away her reputation before three people did not amaze me so very much. And vaguely I knew it was through my personality & for my sake – and the other two were just an incidental audience.

Finally the Lorie & I were left talking alone; Marjorie & Schen became quite silent, sitting one on each side of the glowing fire, with the Lorie and I together on the sofa in front of it, there in that old Oriel room, whose owner had given his life for his country, perhaps, and where generations of men had discussed the problems of the world. Perhaps it was the wandering ghosts of their bygone conversations which made us so very intimate. We talked of the way in which our dearest &

best went out, bravely, gaily, and how we let them go with a smile; she mentioned her brother in Mesopotamia, and I told her how my people had been opposed to Edward, who had always been delicate & sheltered from every breath of wind, joining the Army, and how quietly and uncomplainingly they had let him go when the actual moment came. And she said one realised in these days how much more than mere physical life a man's life meant, and how much life was gained by laying down the physical side of it – how nothing thus given up was ever lost, and those who died were not really gone, but were with us always, and could never be spoilt for us, but would remain canonised for us – 'I know we felt that very much when my brother died,' she said, in quite a broken voice, and put her arms across her face – this Miss Lorimer, who was said by Miss Davies to have crushed all feeling out of herself and to be quite hard – but I think I always knew . . . I very quietly said how true was what someone had said when my fiancé died, that it was not Death, but Disillusionment, that conquered, and one never got that with these, our dead . . . Then we were all silent for a long time; Marjorie and Schen were hiding their faces, and the atmosphere was tense with emotion.

When after a while we began to speak again, it was about Miss Darbishire's brother, and the niceness of Tommies. And soon Miss Lorimer said she really must go, and turned to me, saying how she was looking forward to seeing me back, and would be only too delighted to teach me Greek all over again for Divvers if necessary – & Mr May still remembered how quickly I had learnt it all. And then of all astonishing things, she suddenly kissed me goodbye instead of shaking hands – a thing I would have betted anybody she would never do – and in sudden embarrassment shook hands with Marjorie & Schen, which was distinctly unusual when they all live in the same building, & then realising this said it was Miss Brittain being in a hat which made her feel we were all going away, & she didn't know why she was shaking hands with them – and finally got out of the room, dear old Lorie! And we three all looked at each other a moment and then started to laugh in sudden revulsion of feeling, and I told Marjorie and Schen they ought to be grateful to me for a very exciting tea.

Then I saw the Pen. I was not in the least in awe of her as in the days of old, and sat opposite her on one side of the fireplace and discoursed about hospitals. The Pen made no mention of my fiancé's death, nor did I, except by quite vague & indefinite allusions. With regard to the business on which I went, she seems prepared to do anything I want; she said Somerville would be proud to have me back after my War service even though I was not taking the usual Honours Certificate. In fact the very difference in the sort of certificate I shall get seems to be quite small & technical; my name would be published in the Honours List just like other people's, and the Pen said it would make no difference to me at all in any post I might want to get. So I decided definitely not to come back till the War is over.

Towards the end of the interview Miss Hayes Robinson appeared. She had evidently not heard of Roland's death, & at first congratulated me; then realising the mistake apologised & seemed very distressed at having made it. I really did not mind, for it was a very natural mistake to make, nor is she the first to make it, and I said that I *was* to be congratulated all the same – meaning on having won the love of one whose courage was no less than His intellect & personal brilliance.

Sunday March 5th
In my off-time I went again to see Geoffrey Thurlow, who is going out to-morrow, but still didn't have long with him, as his mother & sister turned up & he was only allowed to have two visitors to tea. In the few minutes before they came we got quite intimate once more. I like him – and I think he likes me; he calls himself a 'weird bird', in which case I would fit in with him, as I am certainly another. Edward & he, he said, were both odd, & always a little apart from the others. When he came to the door with me & asked me if he might come up to town when he was a little more fit and take me to a concert one afternoon, I said he might. The offer pleased me; he is never one to give an invitation out of mere politeness.

Monday March 6th
Sisters & VADs wishing to volunteer for foreign service were asked to put down their names to-day. From here, it might

be Egypt, Malta or Salonika, just as much as France. Of
course there are risks, great risks – but if I had refused to put
down my name I should despise myself as much as I would a
[Territorial] regiment that wouldn't volunteer for foreign
service.

Wednesday March 8th
Met Miss Heath Jones & Miss Bervon at Fuller's & had tea; it
was my half-day. They understood how it is I want to talk about
Roland, instead of always having the subject changed; to me He
is too great a living reality ever to think of as dead quite as I have
always thought of other people who have died.

Thursday March 9th
I had a very pathetic letter from Edward in answer to the one I
wrote about Carey. He wants me to promise that if he too dies I
will go to Uppingham, with Victor if he is alive, & visit the
Chapel and the VIth-form Classroom, and the Captain's study
into which I looked from the Quad. the night before Speech
Day, & where he and Roland so often 'tired the sun with talking
and sent him down the sky'. I wrote & promised that if I were
left I certainly would. I would as much for my own sake as for
his. I wonder if I could bear to see Roland's name on the Chapel
walls – where I imagined it one night nearly a year ago, when I
sat in St John's Church, Buxton, just after He first went to the
Front. I remember how difficult it was not to cry openly in
church; I think my sub-conscious self must have known then
that He was going to die.

   It is strange to think that, as Captain Adam told Mrs
Leighton, Roland became very religious, almost devotional,
in the few weeks before he died, & made a great friend of
the Roman Catholic Chaplain, & used to bring him into the
Officers' Mess. It is almost as if He knew what was going to
happen, & thought there was something in religion after all,
& gave up the Agnosticism we shared . . . Victor thinks His
terrible ordeal was the consummation of His whole life –
that everything He was & did was a preparation for that
end.

Friday March 10th

Clare wrote to me. She has been busy typing His book for Mrs Leighton. She says she believes very much in the Invocation of Saints, & when I last left Keymer to go back to the Hospital, she was so struck by my pathos & loneliness although I am so strong that she prayed to Him to look after me. I like to think of Him as my tutelary deity – my 'genius', as the Romans called it. I wonder why she insists on not treating me as the sceptic I really am.

Sunday March 12th

I woke up this morning with such a sense of Roland all about me. I was alone in the room, as Turner has gone off for a fortnight through being in quarantine. While not asleep but not yet properly awake I had such vivid memories of him, especially of the Sunday morning we stood in the trenches at Lowestoft and talked about callousness, & the afternoon when we sat very near together on camp-stools by the tennis lawn at Heather Cliff, & talked about a Hereafter, but found life itself too sweet to care much whether there was one or not – and then that evening hour when His head was on my shoulder & His arms around me – and then that last day, when the grief of the coming parting made us both almost irritable.

Oh! it is all so unfulfilled!

Everything came back so very vividly. And I wept as I lay in bed, & felt unutterably lonely.

Monday March 13th

I got back just in time for a small operation in the ward – the cutting of an abscess in Holland's thigh. It was an extremely minor operation but rather messy. I had never seen even anything so small before, but such things never seem to affect me physically at all. All I had to do was to hold the hand lamp, as someone had to hold it, & was thus saved from the embarrassment of handling instruments etc. But all the time my mind was with that operation at Louvencourt; it was Roland I saw struggling under the anaesthetic with His beautiful eyes closed and his sturdy limbs all helpless; it was from Roland's wound that I saw the blood pour out in a scarlet stream. . . . So I was glad it was soon over.

Thursday March 16th Brighton
Went over to Keymer in the afternoon. As I walked from Hassocks Station I noticed how the palms were coming out, just as I saw them coming out when a year ago I rode down to Ashwood Dale, just after I had said goodbye to Him. I hate spring . . .

Saturday March 18th
I went over to Keymer again in the afternoon for about 3 hours. The air was soft and springlike as I went along the lane to the Crescent, in the distance the hills were very blue, and again the golden palms oppressed me. Mrs Leighton was very sweet to me & called me 'poor little girl', and said I had been cheated of the best thing in life before I had ever really had it, because I said I felt so unhappy. But little things as well as big make one miserable; for instance, I was wearing a black velvet hat with a fairly large brim, which I bought just before Roland was to come home, because He always liked me in big hats. It suited me very well indeed, but I had never been able to bear to wear it since His death. But to-day Mother said it was a pity to throw it away, so I made myself put it on. But it made me remember very acutely the time I bought it & the feelings of sweet anticipation I had then. . . . 'Nessun maggior dolore . . .' once again!

And then again – to-day a year ago He came to Buxton to say goodbye to me – and having achieved His object of getting to the Front, everything seemed dust and ashes, because it meant farewell. And we walked through the Buxton lanes in the driving snow beneath a grey sky, and we knew there was nothing left but to 'work and wait and hope', and we wondered what we should be doing & where we should be 'this time next year'. Then it was winter at Buxton, and to-day, a year later, it is spring at Keymer, but in our hearts the spring was then and the winter is now.

And now – He has fulfilled some of His many ideals, but the answer to the problems we discussed – if there be an answer – is hidden in His grave. And I am left here, seeing not only my ideals, but seeing how far short of them I fall, how miserably I fail to achieve the high aspirations which I have set myself, perhaps presumptuously. I want to attain to the Highest – and I don't succeed in attaining to the lowest.

Yet – even this I think He would have understood. Lyndall was like that – and He loved her. He loved her frailties as well as her strength. Perhaps he would have forgiven mine. Perhaps he would not have loved me one bit the less because I am unworthy of the ideal of myself that I have set myself. He was so very human. Yes, he would have understood. Oh! if only I could have Him back, how gladly I would give up everybody else if this were the price of Him. With Him & no one else life would be everything; with everyone else but without Him, it is nothing. I wonder what He would have thought if He had known how He was going to make me suffer.

Sunday March 19th
Victor, who happens to be on leave this week-end, telephoned over to Mother, was delighted to hear I was here too, & asked us all to tea. We went to Wilbury Avenue, where they have quite a small house with rather a dreadful view on to the back of some blind & shutter works. I met Victor's Father & Aunts, whom I had seen cursorily at Uppingham, also another aunt I had not met before. They were all quite ordinary but quite charming & very cordial in their manners. Judging by photographs, none of them seem to be very exciting; Victor – who with his big sad dark eyes was very attractive as a child – is quite the most so. When Mother told him I was going back to London by the 6.30 he decided he was going by it too, so we travelled down together in a first-class carriage empty for most of the way. I don't know why but although Victor is a first lieutenant as Roland was, I always feel more compunction about his spending money on me than I [felt] about Roland. Roland when He took one out always had such an air of the millionaire about Him that one quite forgot He wasn't. Victor & I talked about Him most of the time – especially about the last Speech Day at Uppingham.

A year ago – I suffered my first great grief and anguish of loss

– only the first of so much, but I think I suffered as much then as ever I have. And we parted at the station, & did *not* kiss.

Thursday March 23rd Camberwell
23! Once again. Just three months ago to-day, & a Thursday too. Had a somewhat angry conversation with Stella at lunch-time over the bad effect of suffering on my character. Oh! I know! It was happiness, not sorrow, that softened me; I had bitterness enough in my nature before. I didn't need suffering to soften me. I needed joy. I never loved my fellow-men – or fellow-women, rather, for I like most men – in large quantities. And now I like them even less, & let them see it, which is injudicious, but I have somehow ceased to care. Nothing matters – I can't make it matter. All the people that count are out of reach, except on very rare occasions. Fancy being one's self once a month! Charming prospect of keeping one's personality at that rate. Oh! the separating effect of this War – not only by death, but by all the circumstances it has affected. I am so terribly lonely.

'And there shall be no more sea.' Someone in a sermon once said that 'sea' there was a symbol for separation – 'And there shall be no more separation.' Can there be such a world? It seems too good to be true. Never to part from the people with whom one can be one's best self.

Inside I *know* I am not a horrid person. But I wonder if that is any good when one seems horrid on the outside. I wonder what He would have thought of me. At any rate He would have understood. Perhaps He *does* see the metamorphosis by His death of the sweet self developed by contact with His life – and, seeing, understand.

I was off this afternoon, & came up here & wrote, & cried bitterly because I reread all of His letters that I have here. So characteristic with their beautiful handwriting of all He was – so pitiful in their joyful & tender anticipations of a week's leave.

Then I went back to the Hospital – back to one or two dressings that make even me almost sick – that of the man with the hand blown off & the stump untrimmed up, & the other man with the arm off, & a great hole in his back one could get one's hand into, & other wounds on his leg & sides & head. Poor, poor souls!

I leaned out of the window to-night & prayed to Him – at 11.0 o'clock. I always believe that there is something beforehand about the hour at which one is going to die which marks it out from all the rest, & perhaps there is after too. So perhaps He heard – even though I am a sceptic still. I looked out at the dark trees & houses & the distant lights & the black cypress tree in the garden & felt perhaps he was there in the midst of them all. And I asked Him to look after me – for I don't seem able to look after myself after all.

Tuesday April 18th
Such a large blank – nearly a whole month. And this is the day that has been in my mind for months – the day I meant to leave – and I am not leaving. Strange to have come through devious & humiliating paths to that sudden decision to remain, when it was all but too late to change my mind after saying I would go. But after indescribable suffering, indecision, almost madness, at last, if not happy, I am at least at peace. And out of it all I have won that queer conviction, quite against my reason, that 'the dead die not'. For if somewhere He is not living, & feeling, why, when everyone else applauded my decision, should He force Himself upon my mind, set Himself against the choice I had made, and make me feel that He, who means more to me than all the rest put together even though He be dead & they alive, did not approve. Why should I have felt that He was grieved because He said I was turning my back on the higher & more difficult things? But now, at any rate, I can say His poems to myself, say the War Sonnets of Rupert Brooke, without feeling afraid of them, without feeling so bitterly unworthy that I dare not face the thought & meaning of them. For such a right, even remaining to face a life hard, dreary & often unpleasant is a very low price indeed.

But it is a very hard school in which I am learning lessons. 'Redemption . . . with suffering & through time.' At least I feel a little more hope of it to-night than I have felt for months. Meredith would have understood – he who said

> . . . in mould the rose unfolds,
> The soul through blood and tears.

Saw Mother to-day; we had tea at Marshall & Snelgrove's. She thinks me quite madly erratic – but long ago gave up questioning my reasons for what I do.

June 4th–10th
Edward came back on leave for 5 days – so bitter-sweet & all too brief. Got leave from hospital for two days & stayed at the Grafton Hotel with him & Mother. He spoke in veiled but significant language of a great battle – another Big Push – soon to take place, & knew that he was to be in it. He said it would be somewhere in the region of Albert, where he is now. In spite of spending a lot of time with him I hardly had a chance of speaking to him at all, for there were always so many people about.

July 1st
Stella & I came out of Southwark Cathedral, where we had been listening to Brahms' *Requiem* (such a theme for such a day!), to learn from newspapers & porters that a tremendous battle has opened on the Somme – very successfully they say – & that very fierce fighting is going on in the villages in front of Albert. And Edward –? 'De profundis, Domine . . .'
    I had such a kind letter from Geoffrey, afterwards, saying how he had thought of me & my anxiety on that day.

July 3rd
Had a half-day – the last, as it turned out, for some weeks – & went down to see the Leightons – there had been no news of Edward all through this terrible week-end, and I could endure no longer without having them to talk to.

July 4th
When I went to the letter-rack at lunch-time there was – of all things on earth I least expected & most desired to see – a little pencil-scrawled envelope from Edward. I tore it open – it said 'July 1st. I was wounded in the action this morning, in left arm &

right thigh not seriously. Hope to come to England. Don't
worry. Edward.' It was written, I learnt later, from the Casualty
Clearing Station. Heaven at least has had some measure of
mercy on me – for this once.

To-day began the tremendous convoys & days of terrific work
which lasted at their height for about a fortnight, and continued
for the whole of July & a good part of August. I never knew it
was possible to do so much work & to be so tired. But Edward
was safe – away from the struggle for a time. Nothing else
mattered . . . Victor & Geoffrey too are both in England. Just
for a short period of time – I can't hope it will be more – my sad
heart can have peace.

July 5th
There was an early morning convoy of officers into J, which had
been got ready with frantic haste the day before. I went on duty
in 32 as usual, & had not been there many minutes when
suddenly I saw Miss George, who ran up to me & said 'Do you
know your brother's in J?' *Edward* in J! I scarcely knew where to
turn – what to do & think. It was like some impossible novel that
he should have come to *my* hospital. I had just told Miss
Berkeley, who was very pleased & sympathetic but suggested
that the work in that ward would have been very heavy & I had
better wait a while before going, when Matron, kind for once,
rang up to say my brother was in J & I could go to see him. Sister
said I needn't hurry back – busy though we were – & I went, in
haste . . .

There was the dear, in bed, in blue pyjamas, struggling with a
breakfast tray with one hand. The other sleeve was empty, & the
arm below it stiff & bandaged. We could neither of us say
much . . . but he smiled & seemed gayer & happier than he had
been all through his leave. I think the splendid relief of having
the great deed faced & over was uppermost in his mind then,
rather than the memory of all he had been through on that day –
hereafter to be regarded as one of the greatest dates in history. It
was not till a little while afterwards that I & all who loved him
realised that July 1st had changed him utterly & added ten years
on to his life.

I learnt Edward's story by degrees. His battalion took part in the main attack. As far as I remember, about 17 men & 2 officers came through unscathed. . . . Edward's beloved Captain Harris was 'missing' for ages; Edward thought he must have been blown up by a shell, but his body was found, long afterwards. He was wounded by shrapnel in the stomach, & when two of the attacking party stopped to pick him up & carry him in, he told them to 'Go on & not bother about him.' At least one can be thankful that this episode of his heroism came to light. It is such things that help us to live through this War.

Edward himself had to lead the first wave of his company. They were not the very first to attack, and while they were waiting to go over the parapet, whole crowds of wounded began to come in & block up the trench, & not only this, but a certain battalion got into a panic & came running back. What with the blocked trench & the sight of the wounded, the panic began to communicate itself to Edward's men. Had it not been for him they would never have gone. Twice he had to go back to rally them. Finally he got them over the parapet. . . .

He was wounded for the first time when about 90 yards along 'No Man's Land' by a bullet through his thigh; he tried to go on but could not; he fell, & crawled into a shell hole. Quite soon a shell burst very close to him & either a bit of this or a machine-gun bullet went through his left arm above the elbow. It seemed a far worse pain than the bullet in his thigh had been; he thought his arm had been blown off, & for the first time lost his nerve & cried out. He noticed when he had lain there about an hour & a half that the hail of machine-gun bullets was getting less & thought he would try & crawl back. I think it was that crawl back among the dead which aged him more than anything; he says what made more impression on him than anything was seeing the dead hand of a man whose flesh was beginning to turn green & yellow, though he had only been killed that morning.

He was here three weeks. I was too busy to see very much of him but it was a great joy to know he was here. Of course Mother came down to London (not Father, strangely enough) & she & Aunt Edith & Victor & Geoffrey came to see him constantly. At the end of July he was given three months' leave & ordered massage. Towards the end of August Edward had a telegram to say that he had been awarded the Military Cross – for the 'conspicuous gallantry & leadership' he had shown on July 1st in rallying his men at a time of great difficulty & attempting to go on after he was wounded. He got another month's leave when the three were up, & then a month's home service.

End of August
Geoffrey went back to the Front. Edward & I said goodbye to him at Liverpool St Station the day before he went. For me just now life seems one long bidding of farewells. He gave me some lovely crimson & white carnations when he left.

Friday September 15th
Recalled from leave owing to orders for foreign service.

Saturday September 16th–Friday September 22nd
We are all ordered to Malta. Spent a confused week of buying kit. Recalled again on Thursday to learn that we had to start on Sat. 23rd – a week earlier than we were originally told – and were to sail in the *Britannic*.

Sunday September 24th Britannic
First thing in the morning Gower & I wandered over the ship, exploring in the lower wards. A hospital ship is a very wonderful thing, but when I saw the swinging iron cots & realised the stuffiness of the lower decks even when empty, I was thankful that fate had not ordered me to serve on a hospital ship. We heard during the morning that our voyage was going to be much longer than we had hitherto supposed, for the *Britannic*, being too large to put in at Malta, would go straight to Mudros, probably stopping at Naples on the way, and that at Mudros we should tranship and go back to Malta.

I felt no especial pang when I saw England disappear; it was all part of the hard path which I have assigned to myself to tread. So that my chief sentiments were much those of Roland's verse written from my point of view (how truly prophetic He did not know) & which came into my mind as I stood on the boat deck—

> I walk alone, although the way is long,
> And with gaunt briars & nettles overgrown;
> Though little feet are frail, in purpose strong
>   I walk alone.

And again I had that very strong feeling that in spite of the long distance that there was to be between me & all the people I loved, I was not really going very far away, and that no separation, so long as those who were separated were still on earth, could be so very great.

Tuesday September 26th
If only I could see to-day's *Times*. I expect it would be pretty full of 'In Memoriam' notices of those who fell at Loos. How well I remember my great anxiety concerning Roland during those days. Sometimes I wish that he had indeed fallen at Loos, for it would have been nearer His own wish to fall in the wild excitement of a fierce battle, and we, too, should not have been just expecting Him home – that crowning blow of our bitter ordeal.

Friday September 29th
The evening before we came to Naples we got into a thunder-storm, the effect of which lasted for some hours & was worse than the Bay of Biscay. About bedtime, just as we were all at our sea-sickest, an order came that we were all immediately to pack up our boxes in readiness to leave the ship in 10 minutes, in case we transhipped at Naples instead of Mudros. A great groan went up from the community, none of whom felt in the least equal to packing. In fact I didn't attempt it as I felt certain of waking early in the morning, hoping to find it calmer. Stella was incapable of standing up but decided she would do what she could lying on the floor. The sight of her crawling about the floor in pyjamas amongst her luggage, trying to pull things down from pegs without getting up, sent me into fits of laughter. Finally she got very annoyed & threw all my clothes at me.

The transhipping rumour was a false alarm, and at midday on Friday we were all allowed on shore in small parties. Stella & I & some others were taken around by a Sister who lived in

Venice before the War & knew Italian. We spent a long & happy time wandering round the streets; everything was a blaze of colour. In every little piazza there seemed to be an enclosed green space where various kinds of palms & cactus grew, & every available bit of grass was covered with crimson and scarlet salvia. Even the beggars, who of course crowded round, were dressed in faded gay colours; nearly all seemed to be in some way halt, maimed, blind or diseased, & to exhibit their defects almost with pride. Italy is a corrupt country, no doubt.

Monday October 2nd

We were beginning now to get thoroughly bored with the *Britannic* – especially after we had done some bed-making to assist the Staff, who appeared very behind-hand with their work. Let no one who has never been out of England pretend she has any idea what bed-making can be. When you are working in the convalescent wards & have the one-above-another kind to tackle, you cannot get into the middle as two rows are closely alongside one another. You therefore have to stand one at the top & one at the bottom of the bed, & in order to make the top one you have to stand on a ledge fixed to the bottom one, off which you topple every time the ship rolls. The bottom one is even worse; there seems to be no alternative between nearly breaking your back or banging your head with violence. I never knew any expedient so effective in making one hot, tired, & thoroughly bad-tempered.

Tuesday October 3rd

Once again we got out of bed early, this time to see the Archipelago. We saw now that we were being closely escorted, by a British battle cruiser, a British torpedo-boat & a British destroyer. We stayed for some time watching the sun rise over the Greek Islands. In the afternoon after sailing safely through three rows of mines we reached Lemnos, & anchored in Mudros harbour. Seen from a distance the Aegean appeared to gleam with great jewels – golden islands with purple shadows, set in a deep blue sea. When we got nearer we saw that they were of a rocky, hilly, sandy nature, golden-brown rather than red, & in many cases covered with brown scrubby grass. Various camps were about the hills, & crowds of ships in the harbour; one was a British dreadnought, a flagship, probably the *Exmouth*. There were several smaller British & French battleships, also about 7 hospital ships, most of which lay in the curve of the harbour, with the small Greek town on the shore just above them.

We were told that on the Island are the graves of three Canadian Sisters, who died nursing in the camp hospital there. The place was grim & sinister looking, yet there was a queer unaccountable fascination about it which would not allow me to take my eyes from it nearly all the afternoon. And I am very sure that the vision of that momentous curve of Lemnos in the rich desolation of the Aegean will remain in my mind long after the more splendid visions of Naples have almost passed away from it. A mist came over my eyes as I looked over this lonely place where Rupert Brooke died, and I remembered so vividly the first time I heard his poems, when Miss Darbishire read them to me at Oxford one evening in May soon after Roland had gone to the front.

Thursday October 5th Galeka
We were told there is a great outbreak of dysentery at Malta just now, & given a good many precautions to observe with regard to food. Some VADs are supposed to have died, partly owing to neglect of these. There was a glorious blue sea; I leant over the deck rail & thought for a long time of Roland, wondering if I should ever return to England – or if I should not, & so complete the tragic story. I have lost so much already that it were better if it were me, perhaps, than others – only I want to write so much.

Friday October 6th
After lunch I began to feel stiff & very queer & suddenly got a shivering fit on deck. Stella fetched my coat for me but that was no use at all. Finally to her astonishment & perturbation I announced my intention of going to lie down in D Ward – & did so. I did not go to tea & spent all afternoon & evening in a semi-somnolent & very feverish condition, indifferent to everything, even the flies. Just before dinner Stella felt me, said I was burning hot & made me report to Sister Chapman. I did so, was

received quite pleasantly & with the remark 'What, another' & ordered to bed at once. (It afterwards transpired that 16 of us had suddenly been seized with this mysterious disease, much to the alarm of everyone on the *Galeka*.) I went to bed (Stella was ordered to help me undress); anywhere less suitable for being ill in than D deck of the *Galeka* is unimaginable, but I felt much too ill to care. Down there I saw two or three other recumbent figures, one or two groaning miserably. They afterwards proved to be suffering from the same complaint as myself, & none of them was any worse, if as bad; strange the utter abandonment of some people to their ailments.

Saturday October 7th Malta
Temperature 102°. Was not aware of much all day except the vague irritations of various people. We were told that the sick VADs were to go off the boat first (we had now arrived at Malta) and go to a Sick Sisters' hospital, but it turned out that the well ones went first while we sick ones lay boiling & panting in the hold. Stella bade me a regretful au revoir & departed. At last after what seemed hours & hours some orderlies appeared, got us wrapped up in coats & out of bed with our hand luggage and put us into an officers' ward, where we were told we were to stay for the night – much to our disappointment as we were longing to get off the *Galeka*. We were no sooner undressed & settled down in the officers' ward than the order came that we were to dress again – when every movement was a pain – & go off the *Galeka* after all. The orderlies came in & carried us all off on stretchers. I know exactly what it is like to be a convoy now. The CO of the *Galeka* saw us off the boat & wished us all a speedy recovery. I breathed deeply with relief when I was carried out of the *Galeka* into the comparatively pure fresh air of the docks. I was put on to the lower shelf of the usual Red Cross ambulance & driven off, for 7 miles as we afterwards learnt, to Imtarfa Hospital, where are the dysentery & enteric wards for sick Sisters. During the following week we learnt to our cost the immense interest taken in us. We turned out to be one of the most interesting cases of epidemic caused by food poisoning which had taken place during the last few years. So instead of needing to regret that we had arrived to be nursed

instead of nursing, we found that we were really benefiting the cause of science.

Saturday October 14th
At first I thought I should hate Malta, as, when I came in feeling so ill, I thought I had never in the world heard so many bells clanging (afterwards it turned out to be a special feast day) or seen such a glare. But its attraction grows, especially at sunset & sunrise, when the domes & towers are violet-grey & softened with mist, & the skies more wonderful than anything I have ever seen. The tiring glare all day is due to the extreme whiteness of the soil, of roads & cliffs. There are of course no trees here to provide shade – only clumps of tropical shrubs such as cactus, prickly pear, palms and eucalyptus. As soon as the swift night has fallen, this wonderful place seems to hold all the mystery & glamour of the East, though really it is only the fringe of it.

Sunday October 15th
This really is a most fascinating place; I have not had much to do with it yet, but the more one sees of it, the more attractive it becomes. At present the ground looks all very parched & barren after the summer heat, & everywhere there is stubbly burnt-looking grass – though plots of this are frequently cultivated & ploughed, as if for the sowing of seed. The unbuilt-over part of the Island would be one vast tract of this brown grass were it not that all the land is divided up into plots the size of fields by low white stone walls. Someone told me yesterday that this place is supposed to be just like the Holy Land – even to the stone wall divisions. Before I heard this it had struck me as being just like pictures I had seen of Palestine, & several times this evening I passed a barren-looking but slightly cultivated field with some little mosque or shrine in the background which reminded me exactly of illustrations I have seen in children's books of the Parable of the Sower. And one comes so quickly upon one little village after another built on the sides of small hills. You get most wonderful views here, as when you get on top of these little hills you can see all round the Island, & over all is a very vast expanse of sky. The sun here seems to set not only in the West but all over the sky, so that sometimes it is quite difficult to tell

where the West is. This evening I felt infinitely little & unimportant, standing on a long white road beneath an immense dome of shining copper & deepest purple.

Wednesday October 18th
This afternoon Rollett & I went down to Valetta by train after lunch. It seems very crowded, not only with pedestrians but with monks & goats. There is quite a decent tea-shop there; it was crowded with officers & nurses. The invalid officers all look very weary & worn, & when I thought how much better the men looked who had had even the worst sort of time in France, I began to feel that in spite of the heavier fighting the men on the Western Front were the more fortunate, or they do not have disease to contend against, as well as men.

Saturday October 21st
This evening Rollett, Allen & I went for a long country walk to a hill behind Imtarfa. We must have gone quite 8 miles, which was greatly beyond our original intention, as unfortunately we got completely lost; all the roads & tracks here are so alike. This Island is supposed to be quite safe so long as you are not alone, but it is not really advisable (& certainly most uncanny) to be out after dark. We first got on to a very strange plateau at the top of a high rocky hill; it made me think of Conan Doyle's *Lost World*. There was an extraordinary silence up there, & a deserted-looking building gave back a most weird echo. Unhappily night descended upon us, in the sudden & unexpected way it has here, while we were still far from sure of our bearings. The consequence was that in trying to take a short cut we lost the goat-track along which we were struggling, & did not come across another until we had gone over what seemed miles of rough fields & the kind of steep stone walls that fall down the moment you touch them. We were loudly cursed by some distant Maltese, across whose ploughed fields we were, most reluctantly (as anyone who had had some of their sand in his shoes would know), wandering, & chased, greatly to our terror, by wild-looking & loudly-barking dogs. We had to make constant detours to avoid the deep ravines one comes across quite suddenly here; these are partly natural, partly constructed

in order to form a drainage for the torrents that rage over the Island in the rainy season; the sides were of rock, sheer down & quite unprotected. When at last we got into another goat-track it was in a deep valley between two hills, beside what looked like an old river-bed; of course there are no lights here except in the houses, & by this time it was so dark that we could not see the road we were walking on & expected every moment to sprain our ankles on the rough stones. Add to that that this is a country of snakes, & it is easily imaginable that we were glad to get in, which we managed at last by following a Maltese labourer with a boy & a mule for about two miles along the goat-track – fortunately in the right direction, as we made him understand though he spoke no English. We were pretty tired when we got in, but otherwise none the worse.

Sunday October 22nd

I forgot to mention a great event, & that is the coming of the first mail since I have arrived here. There was not a great deal of news, the most momentous of all being that Victor is now in France, attached to the 10th Rifle Brigade. I am very astonished as I had no idea his affairs were so near a climax. I little knew, when I got the Oct. 13th *Weekly Times* in Valetta & scarcely dared look at the casualty list for fear of seeing Geoffrey's name, that there was Victor's to look for as well. Apparently he got his orders the very day after I sailed, & left the following Thursday; Edward seems to have had a strenuous time with him in the interval seeing that he bought the right kind of kit. I am sorry that I have one more person to be anxious about, but glad that his going to the front will lessen – as indeed it must – the gulf of difference in personality & experience that was beginning to widen between him & Edward. Perhaps now (as Geoffrey suggests) he will 'catch up' Edward, & afterwards – if there be an afterwards – it will make a great deal of difference.

Geoffrey says they had their orders to 'go over the top' but these were cancelled; in the second letter he thinks the order is likely to come on again. He seems to try & cover his sense of the glory of life & dread of the dangers out there with the philosophy of 'in this country we're here to-day and gone to-morrow'.

They actually had a little harvest festival in the church-room this morning, so that we exiles may feel we are having it at the same time as our people at home – though, of course, as the Chaplain reminded us, in these semi-tropical places, where things are always ripening & fading & ripening again, it would be possible to have harvest festivals two or three times a year. We had a simple sermon comparing harvest with the Resurrection of the Dead, & the hymn 'On the Resurrection Morning' to end with. I don't believe half the theology implied in these things, of course, & yet it is all a reminder. 'I could not if I would forget' – Roland. But I never would, since in all this hard life He is my great & sole inspiration, & if it were not for Him I should not be here.

Tuesday October 24th

Was discharged from Imtarfa & came down to St George's Hospital, a lovely 9 miles' drive. I was driven by a very skilful driver; even to me, accustomed as I am to motoring, the pace seemed terrific, & these blind-alley-like roads made it all the more alarming. As for anything that was round the corner, it just took its chance!

This is a most beautiful hospital, built on a peninsula of land running right out into the sea. The ground all round is very rocky, with patches of deep red sand in between & vivid green little bushes, quite different from the dusty brown ploughed fields & farmlands at Imtarfa. The sea is right below the rocks but there is a delightful little bay which is quite safe & very shallow though full of large fish; here we have our bathing place, & it is so near that we can go down from our rooms with mackintoshes over our bathing dresses.

Wednesday October 25th

We live in the 'married quarters' (this used to be a barracks); for active service we are really very comfortable, & lucky not to be under canvas. Fuller & I have a totally uncovered stone floor & share a basin, dressing-table etc. There is no wardrobe, only pegs. Our beds are very comfortable; just outside two of our windows (we have 3 big ones & the room is quite large) is a stone balcony, from which you get a most beautiful view right out to sea; we can see all the ships that pass, & the searchlights &

signals at night. Two other rooms occupied by Sisters lead out of ours; everyone walks through everyone else's room without knocking, whatever they are doing; one gets quite used to it. There is no bathroom but just a hip-bath which everyone uses; there is no hot water of course laid on anywhere, but twice a week there is hot water in the boilers behind the dining-room (which is a large tent); you can then have a hot bath if you like to carry the water for it up to your room in cans. There is generally rather a rush for it. The meals here seem good, but will probably need a little supplementing with biscuits.

We all wear white shoes & stockings, low soft collars & Panama hats; no one seems very particular about uniform, unless you are unlucky enough to meet the Principal Matron. The difference between the stiffness & starchiness of the Nursing Profession in England & the freedom here is quite remarkable. No one minds whether you come into meals in your mess-dress or coat & skirt or indoor uniform & no one says anything if you are late. The Sisters treat you as friends & equals instead of as incompetent but necessary evils whose presence they resent; in fact yesterday two Sisters helped me chase a locust out of my room with a mat & a tennis racquet.

You go on duty here on blocks instead of in wards; each block has an upper & lower floor with about 3 wards on each. Of course there are more orderlies than in England. At present the cases are chiefly dysentery, enteric & malaria, but there are going to be more surgical. We have the same number of patients as in London, and a staff of 65 instead of 150. But you have the same off-duty times & more if they can manage it as the climate as well as the work tires you out.

November 22nd
A padre from Spinola came in to see the men in C Block to-night & told us that the Emperor of Austria is dead. I wonder if this can make any possible difference to the duration of the War. Poor old man, he has been a long time in dying.

December 23rd
The anniversary of Roland's death – and for me farewell to the best thing in my life. I am glad I am far from Keymer – far from

London; I could not have borne the associations of either. And now I am in Malta, working hard to try & make other people happy for their Christmas in exile, & in so doing, happier than I have been for months. Yes, even on this foreign service I dreaded so much, on which I told Him I would go if He died. I wonder where He is – and if He is at all; I wonder if He sees me writing this now. It is absurd to say time makes one forget; I miss Him as much now as ever I did. One recovers from the shock, just as one gradually would get used to managing with one's left hand if one has lost one's right, but one never gets over the loss, for one is never the same after it. I have got used to facing the long empty years ahead of me if I survive the war, but I have always before me the realisation of how empty they are and will be, since He will never be there again. One can only live through them as fully and as nobly as one can, and pray from the depths of one's lonely heart that

> Hand in hand, just as we used to do,
> We two shall live our passionate poem through
> On God's serene to-morrow.

1917

April 16th Malta
Had a short letter from Miss Lorimer to say she is going out as an orderly to one of the Scottish Women's Hospitals at Salonika. I want to go there more than ever.

April 18th
I was just going round the wards to-night when a cable came from home to say 'Victor dangerously wounded; serious.' About a week ago I had a letter from him virtually saying farewell. He was at Arras, & last week facts began to come through concerning a great battle in that region. Nothing could say more plainly 'Don't hope.' I could so ill do without Victor; he always seems like the survival of a part of Roland; or rather, in his accurate, clear, & reverent memory of Him, Roland seems to me to live still. I remember how Victor & I last June in St James' Park speculated about Edward's fate in the coming battle on the Somme, & he said then that he thought he would never go to the front, & I that I was glad to know there would be someone left after the War & I should not be quite alone.

Waiting, watching, suspense, mourning – will there never be anything else in life? I am so weary of it all – but I bow my head before the storm now, I don't try to fight it any more. I no longer expect things to go well for me; I don't know that I even ask that they shall. All I ask is that I may fulfil my own small weary part in this War in such a way as to be worthy of Them, who die & suffer pain.

April 22nd
On Thursday I sent a cable home asking for further news of Victor. This morning the answer came from Edward 'Eyesight probably gone, may live.'

So – if he lives – he will be blind – the dear splendid cynical boy, with the beautiful eyes, which make him look, as Mrs Leighton said, as if he sought the Holy Grail. It is better to be anything than blind; I am not sure it is not even better to be dead. And no one would ever suffer so much when helpless & dependent as he. The Three Musketeers have had more than their share of suffering. For us who cannot fight, it is a burden of debt almost more than we can bear, to feel that we owe our safety to the lives & sight & strength of such as Roland, Victor & Edward.

I am anxiously awaiting further news to know if Victor is conscious & what his future – if there is to be one – is likely to be. I feel that I would do anything for him – that I would give up all the things I ever meant to do & be if I could but repay him a little for what he has sacrificed. I feel as if Roland's sad eyes were entreating me out of Eternity to give to Victor some of the strength & comfort He would have given him if only He had been there. Poor motherless Tah! When I remember how good he was to me after Roland's death, and how he comforted me that opening week-end of the Somme Battle, when I was so dreadfully anxious about Edward, it seems terribly hard that I should be so far away from him in the hour of his greatest need. I know how glad Roland would be if I could but be of service to his 'Father Confessor'.

I had a letter from Edward to-night, written before Victor was wounded, to say that he has gone to Stafford on another course & cannot now go to the front before June 15th. So he at least will be with Victor in his darkest hours; I am very very glad of this, for since Roland is dead no one could be the help & comfort to him that Edward can.

May 1st
Had two cables – one to say that Victor's eyesight was hopelessly gone, the other – an hour later – that Geoffrey was killed in action on April 23rd . . .

Sat out on the rocks' edge in front of Night Quarters & suddenly something seemed to tell me to go home. Nothing much doing in Malta – & chances of Salonika seemed further off than ever; decided to go home for Edward's sake & Victor's, & if he wishes it, to devote my life to the service of Victor, the only one (apart from Edward, who is different) left of the three men I loved. For I loved Geoffrey . . . I spent the rest of that day on the rocks, feeling all the time that I was not alone, but that Geoffrey was there & if I looked up I should see him standing beside me . . .

His last letter to me – dated April 20th – arrived that evening. He told me they were going up 'for a stunt' in two or three days, & said his only fear was that he should fail at the critical moment, & that he would like to do well, for the School's sake. Often, he said, he had watched the splendour of the sunset from the school-field. And then, perhaps seeing the end in sight, he turned as usual to his beloved Rupert Brooke for comfort & finished with

> War knows no power. Safe shall be my going . . .
> Safe though all safety's lost; safe where men fall;
> And if these poor limbs die, safest of all.

My dear dear Geoffrey!

> He leaves a white
> Unbroken glory, a gathered radiance,
> A width, a shining peace, under the night.

May 22nd
Left Malta. I hated to go, for I had been very happy there, & it was a real pain to say goodbye to Stella, with whom I have been for so long.

We were taken by transport to Grand Harbour, & after waiting on docks for about an hour, put on the *Isonzo*. It was a rough, wet & stormy day, & as there were no chairs we had to sit on deck on our piled-up luggage. We had not been long out of the harbour when the waves seemed mountains high & the ship pitched & rolled to an angle, as they afterwards told us, of $42°$. All the luggage piled up at the back, to say nothing of ourselves, rolled down the deck right as far as the rails. This happened three times; the last time I sat in almost two inches of dirty water, & slid in it nearly down to the rails, which effectually ruined all the clothes I had on.

May 27th

Woke up at 5.0 when train stopped at Amiens. Seething crowd of British & French officers & soldiers, most of them in a trench-state. Thought of Roland, Edward & Geoffrey as having been here; don't think Victor ever was. Felt very near the War. Left Amiens at last, went through Abbeville & Étaples. Étaples seemed one enormous & very dusty camp; we were much cheered by Tommies in a troop train that we passed, & cheered & waved to by the soldiers in the camps along both sides of the railway. Made me very glad I had elected to be a nurse & remain one, instead of doing something else.

Boat was a leave boat – mostly officers & nurses but some Tommies; another boat crammed with Tommies followed in our wake. Were escorted by 6 destroyers. Met another transport going towards Boulogne; men all waved to us & cheered. Crossing very good & smooth; seemed a very little way after the many hours I had spent on the sea. It seemed very strange to be at Victoria again; same old crowd round barriers, same old tea-rooms, same old everything. One began to believe one hadn't really been away.

Envoi

‑‑‑‑‑‑‑‑‑‑‑‑‑‑‑‑‑‑‑‑‑‑‑‑‑‑‑‑‑‑

'I, too, take leave of all I ever had.'

Lieutenant Roland Aubrey Leighton. 7TH WORCESTERS.
Died of wounds near Hébuterne, December 23rd 1915.
Buried at Louvencourt.

Lieutenant Victor Richardson, MC. 9TH KING'S ROYAL RIFLE
CORPS.
Blinded at Vimy Ridge, April 9th 1917. Died of wounds in 2nd
London General Hospital, June 9th 1917.
Buried at Hove.

Lieutenant Geoffrey Robert Youngman Thurlow. 10TH SHERWOOD
FORESTERS.
Killed in action at Monchy-le-Preux, April 23rd 1917. Buried ?

Captain Edward Harold Brittain, MC. 11TH SHERWOOD
FORESTERS.
Killed in action leading his company to the counter-attack in
the Austrian offensive on the Italian front, June 15th 1918.
Buried at Granezza, Lusiana.

NOTES

(The numbers refer to text pages)

3   MELROSE: The Brittains' 'tall grey stone house'.

3   BUXTON: An attractive tourist town and spa in the Peak District of Derbyshire, with a population in 1913 of about 12,000. Set in a basin over 1,000 feet above sea-level, it is surrounded by hills, moorland and woods.

3   THE PEAK HYDRO: One of several hotels providing 'mineral water and other baths' for the treatment of disease ('hydro' is an abbreviation of 'hydropathic establishment').

3   MAURICE AND DOROTHY: Maurice Ellinger, the son of neighbours, was a close friend of Vera Brittain's brother, Edward. His cousin Dorothy was a musical-comedy actress, and Maurice, who died in old age, was a fine pianist.

4   BERTRAM SPAFFORD: About 30 years old when the First World War began, he served as a Captain in the Irish Guards. After the War he married, and represented the family textile firm on the Manchester Cotton Exchange, dying in 1957. His name is often abbreviated to 'B.S.' later in the diary.

5   ERNEST: Ernest Wynne, one of Edward's school-friends.

6   'WHERE IS THE KING . . .': St Matthew II, 2.

6   MISS HEATH JONES: Founder of St Monica's School, Louise Heath Jones was a 'brilliant, dynamic' teacher. Her ardent feminism and interest in international affairs greatly influenced Vera Brittain. She died in 1931.

6   *Christ and Human Need*: 'Addresses delivered at a conference on Foreign Missions and Social Problems', ed. T. Tatlow (1912).

6   UNIVERSITY EXTENSION LECTURES: In 1878 Oxford University had begun to provide lectures 'for the extension of

teaching beyond the limits of the University'. By 1913 these were being given in many parts of Britain; they were organised by the University Extension Delegacy (later the Department for External Studies) in co-operation with local committees or other voluntary bodies.

6 MR J. MARRIOTT: Later Sir John Marriott (1859–1945). A Fellow of Worcester College, Oxford, he published several books of historical analysis, and was a Conservative MP from 1917 to 1929.

6 ST MONICA'S: The private school for girls (founded in 1902 by Miss Heath Jones) which Vera Brittain attended as a boarder for over 4 years, from the age of 13.

7 UPPINGHAM: Situated in the Rutland market-town of that name, Uppingham School was founded in 1584 and remained a small grammar school until its great Victorian headmaster, the Rev. Edward Thring, developed it into one of the major public schools. In 1913 there were about 400 boys in the School, living in 13 separate Houses. The School's First World War Memorial lists 449 names.

7 THE WORKS: (Thomas) Arthur Brittain, Vera's father, was a director of Brittains Ltd, the family paper-mill near Stoke-on-Trent, Staffordshire (21 miles south of Buxton), until his early retirement in 1915. He died in 1935, some 12 years before his wife Edith.

7 DEVONSHIRE HOSPITAL: Named after the sixth Duke of Devonshire, this large hospital in Buxton was established in 1858 through the conversion of his Stables.

8 *Felix Holt*: *Felix Holt the Radical* (1866) by George Eliot (1819–80); a novel about social reform.

9 CORA: Cora Stoop, a school-friend ('Mina' in *Testament of Youth*).

9 'THE GRANDEUR THAT WAS ROME': From 'To Helen', a lyric by Edgar Allan Poe (1809–49).

9 CAPTAIN SCOTT DEAD: Robert Falcon Scott, Lawrence Oates and three companions died in February–March 1912, having reached the South Pole shortly after Roald Amundsen. Their bodies and effects were discovered that November and the episode quickly became a potent emblem of self-sacrificial heroism.

9 'GREATER LOVE . . .': St John XV, 13.

9 MR PUCKLE: Edward's Housemaster at Uppingham School.

9 STELLA: Stella Sharp, a school-friend ('Betty' in *Testament of Youth*).

10 UNCLE WILL: W. G. Hole, who was related to Vera Brittain by marriage. He published several books of poetry and verse-drama; *The Master*, a play about the Second Coming, appeared first in the *Poetry Review* (Vol. II, 1913, pp. 113–131, 179–193).

11 MISS BERVON: Florence Bervon, eldest sister of Edith Brittain, Vera's mother. She was Co-Principal of St Monica's with Miss Heath Jones from 1904 to 1931, and died in 1936.

12 *The Amazons*: A 'farcical romance in 3 acts' (1895) by Sir Arthur Pinero (1855–1934).

14 MY GRANDFATHER: John Inglis Bervon was an organist and composer of Welsh origin.

15 PROFESSOR CHAPMAN: Later Sir Sydney Chapman (1871–1951), he was Professor of Political Economy at the University of Manchester and author of several books on political economy.

16 HIS ELIJAH'S CLOAK: The great prophet Elijah cast his mantle over Elisha to designate him as successor (I Kings XIX, 19).

17 SPG: The Society for the Propagation of the Gospel in foreign parts, founded in 1701 to assist in the Church of England's missionary work.

17 'AT EVEN . . .': This hymn (*Hymns Ancient and Modern*, 20) by H. Twells (1823–1900) begins 'At even ere the sun was set / The sick, O Lord, around Thee lay; / O, in what divers pains they met! / O, with what joy they went away!'

17 'A WATCH IN THE NIGHT': Psalms XC, 4.

18 CORPS: Officers' Training Corps. Established in 1907 by Richard, later Lord, Haldane (1856–1928), then Secretary of State for War, these university and public-school corps were designed to supply Britain's Regular Army with trained officers.

19 SOMERVILLE: Named after Mary Somerville, a great woman scientist of the nineteenth century, Somerville College was founded in 1879 as a hostel to provide educational opportu-

nities at Oxford University for women. By 1913 the College had achieved the very high academic reputation for which it remains admired, and there were about 100 students in residence.

19   MR LACE'S: A small private establishment preparing pupils rapidly for examinations; a 'crammer'.

19   OXFORD SENIOR, RESPONSIONS: To qualify for entrance to Oxford University, it was necessary to pass either the University's examination, Responsions, or one of the approved equivalents such as the Oxford Senior examination.

19   BYFLEET: A town in Surrey, about 20 miles south-west of London.

20   MOTHERS' UNION: A widespread organisation of Anglican women founded in 1887 to uphold the sanctity of marriage and motherhood.

21   UNCLE WILLIE: W. H. K. Bervon, Mrs Brittain's brother, was a bank manager in London up to his death in 1925. Vera Brittain's relationship with him was close and affectionate.

22   'PERFECT LOVE . . .': From *The Forerunner* (London, 1908), an historical romance about the life and times of Leonardo da Vinci (1452–1519), by Dmitri Merejkowski (1865–1941); see p. 159.

22   MR J. H. WARD, FAIRFIELD: Joseph Harry Ward was Anglican curate of Fairfield (a town just to the east of Buxton with a population of about 6,000) from 1913 to 1914. He later held a variety of pastoral and educational posts, and published several collections of sermons and sermon-outlines. Vera Brittain's novel *Not Without Honour* (1924) presents a fictional version of Mr Ward and his struggles in Fairfield.

22   ROBERT ELSMERE: The novel of this title (1888) by Mrs Humphry Ward (1851–1920) describes the spiritual struggles of an idealistic Anglican clergyman who loses faith in the Christian orthodoxy of his time.

24   PALGRAVE'S GOLDEN TREASURY: A very popular anthology of English poetry (1861) compiled by Francis Palgrave (1824–97).

27   BURBAGE: A village just to the west of Buxton.

29   THE QUEEN: Mary of Teck (1867–1953), wife of King George V (who reigned 1910–36).

33 ABJECT PARASITE: An echo of *Woman and Labour* (1911), by the South African writer Olive Schreiner (1855–1920); see Ch. II. There are many such echoes of Olive Schreiner's writing in this diary, indicating a pervasive influence.

34 'PI-NESS': Ostentatious and excessive piety.

36 POSTMASTERSHIP: Oxford colleges offer open entrance scholarships awarded after competitive examination; those offered by Merton College are termed 'postmasterships'.

36 HOLMAN HUNT: A major painter (1827–1910) of the Pre-Raphaelite Movement.

37 SIR HENRY WOOD: Conductor (1869–1944) and founder of the popular Promenade Concerts.

37 *Tristan and Isolde*: For concert performance, Richard Wagner (1813–83) added to the opera's Overture a purely orchestral version of its conclusion. The latter is conventionally called 'Love-death', but Wagner's own title was 'Transfiguration', for it implies the mystical union of Tristan and Isolde after death.

37 MISS DODD: Lena Dodd was Headmistress of the Grange School, a private school for girls in Buxton that Vera Brittain had attended for two years before being sent to St Monica's.

38 MRS FOWLER: Louisa Fowler, who lived in Fairfield, was a dressmaker and a friend of Mrs Brittain.

39 MR DODD: Arthur Dodd, Mr Brittain's solicitor and friend.

40 PLEB: Coarse person of low birth (abbreviation of 'plebeian').

42 SIR JOHN MATTHEWS: Recently-retired Chief Justice of the Bahamas (1864–1934).

42 *Lyrical Ballads*: This volume of poems (1798) by William Wordsworth (1770–1850) and Samuel Taylor Coleridge (1772–1834) is conventionally regarded as inaugurating the Romantic Movement in English poetry.

43 HIGHWAY-&-HEDGES LOT: Undistinguished, lower-class gathering.

43 'THE RESTLESS SOUNDS . . .': Unidentified; possibly by Vera Brittain in imitation of Wordsworth.

44 GOLDSMITH, JOHNSON: Oliver Goldsmith (1728–74) and Dr Samuel Johnson (1709–84), two dominant figures in eighteenth-century English literature.

44 MR JACK'S ESSAY: *Poetry and Prose, being Essays on Modern English Poetry* (1911) by A. A. Jack (1868–1945) contains essays on Wordsworth and on the thought of Ralph Waldo Emerson (1803–82); see pp. 146–176 and 244–276.

45 VELASQUEZ'S FAMOUS *Venus*: Often called 'The Rokeby *Venus*', this painting by Diego Velasquez (1590–1660) was the first female nude in Spanish art. Its assailant was a prominent Suffragette, Mary Richardson, who was forcibly fed during the six months' imprisonment to which she was sentenced.

46 MISS PENROSE: Emily Penrose ('the Pen') (1858–1942), third Principal of Somerville College (1907–26), was a leader of the fight to achieve the full participation of women in Oxford academic life.

46 THOMSON, COWPER: James Thomson (1700–48) and William Cowper (1731–1800), precursors – especially in their nature poetry – of the Romantic Movement.

47 MISS DARBISHIRE: Helen Darbishire ('the Darb') (1881–1961), Tutor in English literature (1907–26), became Somerville College's fifth Principal (1931–45); her books include major editions and critical studies of the poetry of John Milton (1603–74) and Wordsworth.

47 EXHIBITION: A College entrance award similar to a scholarship but of lesser value.

47 THE DEGREE COURSE: Before 1920 the BA degree was not awarded by Oxford University to women students, although by 1914 they were permitted to write all the examinations and their results were published officially. Anticipating, and promoting, a change of regulation, women's colleges strongly encouraged their students to fulfil all the conditions for the award of a degree, and themselves awarded diplomas to those who passed this 'degree course'.

48 KINGSWOOD: A village on the North Downs, about 20 miles south of London near Reigate, Surrey.

48 IN TOWN: I.e. in London.

50 MISS FRY: Edith B. Fry had taught History and English as a visiting mistress for one term in 1911, and deeply impressed Vera Brittain with her lively intellect, 'understanding of Carlyle and Ruskin', and literary interests (she published

editions of poetry by Browning and others). She lived in a cottage at Burgh Heath, a few miles from St Monica's.

52 *Between the Soup and the Savoury*: A one-act play (1911) by Gertrude Jennings.

52 THOREAU'S *Walden:* A narrative (1854) by the American writer Henry Thoreau (1817–62), describing his idealistic creed of individualism, simplicity and self-reliance.

53 'HIGHER STILL AND HIGHER': Mr Ward was probably quoting from Stanza 3 of 'Abt Vogler' (1864) by Robert Browning (1812–89).

53 HIS MOTHER: Marie Connor Leighton, who died in 1941, published more than 40 popular novels. A brilliant portrait of her can be found in *Tempestuous Petticoat* (1947) by her daughter Clare Leighton.

53 MY DEPARTURE: Vera Brittain spent four days with relatives living at Windermere, in the Lake District.

54 *The Story of an African Farm*, LYNDALL: This novel (1883) by Olive Schreiner deeply influenced Vera Brittain; Lyndall is its idealistic, strong-willed and ill-fated heroine.

57 'REDEMPTION IS FROM WITHIN . . .': *The Story of an African Farm*, near the end of Pt. II, Ch. 9. The complete sentence, from which Vera Brittain quoted frequently in her diary, reads: 'The lifting up of the hands brings no salvation; redemption is from within, and neither from God nor man: it is wrought out by the soul itself, with suffering and through time.'

58 *Raffles*: The play (1906) adapted by E. W. Hornung (1866–1921) and E. W. Presbrey from the former's highly popular novel *The Amateur Cracksman* (1899).

60 MAGGIE TULLIVER, *The Mill on the Floss*: Maggie Tulliver is the ardent, idealistic heroine of this novel (1860) by George Eliot.

63 SOMETHING TO WORSHIP: *The Story of an African Farm*, II, 12.

65 THE LODGE: Edward's and Roland's House at Uppingham School.

66 JOSEPH CHAMBERLAIN: English statesman (1836–1914), famous as the champion of imperial unity and tariff reform.

67 KANT'S THEORY: See the *Critique of Practical Reason* by the German philosopher Immanuel Kant (1724–1804).

70 'FAREWELL . . .': From a speech by Cardinal Wolsey in Shakespeare's *Henry VIII*, III, i.

71 EUROPEAN CRISIS: Archduke Franz Ferdinand, heir to the throne of the Austro-Hungarian Empire, had been assassinated on 28 June 1914 by Gavrilo Princip, a Serbian nationalist, in Sarajevo, capital of the Austrian province of Bosnia (now part of Yugoslavia). Backed by Germany, Austria-Hungary made demands for reparation that Serbia could not fully accept.

71 SERVIA: The name of this Balkan state (now part of Yugoslavia) was conventionally spelt 'Serbia' only from 1915.

72 IRISH QUESTION: The bitterly controversial Home Rule Bill had received its final reading at Westminster in May 1914 but had not been enacted; while in Ireland itself conflict between Nationalists and Ulstermen was threatening to break into civil war.

72 OUR GREATEST RESPONSIBILITIES . . .: From a speech in Ch. XXV of *The Marble Faun* (1860), a romance by Nathaniel Hawthorne (1804–64).

75 KING OF THE BELGIANS: Albert I (1875–1934).

75 SIR EDWARD GREY: Later 1st Viscount Fallodon (1862–1933), he was Foreign Minister (1905–16) of the Liberal Government led by Herbert Asquith (1852–1928) which was in power at the beginning of the War.

75 CABINET RESIGNATIONS: Only three of the more than forty British ministers resigned in disagreement with the Cabinet's decision (2 August 1914) to intervene if Germany invaded Belgium. They were John Burns (1858–1943), the first working-class member of a British Cabinet; Lord John Morley (1838–1922), eminent as statesman and writer; and C. P. Trevelyan (see note to p. 152), who however was a junior minister and not a Cabinet-member. The latter was apparently confused for a time with C. F. G. Masterman (1873–1927), who resigned later for different reasons, but as a member of the Cabinet in August 1914 strongly agreed with its decision.

75 LORD KITCHENER: Field Marshal (1850–1916) famous as conqueror of the Sudan (1898); he became Secretary of State for War on 5 August 1914 but was drowned when on his way to Russia in June 1916.

75   TERRITORIALS: Members of the Territorial Force, which was established in 1906 by Haldane as an auxiliary corps of part-time volunteers. Designed for home defence or voluntary service overseas, it provided from October 1914 the first reinforcements for the British Expeditionary Force of the Regular Army.

75   MANCHESTER GRAMMAR SCHOOL: A well-known and highly respected school for boys, founded in 1519.

77   *The War of the Worlds*: A futuristic 'scientific romance' (1898) by H. G. Wells (1866–1945).

77   SOUTH AFRICAN WAR: The Anglo-Boer War (1899–1902).

77   MRS KAY: The Brittains' elderly cook.

77   RESERVISTS: Britain's Army Reserve was mainly made up of men who had served in the Regular Army and were contractually liable to mobilisation in time of emergency.

78   DREADNOUGHT: Large heavily-armed battleship; after the name of the first one, built in 1905 at the insistence of Admiral Sir John Fisher (1841–1920), First Sea Lord (1904–10 and 1914–15).

81   TWO GERMAN CRUISERS: The *Goeben* and the *Breslau* evaded the British Fleet to reach the Dardanelles and force Turkey's entry into the War (31 October 1914) as Germany's ally.

81   TEMPORARY COMMISSIONS: These appointments to the rank of officer were for 'three years or the duration of the War'.

84   'SUFFERETH LONG . . .': I Corinthians XIII, 4.

85   MARTIN HARVEY, *The Breed of the Treshams*: A well-known actor and manager (1863–1944), he played the leading role of Lieutenant Reresby, a Cavalier, in this very popular costume drama by 'John Rutherford'.

85   GREGORY ROSE: *The Story of an African Farm*, II, 3 to 9.

86   BRILLIANT RUSSIAN VICTORY: The Battle of Gumbinnen (19–20 August 1914).

86   THE DRINA: A river forming the boundary between Serbia and Bosnia. The battle here (17–18 August 1914) was one of several Serbian victories culminating in the rout of the Austrian army in December 1914; but the position was reversed and Serbia defeated the following year, after Bulgaria entered the War on the German side.

87 MONS: 30,000 men of the newly-landed British Expeditionary Force were outnumbered at Mons, in Belgium, by the
advancing German army and forced into an orderly retreat
(23 August 1914). This was one engagement in the 'Battle of
the Frontiers' (14–25 August) in which the French suffered
severe defeat, losing 300,000 men.

87 SIR JOHN FRENCH: Later 1st Earl of Ypres (1852–1925), he
was Commander-in-Chief of British Forces from August
1914 to December 1915.

91 NAVAL VICTORY, REAR-ADMIRAL BEATTY: The British Fleet
was commanded by Admiral, later Earl, David Beatty (1871–
1936) in this battle (28 August 1914) near Heligoland, an
island off the German coast.

91 RICHARD MEYNELL: Like *Robert Elsmere*, *The Case of Richard
Meynell* (1911) is a novel by Mrs Humphry Ward about an
idealistic, evangelical clergyman.

94 RUSSIAN REVERSE AND VICTORY: The Battle of Tannenberg
(28–31 August 1914) was a Russian disaster – over 90,000
prisoners were taken by the Germans, and Russian morale
was severely shaken. But to the south, the battle of the Gnila
Lipa River (26–30 August), near Lemberg, capital of the
Austrian province Galicia, was a Russian triumph which led
to the fall of Lemberg (3 September) and seriously weakened
the Austrian army.

94 THE KAISER: Wilhelm II (1859–1941), Emperor of Germany.

95 MR HAIGH, MR CLAY: Business associates of Mr Brittain;
Alfred Haigh was a director (later Managing Director) of
Brittains Ltd.

95 'THAT SAD WORD, JOY': Possibly a reference to lines in
Roland Leighton's poem 'Goodbye', written on 19 May
1914: 'What matters it that you / Have found love's death
in joy, and I in sorrow?'

96 KITCHENER AT OSTEND: Like most of the war rumours,
incorrect; but Kitchener *had* made a sudden visit to Le
Havre on 1 September 1914 to dissuade Sir John French
from retreating to the River Seine and abandoning co-
operation with the French army.

98 KITCHENER'S NEW ARMY: In August 1914 Kitchener appealed for volunteers to join a new regular force (in effect, the

first national army of Britain); 500,000 men came forward in the first month.

98   GAZETTED: Named in the official gazette as appointed to a command.

98   GERMANS TURNING BACK: The German High Command followed the Schlieffen Plan in ordering a rapid advance through Belgium to outflank the French, but communication became uncertain, supply-lines broke, exhaustion spread, and the premature wheel before Paris led to German defeat at the first Battle of the Marne (6–9 September).

99   THE PLAIN OF CHÂLONS: About 100 miles east of Paris; site of the Roman victory over Attila the Hun in 451 and partial site of the Battle of the Marne.

100   O.T.C.: Officers' Training Corps.

100   MAXIM GUNS: Quick-firing machine-guns invented in the 1880s by Hiram Maxim (1840–1916).

102   THE AUSTRIAN EMPEROR: Franz Joseph (1830–1916).

103   THE CROWN PRINCE: Wilhelm (1882–1951), Crown Prince of Prussia, was commanding the German Third Army near Verdun.

104   FABIAN SOCIETY OF SOCIALISTS: Founded in 1884 to promote 'social reconstruction' by gradual and constitutional means, this influential group included Sidney and Beatrice Webb, G. B. Shaw and H. G. Wells.

104   KREISLER: Fritz Kreisler (1875–1962), the great Austrian violinist.

104   THE BATTLE OF THE AISNE: Also called the Battle of the Rivers (11–25 September) since it was fought near the junction of the Aisne and the Oise, this indecisive battle began the series of north-westward enveloping engagements (the 'Race for the Sea') which established the trenches of a stalemated Western Front.

106   FRIMLEY: A town about 12 miles west of Byfleet, near Farnborough.

110   *The Kreutzer Sonata*: A short novel (1890) by Leo Tolstoi (1828–1910).

111   CZAR: Nicholas II (1868–1918), last Czar of Russia.

111   VON MOLTKE DISMISSED: The German Minister of War, General Helmuth von Moltke (1848–1916), was replaced (14

September 1914) because he had failed to execute the Schlieffen Plan successfully and capture Paris.

111   MISS LORIMER: Hilda Lorimer ('the Lorie') (1873–1954), Tutor in Classics (1896–1934), University Lecturer in Homeric Archaeology (1929–37), author of *Homer and the Monuments* (1950). As a gesture of respect and affection, Vera Brittain later commissioned the portrait of Miss Lorimer that hangs in Somerville College.

111   PASS MODS: Pass Moderations was the examination (usually taken in the undergraduate's first year) that qualified the successful candidate to proceed with work for the Final Examination for the BA degree.

112   MISS HUGHES: Norah Hughes, who later worked in the War Office and in 1915 married a Serbian artist.

112   FIRST PRINCIPAL: Madeleine Shaw Lefevre (1835–1914), Principal from 1879 to 1889.

113   VERDI'S *Requiem*: The popular *Requiem Mass* (1874) composed by Giuseppe Verdi (1813–1901) in honour of his friend the poet and novelist Alessandro Manzoni.

113   DR ALLEN: Later Sir Hugh Allen (1869–1946); organist of New College, Oxford, and distinguished choral conductor, he became Professor of Music in 1918.

113   MISS BYRNE: Muriel Byrne, later a lecturer in English and author of several books, mainly on Elizabethan drama.

113   MISS SIEPMANN: Phyllis Siepmann, who died in 1920, and whose father Otto had published such books as *A Public School German Primer* (1896).

115   MISS ROWE: Dorothea Rowe, later Senior English Mistress at a girls' school and author of several one-act plays.

116   MISS SAYERS: Dorothy L. Sayers (1893–1957), now famous for her detective stories featuring Lord Peter Wimsey.

117   MISS HAYES ROBINSON: Margaret Hayes Robinson, Tutor in Modern History from 1911 to 1916; she married in 1916, had one daughter, and died in 1930.

118   MISS DAVIES: Leila Davies, later a Lecturer in English.

118   MISS BARBER: Marjorie Barber, later a Lecturer in English and editor of works by Chaucer.

118   MISS SCHENZINGER: Teresa Schenzinger ('Schen') became Vera Brittain's closest college friend.

119 OXFORD COUNCIL: The University's Hebdomadal Council strongly influences University policy and negotiates with outside bodies.

119 RADCLIFFE INFIRMARY: The University Hospital (1770), named after John Radcliffe (1656–1714), Queen Anne's Physician.

120 G. K. CHESTERTON: Novelist, essayist, poet and controversialist (1874–1936).

121 MISS JONES: Edith Jones (1884–1936), Research Fellow in French; her *La Vita ancienne de Saint Corentin* was published in 1925.

122 LORD ROBERTS: Frederick, 1st Earl of Kandahar (1832–1914), a general greatly admired for his military success in India and South Africa, and affectionately known as 'Bobs'.

122 MISS WOOD: Katharine Wood became a close friend.

122 'A VEIL OF TERRIBLE MIST . . .': *The Story of an African Farm*, last words of II, 12.

122 MISS WADHAM: Dorothy Wadham was a Secretary in later life.

124 MISS ELLIS FERMOR: Una Ellis Fermor ('E.F.') (1894–1958) became a distinguished university teacher and published several scholarly books, mainly on Elizabethan and Irish drama.

125 FRENSHAM: A town in Surrey about 5 miles south of Aldershot.

127 HOMER BOOK VI: Book VI of the *Iliad* was a set-text for the Pass Moderations examination.

127 SHELDONIAN THEATRE: The University Theatre, built 1664–9 by Sir Christopher Wren (1632–1723), and used for academic ceremonies, concerts, etc.

133 AUNT BELLE: A sister of Mrs Brittain, Isabel Bervon lived with her widowed mother at Purley, a town south of London and a few miles from Kingswood.

133 *David Copperfield*: A play (1914) adapted by L. N. Parker from the novel by Charles Dickens (1812–70); in the popular production at His Majesty's Theatre, the roles of Peggotty and Mr Micawber were played by Sir Herbert Beerbohm Tree (1853–1917).

134   STEERFORTH: Charming, intelligent, egotistical, he seduces and abandons Little Emily.

136   ROLAND'S SISTER: Clare Leighton (1898–1989), artist and writer, well known for her wood-engravings and for books, such as *Country Matters* (1937), written and illustrated by her.

139   'ONE GLORIOUS HOUR . . .': From a stanza quoted by Sir Walter Scott (1771–1832) as the motto to Ch. XXXIII of *Old Mortality* (1816), and by W. E. Henley as epigraph to *Lyra Heroica* (1892), his influential anthology of 'verse for boys'. The stanza is from 'Verses Written During the War, 1756–63' by Thomas Mordaunt (1730–1809): 'Sound, sound the clarion, fill the fife! /To all the sensual world proclaim, / One crowded hour of glorious life / Is worth an age without a name.'

146   'GOD MOVES . . .': One of William Cowper's *Olney Hymns* (1779); *Hymns Ancient and Modern*, 373.

147   SINISTER STREET: A novel (1913) about Oxford University life by Compton Mackenzie (1883–1972).

151   'THE ELOQUENT, THE YOUNG . . .': Thomas Carlyle (1795–1881), *The French Revolution* (1837), Vol. III, Book Fourth, Ch. VIII. This phrase laments the execution in October 1793 of 22 Girondin deputies, and was translated by Carlyle from the *Memoires de Riouffe* (1823).

151   O[W]DS: The Oxford Women's Debating Society.

152   MR TREVELYAN: Later Sir Charles Trevelyan (1870–1958); a Radical Liberal (and later Labour) politician, he had resigned from the Asquith Government (3 August 1914) because he believed that Britain should not go to war with Germany.

153   WOMAN PREACHER, MANCHESTER COLLEGE: The Unitarians, nonconformists prominent in England from the eighteenth century and notable for advanced social views, opened their ministry to women in the late nineteenth century, before any other denomination. Manchester College (1786), unattached to Oxford University, is primarily a Unitarian theological college.

154   MISS ROSE: Beatrice Rose, later a Lecturer in English and Headmistress of a girls' school.

155   PC: Abbreviation of 'postcard'.

156   *Goodnight, Babette!*: A short poetic play by Austin Dobson (1840–1921).

156   VICTORIA, *The Dear Departed*: A 'precocious girl of 10' in the popular one-act comedy of working-class life (1908) by Stanley Houghton (1881–1913).

166   'WHEN THE WAR-DRUM . . .': 'Locksley Hall', ll. 127–8, by Alfred, Lord Tennyson (1809–92).

166   *Adonais*: 'An Elegy on the Death of John Keats' (1821), by Percy Bysshe Shelley (1792–1822).

166   NEUVE CHAPELLE: Surprise attack by the British brought initial success but little ultimate advantage; about 13,000 men were lost on each side (10–13 March).

166   'THE AIR IS FULL OF FAREWELLS . . .': From 'Resignation' by Henry Wadsworth Longfellow (1807–82).

168   'THROUGH MUCH TRIBULATION . . .': Acts XIV, 2.

170   OLIVE SCHREINER SAYS SOMEWHERE . . .: Probably *The Story of an African Farm*, II, 1.

174   *Apology*: By Plato (*c*. 428–348 BC), this presents the self-defence of Socrates (*c*. 470–399 BC) before his condemnation to death.

174   STAINER'S *Crucifixion*: A very popular oratorio (1887) by Sir John Stainer (1840–1901).

177   'AND THE ECHOES OF DESPAIR . . .': *The Story of an African Farm*, II, 2.

180   SAY I AM TWENTY-THREE: In 1915, 23 was the usual minimum age for training as a nurse. After the War this was lowered to 21 when the Nurses Act (1919) imposed general professional standards.

181   'LORD, HOW LONG?': Psalms VI, 3; and in other psalms.

183   TRAVERSE: Sandbag partitions were built in trenches to prevent enfilading and to limit the effects of shell-fire.

183   LYDDITE: An explosive used in shells.

186   *On the Eve*: 'A Romance' (1860) by Ivan Turgenev (1818–83); see Ch. XVIII onwards for the love scenes between hero and heroine.

188   SAP-TRENCH: Saps were dug outwards from existing trenches, often for communication.

190   SECOND BATTLE OF YPRES: The first battle of Ypres (12 October–11 November 1914) had established a large British

salient; this was considerably reduced during the second battle (22 April–25 May 1915), in which the British lost 60,000 men.

191 THE HAGUE CONVENTION: The Peace Conference of 1899, called by Czar Nicholas II, attempted (like its successor in 1907) to control warfare and secure peace through conventions like the one banning the use of poison gases.

192 WOOD JUST OVER THE BELGIAN BORDER: Ploegsteert Wood, the scene of fierce fighting in November 1914.

194 WOMEN'S CHANGED ATTITUDE TOWARDS THE WAR: Leaders of the women's suffrage movement like Emmeline and Christabel Pankhurst had thrown their support behind the war-effort, urging men to enlist and women to work in industry.

196 WALDO IN HIS SHIRT-SLEEVES: In the final chapter of *The Story of an African Farm*, the hero, who is Lyndall's soul-mate, sits in the sun rejoicing in life, then dies.

196 MAY MORNING: A religious ceremony of ancient origin welcoming the arrival of Spring. Vera Brittain's *Verses of a VAD* (1918) and *Poems of the War and After* (1934) contain a poem about this occasion – as well as other poems related to the diary.

198 MISS FARNELL: A senior student then, Vera Farnell became Librarian of Somerville College (1915–28) and Tutor in Modern Languages (1934–47).

198 THE BODLEIAN: The University Library, founded in 1327 and named after its great benefactor Sir Thomas Bodley (1545–1613).

202 'GOODNIGHT, SWEET FRIEND . . .': The closing lines of 'Echoes: XLII' by W. E. Henley (1849–1903).

202 '3.5' SHELLS: Large shells fired by guns with a bore-diameter of 3.5 inches.

203 'BLOTS OUT WISDOM . . .': *The Story of an African Farm*, II, 8.

203 'SURPRISED BY JOY . . .': Opening lines of Wordsworth's sonnet (1815) on the death of his second daughter.

205 WIRE 'CRADLES': Supports for barbed-wire defences.

206 FIVE SONNETS: Rupert Brooke (1887–1915) died of blood-poisoning in the Aegean and was buried on the island of Skyros; *1914*, his famous sonnet-cycle, was first published in

December 1914 in *New Numbers* but had just appeared in book-form (May 1915).

207   GUNCOTTON: A highly explosive compound, later superseded by dynamite.

207   JACK: Jack Sharp, Stella's brother.

208   FRENCH VICTORY, UNSUCCESSFUL BRITISH ATTACK: The beginnings of the battles of Souchez (9 May–30 June 1915) and Festubert (9 May–26 May); both failed, the British losing 10,000 men at Festubert.

209   HANDEL OVERTURE: An arrangement of the overture to the *Occasional Oratorio* (1746) by George Frederick Handel (1685–1759) which celebrated the defeat of the Jacobites by the Duke of Cumberland at Culloden.

209   'SO ANSWERED, NEVERMORE!': From 'James Lee's Wife', Pt. VI, by Robert Browning.

210   LONDON RIOTS: The torpedoing of the *Lusitania* (7 May 1915), with the loss of 1,201 lives, provoked attacks by mobs on German-owned premises in London and other cities over several days. This resulted in the extension of internment (14 May).

211   NATIONAL NON-PARTY GOVERNMENT: The first of two coalition governments during the War, it was formed by Asquith after crises caused by shell-shortages, the growing demand for conscription, and the floundering Dardanelles offensive (begun in March). The second coalition government was formed by Lloyd George after Asquith's resignation in December 1916.

212   TRAIN DISASTER ON THE GREAT WESTERN: The famous Gretna disaster (on the Caledonian Railway, not the Great Western, 9 miles north of Carlisle); 227 passengers died and 246 were injured.

214   LLOYD GEORGE: David, later 1st Earl Lloyd George of Dwyfor (1863–1945), a Liberal statesman of Welsh origin; Minister of Munitions (1915–16), and later Prime Minister (1916–22).

216   STERNDALE BENNETT: Robert Sterndale Bennett (1881–1963), grandson of the Victorian composer Sir William Sterndale Bennett and brother of the popular composer T. C. Sterndale Bennett, was Director of Music at Uppingham School from 1908 to 1945.

217 'CLAIR DE LUNE': One of many organ-pieces by Sigfrid Karg-Elert (1879–1933).

218 D.C.M.: Distinguished Conduct Medal.

221 JCR: Junior (i.e. undergraduates') Common Room.

224 GOING-DOWN PLAY: A lighthearted set of skits to mark the end of the academic year.

225 'OLD OXFORD . . .': From one of the songs in the Going-Down Play.

225 'AND SORROW . . .': Isaiah XXXV, 10.

227 'AND NO ONE KNEW . . .': *The Story of an African Farm*, I, 10, and epigraph to II. Doss, the farm-dog, kills a beetle: 'And it was all play, and no-one could tell what it had lived and worked for. A striving and a striving, and an ending in nothing.'

227 'THEY PASSED . . .': From 'Ode for the Diamond Jubilee of Queen Victoria, 1897' by Francis Thompson (1857–1907).

227 'THE ODE TO THE SETTING SUN': Also by Francis Thompson.

229 GENTLEMAN RANKER: It was unusual for upper-class men to enlist as common soldiers in the ranks rather than as officers.

230 SMITH-DORRIEN: General Sir Horace Smith-Dorrien (1858–1930). He was dismissed by Sir John French for suggesting withdrawal from the Ypres salient to avoid further great losses. French was himself dismissed six months later and replaced as Commander-in-Chief by General Sir Douglas Haig (1861–1928).

231 VA NURSE: The Voluntary Aid Detachments were established in 1910, under the management of the British Red Cross Society and the St John Ambulance Association, to assist the professional military nursing services of the Territorial Force in any emergency. A Women's Voluntary Aid Detachment usually consisted of 23 women, but the initials 'VAD' quickly came to refer to an individual member.

232 'WELL-DESERVED SUCCESS': i.e. in having passed the Pass Mods Examination.

233 SAGE-FEMME: midwife.

233 'OH DAMN! . . .': From 'The Old Vicarage, Grantchester' by Rupert Brooke.

237 FIELD SERVICE POSTCARDS: Postcards containing printed

formulas of communication; words not needed were crossed out.

237 'HONOUR HAS COME BACK . . .': From Rupert Brooke's 'The Dead' (*1914*, III).

240 HAVE NOT GOT 'RED HATS': i.e. are not permanent members of Headquarters Staff.

241 CAMBERWELL, NO. 1 LONDON GENERAL: One of the four Territorial General Hospitals established in London for war-casualties, the No. 1 General was an extension of St Bartholomew's Hospital in Camberwell, a borough south of the Thames. There were over 1,000 beds, and, in July 1915, 122 trained and 90 untrained staff.

241 DEVONSHIRE HOUSE: The British Red Cross organised VAD nursing from Devonshire House in Piccadilly, London.

243 ADMS: Assistant Director of Medical Services.

246 SIGN-ON BUSINESS: 'You sign on for 6 months and are sent anywhere in England, and after 6 months can be sent out to France' (Vera Brittain in a letter).

252 SAPPER SMITH: Sappers were privates in the Royal Engineers.

252 'ONE IS WILLING TO PAY . . .': *The Story of an African Farm*, II, 8.

261 THREE YEARS OR THE DURATION . . .: Ironically echoing the restriction imposed for temporary commissions.

263 CHLORODYNE: A drug used to relieve pain.

264 MR LEIGHTON: Robert Leighton, who died in 1934, was a literary critic, journalist, and author of some 35 popular adventure books for boys.

264 EVELYN LEIGHTON: Trained as a cadet at Osborne and Dartmouth Naval Colleges, he became a Captain in the Royal Navy, fought in the Second World War and was awarded the OBE; he died in 1969.

269 'ICH LIEBE DICH': Possibly the very popular setting (1863) by Edvard Grieg (1843–1907) of a poem by Hans Andersen (1805–75).

272 GEORGE MEREDITH: Well-known poet and novelist (1828–1909).

276 'HAND IN HAND . . .': Final lines of 'Goodbye' by Roland Leighton.

276 'THERE ARE NO DEAD': From *The Blue Bird* (1909), a play by Maurice Maeterlinck (1862–1949).

286 MR BURGIN: C. B. Burgin (1856–1944), author of many popular romances and adventure stories.

287 'FOR WHAT IS OUR FAILURE HERE . . .': From 'Abt Vogler', Stanza 11, by Robert Browning.

290 'A CHILD WHOM A LONG DAY'S PLAY . . .': *The Story of an African Farm*, II, 9.

290 SOMETHING WHICH ONE HAS LOVED: *The Story of an African Farm*, II, 12.

293 'THESE ARE THE THINGS . . .': From the lyric 'A Year and a Day' (1914) by Kathleen Coates.

293 'AND HER EYES . . .': From 'To LL' by Oscar Wilde (1854–1900).

295 I ACTED LYNDALL: See *The Story of an African Farm*, II, 9.

295 'KNOWING NOT THE HOUR . . .': From an anonymous article, entitled 'Smiling Through Her Tears', in *The Times*, 21 May 1915. It describes the pain and courage of women waiting for news from the Front.

297 'A RARER SORT THAN GOLD': From Rupert Brooke's 'The Dead' (*1914*, III); see also Proverbs VIII, 19, and elsewhere in the Old Testament.

298 RED, SWEET WINE OF YOUTH: From Rupert Brooke's 'The Dead' (*1914*, III).

299 'HINC ILLAE LACRIMAE': 'The cause of grief is now clear' (lit. 'Hence those tears'); quoted by Horace and Cicero from the *Andria* of Terence (*c.* 185–158 BC).

300 '. . . SOME CORNER OF A FOREIGN FIELD . . .': From Rupert Brooke's 'The Soldier' (*1914*, V).

300 'WAR KNOWS NO POWER': From Rupert Brooke's 'Safety' (*1914*, I).

304 ADAM: Captain W. Adam, awarded the DSO in 1918.

306 'TE MORITURUM SALUTO': 'I salute you who are about to die'; an adaptation of the gladiators' greeting to the Emperor Claudius (10 BC–AD 54), 'Ave, Imperator, morituri te salutant': 'Hail, Emperor, those who are about to die salute you.'

306 STORM OVER THE WESTERN FRONT: After a summer of recuperation following the failures and appallingly high casualties of the battles of Neuve Chapelle, Second Ypres

and Festubert, the British launched a major attack simultaneously with the French. But the Battle of Loos (25 September–14 October) was another failure, with a loss of 60,000 men.

315 MR VENIZELOS: Intermittently Greek Prime Minister from 1910, Eleutherios Venizelos (1864–1936) later forced the resignation of King Constantine (1868–1923) and in 1917 led Greece into the War on the Allied side.

319 'THE TOP OF THE FULLNESS OF LIFE': Unidentified.

320, MOVE FROM BUXTON . . .: Mr and Mrs Brittain moved
321 temporarily to Brighton after his retirement from the paper-mill. Meanwhile the Leightons had moved to Keymer, near Brighton, in November, shortly after Vera Brittain, worried by Roland's silence, had visited them in Lowestoft.

322 BRIXTON: A workers' residential district of London, near Camberwell.

322 'WE HAVE FOUND SAFETY . . .': From Rupert Brooke's 'Safety' (*1914*, II).

323 MESOPOTAMIA, SALONIKA: In Mesopotamia, the Indian Army, under loose British direction, suffered defeat in November; and the Allied attempt to support Serbia from the Greek port Salonika had ended in retreat.

324 'JOHN': Mr Brittain's occasional nickname for Vera.

327 HASSOCKS, KEYMER: Villages in Sussex; Hassocks is 7 miles north of Brighton; Keymer, where the Leightons lived, is about a mile east of Hassocks.

327 'TO SLEEP IN FRANCE': From 'Territorials', a war-poem by Agnes Falconer.

332 'MORNING HYMN': A song by Sir George Henschel (1850–1934), sung on the Leightons' record by Gervase Elwes (1866–1921). 'Soon night will pass . . .'

332 'O GENTLE CHILD . . .': From Death's lament in Shelley's *Adonais*, stanza 27.

333 COLONEL HARMAN: Later General Sir Antony Harman (1872–1961).

333 ROMAN CATHOLIC CHAPLAIN: Father Albert Purdie (b. 1888), later Headmaster of St Edmund's College, Ware, and author of learned books including *The Life of Blessed John Southwell, Priest and Martyr* (1930).

336 [JANUARY 13TH]: Like the later entry [January], this was found in the diary on separate sheets and has been dated from external evidence.

337 CLEMENT SHORTER: A critic and biographer (1857–1926), he was editor of the *Sphere*.

338 'THE OLD STRONG SOUL . . .': *The Story of an African Farm*, II, 2.

338 'LIFE AND LOVE . . .': From Roland's letter quoted on p. 192, and his poem 'Violets', p. 272.

340 PRÉDESTINÉS: The elect, predestined to eternal life; see 'The Pre-Destined' in *The Treasure of the Humble* (London, 1911) by Maurice Maeterlinck.

340 ARTHUR HALLAM: Tennyson's closest friend, his early death at the age of 22 is commemorated in the elegy *In Memoriam A.H.H.* (1833–50).

341 CAPTAIN ADSHEAD: Later Major H. N. Adshead, he was awarded the Military Cross (1917) and the Italian Silver Medal for Valour (1919).

343 'BLESSED ART THOU . . .': St Luke I, 28.

346 WHAT LYNDALL SAID . . .: *The Story of an African Farm*, II, 6.

347 LOUIS RAEMAEKERS' CARTOONS: The War cartoons of this Belgian artist (1869–1956) were later published as *The Great War* (3 vols, 1916–19).

350 HER BOOK ON ROLAND: Marie Leighton's *Boy of My Heart* appeared anonymously in 1917.

352 'NESSUN MAGGIOR DOLORE . . .' From Dante's *Inferno*, Canto V; the beginning of a speech by Francesca da Rimini. 'Nessun maggior dolore / Che ricordarsi del tempo felice / Nelle misere . . .': 'There is no greater pain than to recall the happy time in misery . . .'

353 DIVVERS: Nickname for an elementary examination in Divinity, then a requirement for the Oxford BA degree.

354 HONOURS CERTIFICATE: The College's diploma certifying that University requirements for the BA Honours degree (superior to the Pass degree) had been fulfilled. Absence for longer than a year would make it impossible to complete these in the permitted time.

355 'TIRED THE SUN WITH TALKING . . .': From 'Heraclitus', the verse-translation by William (Cory) Johnson (1823–92) of an epigram by Callimachus (*c.* 310–240 BC).

359   'AND THERE SHALL BE NO MORE SEA': Revelation XXI, 1.

360   LARGE BLANK: There are no diary-entries between 23
      March and 18 April.

360   'THE DEAD DIE NOT': From 'Holy Sonnet X' ('Death, be not
      proud . . .') by John Donne (1572–1631).

361   '. . . IN MOULD THE ROSE UNFOLDS . . .': Last lines of
      George Meredith's 'Outer and Inner'.

361   BRAHMS' *Requiem*: *A German Requiem* (1861–7) by Johannes
      Brahms (1833–97) is a choral setting of consolatory Biblical
      passages.

361   THE SOMME: This battle (1 July–17 November 1916) has come
      to epitomise the slaughter of trench-warfare in the Great
      War; on one day alone, 60,000 British men were killed or
      wounded.

361   'DE PROFUNDIS, DOMINE . . .': Beginning in Latin of Psalm
      CXXX, which is part of the Anglican burial service; 'Out of
      the deep [have I called unto thee], O Lord . . .'

364   THE *Britannic*: Converted sister-ship of the *Titanic*, she was
      later sunk by torpedo (21 November 1916) when carrying
      over 1,000 wounded soldiers; about 50 people were drowned.

364   MUDROS: Port (now usually 'Moudros') of the Greek Aegean
      island Lemnos.

365   'I WALK ALONE . . .': Opening lines of 'Roundel' by Roland
      Leighton.

367   THE *Galeka*: A small liner converted into a hospital ship.

368   IMTARFA: An inland settlement (usually 'Mtarfa') near
      Rabat.

368   ENTERIC: An infectious fever with severe irritation of the
      intestine; typhoid.

370   VALETTA: The administrative and commercial centre of
      Malta, situated on a peninsula between two deep harbours.

370   *The Lost World*: The prehistoric domain of this adventure
      story (1912) by Sir Arthur Conan Doyle (1859–1930) is an
      almost inaccessible plateau surrounded by a cliff.

372   'I COULD NOT IF I WOULD FORGET': Probably from the
      Chaplain's sermon.

372   ST GEORGE'S HOSPITAL: Above St George's Bay, about 2
      miles west of Valetta.

377   SCOTTISH WOMEN'S HOSPITALS: Medical units, led by Scot-

tish women doctors, which worked mainly in France and
Serbia. They were organised by Dr Elsie Inglis (1864–1916)
with strong support from the Scottish Women's Suffrage
Federation, which she had founded in 1906.

377   ARRAS: This battle (9–24 April 1917), which began on Easter
morning, gained up to 5 miles on a 25-mile front at a cost of
84,000 British casualties.

378   GEOFFREY KILLED: Victor Richardson was wounded on the
first day of the Battle of Arras; Geoffrey Thurlow died as it
ended – two years to the day after Rupert Brooke and sixteen
months to the day after Roland Leighton.

379   'WAR KNOWS NO POWER . . .': From Rupert Brooke's
'Safety' (*1914*, II).

379   'HE LEAVES A WHITE . . .': From Rupert Brooke's 'The
Dead' (*1914*, IV).

383   'I, TOO, TAKE LEAVE . . .': From 'Farewell' (1915), a war-
poem by Robert Nichols (1893–1944).

CHRONOLOGY

(Dates refer to diary entries, numbers to text pages, and the abbreviations 'VB' and 'RL' to Vera Brittain and Roland Leighton)

1915

INDEX